lonely planet

Milan, Turin & Genoa

Nicola Williams

LONELY PLANET PUBLICATIONS
Melbourne • Oakland • London • Paris

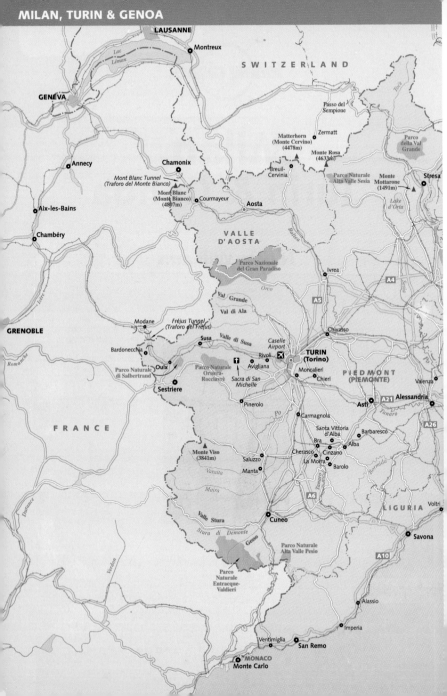

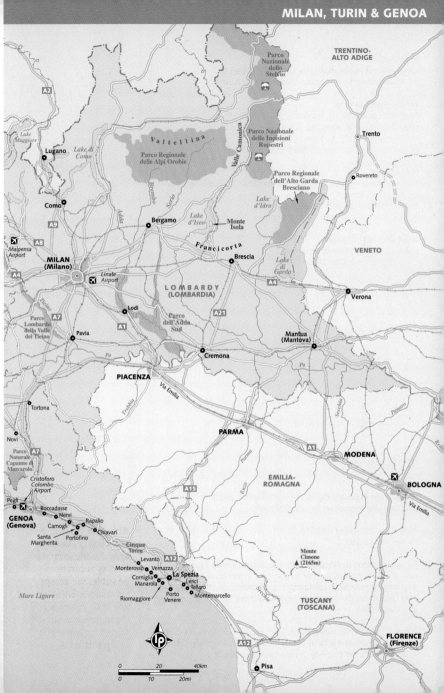

Milan, Turin & Genoa
1st edition – July 2001

Published by
Lonely Planet Publications Pty Ltd ABN 36 005 607 983
90 Maribyrnong St, Footscray, Victoria 3011, Australia

Lonely Planet Offices
Australia Locked Bag 1, Footscray, Victoria 3011
USA 150 Linden St, Oakland, CA 94607
UK 10a Spring Place, London NW5 3BH
France 1 rue du Dahomey, 75011 Paris

Photographs
Many of the images in this guide are available for licensing from
Lonely Planet Images.
email: lpi@lonelyplanet.com.au
Web site: www.lonelyplanetimages.com

Front cover photograph
Inside Galleria Vittorio Emanuele II
Photographer: Stephen Studd (Stone)

ISBN 1 86450 362 9

text & maps © Lonely Planet Publications Pty Ltd 2001
photos © photographers as indicated 2001

Printed by SNP SPrint (M) Sdn Bhd
Printed in Malaysia

Contents

The Author

Nicola Williams

Nicola lives in Lyon, a handy hop from the Alps and the Mediterranean. A journalist by training, she first hit the road in 1990 when she bussed and boated it from Jakarta to East Timor and back again. Following a two-year stint at the *North Wales Weekly News*, she moved to Latvia to bus it round the Baltics as Features Editor of the English-language *Baltic Times* newspaper. Following a happy 12 months exploring the Baltic region as Editor-in-Chief of the *In Your Pocket* city-guide series, she traded in Lithuanian *cepelinai* for Lyonnaise *andouillette*.

Nicola graduated from Kent and completed an MA in Islamic Societies & Cultures at London's School of Oriental & African Studies. She is also the author of Lonely Planet's French regional titles *Provence & the Cote d'Azur* and *The Loire*, and has worked on several others, including *France*, *Romania & Moldova*, *Russia*, *Ukraine & Belarus* and *Estonia, Latvia & Lithuania*.

FROM THE AUTHOR

Special thanks in Milano to Beatriz Barro at Armani, Marcello Mosesso at Versace, Maria Pada Tradli at Gucci, Lucilla Castellari at Teatro alla Scala, Maria Cristina Lani at the Camera Nazionale della Moda Italiana for her insights into the fashion industry, and Patrizia Mutti at the Camera di Commercio, Industria e Agricoltura; in Torino to Martini & Rossi's Florisa Gatti; ACI's Maurizio Bettica; Roberto Strocco at the Camera di Commercio Industria Artigianato e Agricoltura; to Gianni Avagnina at the Instituto Internazionale di Elicicoltura in Cherasco; and in Genoa to Annamaria Torre at the Acquario di Genova, Patrizia Pesca of Pesci Viaggi e Turismo and Lyon-based Tommaso Basevi who helped me get acquainted with his home city. Closer to home, the wedding of Nicola and Francesca Assetta at the Palazzina di Caccia di Stupingi near Turin proved an unforgettable introduction to both Piedmont and Piedmontese cuisine; and a fabulous opportunity for meeting up with Claudia Perucchio of Turin-based EDT who helped me enormously in discovering 'her city'.

Milan, Turin & Genoa is dedicated to my brother, Neil Williams, who reached the summit of Mount Aconcagua (6962m) – the highest point in the southern and western hemispheres – about the same time as I finished writing this book.

This Book

Nicola Williams researched and wrote this first edition of Milan Turin & Genoa.

From the Publisher

This first edition of Milan Turin & Genoa was produced in Lonely Planet's London office and was coordinated by Emma Sangster (editing) and Ian Stokes (mapping and design).

Emma was assisted with editing and proofing by a team comprising Heather Dickson, Imogen Franks, Michala Green and Sam Trafford. Michala and Emma produced the index.

Angie Watts and David Wenk helped out with mapping, James Timmins designed the colour pages and Jimi Ellis created the climate charts. Adam McCrow and Andrew Weatherill designed the front cover and Lachlan Ross drew the back-cover map. Jane Smith and Asa Andersson supplied the illustrations and LPI provided the colour images.

Thanks are also due to Paul Bloomfield, Amanda Canning, Paul Clifton, Tim Fitzgerald, Tom Hall and Rachel Suddart for their expert advice, and to Quentin Frayne for providing the Language chapter.

And finally, a big thank you to Nicola, who battled against the elements to research this book.

Foreword

ABOUT LONELY PLANET GUIDEBOOKS

The story begins with a classic travel adventure: Tony and Maureen Wheeler's 1972 journey across Europe and Asia to Australia. Useful information about the overland trail did not exist at that time, so Tony and Maureen published the first Lonely Planet guidebook to meet a growing need.

From a kitchen table, then from a tiny office in Melbourne (Australia), Lonely Planet has become the largest independent travel publisher in the world, an international company with offices in Melbourne, Oakland (USA), London (UK) and Paris (France).

Today Lonely Planet guidebooks cover the globe. There is an ever-growing list of books and there's information in a variety of forms and media. Some things haven't changed. The main aim is still to help make it possible for adventurous travellers to get out there – to explore and better understand the world.

At Lonely Planet we believe travellers can make a positive contribution to the countries they visit – if they respect their host communities and spend their money wisely. Since 1986 a percentage of the income from each book has been donated to aid projects and human rights campaigns.

Updates Lonely Planet thoroughly updates each guidebook as often as possible. This usually means there are around two years between editions, although for more unusual or more stable destinations the gap can be longer. Check the imprint page (following the colour map at the beginning of the book) for publication dates.

Between editions up-to-date information is available in two free newsletters – the paper *Planet Talk* and email *Comet* (to subscribe, contact any Lonely Planet office) – and on our Web site at www.lonelyplanet.com. The *Upgrades* section of the Web site covers a number of important and volatile destinations and is regularly updated by Lonely Planet authors. *Scoop* covers news and current affairs relevant to travellers. And, lastly, the *Thorn Tree* bulletin board and *Postcards* section of the site carry unverified, but fascinating, reports from travellers.

Correspondence The process of creating new editions begins with the letters, postcards and emails received from travellers. This correspondence often includes suggestions, criticisms and comments about the current editions. Interesting excerpts are immediately passed on via newsletters and the Web site, and everything goes to our authors to be verified when they're researching on the road. We're keen to get more feedback from organisations or individuals who represent communities visited by travellers.

Lonely Planet gathers information for everyone who's curious about the planet – and especially for those who explore it first-hand. Through guidebooks, phrasebooks, activity guides, maps, literature, newsletters, image library, TV series and Web site we act as an information exchange for a worldwide community of travellers.

Research Authors aim to gather sufficient practical information to enable travellers to make informed choices and to make the mechanics of a journey run smoothly. They also research historical and cultural background to help enrich the travel experience and allow travellers to understand and respond appropriately to cultural and environmental issues.

Authors don't stay in every hotel because that would mean spending a couple of months in each medium-sized city and, no, they don't eat at every restaurant because that would mean stretching belts beyond capacity. They do visit hotels and restaurants to check standards and prices, but feedback based on readers' direct experiences can be very helpful.

Many of our authors work undercover, others aren't so secretive. None of them accept freebies in exchange for positive write-ups. And none of our guidebooks contain any advertising.

Production Authors submit their raw manuscripts and maps to offices in Australia, USA, UK or France. Editors and cartographers – all experienced travellers themselves – then begin the process of assembling the pieces. When the book finally hits the shops some things are already out of date, we start getting feedback from readers, and the process begins again …

WARNING & REQUEST

Things change – prices go up, schedules change, good places go bad and bad places go bankrupt – nothing stays the same. So, if you find things better or worse, recently opened or long since closed, please tell us and help make the next edition even more accurate and useful. We genuinely value all the feedback we receive. A well-travelled team reads and acknowledges every letter, postcard and email and ensures that every morsel of information finds its way to the appropriate authors, editors and cartographers for verification.

Everyone who writes to us will find their name in the next edition of the appropriate guidebook. They will also receive the latest issue of *Planet Talk*, our quarterly printed newsletter, or *Comet*, our monthly email newsletter. Subscriptions to both newsletters are free. The very best contributions will be rewarded with a free guidebook.

Excerpts from your correspondence may appear in new editions of Lonely Planet guidebooks, the Lonely Planet Web site, *Planet Talk* or *Comet*, so please let us know if you *don't* want your letter published or your name acknowledged.

Send all correspondence to the Lonely Planet office closest to you:

Australia: Locked Bag 1, Footscray, Victoria 3011
USA: 150 Linden St, Oakland, CA 94607
UK: 10A Spring Place, London NW5 3BH
France: 1 rue du Dahomey, 75011 Paris

Or email us at: talk2us@lonelyplanet.com.au

For news, views and updates see our Web site: www.lonelyplanet.com

HOW TO USE A LONELY PLANET GUIDEBOOK

The best way to use a Lonely Planet guidebook is any way you choose. At Lonely Planet we believe the most memorable travel experiences are often those that are unexpected, and the finest discoveries are those you make yourself. Guidebooks are not intended to be used as if they provide a detailed set of infallible instructions!

Contents All Lonely Planet guidebooks follow roughly the same format. The Facts about the Destination chapter or section gives background information ranging from history to weather. Facts for the Visitor gives practical information on issues like visas and health. Getting There & Away gives a brief starting point for researching travel to and from the destination. Getting Around gives an overview of the transport options when you arrive.

The peculiar demands of each destination determine how subsequent chapters are broken up, but some things remain constant. We always start with background, then proceed to sights, places to stay, places to eat, entertainment, getting there and away, and getting around information – in that order.

Heading Hierarchy Lonely Planet headings are used in a strict hierarchical structure that can be visualised as a set of Russian dolls. Each heading (and its following text) is encompassed by any preceding heading that is higher on the hierarchical ladder.

Entry Points We do not assume guidebooks will be read from beginning to end, but that people will dip into them. The traditional entry points are the list of contents and the index. In addition, however, some books have a complete list of maps and an index map illustrating map coverage.

There may also be a colour map that shows highlights. These highlights are dealt with in greater detail in the Facts for the Visitor chapter, along with planning questions and suggested itineraries. Each chapter covering a geographical region usually begins with a locator map and another list of highlights. Once you find something of interest in a list of highlights, turn to the index.

Maps Maps play a crucial role in Lonely Planet guidebooks and include a huge amount of information. A legend is printed on the back page. We seek to have complete consistency between maps and text, and to have every important place in the text captured on a map. Map key numbers usually start in the top left corner.

Although inclusion in a guidebook usually implies a recommendation we cannot list every good place. Exclusion does not necessarily imply criticism. In fact there are a number of reasons why we might exclude a place – sometimes it is simply inappropriate to encourage an influx of travellers.

Introduction

Forget any preconceived notion you might have of an impoverished place that struggled to get into Euroland: northern Italy is a vastly different catwalk model from that leggy bit of Italy kicking little Sicily. Glamorous, rich and *very* get-up-and-go, this is the powerhouse that drives the nation. Three prima donnas sit on its board, which – let's be frank darling – are as scornful of the siesta-driven south as one would expect of supermodels.

Milan, Turin and Genoa (those 'three prima donnas') earned themselves seats in Italy's engine room through nothing less than hard graft. Toil of the grubby-nails variety transformed the region's swampy plains around the River Po into fertile agricultural land in the 17th century, while post-WWII industrialisation saw workers pour in from the south as its car-manufacturing industry boomed. Factories busily produced furniture, mammoth exhibition halls were constructed to show off the region's wares and by the 1960s there was no disputing the trio's status as queen bee. Milan's meteoric rise to fame as Europe's fashion capital in the 1970s capped it off.

Geographically speaking, the cities are branded with the label 'industrial triangle'. Milan (Milano) spearheads the neat three-pointed shape. The largest of the three, she peers down on Turin (Torino), 140km west, and Genoa (Genova), 150km south on the Ligurian coast. Each is an easy train or car journey from the other, allowing for quick and easy flitting between and flirting with all three. The country's lake district lies to the north of Milan; the Italian Alps surround Turin; and a coastline studded with cliff-top villages and terraced vineyards loiters around Genoa and its busy port.

Milan is innovative and fabulous. Shopping, fashion and design, coupled with the world's fourth largest cathedral and Europe's most esteemed opera house, take pride of place in this magnificent city that easily outpaces Rome in the trends it sets and names it attracts. Most of Italy's largest corporations are headquartered here, as are world-renowned fashion designers. Twice yearly, all eyes turn to this city as Armani, Gucci, Versace, Dolce & Gabbana et al lay bare their new designs to the world during the Milan fashion shows. Cutting-edge creations in furniture are revealed at Milan's Salone Internazionale del Mobile, Europe's largest furniture fair, which causes chaos in the city each April. A rash of fine art museums and Leonardo da Vinci's masterpiece the *Last Supper* complete the picture.

Cars, chocolate and the Holy Shroud are Turin's key drawing cards. An elegant city that shared a history with neighbouring France for several centuries, it's an often overlooked hub offering unexpected surprises for those who venture this far west. The Savoy kings transformed the city into Europe's capital of Baroque architecture. Christ's supposed burial cloth arrived here in 1578, while the turn of the 19th century spawned Italian industry with the foundation of auto-giant FIAT. Unlike Milan, this city has a green advantage – parks, riverside promenades and Alpine mountains that will host the 2006 Winter Olympics.

Genoa is the least pompous yet least lovable (to many) of northern Italy's three great cities. A powerful medieval republic with outposts around the globe, it encountered a nasty fall from grace in the 17th century and never quite recovered. Unlike manicured Milan and Turin, where painted lips and a perfect complexion hide inevitable flaws, Genoa's seamier side of life is very much in your face. Yet its crumbling palaces and backstreet alleys are charming in their own quirky way and yield a wealth of century-old churches and museums to explore. East along the coast is Cinque Terre, one of Italy's most precious (and popular) beauty spots.

Hot tips for wooing these northern Italian beauties? Don't be intimidated, walk tall and – if all else fails – invest in that all-essential pair of shades to pout behind.

Facts about the Cities

HISTORY
Early Inhabitants

Archaeological finds show that Palaeolithic Neanderthals lived in the region about 70,000 years ago. By 1800 BC Italy had been settled by pre-Indo European Italic tribes, including the bold and courageous Ligures (Ligurians), who claimed most of north-western Italy (including Piedmont and Valle d'Aosta) as their own, and the Etruscans – the largest and most powerful pre-Roman tribe – who had their finger in the Po Plain. The coast was colonised from around 600 by Greeks from Phocaea in Asia Minor who established a trading post in Xenoa (Genoa).

The earliest conflict in the region was sparked off by the Celts. With the help of Ligurian warriors, they seized Spain from the Carthaginians in 500 and waged war against the Etruscans of northern Italy a century later. Milan was one of the first setlements to be destroyed and resettled between 388 and 386 by the Insubres, one of several Celtic tribes to settle in the area north of the River Po (known as Cisalpine Gaul). In 222, Roman legions marched in, defeated the Insubres and occupied the town, which they called Mediolanum (middle of the plain).

The Roman's greatest enemy during this period was Carthage, a kingdom of traders based in North Africa. When the Second Punic War broke out between the two powers from 218 to 202, it was through the Italian Alps that Hannibal, the Carthaginian general, marched on his way from Spain to Rome. During the 15-day crossing, he lost about 15,000 of his 40,000 troops and almost all his war elephants in snowstorms, prompting him to persuade the Celts and Ligurians to side with him in the crushing, anti-Rome, military campaign that ensued. En route, Hannibal stumbled across Taurasia (Turin), a settlement on the River Po where the Celtic-Ligurian Taurini tribe lived. He burnt the village to the ground.

The Romans sought revenge in 197 with the defeat of the Celts at the Battle of Lake Como. In 191, Rome conquered all of Cisalpine Gaul and in 180 deported some 40,000 Ligurians from the region. In 58, Julius Caesar founded the military colony of Colonia Giulia (Turin) and granted Roman citizenship to its inhabitants.

The Roman Empire

During the 40-year-long rule of Augustus from 23 BC, the arts flourished and marble temples, public baths, theatres and arenas were built. The emperor refounded Caesar's Colonia Giulia as Augusta Taurinorum (Turin) and fortified the Roman castrum in the 1st century AD with 6m-high walls, pierced by four gates including Porta Palatina. The city's amphitheatre was built during the same period, although its theatre dated to the reign of his successor Tiberius' (14–37). Remnants from both are among the archaeological finds displayed in Turin's Museo d'Antichità.

On the coast, Genoa and La Spezia – both on Via Julia Augustus, linking Italy with the empire's western provinces – were developed as key ports. Portus Veneris (Porto Venere) was built on the western shore of the Golfo della Spezia as a base for the Romans en route from Gaul to Spain. Inland, Mediolanum's key position on trade routes between Rome and north-western Europe ensured increasing prosperity: the city served as seat of the imperial court and capital of the Western Roman Empire from 286 until 402. The city was fortified by Augustus in the 1st century and again by Maximianus in the 3rd.

It was in Mediolanum that the momentous edict granting Christians freedom of worship was signed in 313. Known as the Edict of Milan, the agreement between Emperors Constantine I and Licinius established Christianity as a recognised religion in the Roman Empire. The edict was the initiative of Milan-based emperor Constantine I who'd converted to Christianity after he saw the Christian monogram in a vision, together with a message telling him 'with this sign you will conquer'.

With religious freedom enshrined in law, churches (previously confiscated from persecuted Christians) were returned to their rightful owners and new ones built. Many of Milan's finest churches date to this dynamic period, due in part to the tremendous influence of Ambrose, bishop of Mediolanum (see the boxed text 'A Saint of the World'), who commissioned Chiesa di San Lorenzo Maggiore and Basilica di Sant'Ambrogio. His counterpart in Augusta Taurinorum, Bishop Maximus, was equally active and likewise canonised.

Lombard Rule

With the decline of the Roman Empire (recognised as ending in 476), the imperial residence was moved from Milan and northern Italy's cities fell from the hands of one barbaric invader to another. The Lombards (Longobards) ransacked Milan in 402, forcing its bishops and clergy to seek refuge on the coast in Genoa, and razed it to the ground in 538. The city was finally conquered by the Lombards in 569 and they ruled it until the end of the 7th century. Turin

fell into their clutches in 570, followed by Genoa in the middle of the 7th century.

Settling mainly around Milan, Pavia and Brescia, the Lombards were a Swabian people who originally inhabited the lower basin of the Elbe but, rather than imposing their culture on the locals, quickly adopted the local way of life. Their more communal concept of land and property tenure was soon overthrown by the Romans' high regard for private property, either absolute or leased. The Lombards soon became city-dwellers, building churches and public baths. The city of Pavia was their chosen capital until 754 when, with the pope's support, they were unseated by invading Franks led by the Frankish king Pepin. Pepin's son, Charlemagne, was crowned emperor by Pope Leo III on Christmas Day 800 and the concept of the Holy Roman Empire came into being.

City States & Comuni

In the 12th century, Barbarossa was the big name to be feared – big enough for the Genoese to encase their city in a sturdy ring of walls dubbed 'Barbarossa's walls'. Frederick 'Barbarossa' I was a Swabian duke who wed a Burgundy duchess and made advances on

A Saint of the World

When the future St Ambrose (Sant'Ambrogio) was appointed bishop of Milan in AD 374 his credentials were hardly in order – he hadn't even been baptised. Small matter; this former governor of Liguria had so impressed everyone with his umpiring skills between Catholics and Arians (a Christian sect that denied Christ's oneness with God) that he received all the sacraments and mitre in an unusually accelerated procedure.

At that time, Milan was the effective capital of the western half of the crumbling Roman Empire and Ambrose became a leading figure in imperial politics. He and the emperor of the western Roman Empire, Gratian, embarked on a crusade to eradicate paganism and the Arian heresy.

His influence grew and he was later able to challenge the authority of Theodosius – the eastern emperor and guarantor of the western empire after Gratian's assassination – with impunity. In one incident, the emperor ordered Christians to rebuild a synagogue they'd burnt. Ambrose demanded the order be revoked and, threatening to thump the pulpit and stir popular feeling, convinced the emperor to see things his way.

Ambrose, the public functionary who had never been a priest, was a powerful and charismatic bishop. He was the incarnation of the triumph of spiritual over secular power. He presaged the Church's future political role in European affairs and inspired the composition of the *Te Deum*. He died in 397.

northern Italy from 1154 in the hope of expanding his empire that already included Germany and Burgundy. 'Red Beard', as the Italians nicknamed him, was crowned emperor of the Holy Roman Empire in 1155 by Pope Adrian IV. His bid to control Milan, Pavia, Brescia and other northern Italian cities was met with fierce hostility, prompting Barbarossa to burn Milan down in 1162. The Milanese retaliated in 1167 with the Lega Lombarda (Lombard League), an anti-imperial coalition of northern Italian cities supported by the papacy.

At the Battle of Legnano (1176), imperial forces were finally defeated at the hands of triumphant Milanese troops and Barbarossa was sent packing. Milan was now free to become an independent city-state or city-republic governed by a *comune* – a town council which the Milanese Bishop Heribert pioneered from his city's ancient episcopal seat on Piazza Reale in the 11th century. This form of political institution – adopted by Genoa in 1099 and Turin by the 12th century – became typical across northern Italy between the 12th and 14th centuries. Some freed themselves from feudal control and others set themselves up as autonomous powers, but with the protection of the pope or emperor.

The Crusades of the 11th to 14th centuries saw ambitious Christians embark on eastbound military expeditions to reclaim the Holy Land from the Muslims. For increasingly important maritime powers, such as Genoa, these campaigns established new trade routes and commercial ties. During the First Crusade (1097–1104) it was a Genoese fleet that helped Crusaders clinch the port of Antioch and conquer a besieged Jerusalem in July 1099, following which its entire population was massacred. In 1101, Guglielmo Embriaco returned from Cesarea to Genoa, bringing with him great bounty – the *Sacro Catino*, a chalice said to have been used by Jesus at the Last Supper and given to Solomon by the Queen of Sheba. Believed by the crusaders to be made of emeralds, it was not until the 19th century that the Genoese recognised it as green glass (priceless nonetheless).

Highly favoured commercially for their position on the route into Europe from the Mediterranean coast, northern Italy's cities rapidly gained a new wealth. A middle class was born, composed of rich merchants and artisans who, very soon, passed from commercial rivalry to internal political struggles. These conflicts ended up favouring restricted oligarchies in which one family prevailed, charged by the city with exercising a form of government called the *Signoria*. This was the highest level of republican government of the city-states, prevalent in both Milan and Genoa where Signorie persecuted rival families and opponents while simultaneously expanding their territories at the expense of weaker neighbours.

In Turin, events took a dramatically different twist. Riddled with disputes, its early comune was quickly scooped up by France's House of Savoy who claimed ownership of the Piedmont region through the marriage of Otto of Savoy to Adelaide of Turin in 1060. In 1248, the Savoys scored control of Turin's Signoria, backed by Frederick II, emperor of the Holy Roman Empire, and – with the exception of a brief interlude between 1255 and 1274 – Savoy dukes ruled Turin almost exclusively until the 19th century.

Dynasty

A bitter power struggle between the pope and the Holy Roman Emperor in the Middle Ages saw two camps emerge: Guelfi (Guelph) in support of the pope and Ghibellini (Ghibelline) in support of the emperor. This exploded into a soap opera of murders, mysteries and backstabbing dramas between the cities' leading families. Despite such internal quarrels, the period still witnessed tremendous growth.

In Milan, the powerful Visconti dynasty (1277–1447), representatives of the Ghibelline nobility, wrenched control of the city from the ruling Della Torre family who represented the popular party of the city-state and took up residence in Palazzo Reale. Ottone Visconti was made archbishop of Milan in 1262 and his nephew, Matteo, was made imperial vicar by Henry

VII, following which he destroyed the power of the Della Torre and extended Milanese control over Pavia and Cremona.

Work started on Castello Sforzesco in 1368 and was later enlarged under Giangaleazzo Visconti (1351–1402), who also commissioned what would become the world's fourth largest cathedral. In 1382, when rival brother Bernabò threatened to wed his daughter to Louis of Anjou's son – hence creating an unwanted alliance with France – Gian Galeazzo flung his brother in prison, where he died (allegedly poisoned) several months later. With this threat safely removed, the Milanese duke extended his lordship over Siena and Pisa in 1399, substantial parts of Umbria in 1400 and Bologna in 1402, turning Milan from a city-state into a strong European power. Although the Visconti were disliked as dictators, Milan managed to resist French attempts at invasion.

In Genoa, the Fieschi family plotted the overthrow of town captain Giuglielmo Boccanegra in 1262 and established their own uneasy comune instead. This victory for the Guelph family was short-lived though and in 1270 the Fieschi were pushed out by the Spinolas and Dorias – opposition Ghibellini families – who took control of the city. Several decades of plotting later, the Fieschi teamed up with the Grimaldi clan to drive their rivals out in 1317. Rule of the port city continued to be bandied back and forth in this fashion until 1339 when a *dogate* was established. This more bureaucratic form of government saw a *doge* elected to head the city, assisted by several advisory bodies.

At sea, a succession of naval victories saw Genoa destroy its traditional commercial rivals – the powerful maritime republics of Venice, Pisa and Amalfi – that had competed with the city for control of the Mediterranean ever since the Crusades. Pisa was crushed by a Genoese fleet in the Battle of Meloria in 1284, followed by Venice at Curzola in 1298. The latter battle famously saw Venetian ship commander Marco Polo, along with 7000 other Venetians, captured and imprisoned in Genoa's Palazzo San Giorgio.

Glories turned ghastly in 1347, when 12 Genoese ships docked at a port in Sicily from a Black Sea voyage to one of the republic's many far-flung trading posts. Scores of dying sailors were on board. The Black Death, as the plague became known, had arrived in Europe. Despite desperate measures taken to fight the deadly disease – such as walling up the homes of victims (and those yet to catch it) in Milan – the plague wiped out over half the cities' population and left decades of economic depression, famine and deprivation in its wake.

Golden Ages & Foreign Domination

Christopher Columbus was born in 1451 in the troubled republic of Genoa, which had recovered from the plague only to find itself subordinate to either Milan (1421–35, 1464–78, 1487–99) or France – mightier powers that 'took it in turns' to control the city almost continuously from 1421 to 1507. The Spanish dealt the final straw in 1522 when they attacked the port, prompting Andrea Doria (1466–1560) to step in and strike a deal with them. In 1528, he created an aristocratic constitution making Genoa an independent mercantile republic allied to the emperor. It lasted until 1797.

Genoa reached its peak under Doria in the 16th century, managing to benefit from Spain's American fortunes by financing Spanish exploration. Coinciding happily with the Renaissance, this age of power and wealth lasted well into the 17th century and produced innumerable palaces and great works of art by the likes of Rubens, Caravaggio and van Dyck. As new threats were posed by France and the House of Savoy, walls were built around the city between 1626 and 1632. They did little to protect Genoa against Louis XIV's bombardment of the city in 1684, however.

In Milan, the policies of the Visconti, followed by those of the Sforza family from 1450, allowed the city to develop economically and territorially. The borders of the Signoria were extended from Genoa to Bologna and from Ticino in Switzerland to Lake Garda. During these tireless years of

He Belongs to Genoa!

Christopher Columbus (Cristoforo Colombo to Italians) exhibited a bad case of the travel bug from an early age. Steeped in Marco Polo's writings and Pliny's *Natural History*, the Genoese adventurer (born 1451) conceived an ambitious project to reach the Orient by sailing west instead of east.

Broad-minded as Genoa's rulers might have been, this preposterous idea was just too much for them, forcing Columbus to seek other patrons. He first tried his luck in Portugal in 1484 but it was only after knocking for a very long time on the appropriate door in Spain that he received a sympathetic hearing – scoring backing for his journey of a lifetime from the Catholic Monarchs, Fernando and Isabel.

On 3 August 1492 Columbus (Cristóbal Colón to Spaniards) set off with 100 men and three small caravels *Niña, Pinta* and *Santa Maria*. Two months later he and his entourage landed in the Bahamas. Over the following eight years he discovered Cuba, Haiti, Jamaica and some of the Antilles, still convinced he was in Asia.

Sent back to Spain on charges of committing atrocities (although subsequent Spanish colonisers evidently developed a thicker skin in this regard), he was later pardoned. He made one last voyage between 1502 and 1504, tracking the central American coast and reaching Colombia. When Columbus died, forgotten and embittered, two years later in Valladolid, Spain, he still had no idea of the new world that he'd discovered.

Christopher Columbus is everyone's hero, from Genoa and the USA to Spain and Latin America. Common lore has him as the son of various cities and, although most accept Genoa as his birthplace, there are those in Barcelona, Spain, who insist he's theirs.

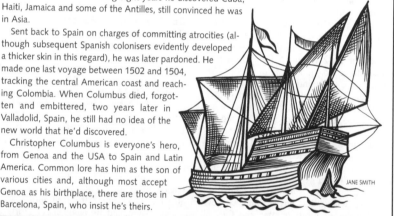
JANE SMITH

hard work, hydraulic and irrigation projects converted the Po Plain from swampy woodland into an extremely productive agricultural collective with some of the most fertile farmland in Italy. Among other things, the cultivation of rice and mulberries was introduced. Parmesan became one of Europe's most precious cheeses and butter from the plains of Lombardy was exported as far as Rome. Leonardo da Vinci helped Francesco Sforza with numerous engineering projects and started painting the *Last Supper* (1494).

Changing Hands Unlike Genoa, Milan failed to resist Spanish domination and in 1535 (upon the death of Francesco II, the last of the Sforza line and a puppet of France since 1500) the grand old duchy fell under Spanish rule.

The Spaniards ringed Milan with another circle of defensive walls. In the mid-16th century, the city became a stronghold in northern Italy for the dogmatic Counter-Reformation led by Carlo Borromeo (1538–84), archbishop of Milan from 1560. Borromeo played a key role in the Council of Trent (1542–65), the body that documented the theology of the Counter-Reformation movement and effectively dictated the Roman Catholic Church's catechism. Born on the shores of Lake Maggiore, Borromeo was canonised in 1610 and his cousin Frederico Borromeo (1564–1631) became the next archbishop, establishing Italy's first public library, the Biblioteca Ambrosiana.

During the famine of 1627 to 1628, he and his merry band of devoted clergymen doled out daily food to 2000 starving Milanese. Most no doubt died three years later when the plague swept through Milan, killing more than 50% of the 250,000-strong population.

A year after Milan fell into Spanish hands, Turin was seized by Francis I of France – a period which saw the sacred Holy Shroud, the cloth in which Jesus was supposedly buried, brought from the French town of Chambéry to Turin in 1578. The move was allegedly for no other reason than to shorten the pilgrimage of Carlo Borromeo who'd vowed to walk from Milan to the shroud to thank God for escaping another bout of plague in 1576. Turin remained under French domination until 1559 when the Treaty of Cateau-Cambrésis returned the city to the Duchy of Savoy. As if to reaffirm its rightful place on the European map, Emanuele Filiberto shifted the Savoy capital from Chambéry to Turin and transformed the city into a capital. He built a star-shaped citadel and commissioned a rash of elegant palaces and public buildings. This magnificent glorification of the city was continued by his successors, Carlo Emanuele I (1580–1630), Vittorio Amedeo II (1630–37) and Carlo Emanuele II (1638–75), noted for the Baroque *palazzi* (palaces) and sprawling hunting lodges created by royal architect Filippo Juvarra.

In 1701, the War of the Spanish Succession broke out. Allied with Austria, Turin was besieged by French and Spanish troops in 1706, inciting its population to seek refuge in the citadel and prompting Turinese miner Pietro Micca to blow up a tunnel – and himself – to stave off French advances and preempt their eventual defeat. At the end of the war, under the Treaty of Utrecht (1713), Vittorio Amedeo II became king of Sicily – a

Turin's Holy Shroud

The Holy Shroud (*sindone* in Italian) is Christianity's greatest icon of faith and object of devotion. Luring three million pilgrims to Turin when it was publicly displayed in 1978 and 2.1 million pilgrims from 67 different countries in 1998, another million visited when the sacred cloth was hauled out again to mark 2000 (with each showing, numbers drop as those who've 'seen it once' fall away). It has an official Web site at www.sindone.org.

Shroud scholars worldwide endlessly debate the true origins of the shroud, believed to be the burial cloth in which Jesus' body was wrapped. Tests in 1981 uncovered traces of human blood (type AB) and pollen from plants known to exist only in and around Jerusalem. While many date the shroud to AD 1260–1390, carbon dating carried out in 1988 dated it to the 13th century – making it far from sacred. Most agree the white cloth, 4.37m long and 1.10m wide, to have been woven in the Middle East using ancient Egyptian techniques.

How the image of a human body – with fractured nose, bruised right cheek, lance wound on chest, scourge marks on back, thorn wounds on forehead and nail wounds on both wrists and feet – was formed on the cloth remains the biggest mystery. Antishroudies claim it's neither the blood of Christ nor a cheap medieval fake but, rather, the first ever attempt at photography (using a camera obscura) by Leonardo da Vinci.

Crusaders brought the shroud to Europe. From 1453 it belonged to Louis of Savoy who folded the cloth into squares and stashed it in a silver treasure-trove in a chapel in Chambéry (France). The tie-dyed-style brown patterns visible on it today were caused by a fire in 1532 that saw a drop of hot silver fall into the casket and through the folded layers. Safe-guarded in Turin since 1578, the shroud is laid out flat today in a vacuum-sealed box which, in turn, is stored in a controlled atmosphere. When fire yet again engulfed the chapel in which it was kept in 1997, firemen with faith plucked it to safety.

title and territory he held onto until 1720 when the Spanish took it from him and gave him Sardinia and its crown instead.

The same treaty catapulted Milan into Austrian hands. Under the royal dictatorship, Maria Theresa of Austria bestowed Milan with its finest attraction in 1778, La Scala (see under Arts later in this chapter).

Napoleon Italy had been the source of many enlightened political ideas, but the concept of national sovereignty had not been one of them. But when the 27-year-old, Corsican-born French general Napoleon Bonaparte entered Milan on 15 May 1796, nationalist seeds were sown.

Napoleon acceded to the calls of Italian deputies in the north and in 1797 proclaimed the Cisalpine Republic, a nominally independent republic embracing the Duchy of Milan, most of Lombardy, Bologna, Emilia and Modena. It had its own government, constitution and capital city (Milan) and was recognised by France and Austria under the Treaty of Campo Formio

(1797). In 1798, Napoleonic troops led by General Joubert marched into Turin and forced the Savoys into exile. By 1802 the Cisalpine Republic had been superseded by the Italian Republic and in 1805, following Napoleon's conquest of Venice and Genoa, the Kingdom of Italy came into being – the first mention in history of a political entity known as Italy, albeit with Napoleon as its head. The self-elected dictatorial president and sovereign crowned himself king of Italy in Milan's *duomo* (cathedral) in 1805, a building which Napoleon was ironically responsible for getting completed after several hundred years of toil.

Any hopes of independent, constitutional rule were brutally dashed in 1815 with Napoleon's defeat at Waterloo. The Congress of Vienna annexed Milan back to Austria, and Turin and Genoa to the House of Savoy.

Unification

1815 was a big step backwards but it encouraged the rapid growth of secret societies and bred two of Italian history's greatest figures, Garibaldi and Mazzini (see the boxed text 'Mazzini'). The nationalist Risorgimento (literally 'Revival') movement, which had taken root under Napoleon, also gained tremendous ground thanks to Camillo Benso di Cavour (1810–61), a Turin lad who served as the first prime minister of the unified Italy he'd helped to carve out.

The 1848 revolutions in Europe sparked off the so-called 'Cinque Giornate di Milano' (five days of Milan), which saw the Milanese revolutionaries clash with Austrian troops for five days from 18 to 22 March. About 500 Milanese died and the Austrian Marshal Radetzky and his hated state fled the city. In the months leading up to the violent street fighting, troops had fired on crowds gathered to honour the city's new archbishop. In January 1848, city-dwellers had boycotted tobacco, a vital source of revenue for the state. Six were shot and scores wounded in subsequent clashes sparked off by troops puffing away in front of nicotine-craving smokers on the

Napoleon Bonaparte's Cisalpine Republic was the catalyst for Italian unification

Mazzini

Revolutionary Giuseppe Mazzini (1805–72), key proponent of nationhood and political freedom, was the Risorgimento's champion. Yet his fight for Italian unification exiled Mazzini from his homeland for much of his life.

Son of a Genoese doctor, Mazzini studied at Genoa university until 1827 when he joined southern Italy's secret republican Carbonari movement. Three years later his political activities saw him exiled from Piedmont to Marseilles, in neighbouring France. Far from giving up the fight, the Genoese rebel founded Giovane Italia (Young Italy), a society of young men whose aims were the liberation of Italy from foreign and domestic tyranny and its unification under a republican government. Significantly, however, this was to be achieved through education and, where necessary, revolt by guerrilla bands. Secret branches of Giovane Italia were set up in Genoa and other cities – all masterminded by the exiled Mazzini.

During the 1830s and 1840s Genoa's freedom-lover organised several abortive uprisings. By 1834 he'd gained an ardent follower in the shape of Giuseppe Garibaldi (1807–82) who, like Mazzini, was tried in absentia and sentenced to death following an unsuccessful uprising in Piedmont in 1834.

Mazzini lived out the rest of his life in England (from 1837), writing articles and soliciting support in order to raise the consciousness of Europeans about the Italian question.

streets. Three months later the provisional government installed by the revolution had been overthrown and Radetzky was back in Milan. Rebels were also squashed in Brescia, a Roman town east of Milan that earned itself the nickname of 'The Lioness' for its 10-day anti-Austrian uprising.

In *Il Risorgimento*, one of several publications to spring up in 1847 out of the growing Italian nationalist movement, Turin's Camillo Benso di Cavour and nationalist writer Cesare Balbo pressed for a constitution. In 1848, they published their *Statuto* (Statute) advocating a two-chamber parliament, with the upper chamber to be appointed by the Crown and the lower chamber to be elected by educated taxpayers. In 1861, the *Statuto* was to become the constitutional basis of the Kingdom of Italy, but not before 13 more years of warring between the various European princes had resulted in the deaths of many more Italians.

Giuseppe Garibaldi (1807–82) proved the turning point on Italy's drive for unification. Returning to Italy in 1848 from his famous exploits in South America, Garibaldi was the hero Italians needed. His personal magnetism drew more Italians into the fight for nationhood than ever before.

Despite significant personal animosity,

Garibaldi and Cavour fought side by side, each in their chosen arena, to break the stranglehold of foreign domination. The brilliant diplomacy of Cavour, coupled with the independent efforts of Garibaldi and his popular base, finally caught the attention of European communities, particularly the British, who became staunch supporters of a free and united Italy.

When King Carlo Alberto (ruled 1831–49), the sympathetic Piedmontese monarch, granted a constitution based on the *Statuto* in March 1848, Cavour stood for election. In 1850, he was given three ministries – navy, commerce and finance – in the government headed by Massimo d'Azeglio. When Cavour's centre-left faction joined forces with the centre-right, headed by Urbano Rattazzi, behind d'Azeglio's back, the prime minister resigned and Cavour was asked by the king to take the top government post. As prime minister, Cavour focused on forging an alliance with the French emperor Napoleon III, in a move destined to overthrow Austrian domination of Piedmont. Troops under Victor Emmanuel II (Carlo Alberto's successor) and Napoleon III crushed Austrian forces at the Battle of Magenta in 1859 and Milan was incorporated into the nascent Kingdom of Italy.

The Kingdom of Italy was declared on 17 March 1861. Victor Emmanuel II became the first king of Italy and Turin became the kingdom's capital, a status it kept until 1865 when the parliament and capital shifted to Florence.

Industrialisation

Rapid growth marked the post-unification period. Victor Emmanuel II celebrated unification in Milan by bulldozing the neighbourhood around the cathedral and replacing it with a central square and drawing room, Piazza del Duomo and Galleria Vittorio Emanuele II (1864–78). The first edition of the *Corriere della Sera* newspaper rolled of the presses in 1875 and tasty Pecks opened its doors in 1883 – the same year that electric lighting was installed in Milan's opera house. Railway lines were laid between 1860 and 1873 to link Milan, Turin and Genoa.

Turin's answer to its loss of political significance was aggressive industrialisation, becoming first a centre for industrial production during the WWI years and later a hive of trade-union activity. In 1899, the Fabbrica Italiana di Automobili di Torino (FIAT; Italian Automotive Manufacturer of Turin) was established. Among its competitors was the Società Anonima Lombarda Fabbrica Automobili (ALFA; Lombardy Car Manufacturing Company), another car manufacturer founded near Milan by a bunch of industrialists who joined forces with Nicola Romeo (inventor of the portable air pump used by the Italian army in WWI) in 1919. Two corners of what would become to be dubbed Italy's 'industrial triangle' were born.

On the coast, La Spezia was transformed from anonymous port to bustling provincial town with the construction between 1860 and 1865 of what would soon be Italy's largest naval base. Europe's social elite flocked to the coast, giving rise to resorts such as San Remo and Santa Margherita. Its natural beauty had long lured writers and artists such as Shelley, Byron, Dante, George Sand and DH Lawrence.

Blue skies clouded over with the approach of the 20th century. Increasing social and economic unrest in Europe erupted in 1898 with protests across Italy at high bread prices. Demonstrations turned bloody in Milan when General Bava Beccaris fired canons on crowds gathered on Piazza del Duomo. Despite the hundreds killed, the general was subsequently decorated by Umberto I, leading to the Italian king's assassination by an anarchist in Monza, north of Milan, in 1900.

The mounting crisis was reflected in the political arena by constant fluctuations between socialist democrats and right-wing imperialists who gained then lost support of the discontented populace. A backlash against socialism after the 1894 general elections saw numerous political activists imprisoned, including Como-born Turati Filippo (1857–1932) who co-founded the Italian Socialist party in 1892. Giovanni Giolitti (1842–1929), a graduate of Turin university, was one of Italy's longest-serving prime ministers (heading five governments between 1892 and 1921) and managed to bridge the political extremes. The Piedmontese politician granted male suffrage in 1913.

The curtain rose on Puccini's *Madame Butterfly* at Milan's La Scala in 1904.

WWI & WWII

Mussolini (1883–1945) made Milan a hotbed of fascism after WWI. Working in the city as editor of the socialist newspaper *Avanti!*, which he founded in Milan in 1911, Mussolini broke with the Socialist Party in 1914 after publicly declaring his support for Italy's alignment with the Allied forces. He then set up *Il Popolo d'Italia* (1914–43), a propaganda publication financed by French, British and Russian interests. In 1919, he founded the Fascist Party whose black shirts and Roman salutes would symbolise violent oppression and aggressive nationalism for the next 23 years. Party meetings were held in Milan's Palazzo Castini.

Fascism's rise to power was paralleled by that of trade unionism. In Turin, FIAT had profited enormously from WWI, increasing its 4000-strong workforce 10-fold by 1918.

tress by partisans on the shores of Lake Como in April 1945. The pair were shot and their corpses hung upside down from the roof of a petrol station on Milan's Piazzale Loreto.

Italy's Industrial Triangle

Swift postwar economic recovery hailed the dawning of a new age for the northern cities, which were rebuilt to emerge as the country's industrial giants and create Italy's 'industrial triangle'. Genoa swallowed up numerous coastal villages as the city grew at lightening pace and Italy's industrial workforce, based almost exclusively in the north, swelled from about 32% of the country's total workforce in 1950 to over 50% in 1960.

A major feature of this period was the boom in Italy's car industry. This sparked massive migration from the poorer south to the wealthier north. Under managing director and founder Giovanni Agnelli, FIAT became the driving force behind Italian industry, its output leaping from 425,000 cars in 1960 to 1.7 million by 1970. In 1969, FIAT bought out Ferrari and, in 1978, it swallowed up Lancia, a fellow Turin-based financially troubled car manufacturer founded in 1906. FIAT's takeover of Milan's Alfa Romeo in 1986 heralded the monopoly that Turin's FIAT clearly enjoyed.

The construction of large exhibition centres in all three cities signalled the birth of northern Italy's massive trade-fair industry. The 11.7km-long Mont Blanc Tunnel opened in 1965, prompting an immediate and dramatic increase in tourism and traffic in the formerly quiet Valle d'Aosta, west of Turin, as the road tunnel became a major road-freight thoroughfare between Italy and France. When a second road tunnel, the 12.9km-long Fréjus Tunnel, was burrowed out between the neighbouring countries in 1980, there was no escaping Turin's continuing growth as a transport hub. Trains between Paris and Turin have whizzed beneath Piedmont, courtesy of the Mont Cenis Tunnel (1857–71), since the end of the 19th century.

Rejecting his socialist ideals, Benito Mussolini founded Fascism and dragged Italy into WWII

But factory workers had opposed Italy's entry into the war in 1915 and had protested by striking for two days. Soaring living costs coupled with lousy wages after WWI saw the membership of the dissident Unione Sindacale Italiana grow from 300,000 members in 1919 to over 800,000 in September 1920, when workers country-wide went on strike. In Turin alone, over 150 factories were occupied, including Michelin's rubber-tyre plant. Industrial unrest on FIAT's factory floors spawned the Italian Communist Party under the leadership of Antonio Gramsci.

Allied bombings during WWII destroyed much of central Milan, Turin and Genoa, although treasures such as Leonardo's *Last Supper* miraculously survived. The opera houses in all three cities were bombed to smithereens.

Genoa was the first northern city to rise against the Germans and the Italian Fascists towards the close of WWII, liberating itself before the arrival of Allied troops – the rest of northern Italy was liberated in May 1945 after Allied troops broke through German lines. Mussolini tried to flee to Switzerland but was captured with his mis-

Political Scandal

With the waning of economic muscle in the late 1960s, Genoa's big industries folded, port activity dropped and the waterfront fell into a slow decline. In Turin, industrial unrest on FIAT's factory floors gave birth to the left-wing terrorist group, Brigate Rosse (Red Brigades) in 1970. Neo-fascist terrorists had already struck on 12 December 1969, when a bomb exploded in a bank in Milan's Piazza Fontana, killing 16 people. The incident is believed to have been an act of right-wing extremists directed by forces within the country's secret services.

Brigate Rosse continued to operate throughout the Anni di Piombo (Years of Lead; 1973–80), with 1977 seeing a major recruiting campaign inject new zest into the movement and students occupying universities in Milan in opposition to education reforms proposed by the government. One of the region's more unfortunate sons, General Carlo dalla Chiesa from Saluzzo, south of Turin, was appointed to wipe out the terrorist groups. His implacable pursuit of the Mafia led to his assassination in 1982.

The 1990s was marred by one of Italy's greatest political scandals that exposed Milan as a city corrupt to the core. Tangentopoli (literally 'kickback cities') broke in early 1992 when a functionary of the PSI was arrested on charges of accepting bribes in exchange for public works contracts. Led by Milanese magistrate Antonio di Pietro – later dubbed 'the reluctant hero' – the extensive investigations were known as Mani Pulite (Clean Hands). Literally thousands of top politicians, officials and businesspeople were implicated, Gianni Versace and Giorgio Armani among them.

The scandal effectively ripped Italy's main political parties to shreds and wiped out the centre of the Italian political spectrum, allowing Umberto Bossi's Lega Nord (Northern League) to emerge as a force to be reckoned with on a national level in the 1992 elections. The federalist, anticorruption party has enjoyed strong support in northern Italy ever since (see the boxed text 'Another Country'). Following the 1994 elections, it formed part of the right-wing governing coalition Polo per le Libertà (Freedom Alliance) but pulled out nine months later, leading to the government's collapse. It had been headed by Milanese billionaire Silvio Berlusconi (see the boxed text 'Go Italy').

Organised crime continues to haunt northern Italy, particularly Milan where a Sicilian Mafia terrorist bomb exploded outside the Padiglione d'Arte Contemporanea in 1993, killing five people.

Nine people were murdered in nine consecutive days in January 1999, prompting Milanese mayor Albertini to seek advice from New York's hardliner Rudolph Giu-

Another Country

Utopia for the Lega Nord (Northern League) is Padania – another country, separate from poor old southern Italy, whose rich northern Italian inhabitants have their own government and nobody to subsidise.

Padania was proclaimed in September 1996 by the political party's outspoken leader and founder, Umberto Bossi. It has since come to spearhead the Lega Nord's right-wing secessionist ideology. Padania would be governed by a federal assembly, further split into a national and regional assembly. Popular vote would elect the national assembly, comprising 200 deputies, every five years.

Since the Lega Nord's foundation in 1991, it has been criticised for its blatantly anti-Semitic and antiforeigner stance. In 1993 local elections, its candidate, Marco Formentini, became mayor of Milan after winning 40% of votes. In the 1996 national elections the party won 8.4% of national votes (19.5% in northern Italy), only to be thwarted by Silvio Berlusconi who dropped all support for the Lega Nord's policies once in power. In 2001, the Lega Nord, online at www.leganord.org, nonetheless remained part of the current opposition Polo per le Libertà (Freedom Alliance).

Go Italy

When Milan-born Silvio Berlusconi (born 1936) strode purposefully into the political arena with Italy's Forza Italia (Go Italy) in 1993, he already held a huge advantage: money. He made it in several ways – through property in the 1960s, television in the 1970s (his holding company Fininvest pioneered game shows on TV in Italy and gobbled up three rival stations to emerge as a monopoly alongside state-owned RAI TV), football and retailing in the 1980s (he owns AC Milan and La Standa chain of department stores) and publishing in the 1990s (the mogul bought up the Monadori publishing group to add to the Publitalia ad agency he already owned).

Berlusconi's brief reign as Italy's prime minister in 1994, under the right-wing governing coalition Polo per le Libertà (Freedom Alliance), was followed by less-brief court appearances which – riding on the back of Tangentopoli – saw the media tycoon grapple with charges of bribery and a suspended prison sentence in 1998.

In the 2001 elections, Milan's self-made big shot (and Italy's richest man) is up against Rome's former mayor: Silvio Berlusconi runs as leader of the opposition right-wing Polo per le Libertà; Francesco Rutelli (who ushered Rome through its jubilee celebrations in 2000) is the centre-left's candidate. The odds are heavily on for 'Milano's Silvio' as next prime minister.

liani, following which 'tolleranza zero' (zero tolerance) became the buzzword of the day. Nevertheless, in December 2000 a bomb was discovered on the roof of Milan's duomo – an explosive fact of city life.

GEOGRAPHY

Milan, Turin and Genoa (Milano, Torino and Genova in Italian) are northern Italy's three largest cities.

Milan, the largest and most eastern of the trio, sits in the heart of the heavily populated and industrialised Po Plain (Pianura Padana), bounded by the Alps (Alpi in Italian), the Apennine mountains and the Adriatic Sea that separates Italy from Slovenia and Croatia. North of the city is Italy's lake district; Lake Maggiore flows out along the River Ticino and into the Po.

The River Po, Italy's largest river runs across the Po Plain. Turin, 140km west of Milan, sits on its left bank, on the confluence of the Rivers Dora Baltea, Sangone and Stura di Lanzo. It is surrounded to the west and north by the Piedmontese Alps, which peak at 4633m with Mount Rosa (Monte Rosa), north of Turin on the Swiss border. These Alps stretch from the Adriatic Sea north of Trieste to the Gulf of Genoa and divide northern Italy from France, Switzerland, Austria and Slovenia. The highest

Alpine peak is Mont Blanc (Monte Bianco), on the border with France at the western end of Valle d'Aosta. It is 4807m high.

Genoa, 150km south-west of Milan and 170km south-east of Turin, sits on the cliff-caked coastline of the Ligurian Sea (Mar Ligure). The city overlooks the Gulf of Genoa (Golfo di Genova), east of which stretches the Riviera di Ponente to neighbouring France and west of which stretches the Riviera di Levante. East of Genoa, the Apennine range (Appennini) form a backbone extending for 1220km along the lanky leg of Italy.

CLIMATE

The Alps shield Milan and its lakes from the extremes of the northern European winter, but temperatures can rise to a stifling 30°C in July and August, prompting city dwellers to flee the dust and city heat. Summers are also hot and humid in Turin. Genoa enjoys a mild, Mediterranean climate similar to southern Italy.

In the Alps, temperatures are lower and winters are long and severe. The weather is warm from July to September, although rainfall can be high in September. While the first snowfall is usually in November, light snow can sometimes falls in mid-September and the first heavy falls can

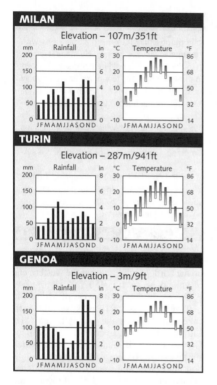

occur in early October. There's sufficient snow to ski on the slopes most years from mid-December to early April.

Milan's fog is legendary and can cast a cloud over the city any time of year ('the fog was so dense that the spire of the far-famed cathedral might as well have been in Bombay' wrote Charles Dickens of his trip to Milan in 1844). The torrential rain that broke the River Po's banks in October 2000, washing 15,000 people out of their homes around Turin and closing 170 roads in the region, claimed 25 lives. It was the worst catastrophe to hit Piedmont since 1994, when floods killed 68 people.

ECOLOGY & ENVIRONMENT

Air pollution menaces all three cities, although carbon emissions remain the filthiest headache in polluted Milan – a city which, according to a World Health Organisation survey conducted in 1998, ranked among the world's worst five polluted cities. Milan's dirty air effectively boils down to too many cars on the road; Italy ranks third in the world after the USA and Australia for the number of cars per capita. In 1999 a token handful of electric cars were introduced in both Milan and Turin, followed in 2000 by a series of car-free Sundays in both city centres: emissions dropped by an astonishing 40% in Milan and 56% in Turin in one day alone (only to soar sky-high again when maniac motorists hit the city come Monday morning).

On the Ligurian coast the beaches at Riomaggiore, Monterosso al Mare and Vernazza in Cinque Terre were ranked as Italy's three cleanest beaches in 2000 by the Lega Ambiente (League for the Protection of the Environment). Visit online at www.legambiente.com.

FLORA & FAUNA

The region's flora and fauna is surprisingly varied, although urbanisation, industry and an ever-expanding tourism infrastructure threaten fragile species outside protected areas.

Milan is the least green of the three cities. Westwards lies the Parco Lombardo della Valle del Ticino, a 90,000-hectare park formed in 1974 to protect the River Ticino and its 100km-long valley which flows south from Lake Maggiore to the River Po. Pavia, on the Ticino's left bank, is the park's only town. Wildlife includes 140 bird species, 26 types of mammal and one of Italy's most notable examples of fluvial forest. The park's northern tip embraces the foot of Lake Maggiore, one of several pre-Alpine lakes north of Milan where subtropical flora such as azaleas, magnolias and acacias flourish. Italy's tallest palm trees grow on the fertile Borromeen island of Madre and there's a lush collection of rare and endemic species (Lombard garlic, bellflower) in Villa Carlotta's lush gardens overlooking Lake Como.

Turin's surrounds range from the limestone Langhe region, south of the city, where clay soils nurture rich vineyards and truffle crops, to the westward Alpine ranges of Valle d'Aosta. The Alps are home to marmots, chamois and roe deer. Oak and beech trees, dwarf pines and rhododendrons carpet much of the Italian range. The Parco Nazionale Gran Paradiso protects 70,000 hectares of Alpine terrain between Valle d'Aosta and Piedmont; as early as 1856 Victor Emmanuel II declared the area a royal hunting reserve, thus saving the ibex (mountain goat) from extinction.

Palm trees, lemon trees, juniper bushes and other typical Mediterranean flora sprout all over the place in warm Genoa. Cypress trees and pines (aleppo and maritime) grow along the lower-lying coast and everything from elm and ash to larch is abundant inland – making Liguria Italy's most heavily wooded region (52.3%). Vineyards and olive groves are grown in cultivated terraces on the rocky hillsides around Cinque Terre.

Marine fauna includes the great white shark, though attacks are extremely rare.

East of Genoa, the Mediterranean biodiversity of Cinque Terre is protected by the Riserva Marina delle Cinque Terre and the Parco Naturale Regionale di Portofino, which protects over 700 floral species on the Portofino promontory. The wild boar, stripeless tree frog, kestrel and Italian cave salamander all live here.

GOVERNMENT & POLITICS

Milan, Turin and Genoa are the respective capitals of the Lombardy *(Lombardia)*, Piedmont *(Piemonte)* and Liguria regions *(regioni)* – three of 20 administrative regions in Italy. Each elects its own regional council, regional cabinet and president. Valle d'Aosta is one of five Italian regions to be semi-autonomous or autonomous, with special powers granted under the constitution. Its regional assembly is similar to a parliament and has a wider range of administrative and economic powers (such as keeping 90% of local taxes within the region).

Regions are divided into provinces and city councils *(comuni)*. Milan heads the Provincia di Milano, further split into 188

comuni; Turin heads the Provincia di Torino; and Genoa is at the helm of the Provincia di Genova. Each is served by a prefect who selects a provincial assembly. Elections for all three tiers of local government are held simultaneously every five years.

Italy itself is a parliamentary republic, headed by a president who appoints the prime minister. The parliament, which had its seat in Turin between 1861 and 1865, consists of two houses with equal legislative power – a 630-strong chamber of deputies and a senate with 315 senators. The president, last elected in 1999, serves a seven-year term. The last parliamentary elections, held every five years, took place in Spring 2001.

ECONOMY

Serving as Italy's economic capital (Milan), the birthplace of Italian industry (Turin) and the largest Mediterranean port (Genoa), it is natural that the cities should rank among the country's wealthiest. Lombardy's contribution to national GDP (20.2%) is higher than any other region in Italy (only one other notches up a double figure); Piedmont and Liguria contribute 8.6% and 3.3%, respectively. Wealthy Lombardy generates 3.3% of European GDP, with annual production per capita (€22,000) equalling that of London.

Despite negative growth in production for all three regions in 1999 (down by 0.4%, 0.8% and 2% in Lombardy, Piedmont and Liguria compared to 1998), a boom in trade in the first quarter of 2000 – a 7% increase compared to 1999 for Milan – was enough to convince analysts that prosperous northern Italy was back on track. Unemployment in its leading city averaged an impressive 5.6% (compared to 11.4% nationally) in 1999 and, more recently, Milan was ranked third (after London and Paris) in Europe's 'innovation index' – linked to the number of patent requests it yields.

Some 8% of all Italian companies and 512 of Italy's 1630 multinational companies are based in Milan. The 1970s saw the tertiary and service sectors grow rapidly, swamping industrial mass production of the

1960s and accounting for 69% of business in Milan today. Outpacing both in growth since the 1990s is Italy's technology sector – headquartered in the city alongside 13% of the country's financial firms and the Milan stock exchange, which handles 90% of the national market. Trade fairs reap an annual revenue of €150 million and pull in 3.6 million visitors per year. Furniture, textile and clothing production are other key industries in the Milan province, coupled with its metallurgy industry (17.5% of national production).

Business is likewise on the up for Turin, a city that spawned Italian industry out of the Topolino (literally 'little mouse' but understood as 'Mickey Mouse' in Italian) and its predecessors, built by FIAT at its factory in Turin from 1899. In 2000 FIAT Auto, one of several companies within the FIAT Group, boasted an annual turnover of €18.5 billion (72% of total group revenues) and employed 95,400 people – making it Piedmont's largest employer. The only other five-digit employers in the region are Telecom Italia, Olivetti, San Paolo and Iveco FIAT (industrial vehicles). In March 2000, the FIAT Group traded in 20% of its shares for a 5.1% stake in the USA's General Motors, creating a joint venture anticipated to yield US$2 billion within five years.

Food and drink is Turin's other traditional industry. Nutella is produced at the Ferrero factory in Alba, south of Turin (Ferrero being Piedmont's 18th largest employer with a workforce of 2300); Italy's largest coffee roaster Lavazza is here; as are Martini & Rosso (see the 'Martini & Rosso' boxed text in the Turin chapter) and Cinzano, founded in Turin in 1757 and part of the Cinzano-based United Distillers & Vintners (UDV) group today. In the realm of telecommunications, Omnitel Pronto Italia, Italy's largest mobile phone company after Telecom Italia, employs 8000 people headquartered in Ivrea in Valle d'Aosta. In late 2000 it won one of five licences issued for third-generation mobile phones. Despite these industries, unemployment in Turin was only marginally below the national average at 11.2% in 1998 (7.6% in Piedmont).

Agricultural production in the Genoese economy – the smallest of the three urban economies – totalled L1.5 billion in 1999 (2% of national agricultural production). Flowers, olives and grapes are the predominant crops grown by 4% of the region's workforce – with the Riviera di Ponente notably harvesting 50% of Italy's cut flowers. The continuing national decline in heavy industry dealt a bitter blow to the traditional ship-building, engineering and metallurgical industries centred around both Genoa and La Spezia ports which, in 1999, decreased by 2% (compared to a 4.1% increase in 1998). Industry accounts for 23% of regional (Ligurian) GDP today.

Genoa is now turning its attention to tourism. The massive regeneration of the port area in anticipation of the 1992 Expo saw vast amounts of money poured into the port area which, coupled with its partial privatisation and restructuring of port operations, registered increases in container business and signalled a recovery of some of the port's former glory. In 1999, the number of ferry and cruise-ship passengers arriving at Genoa's ports rose by 14.7% and 56% respectively, while airport passenger traffic increased by 13%. Equally indicative of Genoa's turnaround is Liguria's unemployment rate, which fell from 10.2% in 1998 to 9.9% in 1999.

POPULATION & PEOPLE

Milan is second only to Rome in population. It forms part of one of Italy's most densely populated provinces (1881 inhabitants per sq km) and sits at the heart of its most populated region – 15.7% of the country's populace lives in Lombardy, compared to 7.4% in Piedmont and 2.8% in Liguria.

While the Turinese live a little bit in each other's pockets, the surrounding Piedmont region has lots of empty space: 170 inhabitants per sq km, compared to 194 nationally. In Liguria, 90% of people are clustered on the coast, with 55.8% living and working in the province of Genoa – an area still relatively unpacked (500 inhabitants per sq km) compared to other cities.

A huge influx of workers from both southern Italy and bordering countries in the 1960s saw the numbers of foreigners in all three cities rise. With low unemployment rates coupled with the lucrative work opportunities that cities such as Milan and Turin offer, this is a trend that continues to a lesser extent today: northern Italy's foreign population rose by 20% in 1999 (compared to 15% in central and southern Italy). Nationally, 2.2% of Italy's total population was foreign as of 1 January 2000.

Of the three cities, Milan touts the largest foreign population (20 in every 1000 inhabitants), fairly evenly split between Europeans (23.8%), Africans (25.5%) and Asians (35.2%). Its significant Chinese and Filipino communities are the fastest growing. Some 12,333 foreigners live in Genoa.

EDUCATION

School attendance is compulsory between the ages of six and 15, although the government announced plans in September 2000 to extend the latter to 18. Everyone can attend nursery school from the ages of three to five, and higher secondary school from the ages of 14 to 19.

Italy has a long tradition of university education and can claim to have the world's oldest universities, among them Turin's Università degli Studi di Torino founded in 1405 (the world's oldest dates to the 11th-century in Bologna). Milan alone has seven universities and higher education institutions. Courses last four to six years.

ARTS
Music & Theatre

What with its production of violins and La Scala's monumental contribution to opera (see the boxed text 'La Scala' later in this chapter), northern Italy has played a pivotal role in the history of music.

As bishop of Milan from 374, St Ambrose composed music based on ancient Greek chants, later known as Ambrosian chants. Instrumental music followed hot on the heels of the creation of the first modern string instrument in the Cremonese workshop of Andrea Amati (1511–77), near Milan, in 1566. Other famous Cremonese violinmakers include Francesco Rugeri (1620–95), Andrea Guarneri (1626–98) and Antonio Stradivari (1644–1737). When the 16th century ushered in a musical revolution in the development of opera – an attempt to recreate the drama of ancient Greece – it was again Cremona that stepped forward with the genre's earliest successful composer, Claudio Monteverdi (c1567–1643), who drew from a variety of sources.

In Genoa, Niccolò Paganini (1782–1840) knew just about all there was to know about the violin by his 13th year. Two years later he launched a concert career that took him to every corner of Italy and to Europe's great stages. In addition to extracting chords, harmonies, arpeggios and rhythms hitherto undreamed of from a violin, Paganini was a virtuoso on the guitar. A prolific composer, he left behind six concertos, 24 quartets for violin, viola, guitar and other strings, 12 sonatas for violin and guitar and a long list of further sonatas. Liszt and Chopin applied much of what they learned from Paganini's genius to the piano.

Despite a rejection early in his career from Milan's prestigious conservatory, Giuseppe Verdi (1813–1901) became an icon midway through his life. Born in a village in northern Italy, he spent most of his life in Milan where he achieved his greatest works, including *Aïda*, *La Traviata* and *Otello* (1887). Almost all his operas were premiered at La Scala, including *Oberto*, his first in 1839. Following the death of his wife, Verdi spent four heart-broken years living in Milan's Grand Hotel, where a stroke killed him aged 87. A funeral procession of 300,000 was led through Milan by an 800-strong choir, conducted by La Scala's Arturo Toscanini.

Aïda inspired Puccini (1858–1924), the other star of the modern operatic era, to turn his hand to opera. He studied at the Milan Conservatory from 1880 to 1883 and saw the curtain rise on his first creation at La Scala in 1884. His subsequent achievements – *La Bohème* (1896) premiered in Turin, *Tosca* (1900) and *Madame Butterfly* (1904) – ensured Puccini a firm place in

La Scala

The curtain rose on Milan's legendary opera house in 1778, just a few years after a raging fire burnt down the Teatro Regio Ducale, a theatre situated in the same spot. Following the 1776 disaster, Maria Teresa of Austria clubbed together with the most noble of her subjects to build a new theatre – this elitist 'buy-your-own-box' system remained firmly intact until 1928, despite the Cisalpine Republic banning family coats-of-arms on boxes in 1798.

A seasonal approach to performances at La Scala was adopted in 1788, much to the consternation of Milanese theatre-goers for whom the theatre was a place to gossip, gamble (forbidden everywhere but in theatres until 1814, when it was banned altogether) and dine. Its interior was lit with 1080 oil lamps (replaced with electric lighting in 1883) and the legendary 362-lamp crystal chandelier in the auditorium was added in 1821.

Between 1823 and 1825, 32 of the 52 operas performed at La Scala were by Gioacchino Rossini (1792–1868), best known for introducing both comedy and many new instruments into opera. Vincenzo Bellini (1801–35) followed with world debuts of three operas, including his masterpiece *Norma* (1831), detested by the Milanese audience. When Giuseppe Verdi arrived in 1839 with his two-act opera *Oberto, Conte di San Bonifacio*, success was assured. In 1873, the controversial German composer Richard Wagner (1813–83) performed *Lohengrin*, the 1880s applauded the premieres of Luigi Manzotti's ballet and opera *Excelsior* (1881) and *Amor* (1886), and in 1889 Puccini arrived on the scene. Ironically the latter's *Madame Butterfly* was a total flop when premiered here in 1904 and wasn't performed in Milan for another 21 years.

La Scala's orchestra pit was sunk in 1907. Arturo Toscanini opened his debut season as conductor at La Scala in 1898. He returned in 1921 as artistic director, only to flee Fascism, Milan and Italy in 1929. When the grand old opera house reopened its doors in 1946 (having been bombed and rebuilt), it was an emotional 79-year-old Toscanini who conducted the inaugural concert. After his death in New York in 1957, his coffin was flown to Milan and laid in the foyer of La Scala where thousands flocked to pay their last respects. La Scala's greatest conductor is buried in Milan.

Soprano Maria Callas made her debut at La Scala in 1949 (in Verdi's *Aïda*), returning in 1953 to sing in Cherubini's *Medea* conducted by Leonard Bernstein. The same year Franco Zefferelli worked as scenographer on Rossini's *Italiani in Algeri*. From 1968 until 1985, Claudio Abbado (born 1933) served as musical director, La Scala being but one of many prestigious orchestras (including the Berlin Philharmonic and the London Symphony Orchestra) that the Milanese musician conducted. Since 1986, the position has been held by Italy's leading conductor, Naples-born Riccardo Muti (born 1941). Equally at home conducting opera or symphonic music, Maestro Muti enjoys a distinguished career at home and abroad.

musical history. *Turandot*, completed after his death, was seen for the first time at La Scala in 1926.

Modern theatre's most enduring contemporary representative is Dario Fo, born in 1926 in San Giano, Lake Maggiore. Often in the form of a one-man show, but also in company (most often with Franca Rame), his work is laced with political and social critique. He has had a number of hits in London's West End, including *Morte Accidentale di un Anarchista* (Accidental Death of an Anarchist), *Non Si Paga, Non Si Paga* (Can't Pay, Won't Pay) and *Mistero Buffo*. Much to the consternation of the Italian literary establishment, Fo won the 1997 Nobel Prize for Literature. At the last count, he was contemplating running for mayor of Milan.

Literature

Medieval to Modern Two of Italian literature's greatest architects, Francesco Petrarca (Petrarch; 1304–74) and Giovanni Boccaccio (1313–75) found themselves in Milan in 1359.

Fleeing from France to northern Italy in 1353 to escape the plague that had already killed his muse Laura, Petrarca worked in Milan for seven years. During this time he completed the sonnets of *Il Canzoniere*, considered typical of his formidable lyricism that permanently influenced Italian poetry. The poet's personal annotated copy of Virgil's *The Georgics* is kept in Milan's Biblioteca Ambrosiana, as are letters from Boccaccio, a friend of Petrarca who visited him frequently during this period. Boccaccio's experiences in the big city are related in *Il Decamerone*, 100 short stories chronicling the exodus of 10 young Florentines from their plague-ridden city. Genoa also features in the work of Italy's first novelist.

Amid the feverish frenzy of treatises on architecture and politics, translations of Greek classics, and works by Hebrew and Arabic scholars nurtured by the Renaissance, came the scientific theories of Leonardo da Vinci (1452–1519). He lived in Milan between 1482 and 1499 and encoded his ideas from 1489 in the *Atlantic Codex* (not to be confused with his *Leicester Codex* which Bill Gates allegedly bought for over US$30 million in 1994). This scientific manual also forms part of the Biblioteca Ambrosiana collection.

Tragedy dramatised 18th-century literature which saw Piedmont's Vittorio Alfieri (1749–1803) create a new genre, unknown until then. Ranked as Italy's greatest tragic poet, the Asti-born writer penned 22 tragedies from 1778, of which *Don Grazia Saul* was considered his masterpiece.

Poetry remained the main avenue of literary expression until Alessandro Manzoni (1785–1873) came along with *I Promessi Sposi* (The Betrothed), a historical novel on an epic scale. The Milanese writer laboured over the novel between 1825 and 1840 in order to establish a narrative language accessible to all Italians. The result was a manuscript with a barely disguised, strong nationalist flavour that rallied the nation when it appeared in the 1840s. The novel was set in 17th-century Milan. Upon Manzoni's death, one of his closest friends, Verdi, composed *Requiem* as a tribute to his great friend.

20th Century & Beyond Italy's richest contribution to modern literature has been through the novel and short story. Turin especially has produced a wealth of authors. Cesare Pavese, born in a Piedmont farmhouse in 1908, took Walt Whitman as his guiding light. Involved in the anti-Fascist circles of prewar Turin, his greatest novel, *La Luna e Il Falò* (The Moon and the Bonfire), was published in 1950, the year he took his life. *An Absurd Vice: A Biography of Cesare Pavese* by Davide Lajolo, published in 1983, is a meaty account of the writer and the Turin and Piedmont in which he lived.

Like Pavese, Turinese doctor Carlo Levi (1902–75) experienced internal exile in southern Italy under the Fascists. The result was a moving account, published in 1979, of a world oppressed and forgotten by Rome, *Cristo si è Fermato a Eboli* (Christ Stopped at Eboli).

Primo Levi, a Turinese Jew, ended up in Auschwitz during the war. *Se Quest'è Un*

Uomo (If This is a Man), published in 1958, is the dignified account of his survival, while *La Tregua* (The Truce), published in 1963, recounts his long road back home through Eastern Europe. *Other People's Trades*, a collection of essays published in 1985, includes an account of the house on Corso Umberto in Turin where he was born in 1919. Levi committed suicide in 1987.

Palermo-born Natalia Ginzburg (1916–91) spent most of her life in Turin. Much of her writing is semi-autobiographical. *Tutti i Nostri Ieri* (All Our Yesterdays; 1952), *Valentino* (1951) and *Le Voci della Sera* (Voices in the Evening; 1962) are just three novels from her range of fiction, plays and essays. Her particular gift is in capturing the essence of gestures and moments in everyday life.

In between working as a reporter on Milan's *Corriere della Sera* from the age of 22 until his death, Dino Buzzati (1906–72) produced *Tartar Steppe*, an epic novel about a soldier posted to a far-off land, only to await a battle for several decades. Largely written in 1938, it's translated into 20-odd languages.

A writer of a different ilk is Italo Calvino (1923–85), Cuban-born but raised in San Remo on the Ligurian coast. A Resistance fighter and then Communist Party member until 1957, Calvino's works border on the fantastical, thinly veiling his main preoccupation with human behaviour in society. *I Nostri Antenati* (Our Ancestors; 1960), a collection of three such tales, is perhaps his greatest success.

Genoa's best-known writer is Nobel-prize winner Eugenio Montale (1896–1981). His poems can be read in translation in the recently published *Collected Poems 1920–54* and *Satura 1962–70*.

Another Ligurian name to look out for is Edmondo de Amicis (1846–1908) whose novel, *Cuore*, was translated in 1895 under the title 'Heart' and later as 'Enrico's Schooldays'. Tagged 'an Italian schoolboy's journal – a book for boys', it tells the emotional tale of a boy's days at a Turin school. The novel later served as a very loose basis for the film *3000 Leagues in Search of Mother*, which opens in the port of Genoa.

Italian literature of the 1980s was briefly dominated by the Milan-based intellectual Umberto Eco, born in Bologna in 1932. He shot to popularity with his first and best-known work, *Il Nome della Rosa* (The Name of the Rose, 1980). It was made into a successful film starring Sean Connery.

Paola Capriolo, born in Milan in 1962, explores the power of theatre in her novels, presenting Puccini's opera in an uncanny light in her novel *Vissi d'Amore* (Floria Tosca; 1997), and exploring the macabre sense of stage in *La Spettatrice* (The Woman Watching; 1998). Both are musts for opera buffs.

Turin's Alessandro Baricco (born 1958) is one of Italy's boldest contemporary writers. His bestseller *Seta* (Silk), a poetic love story about silk worms published in 1996, has been translated into 27 languages and is being adapted for screen. His latest novel *City* (2000) – 'city' being the Italian title – will be published in English in 2001.

Architecture

The region's greatest contribution to early architecture is, without a doubt, Milan's Gothic duomo, built by a rash of different architects between 1397 and 1812 to become the world's fourth largest cathedral today.

The Renaissance (c1400–1600) saw *palazzi* mushroom, as leading families in the city-states sought to show off their wealth with grandiose dynastic palaces. Among the most notable are those studding Genoa's Via Garibaldi – a grand boulevard created by Galeazzo Alessi (1512–72). A pal of Michelangelo when in Rome, Alessi worked in Genoa for several years, laying out the port area and building palace after noble palace in the old city.

A century later it was Turin's turn to make its architectural mark as Guarino Guarini (1624–83) enlarged the city and gave it its distinctive Baroque appearance. Carlo di Castellamonte worked on Castello di Rivoli (1670) and Filippo Juvarra (1678–1736), as royal architect, graced the Savoy capital with masterpieces such as the revolutionary scissors staircase inside Palazzo Reale, Palazzo Madama (1718–21), Palazzina di Caccia di Stupingi (1729) and the Basilica di Superga (1715–31).

A flurry of creative architecture marked the early 18th century, finding expression in Milan through the work of Giuseppe Piermarini (1734–1808), a pupil of Italian architect Luigi Vanvitelli. Among other edifices, Piermarini built Teatro alla Scala (1778).

The beginning of modern architecture in Italy was epitomised by the late-19th-century shopping galleries that sprung up in all three northern cities. The most sumptuous is Milan's Galleria Vittorio Emanuele II, designed between 1864 and 1878 by Giuseppe Mengoni who gave the covered mall its distinctive iron-and-glass roof.

The Art Nouveau movement of the 20th century (called *Lo Stilo Liberty* in Italy) had scarcely got off the ground when Mussolini and the Fascist ones inaugurated grandiose buildings such as Milan's Stazione Centrale (1927–31) and the FIAT factory in Lingotto (1929–30) which, with a race track whizzing around its roof, symbolised Turin's contri-

bution to Italian industry. Milan was graced with two delightfully ugly skyscrapers – the 20-storey Torre Velasca with its distinct bulge in the 1950s, followed by Gio Pirelli's 1960 creation – and renowned Rationalist architect Pier Luigi Nervi (1891–1979) built Turin's exposition hall in 1949.

Contemporary architects have endowed all three cities with some stunning constructions, Genoa unquestionably leading the way thanks to Italy's leading architect, Genoese-born Renzo Piano (see the boxed text 'Renzo Piano'). In Milan, world-renowned designers have called on the likes of New York's Peter Marino and London's David Chipperfield to create state-of-the-art homes, boutiques and showrooms for them.

Design

Despite an early lead by Turin in this field, with its hosting of the first Internazionale d'Arte Decorativa Moderna in 1902 which saw Art-Nouveau works by Turinese furniture designers such as Vittorio Valabrega and Agostino Lauro in the limelight, Milan soon dominated the scene. The latter started

Renzo Piano

A daring use of glass is the distinctive trademark of world-renowned Genoese architect, Renzo Piano (born 1937). Son of a builder and graduate of Milan Polytechnic's architecture school, he raised eyebrows for the first time with Paris' Centre George Pompidou (1978) – a 'shocking' state-of-the-art construction at odds with the historic city quarter in which it boldly stood. Since then, eyebrows have remained raised.

The maverick of world architecture has trotted around the globe: the Menil Museum in Houston, Texas (1996); Basel's Beyeler Museum in Switzerland; Lyons' Cité Internationale and contemporary art museum (1996), France; and Japan's Kansai airport (1994), built on a 15 sq km man-made island in Osaka Bay. Piano's been overseeing the transformation of Berlin's Potsdamer Platz since 1992.

Closer to home, Piano converted Turin's FIAT factory at Lingotto into a conference centre (1988–96) topped, no less, with a bright blue bubble of glass; and revamped Genoa's Porto Antico area (1988–92), transforming cotton warehouses into a shopping and congress centre, building an aquarium and other waterside attractions. In mid-2001 world leaders attending the G8 Summit in Genoa saw Piano's latest creation unveiled – a 'bubble' of glass floating on water at the Porto Antico, filled with a fluttering kaleidoscope of butterflies.

Piano masterminds his architectural wonders from the Renzo Piano Building Workshop (1989–91), his glass office on rocks overlooking the sea, midway between Voltri and Vesima, west of Genoa. He has a second office (and a second home) in Paris. He won the Pritzker Architecture Prize in 1998 – the highest accolade an architect can win.

to make a name for itself before WWII, but it was only after the war that its design business came into its own.

Gio Ponti (1891–1979) is the considered architect of Italian design. Founding one of Italy's first architectural magazines *Domus* alongside *La Casa Bella* in 1928, the Milanese architect advocated a fusion of the avant-garde Rationalism movement with tradition, from which a distinct 'Italian style' would emerge. In 1946, Piaggio, an aircraft manufacturer which found itself in tatters after WWII, produced the first Vespa (literally 'wasp') – a cheap lightweight scooter that sold 2000 in its first year of production, 10,000 in its second and one million by 1956. Starring in over 90 films – including *Vacanze Romane* (Roman Holiday) with Audrey Hepburn in 1953 – in Italy's industrious postwar years, Piaggio's Vespa zipped into fashion as a potent symbol of Italy's free spirit.

Attention was turned to kitchen design and household appliances in the 1950s and '60s. Specialist lamp producers such as Brescia-based Arteluce, Flos and Milan's Artemide – still strong today – lured top designers into their fold, while plastic and rubber emerged as new mediums for furniture design. Together with Kartell, a Milan design house founded in 1949, Marco

ASA ANDERSSON

With sultry designs and shapely lines, Italian furniture is more sculpture than sofa!

Zanuso (1916–98) created a children's plastic chair in 1964. Three years later the Milanese designer worked with furniture manufacturer Arflex (founded 1950) to create *Lady*, an armchair made from sponge rubber. Another Milan furniture producer, Zanotta (founded 1954) went one step further in 1967 and produced an inflatable armchair from transparent PVC. When it later came out with a saggy shapeless beanbag filled with thousands of polystyrene balls in 1968, it scored an unprecedented coup.

Milan hosted its first Salone del Mobile (furniture fair) in 1961. Hot on its heels followed Pop Art, which found expression in furniture through designs such as Gaetano Pesce's *Donna*, an armchair sculpted in a womanly shape from polyurethane and attached to a 'ball-and-chain' pouffe (reproduced only in red today). The designers of the subsequent Radical avant-garde movement in the late '60s and early '70s wiped out any last remaining traces of rationalism in works like *Bocca*, a sultry sofa shaped like a pair of red lips produced by the Turin-based design house Gufram (founded 1966). Works like this formed the backbone of an exhibition entitled 'Italy: The New Domestic Landscape' held in New York's Museum of Modern Art in 1972. Italian design had made its mark internationally.

The 1980s saw the consolidation of Milanese design houses such as Alchimia, Memphis, Design Group Italia and Zanotta, all of whom have designers of the highest calibre on their books. Ettore Sottsass (born 1917), a Turin university graduate based in Milan since 1961, created his angular *Carlton* set of shelves in 1982; Memphis still produces it (it sells for an extraordinary €11,000 today). Milanese architect and designer Alessandro Mendini (born 1931) worked closely with Italian tableware guru Alessi during this period, as did Milan's Aldo Rossi (1931–97) and Liguria's Stefano Giovannoni (born La Spezia 1954), whose Studio King Kong created the little man who adorns Alessi's leading product line. Notable designs to come out of the world's design capital in the 1990s included Ron

Arad's *Bookworm* book shelf, produced by Kartell in 1994 and among 1000 pieces displayed in Kartell's Milan museum which opened in 2000 to chronicle plastic design.

Fashion

Milan's meteoric rise to European fashion capital rode on the back on the wave of creative activity that the city witnessed from the 1960s. With the gradual departure of many haute-couture fashion houses from Florence in the mid-1950s, coupled with the emergence of a new mass market in high fashion, Italy's largest fashion show – a twice-yearly Florentine event since 1951 – made a leggy leap to the industrial north.

The first international fashion show waltzed down Milan's catwalk in 1971. In 1982, the industry was revolutionised with the more wearable and reasonably priced *prêt à porter* ('ready to wear') collection of Giorgio Armani. The Milan-born fashion designer, who moved from window dresser at Milan's La Rinascente department store to Nino Cerruti's men's wear studio in 1961, branched out on his own in 1975. The Giorgio Armani empire set another precedent in 2000 when it opened its flagship store, Emporio Armani, in Milan – 6000 sq m of space pioneering designer shopping for fashion, flowers and wine 'under one roof'.

Gucci, the industry's other big name, moved from Florence to Milan's Via Monte Napoleone in 1951. Prada, a million-dollar holding for dozens of smaller design houses including Jil Sander and Miu Miu, has its origins in a family-run shop that opened in Milan in 1913. Laura Bijoti and Krizia (lesser-known in Europe but huge in Russia and the wealthy Far East), Roberto Cavalli (trendy designs at fashion's cutting edge) and Dolce & Gabbana are other design houses ranked alongside Italy's richest. See the special section 'Shopping in Milan'.

Italian fashion is overseen by the Milan-based Camera Nazionale della Moda Italiana (CNMI), organiser of Milan's dazzling fashion weeks. Shows are seasonal, the most prestigious being the Milano Collezioni Donna, which sees the world's top designers unveil their prêt à porter women's collections in Milan each February/March and September/October. The men's fashion show – Milano Collezioni Uomo – takes place in January and June/July. Some 120 events are crammed into each show, which typically lasts 10 to 12 days. Most designers share the Fiera di Milano catwalk, but an exclusive bunch model their collections elsewhere – in private palaces or in their own state-of-the-art boutiques around the city's famous 'golden quad'.

Increasing competition has forced the fashion industry to become prêt à porter focused; exclusively haute-couture houses number just one in 10 (Italy's twice-annual, haute-couture shows are held in Rome). Early 2000 saw the debut of Milano Freestyle, a show devoted to designer sportswear. More recently, Pitti Bimbo – children's fashion – has graced Milan's catwalk.

Painting

The history of painting in northern Italy is well-illustrated by the extensive art collections displayed in Milan's Pinacoteca di Brera and the Galleria Sabauda in Turin. Among the religious frescoes to emerge in the 14th century were those by Giovanni da Milano (1346–69), also known as Giovanni da Como after the lakeside village where he was born. Heavily influenced by the naturalism of Giotti (1266–1337), the Lombard artist who cast aside the two-dimensional restrictions of painting, he played with the use of light to create a new depth and drama to the genre. The plague that swept through Milan in 1348 had a huge effect on his work.

Brescia-born Vincenzo Foppa (c1427 –1515) and Andrea Matagna (1430–1506), who painted his first fresco at the age of 17, dominated the Milanese School in the 15th century. Matagna's masterpiece, *The Dead Christ*, was completed towards the end of his life and was intended for his own tomb. Its startling perspective took foreshortening to a new level. The morbid work of art hangs in the Pinacoteca di Brera.

The Renaissance ushered in Leonardo da Vinci (1452–1519), who arrived in Milan to paint the *Last Supper* in the refectory of

JANE SMITH

Leonardo da Vinci lived in Milan from 1482 to 1500, where he painted the *Last Supper*

Santa Maria delle Grazie. The artist's ability to represent the psychological characteristics of Jesus and his 12 disciples and create illusions of space marked the start of the High Renaissance. Another work from this era to survive is one by a Leonardo pupil – Bernardino Luini. A leading figure in 16th-century northern Italian art, Luini was active in Milan from 1512 until his death around 1532. His cycle of frescoes inside the Chiesa di San Maurizio decorates the entire church interior; his fresco of St Catherine is outstanding. The influence of Leonardo finds expression in the faces of the Madonna and child, depicted in his *Virgin of the Rose Garden* (c1508). Another Lombard painter of note during this period was Bramantino (1465–1530), whose *Crucification*, displayed in the Pinacoteca di Brera is considered to be among his most representative works. In Turin's Galleria Sabauda, one room is dedicated to Piedmontese 'followers' of Leonardo.

The Milanese painter Michelangelo Merisi di Caravaggio (1573–1610) heralded a movement from the confines of the High Renaissance towards a new naturalism. His paintings, using street urchins and prostitutes as models for biblical subjects, were often rejected for being too real. However, his innovative use of light and shade, coupled with a supreme drawing ability, did see him courted by contemporary collectors and an influence for centuries. The expression on Christ's face in *Supper at Emmaus* (1606) and *Canestra di Frutta* (Fruit Basket) both demonstrate his cruel realism.

Mannerism ushered in Bergamo-born Evaristo Baschenis (1617–77), whose *Still Life with Musical Instruments*, with its exact depiction of every last detail, saw it later hailed as one of Italian art's most important 17th-century works. Giacomo Ceruti (1698–1767) picked up where Caravaggio had left off in dragging urchins off the street as models, earning him the nickname 'Pitocchetto' (from the Lombard word for louse). Unlike those of his predecessor, however, his realist depictions of pitiful young boys with chicken baskets and the like were praised and he quickly won acclaim as an admired portrait painter.

Cinema

The Italian film industry was born without a bang in Turin in 1904. Screenings of silent B&W pictures had taken place in Milan, Turin and Rome as early as 1896, but it was not until the start of the 20th century that Turin's production studios – such as Ambrosio and Italia Film – mushroomed, peaking at 50 by 1914.

The first blockbuster to be produced in Turin was silent *Cabiria* (1914) which – at 123 minutes long – was Italy's longest film made up until that date. The advanced techniques it used (such as a dolly) laid the path for the monumental epics that would follow. The film was directed by Asti-born film director Giovanni Pastrone (1882–1959). By 1930, the industry was virtually bankrupt so Mussolini nationalised it.

Milan gave birth to Luchino Visconti (1906–76), the great 'aristocrat' of Italian cinema and the most 'aristocratic of Marxists' whose work steered in neo-realism. He made movies from 1942 until his death, including the memorable adaptation of Tomasi di Lampedusa's *Il Gattopardo* (The Leopard, 1963), starring Burt Lancaster and set in the Risorgimento era. In the late 1940s, Visconti was joined by Franco Zeffirelli (born 1923), who worked with the Milanese director as actor and stage manager. As an accomplished theatre director, Visconti introduced French playwrights such as Cocteau and Sartre into Italy, and in the 1950s produced operas starring sopranos of Maria Callas calibre.

Federico Fellini (1920–94) waved the creative baton in the 1950s. When *La Dolce Vita* was world-premiered in Milan in 1960, it was met with boos and 'basta' shouts by the Milanese audience, shocked by Fellini's disquieting style, which abandoned realistic shots for explicitly pointed images.

Roberto Benigni worked closely with Milan's notable Jewish community to make the Oscar-winning *La Vita e Bella* (Life is Beautiful) in 1998. The film was accosted by right-wing protestors when premiered in Milan. One of Italy's great silver-screen idols was Vittorio Glassman, born in Genoa in 1922. The actor made more than 50 films in a career that spanned several decades and featured highlights such as *War & Peace* (1956), *Profumo Di Donna* (Scent of a Woman) which won Best Actor at Cannes in 1975 and was remade in 1992 with Al Pacino, *The Palermo Connection* (1991) and *Sleepers* (1996). He died of a heart attack in 2000.

SOCIETY & CONDUCT

The Milanese, Turinese and Genoese are three very different breeds, although certain stereotypical traits are upheld by all three: wild gesticulations while speaking at lightening speed, a dare-devil passion for food, and an uncontrollable need to drive like maniacs. There's a lot more to it than meets the eye however (should you actually get to meet their eye, given those very dark shades that most beauties bask behind, sun or no sun).

Typically, each slams the other. The Milanese are classed as cold, ruthless creatures driven by the sole desire to make shed-loads of money and be filthy rich – an image that

the city's cocktail-quaffing jetset reaffirms with its 'bop-till-you-drop' party pace and love for big fast cars. Bribes form the backbone of business most assume, a 'fact' of city life voiced by Milanese designer Giorgio Armani when his dirty linen was hung up to dry during Tangentopoli's messy aftermath.

The Turinese are down-to-earth creatures living in a provincial backwater, so say scornful Milanese. Despite this and the other common misconceptions showered on Turin, the refined Turinese are staunchly proud of their unexpectedly elegant city, believing no other in Italy to be as wonderful as theirs.

The rough-and-tumble Genoese, meanwhile, duck 'n' dive to get things done and can be as difficult to decipher as Genoa's *caruggi* (old city alleys) are to navigate. 'Rogues' is what an uppity Milanese might say, yet the natural exuberance and ingenuity of these sea-faring people carries an irresistible charm and warmth.

Hard-working, resilient, resourceful and optimistic with a good sense of humour are classic labels that all three wear. Most are passionately loyal to their friends and families, carry a strong distrust of authority and, when confronted with a silly rule, an unjust law or a stupid order, they don't complain or try to change things, they simply try to find the quickest way around them. The Turinese trend of simply abandoning one's car in the middle of the street, should no authorised parking space be available, is a classic example.

Dos & Don'ts

Italians tend to be tolerant but, despite an apparent obsession with (mostly female) nakedness, especially in advertising, they are not excessively free and easy.

Shopping in Milan and – to a lesser extent – in Turin requires certain etiquette; killer glares from shop assistants will establish if you're doing things right or wrong. Saying that, when waltzing into Missoni, Moschino or Miu Miu, don't expect a necessarily warm welcome. The odd shop assistant might smile, but most adopt an icier approach. Stroking and fondling is frowned upon in most upmarket boutiques – ask if you want to try on a garment or inspect it more closely.

In rainy weather, umbrellas are allowed no further than the threshold. Practically every public place in all three cities – be it a shop, cafe, restaurant or museum – sports a purpose-built umbrella stand inside its entrance. Should you fail to deposit your wet 'n' soggy brolly here, you and it will be quick-marched back to the entrance quicker than you can say Giacomo Robinson. At one of the Armani shops in Milan, a burly doorman doles out umbrella-shaped plastic bags, complete with white cord for slinging over one's shoulder.

Dress modestly in churches – no shorts, short skirts or bare shoulders (cover them with a scarf). When visiting the duomo in Milan or another church during a mass or other service (which you should refrain from doing), try to be as inconspicuous as possible.

Topless sunbathing, while not uncommon on some Ligurian beaches, is not always acceptable. Take your cue from other bathers; should you strip off your top, boob-baring is not generally interpreted as provocative.

Walking the streets near beaches or around Cinque Terre in a bikini or skimpy costume, bare-chested or bare-footed is simply not on.

RELIGION

A visit to Milan's duomo on Sunday – packed with worshippers of all ages – banishes any doubt that Catholicism, the state religion until 1985, might be anything other than alive and very well. The Lateran Treaty of 1929, between Mussolini and the Catholic Church, recognised Italy's capital as the centre of the Catholic world. After Rome, Milan is Italy's largest and most important diocese.

Despite church attendance falling from 70% after WWII to 25%, Pope John Paul II (since 1978) has successfully steered the church into the 21st century, winning the hearts of Catholics around the world with his indefatigable papal tours and punishing schedule, in spite of painfully advanced age and failing health. Although most Italians greatly respect the Polish pontiff (the papacy is a kind of royal family to Italians), most yearn for one of their own to be at the helm – as was the case between 1963 and 1978 when Giovanni Battista Montini, born in Brescia in 1897 and archbishop of Milan from 1954, became Pope Paul VI. The hot favourite in early 2001 for the next pontificate was Cardinal Carlo Maria Martini, Turin-born and ordained Milan archbishop in 1980. Rival Cardinal Dionigi Tettamanzi, archbishop of Genoa and academic theologian who's assisted the Pope in writing several works, blew his chances in March 2000 when a set of devilish rules he wrote about resisting Satan were slammed by the Church as a load of garbled tosh. Some 85% of Italians profess to be Catholic.

Muslims, who have a mosque in Milan (one of three countrywide), numbering about 700,000, are Italy's second largest religious community – to the horror of the right-wing Lega Nord (see the boxed text 'Another Country' earlier in this chapter). Other denominations include 500,000 evangelical Protestants, about 220,000 Jehovah's Witnesses, and other, smaller groups, including a notable Jewish community in Milan and the Valdesi (Waldenses), Swiss-Protestant Baptists in Piedmont.

LANGUAGE

Many Italians speak some English because they study it in school, but it is more widely understood in the major centres such as Milan. Staff at hotels and restaurants often speak a little English, but you will be better received if you at least attempt to communicate in Italian. Given their proximity to France, many Turinese speak French. The latter is afforded equal right with Italian in Valle d'Aosta, a region west of the city, where Italian was only introduced in 1861.

See the Language chapter for an introduction to the Italian language and some vocabulary.

Facts for the Visitor

WHEN TO GO

Milan, Turin and Genoa are alluring places to visit at any time of year, with the exception of late July and August when the weather boils, city dwellers abandon their cities and many shops, restaurants and galleries. Scores flock to the Genoese coast – packing its beaches with oiled bodies and prompting prices to soar sun-high. May to June are among the most attractive months to stroll the city streets, although finding accommodation in Milan is horrendously difficult due to the flurry of big trade fairs that fall at this time.

Those planning a city break should plump for the weekend, which is when mid-range and top-end hotels in northern Italy's commercial cities empty of business travellers and lower their rates to lure other guests in.

July and September are the best months for walking in the Alps and Turinese foothills. Skiers and snowboarders fly down slopes in Valle d'Aosta from late December to early April.

You may prefer to organise your trip or itinerary to coincide with one or more of the many festivals that litter the cities' cultural calendars – Milan's fashion days are a fabulous time to visit, except for the fact that accommodation needs booking several months in advance. Shoppers seeking a sinful splurge should consider January and its sales.

MAPS

Abroad, you'll only be able to pick up a Milan city map. In the country, none of the tourist offices distribute decent city maps, but bookshops sell a wide range. The Touring Club of Italy (TCI; see Tourist Offices later in this chapter) and the Automobile Club Italia (see Car & Motorcycle under Getting Around in the city chapters) are invaluable sources for maps and guides.

City Maps

Milan A detailed map of Milan is essential if you want to venture outside the central 'inner ring' without getting lost. The TCI publishes handy pocket-size maps (1:12,000; L4500) of Milan and Turin city centres.

There are countless other possibilities for Milan: French rubber-tyre giant Michelin rolls out an excellent 170-page pocket-size atlas *Milano e dintorni* (L10,000) with metro map, street index and city centre/suburb maps marked with one-way streets. Its blue-jacketed folded sheet map, *Milano e dintorni* (No 46; L12,000), also with street index and 1:15,000 city centre map, is available abroad and on the Internet at www.michelin-travel.com.

Another interesting choice is *Numeri civici di Milano* (1:5000; L38,000), an A4-size book with 200 pages of city maps, public transport routes and road maps (1:200,000) for the Lombardy region. It's published by Milan-based Edizioni Dilguro Milano (☎ 02 336 02 022). Other maps available in Milan include *Milano e comuni limitroti* (1:16,000; L12,000) by Edizioni Cartografione Milanesi, *Milano* (1:12,000; L9900) by Instituto Geografico de Agostini, the green-jacketed *Milano* (L9500) by Florence-based publishers Litografico Artistica Cartografica, and Belletti Editore's yellow-jacketed *Milano con tangenziali* (L9000).

Turin TCI's map of Turin (see Milan earlier) is one of the best. Otherwise, try *Torino pianta della città* (1:15,000), published by Litografia Artistica Cartografica, or the Instituto Geografico de Agostini's laminated *Torino* map, with a 1:12,000 city-centre spread. It costs L5900 and is an inspired idea for Turin's rainy days.

Genoa Belletti Editore publishes the yellow-jacketed *Genoa City Map* (1:5000) and the Instituto Geografico de Agostini puts out *Genova pianta di città* (1:10,000). Particularly useful for its comprehensive street index is the Genoa city map (1:12,000; L10,000) published by Studio FMB Bologna in its orange-jacketed EuroCity map series.

Regional Maps

Michelin's *North-West Italy* (No 428 in its orange-jacketed series), at a scale of 1:400,000, is widely available abroad and covers the entire region included in this book.

Within Italy, one of the best of the maps covering the Milan-Turin-Genoa region is TCI's orange-jacketed *Italia Settentrionale* (1:400,000).

The latter also publishes 1:200,000 regional maps (L12,000), which have road-distance tables and place-name indices: the green-jacketed *Piemonte e Valle d'Aosta* covers Turin and Valle d'Aosta, *Liguria* stretches south to Genoa, west to France and east to La Spezia, and *Lombardia* covers Milan.

Litografico Artistica Cartografica publish a map, *Riviere di Ponente-Costa Azzura* (1:145,000), which covers the strip of coast between Genoa and Nice (France). Its *Le Cinque Terre e il Golfo della Spezia* (1:40,000) covers the Cinque Terre coastline in excellent detail.

RESPONSIBLE TOURISM

Carving your name in stone in Milan's *duomo* (cathedral) or any other historical monument is nasty, mean and irresponsible – so don't graffiti. Likewise, resist the urge to touch the *Last Supper*, the frescoes covering the interior walls of Milan's Monastero Maggiore and other works of art which, despite the lack of glass protecting them, are precious.

You can reduce your own impact on the region – and keep your own stress level down – by using public transport. In Milan, abandon your car in an out-of-town car park (use those adjoining Bisceglie, Lampugnano or San Donato metro stations for the Fiera di Milano) and travel by metro into the centre.

Out of the cities, be it in the Turinese mountains or the Genoese coast, respect the law of the land. Don't litter or light fires and stick to marked trails and footpaths. In Cinque Terre, do not drive into the villages; those that are accessible by car are limited strictly to residents.

TOURIST OFFICES
Local Tourist Offices

Milan The central Azienda di Promozione Turistica (APT; provincial tourist office; ☎ 02 725 24 301/2/3, ⓔ apt.info@libero.it), Via Marconi 1, sells various locally produced guides (see Newspapers & Magazines later in this chapter) and maps, and stocks a vast collection of free brochures on Milan and its northern lakes. It opens 8.30 am to 7 pm weekdays, 9 am to 1 pm and 2 to 6 pm Saturday, and 9 am to 1 pm and 2 to 5 pm Sunday and holidays, October to April; and 8.30 am to 8 pm weekdays, 9 am to 1 pm and 2 to 7 pm Saturday, and 9 am to 1 pm and 2 to 5 pm Sunday and holidays, the rest of the year. The city council provides reams of practical information bilingually at www.comune .milano.it. There's information on the province at www.provincia.milano.it, and information on Lombardy at www.inlombardia.it.

Don't bother trying to extract tourist information by telephone from the busy Piazza del Duomo office; staff there will only ask you to fax your query to them. Instead call one of its less busy branch offices, such as the tourist office (☎ 02 725 24 360) at Stazione Centrale, which open 8 am to 7 pm Monday to Saturday, and 9 am to noon and 1.30 to 6 pm Sunday; or at Malpensa (☎ 02 748 67 213) or Linate (☎ 02 702 00 443) airports, both open 9 am to 5 pm weekdays.

TCI (☎ 02 535 99 71 for tourist information, ⓔ infotouring@touringclub.it), Corso Italia 10, opens 9 am to 7 pm Monday to Saturday. Visit its helpful Web site at www.touringclub.it.

Turin The main tourist office (☎ 011 53 59 01, 011 53 51 81, fax 011 53 00 70, ⓔ info @turismotorino.org), Piazza Castello 161, opens 9.30 am to 7 pm Monday to Saturday, and 9.30 am to 3 pm Sunday. Its booth at Stazione Porta Nuova (☎ 011 53 13 27) opens 9.30 am to 7 pm (3 pm Sunday). The airport branch (☎ 011 567 81 24) opens 8.30 am to 11.30 pm. There are useful Web sites in Italian (www.turismotorino.org) and English (www.comune.torino.it).

TCI (☎ 011 562 72 07, ⓔ negozio.torino @touringclub.it), Piazza Solferino 3b, opens

9 am to 1 pm and 2 to 7 pm weekdays, and 9 am to 1 pm Saturday.

Genoa The main Informazioni e Assistenza ai Turisti (IAT; local tourist office; ☎ 010 24 87 11, e aptgenova@apt.genova.it), Palazzina Santa Maria, on the waterfront at Porto Antico, opens 9 am to 6.30 pm daily. Its glass booths at Piazza Giacomo Matteotti (☎ 010 557 40 00) and in front of Magazzini del Cotone (☎ 010 248 56 11) open 9 am to 8 pm daily.

The tourist office at the airport (☎ 010 601 52 47) and in the ferry passenger terminal (☎ 010 530 82 01, e inliguria@tin.it) both open 8 am to 8 pm Monday to Saturday. Their small Stazione Principe counterpart opens 9.30 am to 1 pm and 3.30 to 6 pm Monday to Saturday, and 9.30 am to 12.30 pm Sunday.

The tourist office Web site (Italian only) is at www.apt.genova.it. The city council provides information on its site at www.comune.genova.it) and there's information on Liguria (☎ 800 46 98 38 toll-free) online at www.regione.liguria.it and at www.turismo.liguriainrete.it.

The Touring Club Italiano (☎ 010 595 52 91, e negozio.genova@touringclub.it), Palazzo Ducale 62r, opens 9 am to 1 pm and 2 to 7 pm weekdays, and 9 am to 1 pm Saturday.

Tourist Offices Abroad

Information is available from Italian state tourist offices abroad, run by the Ente Nazionale Italiano per il Turismo (ENIT; Italian State Tourism Board), with a Web site at www.enit.it.

Australia
(☎ 612-92 621 666, e lenitour@ihug.com.au) Level 26-44, Market Street, Sydney NSW 2000

Canada
(☎ 416-925 4882, e enit.canada@on.aibn.com) 175 Bloor Street East, Suite 907, South Tower, M4W 3R8 Toronto, Ontario
Web site: www.italiantourism.com

France
(☎ 01 42 66 66 68, e enit.parigi@wanadoo.fr) 23 rue de la Paix, 75002 Paris

Germany
Berlin: (☎ 030-247 83 97, e enit-berlin@t-online.de) Karl Liebknecht Strasse 34, 10178 Berlin
Frankfurt am Main: (☎ 069-25 91 26, e enit.ffm@t-online.de) Kaisertstrasse 65, 60329 Frankfurt am Main

Netherlands
(☎ 020-616 8244, e enitams@wirehub.nl) Stadhouderskade 2, 1054 ES Amsterdam

Switzerland
(☎ 01-211 7917, e enit@bluewin.ch) Uraniastrasse 32, 8001 Zurich

UK
(☎ 020-7408 1254, e enitlond@globalnet.co.uk) 1 Princes St, London W1R 8AY

USA
Chicago: (☎ 312-644 0996, e enitch@italiantourism.com) 500 North Michigan Ave, Chicago, IL 60611
Los Angeles: (☎ 310-820 2977, e enitla@earth link.net) Suite 550, 12400 Wilshire Blvd, Los Angeles, CA 90025
New York: (☎ 212-245 4822, e enitny@italiantourism.com) Suite 1565, 630 Fifth Ave, New York, NY 10111
Web site: www.italiantourism.com

TRAVEL AGENCIES

TCI (see the section on Tourist Offices earlier in this chapter) operates as a travel agency too.

For student and budget travel, CTS Travel has branches in Milan at Ripa di Porta Ticinese 100 (☎ 02 837 26 74) and Via San Antonio 2 (☎ 02 58 47 51), in Turin (☎ 011 812 45 34) at Via Montebello 2, and in Genoa (☎ 010 56 43 66) at Via San Vincenzo 119. Visit online at www.cts.it.

CIT Viaggi (☎ 02 86 37 01), inside Galleria Vittorio Emanuele II, is another Milanese agency that's worth trying. In Turin, Passaggi (☎ 011 53 46 63, e passtorino@tin.it) at Stazione Porta Nuova sells domestic and international train tickets. In Genoa, Nouvelles Frontières (☎ 010 553 64 74), Via Brigata Bisagno 19, and Pesci Viaggi e Turismo (☎ 010 56 49 36, e pesciros@tin.it), Piazza della Vittoria 94r, are reputable agencies.

DOCUMENTS

Citizens of the European Union (EU) can travel to Italy with their national identity cards alone. People from countries that don't issue ID cards (such as the UK) and non-EU nationals must have a full valid passport.

Visas

There are no entry requirements or restrictions on EU nationals. Citizens of Australia, New Zealand, Israel, the US, Canada and Japan can stay in Italy for up to 90 days without a visa. Except for people from a handful of other European countries (such as Iceland, Norway and Switzerland), everyone else needs a Schengen visa, valid for 90 days and accepted for travel in all other Schengen countries. Legal residents of one Schengen country don't require a visa for another Schengen country.

You can only apply for a Schengen visa in your country of residence and can apply for no more than two Schengen visas in any 12 month period – they're not renewable inside Italy. If you intend visiting more than one Schengen country, you are supposed to apply for the visa at a consulate of your main destination country or, if you have no main destination, the first country you intend to visit.

Study Visas Non-EU citizens who want to study at a university or language school in Italy must have a study visa. These visas can be obtained from your nearest Italian embassy or consulate. You will normally require confirmation of your enrolment and proof of payment of fees and adequate funds to support yourself before a visa is issued. The visa will then only cover the period of the enrolment. This type of visa is renewable within Italy but only with confirmation of ongoing enrolment and proof that you are able to support yourself (bank statements are preferred).

Resident Permits Anyone who takes up residence is advised to register with a *questura* (police station), in accordance with an anti-Mafia law that aims to keep watch on everyone's whereabouts. Failure to do so carries no consequences, although some landlords may be unwilling to rent out a flat to you if you cannot produce proof of registration.

A *permesso di soggiorno* (resident permit) is necessary if you plan to study, work (legally) or live in Italy. Obtaining one is never a pleasant experience, although for EU citizens it's a fairly straightforward procedure. Exact requirements vary between cities, so ask at your local questura. In Milan, contact the Ufficio Stranieri (Foreigners' Office; ☎ 02 6 22 61, metro MM3 Turati), Via Montebello 26. In general, you need a valid passport containing a visa stamp indicating your date of entry into Italy, a special visa issued in your own country for those planning to study, four passport-style photographs and proof of your ability to support yourself financially.

For information on work permits (EU citizens do not need one), see Doing Business later in this chapter.

Travel Insurance

This covers you for medical expenses, theft or loss of luggage, and for cancellation of and delays in your travel arrangements. Cover depends on your insurance and type of ticket, so ask your insurer and ticket-issuing agency to explain where you stand. Ticket loss is also covered by travel insurance.

Travel insurance papers and the international medical aid numbers that generally accompany them, are valuable documents, so treat them like your passport.

Paying for your ticket with a credit card often provides limited travel insurance and you may be able to reclaim the payment if the operator doesn't deliver. Ask your credit card company what it covers.

Driving Licence

When driving in Italy, always carry proof of ownership or rental of the vehicle that you're driving. EU member states' driving licences are recognised throughout. Those with non-EU licences are supposed to obtain an International Driving Permit (IDP) – issued by your national automobile association – to accompany their national licence.

Hostel Cards

A Hostelling International (HI) card is required if you want to stay in hostels affiliated to the Associazione Italiana Alberghi per la Gioventù (AIG; ☎ 06 487 55 12, e aig@uni.net). Buy a card in your home country by joining your national Youth Hostel Association (YHA) or pay L5000 for a one-night stamp once you roll up at the hostel door in Italy – six stamps make you a full international member. As a member you get various discounts in Italy, including on rail passes, some museums and Genoa's aquarium (L2000 reduction). Bookings for all three hostels can be made through the HI Web site, which is at www.hostelsaig.org.

Student, Teacher & Youth Cards

The International Student Identity Card (ISIC), for full-time students, and the International Teacher Identity Card (ITIC), for full-time teachers, are issued by more than 5000 organisations worldwide. The cards entitle you to a range of discounts, from reduced museum admission fees to cheap air fares.

Anyone aged under 26 can get a Euro<26 card (called Carta Giovani in Italy), which gives similar discounts to the ISIC card and is issued by most of the same organisations.

In Milan, Turin and Genoa, branches of Centro Turistico Studentesco e Giovanile (CTS), with a Web site at www.cts.it, issue all three cards (see Travel Agencies earlier in this chapter). However, you must join CTS first (L50,000).

Seniors Cards

Those aged over 60 or 65 can get many discounts (especially on museum admission fees) by presenting a passport or ID card as proof of age. You likewise only need proof of age to buy a Carta d'Argento (a discount rail pass for those aged over 60 or 65; see Other Parts of Italy under Train in the Getting There & Away chapter).

Copies

All important documents (passport data page and visa page, credit cards, travel insurance policy, travel tickets, driving licence and so on) should be photocopied before you leave home. Leave one copy with someone reliable at home and keep another with you, separate from the originals.

There is another option for storing details of your vital travel documents before you leave – Lonely Planet's online Travel Vault. It's the best option if you travel in a country with easy Internet access. Your travel vault is password-protected and accessible online at anytime. Storing details of your important documents in the vault is much safer than carrying photocopies. You can create your own travel vault for free by visiting the eKno Web site at www.ekno.lonelyplanet.com.

EMBASSIES & CONSULATES
Italian Embassies & Consulates

Here's a selection of Italian diplomatic missions abroad – Italy maintains consulates in additional cities in many of the countries listed:

Australia
Embassy: (☎ 02-6273 3333, e ambital2@dynamite.com.au) 12 Grey St, Deakin, Canberra 2600
Consulates: (☎ 03-9867 5744, e itconmel@netlink.com.au) 509 St Kilda Rd, Melbourne 3004; (☎ 02-9392 7900, e itconsyd@armadillo.com.au) Level 45, The Gateway, 1 Macquarie Place, Sydney NSW 2000

Canada
Embassy: (☎ 613-232 2401, e ambital@italyincanada.com) 21st Floor, 275 Slater St, Ottawa, Ontario KIP 5H9
Web site: www.italyincanada.com
Consulates: (☎ 514-849 8351/2/3, e cgi@italconsul.montreal.qc.ca) 3489 Drummond St, Montreal, Quebec H3G 1X6; (☎ 416-977 1566, e consolato.it@toronto.italconsulate.org) 136 Beverley St, Toronto, Ontario M5T 1Y5
Web site: www.toronto.italconsulate.org

France
Embassy: (☎ 01 49 54 03 00, e stampa@dial.oleane.com) 47–51 rue de Varenne, Paris 75007
Consulates: (☎ 01 44 30 47 00) 17 rue du Conseiller Collignon, 75116 Paris; (☎ 04 78 93 00 17) 5 rue Commandant Faurax, 69452 Lyons

Germany
  Embassy: (☎ 030-25 44 00) Hiroshimastrasse 1–7, Berlin 10785
  Web site: www.ambasciata-italia.de
Ireland
  Embassy: (☎ 01-660 1744, e italianembassy@tinet.ie) 63/65 Northumberland Rd, Dublin 4
Netherlands
  Embassy: (☎ 070-302 1030, e italemb@worldonline.nl) Alexanderstraat 12, The Hague 2514 JL
  Web site: www.italy.nl
New Zealand
  Embassy: (☎ 04-473 5339, consular section 49 47 176, e consular@ambwell.co.nz) 34–38 Grant Rd, Thorndon, Wellington
  Web site: www.italy-embassy.org.nz
Switzerland
  Embassy: (☎ 031-352 4151, e ambital.berna@spectraweb.ch) Elfenstrasse 14, Bern 3006
UK
  Embassy: (☎ 020-7312 2209, e emblondon@embitaly.org.uk) 14 Three Kings Yard, London W1Y 2EH
  Web site: www.embitaly.org.uk
  Consulate: (☎ 020-7235 9371) 38 Eaton Place, London SW1X 8AN
USA
  Embassy: (consular section ☎ 202-612 4400/5, e visa@itwash.org) 3000 Whitehaven Street, NW Washington, DC 20008
  Web site: www.italyemb.org
  Consulates: (☎ 310-820 0622, e cglos@aol.com) Suite 300, 12400 Wilshire Blvd, Los Angeles, CA 90025, Web site www.conlang.com; (☎ 212-737 9100, e italconsny@aol.com) 690 Park Ave, New York, NY 10021, Web site: www.italconsulnyc.org; (☎ 415-931 4924, e consolato@italcons-sf.org) 2590 Webster St, San Francisco, CA 94115, Web site: www.italcons-sf.org

Consulates in Milan, Turin & Genoa

Most embassies are in Rome but many countries have consulates in Milan, Turin or Genoa:

Australia
  (☎ 02 77 70 41, 02 777 04 217, toll-free 800 87 77 80, e australian-consulate-general@austrade.gov.au, metro MM1 San Babila) Via Borgogna 2, 20122 Milan
Canada
  (☎ 02 6 75 81, e milan-cs@dfaitmaeci.gc.ca, metro MM2/3 Centrale FS) Via Vittor Pisani 19, Milan 20124
  Web site: www.canada.it
France
  (☎ 02 655 91 41, metro MM3 Repubblica), Via Cesare Mangile 1, 20121 Milan
  (☎ 011 573 23 11) Via Roma 366, 10123 Turin
  (☎ 010 247 63 27, 010 247 63 40) Via Garibaldi 20, 16124 Genoa
Germany
  (☎ 02 623 11 01, metro MM2 Moscova) Via Solferino 40, 20121 Milan
  (☎ 011 53 10 88) Corso Vittorio Emanuele II 98, 10121 Turin
  (☎ 010 545 19 13) Via San Vincenzo 4/28, 16121 Genoa
Netherlands
  (☎ 02 485 58 41, e nlgovmil@iol.it, metro MM1 Conciliazione) Via San Vittore 45, 20123 Milan
  (☎ 010 56 68 38) Viale Sauli 4, 16121 Genoa
New Zealand
  (☎ 02 480 12 544, e milano@tradenz.govt.nz, metro MM1 Conciliazione) Via Guido d'Arezzo 6, 20145 Milan
  Web site: www.tradenz.govt.nz
Switzerland
  (☎ 02 777 91 61, metro MM1 Palestro) Via Palestro 2, 20121 Milan
  (☎ 011 71 55 70) Via Sacra San Michele 66, 10141 Turin
  (☎ 010 54 54 11) Piazza Brignole 3/6, 16122 Genoa
UK
  (☎ 02 72 30 01, metro MM1/3 Duomo) Via San Paolo 7, 20121 Milan
  (☎ 011 650 92 02, e timp@teleion.it) Via Saluzzo 60, 10125 Turin
  (☎ 010 41 68 28) Via di Francia 28, 16149 Genoa
USA
  (☎ 02 29 03 51, metro MM3 Monte Napoleone), Via Principe Amedeo, 2/10, 20121 Milan
  Web site: www.usis.it/milan
  (☎ 010 58 44 92) Via Dante 2/43, 16121 Genoa

CUSTOMS

Goods bought in and exported within the EU don't incur additional taxes, provided duty has been paid somewhere within the EU and the goods are for personal consumption.

Travellers arriving in Italy from outside the EU can import duty free 200 cigarettes, 1L of spirits, 2L of wine, 60mL of perfume, 250mL of toilet water, and other goods up to a total value of L340,000 (€175); anything over this limit must be declared on arrival and the appropriate duty paid (carry all receipts).

MONEY
Currency
Italy's national currency remains the *lira* (plural *lire*) until 28 February 2002, when it will be hurled on the scrapheap of history (see the boxed text 'Euroland'). Until then, there are notes of L1000, L2000, L5000, L10,000, L20,000, L50,000, L100,000 and L500,000 and coins in denominations of L50, L100, L200, L500 and L1000.

Exchange Rates
The Universal Currency Converter posts daily exchange rates at www.xe.net/ucc. In early 2001 exchange rates included:

country	unit		lira
Australia	A$1	=	1119
Canada	C$1	=	1396
euro	€1	=	1936
France	1FF	=	295
Germany	DM1	=	990
Ireland	IR£1	=	2458
Japan	Y100	=	1841
New Zealand	NZ$1	=	907
UK	UK£1	=	3089
USA	US$1	=	2134

Exchanging Money
A combination of cash, cheques and plastic will serve you grandly in Milan, Turin and Genoa. If you're arriving by car from France, bring some lire with you to avoid the embarrassing situation of rolling up at the toll booth and not being able to pay (not all toll booths in Italy accept credit cards).

There's little advantage in bringing wads of foreign cash. Exchange commissions are often lower than for travellers cheques, but the risk of losing the lot far outweighs such petty gains. Money can be easily changed at banks, post offices and bureaux de change. Banks generally offer the best rates, but shop around. Currency exchange booths often advertise 'no commission' and simply tout an inferior rate of exchange to compensate.

Euroland

As of 1 January 2002, the euro (€) – Europe's new currency for 11 European Union (EU) countries – will be legal tender in Italy. The lira will remain in circulation until 28 February 2002 when it will be hurled on the scrapheap of history – although L50 and L100 coins will be withdrawn before 2002. After this, any bank in Italy will trade in your tattered old lire banknotes for spanking-new, bridge-adorned euro bills.

The same euro coins (one, two, five, 10, 20 and 50 cents, €1 and €2) and bills (€5, €10, €20, €50, €100, €200) can be happily used in Euroland's 11 countries: Austria, Belgium, Finland, France, Germany, Ireland, Italy, Luxembourg, the Netherlands, Portugal and Spain. ATMs in Italy will only issue €10,€20 and €50 banknotes.

Until then, one euro is 13.76ATS, 40.34BEF, 5.95FIM, 6.56FF, 1.96DEM, 0.79IEP, L1936, 40.34LUF, 2.20NLG, 200PTE and 166.4ESP.

You can log into Euroland online at www.europa.eu.int/euro/html/entry.html and the Lonely Planet Web site, www.lonelyplanet.com, has a link to a currency converter.

Travellers cheques – the safest means of transporting your hard-earned cash – can be easily cashed at banks and bureaux de change. Keep the bank receipt listing the cheque numbers separate from the cheques and, likewise, a list of numbers of those you've cashed; this reduces problems in the event of loss or theft. Travellers cheques in lire and euros usually command no commission charge when cashing them. Travellers carrying better-known cheques, such as Visa, American Express (Amex) and Thomas Cook, will have little trouble cashing them in. If you lose your Amex cheques, call ☎ 800 87 20 00, a 24-hour toll-free number valid from all three cities.

Visa, MasterCard, Eurocard, Cirrus and other major credit cards are widely accepted in Milan, Turin and Genoa – except in many budget hotels and pizzerias which accept payment in hard cash only. ATMs (automated teller machines) are abundant in all three city centres, although it's not uncommon for ATMs to reject foreign cards. If your card's spat back, try another machine displaying your credit card's logo – the chances are it will work. To find out the location of the nearest ATM, call ☎ 1102.

If your credit card is lost, stolen or swallowed by an ATM, call ☎ 800 87 08 66 toll-free for MasterCard; ☎ 800 87 72 32 toll-free for Visa; and ☎ 800 82 20 56 toll-free for cards issued in Italy by an Italian bank. The toll-free emergency number to report lost or stolen Amex cards varies according to where the card was issued. Check with Amex in your home country, contact Amex's Rome-based 24-hour call centre (☎ 06 7 22 82) or the Amex office in Milan (☎ 02 87 66 74, metro MM1 Cordusio), Via Brera 3, which is open 9 am to 5.30 pm Monday to Thursday, 9 am to 5 pm Friday. Updated information is online at www.americanexpress.com.

International transfers can be made through Amex, Thomas Cook (☎ 800 00 44 88 toll-free) or Western Union (☎ 800 22 00 55 toll-free), a service which functions through Mailboxes Etc (which has stores in all three cities and a Web site at www.it.mbe.com).

Milan Central Milan is dotted with exchanges. Change and Money Shop on the western side of Piazza del Duomo (metro MM1/3 Duomo), both open 9 am to 9 pm. At Stazione Centrale (metro MM2/3 Centrale FS), the Exact exchange opens 7 am to 10.30 pm and offers a Western Union money transfer service. There are bureaux de change at both airports.

Banca Commerciale Italiana (metro MM1/3 Duomo), on the corner of Via Alessandro Manzoni and Piazza della Scala, has a 24-hour booth, with an automatic banknote exchange machine and ATMs inside. There are other 24-hour banknote exchange machines outside Banca Cesare Ponti, Piazza del Duomo 19 (metro MM1/3 Duomo) and Banca Populare di Luno e di Varese, Piazza Luigi Cadorna (metro MM1/3 Cadorna Triennale).

Many foreign banks have a Milan branch, including HSBC on Via Santa Maria alla Porta; National Westminster Bank, Via Turati 16/18; American Express Bank, Piazza San Babila 3; Deutsche Bank, Via San Prospero 2; and Credit Suisse, Via Turati 9.

Mailboxes Etc has stores scattered throughout the city, including at Piazza Caiazzo 3 (☎ 02 670 71 039, metro MM1/3 Centrale FS), open 9 am to 6.30 pm weekdays, 9 am to 6pm Saturday; and at Corso Sempione 38 (☎ 02 34 53 84 30, metro MM1 Pagano), open 9 am to 12.30 pm and 2 to 7 pm weekdays, 9 am to 1 pm Saturday.

Turin Banca CRT (Casa di Risparmco di Turino), in front of Hotel Nazionale, has ATMs and a 24-hour automatic banknote exchange machine outside. Other banknote machines, accessible 24 hours, are in front of San Paolo Bank at Via Santa Teresa 1g and opposite the waiting room near the tracks at Stazione Porta Nuova.

There is a bank with an ATM and exchange booth (open 7.10 am to 1.40 pm and 2.10 to 8.30 pm) at Stazione Porta Nuova. There are numerous commercial banks along Via Roma and Piazza San Carlo.

Mailboxes Etc (☎ 011 517 41 40, e mbe239@yahoo.com), Via Arsenale 25, opens 9.30 am to 1.30 pm and 2.30 to 7 pm weekdays.

Genoa There are banks which give cash advances and exchange travellers cheques, and plenty of ATMs all around town, at the airport and ferry terminal. In the town centre, there's an automatic banknote exchange machine outside Banca di Roma, Piazza Ferrari 32. Deutsche Bank has branch offices at Via Garibaldi 5 and Via Fieschi 14r.

Mailboxes Etc, Via Posco 21, opens 9 am to 1 pm and 3 to 4.45 pm weekdays.

Security
Pickpockets are pests in all three cities, particularly in Milan where crowded streets

and metro stations are prime breeding grounds. On the streets, keep as little on you as possible – preferably in a shoulder wallet or under-the-clothes money belt or pouch (external money belts only attract attention to your belongings). If you eschew the use of any such device, keep money in your front pockets and watch out for people who seem to brush close to you. Teams of delinquents employ an infinite number of tricks whereby one distracts you and the other deftly empties your pockets.

Back at your hotel, if your accommodation has a safe, use it. If you must leave money and documents in your room, divide the former into several stashes and hide them in different places. Lockable luggage is a good deterrent. Keep only a limited amount of your money as cash and the bulk in more easily replaceable forms, such as credit cards or travellers cheques.

Costs

If money's no object, then Milan is the city for you. What with excellent restaurants, luxurious hotels, exquisite cafes and a dearth of deadly designer shops, it's easy to blow a fortune – in a *very* short time. Such irresistible temptations, coupled with the fact that these cities are among Europe's most expensive, makes pre-trip budgeting essential if you want to enjoy yourself without having to be always counting how many lire you don't have.

A traveller wanting to stay in mid-range hotels, dine twice daily, not feel restricted to one museum visit a day and enjoy the odd drink or three should reckon on a minimum daily average of L300,000 to L400,000.

A *very* prudent backpacker might scrape by on around L70,000 per day, but only by staying in hostels, eating one simple meal a day, buying a sandwich or pizza slice for lunch, and minimising museum visits.

Tipping & Bargaining

You're not expected to tip on top of restaurant service charges (see Food later in this chapter) but it's common to leave a small amount, perhaps L3000 per person. If there is no service charge, consider leaving a 10% tip. In bars, Italians often leave small change as a tip – especially if the aperitif was accompanied by several platefuls of hors d'oeuvres. The tipping of taxi drivers is not common practice, but the porters in top-end hotels frequently expect big fat tips.

In hotels, always ask if there is a special price for a room if you plan to stay for more than a few days. This particularly applies to mid-range and top-end hotels in all three cities where rates are usually dictated by what trade fair is on and, occasionally, what your native language is.

While bargaining in shops is not acceptable, proprietors can be disposed to giving discounts if you are spending a horribly large amount of money.

Taxes & Refunds

When leaving the EU, non-EU residents can claim a refund of about 13% on the approximate 20% value-added tax (IVA) slapped onto just about everything in Italy. This refund is limited to big spenders however – you must spend more than L300,000 in one day in one shop to claim.

Refunds only apply to items purchased at retail outlets affiliated to the system. Shops (including big designers from Fratelli Rossetti and Sergio Rossi to Gucci) usually display a 'Tax-free for tourists', 'Cash Back' or 'Global Refund' sign but if not ask the shopkeeper. Fill out a form at the point of purchase and have it stamped and checked by Italian customs when leaving Italy.

Several companies specialise in immediate cash refunds. These include Global Refund (☎ 167 01 84 15 toll-free), which has offices at Milan's Malpensa and Linate airports and an information booth in Milan's La Rinascente department store; and CashBack, with a Web site at www.cashback.it, which issues refunds through Eurochange exchange booths at Malpensa and Turin's Caselle airport. Alternatively, return the form by mail to the vendor, who will make the refund, either by cheque or to your credit card.

POST & COMMUNICATIONS
Post

Italy's postal service is slow, unreliable and expensive. Information (in Italian) about postal services can be obtained by calling ☎ 160 and via the Internet at www.poste.it.

Post offices and tobacconists sell *francobolli* (stamps). It costs L800 to send a postcard or letter weighing up to 20g to EU countries (L900 to the rest of Europe), L1300 to the USA and L1400 to Australia and New Zealand. Urgent mail (maximum 20kg for international destinations) can be sent by Postacelere (☎ 800 00 99 66 toll-free), an express mail service available at post offices. Letters weighing up to 500g cost L30,000/46,000/68,000 to the UK/USA/Australia. Count one to three days for European destinations. You can even follow your parcel on its journey overseas online at www.postacelere.com.

International couriers such as DHL (☎ 800 34 53 45 toll-free), Federal Express (☎ 800 83 30 40 toll-free) and UPS (☎ 800 82 20 54 toll-free) have offices in all three cities and Web sites at www.dhl.it, www.fedex.com and www.ups.com respectively Call the toll-free number for collection.

Milan The main post office is on Piazza Cordusio (metro MM1 Cordusio) but its branch offices at Via Cordusio 4 and at Stazione Centrale open longer hours: 8 am to 7 pm weekdays and 8.30 am to noon Saturday.

Turin The main post office, Via Vittorio Alfieri 10, opens 8.10 am to 7.20 pm weekdays and 8.10 am to 7 pm Saturday. There are many more branches around town, including next to Stazione Porta Nuova at Via Saachi 2b and south of the station at Via Saluzzo 37.

Genoa The main post office at Via Dante 4a opens 8.15 am to 7.40 pm Monday to Saturday. The branch office on Via San Lorenzo opens 8 am to 1.30 pm Monday to Saturday. Opening hours at the Stazione Principe branch are 9 am to 7.20 pm Monday to Saturday.

Telephone & Fax

State-run Telecom Italia, with a Web site at www.telecomitalia.it, is Italy's largest telecommunications organisation and its orange public payphones are liberally scattered in the streets and train stations in all three cities. Phones accept Telecom Italia phonecards (values of L5000, L10,000 and L15,000) and Unica calling cards (☎ 800 34 13 41 toll-free) which cost L25,000 and can be used to make calls from private phones too. Both types of card are sold at post offices, tobacconists, newspaper stands and vending machines at train stations and in Telecom offices. Some payphones send faxes (price of call plus L2000 per A4 page).

Public telephones operated by other telecommunications companies such as Infostrada (Web site: www.infostrada.it) and Albacom (Web site: www.albacom.it) are located at airports and stations. These phones only accept Infostrada/Albacom cards respectively, again sold at tobacconists and newsstands.

Italy has no area codes to the extent that the 'code' (such as ☎ 010 for Genoa) is an integral part of the telephone number and must always be dialled. Mobile-phone numbers start with a four-digit prefix, such as 0330, 0335 or 0347, and *numeri verdi* (toll-free numbers) kick off with 800. The prefix 147 indicates a national number charged at a local rate. To reach directory enquiries, dial ☎ 12.

To call Italy from abroad, dial Italy's country code (☎ 39) and the telephone number (*including* the initial 0). For mobile phones, drop the 0. To make an international call from Italy, dial 00, the country code, city code and telephone number. To make a reverse-charge (collect) international call from a public telephone, dial ☎ 15 for European countries (☎ 170 for elsewhere). For international directory enquiries, call ☎ 176.

Aimed primarily at Anglophones and other expats, *English Yellow Pages* is published annually and sold in bookshops and online at www.englishyellowpages.com. It covers Milan and Genoa, but not Turin.

Mobile Phones

Italy has four mobile-phone networks: TIM (Telecom Italia), Omnitel, Wind and Blu. Between them, there's a mind-boggling number of monthly subscriptions and package deals to choose from. In early 2001, mobile-phone calls averaged: L200 per minute from one mobile to another on the same network, L300 per minute for national calls to fixed phones and mobiles on other Italian networks, and L600 to L1000 per minute for international calls to Europe. From a fixed phone, Telecom Italia charged a L127 connection fee plus about L550 per minute to call a mobile (L290 per minute at off-peak times).

With the exception of a couple of top-end hotels in Milan, which dole out mobiles as a perk to guests, renting a phone is impossible. However, all four providers sell SIM cards (meaning you have an Italian mobile-phone number) which can be recharged with prepaid calling cards. At the time of writing TIM, with a Web site at www.tim.it, offered a L100,000 TIM-card package – a SIM card loaded with L50,000 credit. Subsequent cards (L50,000 and L100,000) to top up mobile credits can be purchased at tobacconists and newsstands.

To buy a SIM card from any network, you need your passport or identity card and an address in Italy (a hotel address will do).

Rates Telecom Italia slashed its rates in early 2001, reducing the cost of local calls to L31 per minute (L18 between 6.30 pm and 8 am weekdays, after 1 pm on Saturday and all day Sunday) and calls between Milan, Turin and Genoa to L220 per minute (L134 at off-peak times). For international calls, it costs an initial L500 plus L400 per minute to Western Europe, Canada and the USA, and L1400 per minute to Australia and New Zealand.

There are cut-price call centres in all three cities. These grungy centres, always in the dodgiest part of town (around the train station usually), are run by a variety of companies and offer lower rates for international calls than Telecom Italia. Many open 24 hours and attract an unsavoury clientele.

Milan The main Telecom office, which is in Galleria Vittorio Emanuele II (metro MM1/3 Duomo), opens 8 am to 9.30 pm. The office at Stazione Centrale opens 8 am to 9.30 pm. Neither is staffed.

There are cut-price phone offices in the streets around Stazione Centrale, especially on Via Dom Scarlatti.

Turin There are unstaffed Telecom centres at Via Roma 18 and Stazione Porta Nuova, both open 8 am to 10 pm. There's a crop of cut-price phone offices in the streets southeast of the station, including at Via Saluzzo 18 and 20 (open 24 hours).

Genoa The most central Telecom office is inside the main post office and opens 6 am until 8.30 pm. Another at Stazione Brignole opens 8 am to 9.30 pm.

eKno Communication Service

Lonely Planet's eKno global communication service provides low-cost international calls – for local calls you're usually better off with a local phonecard. eKno also offers free messaging services, email, travel information and an online travel vault, where you can securely store all your important documents. You can join online at www.ekno.lonelyplanet.com or by phone from Italy by dialling ☎ 800 87 56 91. Once you have joined, to use eKno from Italy dial ☎ 800 87 56 83. Always check the eKno Web site for the latest access numbers and updates on new features.

Email & Internet Access

The electronic world is as firmly implanted in Italy as elsewhere in Western Europe, with most young Italians being wised up about the ways of the www – charmingly pronounced 'voo voo voo' in Italian.

If you plan to carry your notebook or palmtop computer with you, remember that the power-supply voltage in hotels may vary from that at home, risking damage to your equipment. A universal AC adapter for your appliance allows you to plug it in anywhere without frying the innards. You'll also need a plug adapter – buy it before leaving home. For information on travelling with a computer visit www.teleadapt.com or www.warrior.com.

Major Internet service providers (ISPs), such as CompuServe (Web site: www .compuserve.com) and AT&T (Web site: www.attbusiness.net), have dial-in nodes in all three cities. Compuserve users should try ☎ 02 869 05 61 in Milan, ☎ 011 561 62 31 in Turin and ☎ 010 58 81 62 in Genoa. The numbers for AT&T users are: ☎ 02 703 09 507 in Milan, ☎ 011 779 60 00 in Turin and ☎ 010 570 79 14 in Genoa. Numerous Italian service providers – including Telecom Italia, Posteitaliane and CyberNet Italia (☎ 02 48 28 11) at www.cyb.it – are listed in the *English Yellow Pages.*

If you intend relying on cybercafes to access your regular Internet mail account, you'll need your incoming (POP or IMAP) mail server name, account name and password. Armed with this information (available from your ISP or network supervisor), you should be able to access your account from any Net-connected machine, provided it runs some kind of email software (try www.mailstart.com). An easier option for collecting mail is to open a free eKno Web-based email account online at www.ekno .lonelyplanet.com. You can then access your mail from any Net-connected machine running a standard Web browser.

Milan Surf the Net for free at Rizzoli (metro MM1/3 Duomo), Piazza del Duomo. It opens 10 am to 11 pm (8 pm Sunday).

Nashuatec (☎ 02 583 15 546, ⓔ digi copy1@galactica.it, metro MM3 Missori), Via Larga 9, is a photocopy shop with Internet access (L7000 an hour). It opens 8 am to 6.30 pm weekdays, 9 am to 1 pm Saturday.

Mailboxes Etc, at Corso Sempione 38, charges L15,000 per hour for Internet access.

Turin @h! (☎ 011 815 40 58, ⓔ info @ahto.it), Via Montebello 13, charges L12,000/50,000 for one/five hours online

time and opens 10 am to 1 pm and 2 to 7 pm weekdays.

Mailboxes Etc (see Money earlier in this chapter) charges L15,000 per hour or L250 per minute .

Genoa Internet Village (☎ 010 570 48 78), on the corner of Corso Buenos Aires and Piazza Borgo Pila, charges L4000/8000 for 15/30 minutes or L15,000 per hour. It opens 9 am to 1 pm and 3 to 7 pm weekdays. Mailboxes Etc (see Money earlier in this chapter) also offers an email and Internet service.

The hourly rate at Internet Point Il Faro (☎ 010 251 83 14), Via Polleri 17r, is L12,000. Prepaid cards cost L22,000/ 32,000 for two/three hours. It opens 9 am to 1 pm and 4 to 7.30 pm weekdays and 3 to 7 pm Saturday.

At Porto Antico, surf at the Marina Molo Vecchio's harbour office (see the Activities section in the Genoa chapter). Prepaid cards, valid for one hour, cost L20,000.

Near Piazza Vittoria, Centro Copio (☎ 010 58 10 12), Via Ruspoli 108, is a photocopying shop with Internet access. It opens 9 am to 12.30 pm and 2.30 to 7 pm weekdays and 9 am to 12.30 pm Saturday.

Internet Point (☎ 010 576 13 96), Via SS Giacomo e Filippo 22r, is a small telephone outlet where you can surf for L15,000 an hour. It opens 9.30 am to 1 pm and 3.30 to 7.30 pm weekdays and 9.30 am to 1 pm Saturday.

INTERNET RESOURCES

The World Wide Web is a rich resource. You can research your trip, hunt down bargain air fares, book hotels, check on weather conditions or chat with locals and other travellers about the best places to visit and avoid.

There's no better place to start your Web explorations than the Lonely Planet Web site (www.lonelyplanet.com). Here you'll find succinct summaries on travelling to most places on earth, postcards from other travellers and the Thorn Tree bulletin board, where you can ask questions before you go or dispense advice when you get back. You can also find travel news and updates to many of our most popular guidebooks, and the subWWWay section links you to the most useful travel resources elsewhere on the Web.

Numerous sites are embedded in the text throughout this guide. The following are also useful links:

www.cityvox.com – key site on Milan and Turin for detailed listings and reviews of the hottest clubs, bars and restaurants of the moment

www.englishyellowpages.it – fully searchable electronic version of the paper edition, covering Milan and Genoa

www.lascala.milano.it – everything you'll ever need to know (including how to score tickets) about Europe's most famous opera house

www.milandaily.com – superb English-language site carrying the latest Milan-related headlines from Reuters and other newsagencies, links to all the Italian press, top sports stories and loads more pertaining to Milan and its surrounds

www.travel.it – handy travel tips for Italy-bound travellers

BOOKS

Most books are published in different editions by different publishers in different countries. As a result, a book might be a hardcover rarity in one country while it's readily available in paperback in another. Fortunately, bookshops and libraries search by title or author, so your local bookshop or library is best placed to advise you on the availability of the books that follow.

All three cities tout a diverse range of bookshops (listed under Shopping in the respective city chapters), many of which sell English-language books. See Literature under Facts about the Cities for literary works by Italian authors.

Lonely Planet

The *Italian Phrasebook* lists all the words and phrases you're likely to need. Another essential read is Lonely Planet's *World Food Italy*, a full-colour book with information on Piedmont, Lombardy and Ligurian cuisine, as well as the whole range of Italian food and drink.

Walking in Italy is useful for walkers wanting to explore Italy's great outdoors.

Italy, Rome, Florence, Venice, Tuscany, Sicily, Europe on a Shoestring, Mediterranean Europe and *Western Europe* are other guides recommended for those planning further travel in Italy and Europe.

Guidebooks

The Instituto Geografico de Agostini and TCI publish guides to Turin and Milan in English, with a bias on heritage and history rather than nuts-and-bolts information. Genoa-based publishing house Sagep's 220-page *Genoa Guide* (1999) by Gian Antonio Dall'Aglio is worth reading.

Locally produced *A Key to Milan* is updated every two to four years and is loaded with practical facts, as is *Where, When, How Milano*, costing L3000 at tourist offices. *Milanopass* (L19,000) is a hip listings guide, published annually in Italian and containing 300-plus pages of listings. Motorists can invest in Sagep's *Guide to Liguria – 25 Excursions by Car*, by Gian Antonio Dall'Aglio.

If you understand Italian, you can't get better than the excellent red guides published by the TCI. Its *Alberghi et Ristoranti d'Italia* (L34,000) listing 5249 hotels and 3215 restaurants country-wide is also useful. Those who enjoy eating their way around, won't do better than *The Italian Wine Guide* (L42,000), a 600-page book with exhaustive information on where to drink wine and what to drink it with.

Travel

'Grand tour' classics such as Johann Wolfgang von Goethe's *Italian Journey*, Charles Dickens' *Pictures from Italy* (first published in 1846) and Henry James' *Italian Hours* (written between 1872 and 1909) all pass through Milan, Turin and Genoa. James travelled through Turin – 'city of arcades, pink and yellow stucco, innumerable cafes' – en route from Chambéry in France to Milan, and journeyed south to 'crooked' Genoa, 'most incoherent of cities'. Milan at the start of the 20th century is captured by Edith Wharton in her collection of travel tales, *Italian Backgrounds*, published in 1905.

DH Lawrence wrote three short travel books while living in Italy, now combined in one volume entitled *DH Lawrence and Italy* (1997), with an introduction by Anthony Burgess. *Twilight in Italy* focuses the author's time spent in the lakes north of Milan. You can also pick up Lawrence's *Sketches of Eruscan Places & Other Italian Essays*, seven essays he wrote in 1927.

Italy: The Fatal Gift and *The Last Italian* by New Yorker William Murray are collections of essays which Murray wrote for magazines and newspapers from the 1960s to 1990s. His 'Queen of the Bogs' essay (yes, that is Milan he's talking about) is among several excerpts to appear in *Italy in Mind* (1997), an anthology of Italy-inspired travel writing edited by Alice Leccese Powers.

Only women writers feature in *Desiring Italy* (1997), another collection of stories and essays (most of which are out of print in their original form) about Italy, edited by Susan Cahill. It includes excerpts by Edith Wharton; an essay written in 1718 on Genoa by Lady Mary Wortley Montagu (an embassy wife who lived apart from her husband in Brescia, near Milan) and an excerpt from Elizabeth von Arnim's *The Enchanted April* (1922), a novel set in Portofino.

A Farewell to Arms (1929) by Ernest Hemmingway is essential reading for the Milan-bound. Based on Hemmingway's true-life experience as a volunteer ambulance worker stationed in northern Italy during WWI, it paints a vivid picture of Milan which is where the author wound up in hospital – and fell in love.

Cuban-born essayist, journalist and novelist Italo Calvino depicted Italy's northern cities in several of his works. *Numbers in the Dark* (1996), a collection of stories and fables translated by Tim Parks, brilliantly depicts Milan ('houses that turn their backs on you in fields of fog'), Turin ('straight streets that never end') and Genoa ('streets that go up and down and houses above and below'). Calvino lived for many years in San Remo, a town west of Genoa.

History & Politics

Few titles deal exclusively with Milanese, Turinese and/or Genoese history, but there's plenty of general Italian history books. *History of the Italian People* (1991) by Giuliano Procacci and *The New Italians* (1995) by Charles Richards are two good places to start. *A History of Contemporary Italy: Society & Politics 1943–1988* (1990) by Paul Ginsborg is an absorbing and well-written book that will help Italophiles place the country's modern society in perspective.

Art & Architecture

Leonardo is the main man and the Cenacolo Vinciano bookshop sells a dearth of titles about him including: *Leonardo – The Artist & the Man* (1994) by Serge Bramly, a heavy-weight biography; *Fortune is a River – Leonardo da Vinci & Niccolò Machiavelli's Magnificent Dream to Change the Course of Florentine History* (1999) by Roger D Masters which looks at Leonardo da Vinci's engineering and invention achievements; light-hearted *Leonardo – Portrait of a Master* (1999) by Bruce Nardini which traces da Vinci's life from Ambroise in France to Milan; and *Leonardo: The First Scientist* (2000) by Michael White which focuses on Leonardo's inventive and scientific talents.

One of da Vinci's pupils is the subject matter of *Bernardino Luini & Renaissance Painting in Milan: The Frescoes of San Maurizio Al Monastero Maggiore* (2000) edited by Maria Teresa Fiorio and Sandrina Bandera. Its 320 pages of informative text and images analyse the Renaissance frescoes inside Milan's Maggiore Monastery.

M (2000) by Peter Robb is a stunning biography of 16th-century Milanese painter, Michelangelo Merisi, better known as Caravaggio after the small town east of Milan where he spent part of his childhood.

Italian Art: Painting & Architecture from Origins to Present Day (2000) edited by Gloria Fossi, with texts by Mattia Reiche, Gloria Fossi and Marco Bussagli provides a broader overview of Italian art history through the ages. Most bookshops in Milan sell it (L48,000).

Ellipsis' pocket-size *Milan: A Guide to Recent Architecture* (1998; L9900), by Thomas Muirhead, looks at 25 buildings in central Milan, constructed in the city between 1987 and 1997. Architecture is covered in a similar vein in Allemandi's *Torino Architectural Guide*, compiled by 20 professors from Turin University's architectural faculty (L40,000).

Design & Fashion

The Milanese publisher Edizioni L'Archivolto (☎ 02 290 10 424, ⓔ archivolto@ homegate.it), Via Marsala 3, brandishes an unbeatable range of books on Italian design in its impressive portfolio. Hardback A4 titles, available locally and on the Internet, are co-written by Silvio San Pietro and include *Contemporary Italian Product Design* (1999); *Contemporary Italian Furniture* (1996); *Disco Design in Italy*; *New Shops Made in Italy* and *Urban Interiors in Italy*. Each book costs L190,000 in Milan bookshops.

Thames & Hudson publishes two titles worth picking up for a broader introduction to fashion design and the industry: *A Century of Fashion* (1999) by François Baudot and *20th Century Fashion* (1999) by Valerie Mendes & Amy de la Haye. Racy's *The House of Gucci* (2000) by Sara Gay Forden tells the tragic tale of Maurizio Gucci and his handbag clan – an intriguing read set mainly in Milan.

Numerous books about Armani et al are sold in the bookshop inside Milan's Emporio Armani.

FILMS

For a taste of Turin with a ghoulish twist, look no further – if you dare – than the horror movies by legendary Italian film director Dario Argento (born 1940). He shot several films in Turin, including *Deep Red* (*Profondo Rosso*: 1975) and his most recent gruesome creation, *I Can't Sleep (Non Ho Sonno)* with Max von Sydow (star of *The Exorcist*), which was filmed in Turin in mid-2000.

Less scary films worth watching before you arrive include *Miracle in Milan* (1951; Italian with English sub-titles), *The Italian Connection* (1973) and *Wipeout* (1991). *The Italian Job* (1968) with Michael Caine and his Mini Cooper is a must. *Made in Milan* (1990) by Martin Scorsese is a short documentary based around an interview the American film director shared with Giorgio Armani.

In Italy, there's no better seat to see B&W classics filmed in Turin than at the Museo Nazionale del Cinema where you can sit in a typical Piedmontese cafe and watch films (in Italian) from the 1940s to the 1990s. If you understand some Italian, Luigi Comencinci's *La Donna della Domenica* (1975) and Gianni Amelio's Rosso *Cosi Ridevano* (1998), about Sicilian emigrees in Turin between 1958 and 1964, are two big films worth watching.

A history of the Turin-born Italian film industry is included under Cinema in the Arts section of Facts about the Cities. Information on film festivals is included under Special Events later in this chapter.

NEWSPAPERS & MAGAZINES

Milan-based *Corriere della Sera*, online at www.corriere.it, is Italy's leading daily, with the best foreign-news pages and the most comprehensive (and comprehensible) political coverage. Turin's *La Stampa*, online at www.lastampa.it, is a 50-page broadsheet which has been going strong since 1867. The day's financial news can be read in *Milano Finanza*, online at www.milanofinanza.it.

The English-language *International Herald Tribune* is available from newsstands Monday to Saturday and has a daily four-page Italian news supplement. Early-morning delivery through your letterbox (☎ 167 78 00 40 toll-free, ⓔ subs@iht.com) is only possible in Milan.

You can normally pick up foreign newspapers of the day (including the *Guardian*, *Times* and *Daily Telegraph*) in Milan and at the airports, and papers that are a day or two old in Turin and Genoa.

Several English-language magazines circulate in Milan: *Easy Milano* is an easy-to-find freebie, published twice monthly and found in embassies and hotel lobbies. The twice-yearly *Focus on Italy* is the

British Chamber of Commerce for Italy's 'guide to business and pleasure' (see Doing Business later in this chapter). *Hello Milano*, online at www.hellomilano.it, is a crass but better-than-nothing newspaper-guide to the city; it's free and published monthly.

RADIO & TV

Italy's three state-owned radio stations are RAI-1 (89.7 FM), RAI-2 (91.7 FM), with news in English at three minutes past the hour from 1 to 5 am, and RAI-3 (93.7 AM) with a combination of classical and light music, news broadcasts and discussion programmes. There are Internet relay links from www.radio.rai.it.

The BBC World Service can usually be picked up on short wave at 648kHz most times of day, at 12095kHz between 4 am and 5 pm, and at 9410kHz from 6 to 9 am and 3 to 10 pm; and via Internet relay at www.bbc.co.uk/worldservice. Voice of America (VOA) can usually be found on short wave at 15.205MHz.

Along most of the coast west of Genoa, you can get Riviera Radio on 106.5 FM. This English-language radio station broadcasts 24 hours a day from its Monte Carlo station in neighbouring Monaco. It broadcasts BBC World Service news every hour and has Internet relay at www.riviera-radio.com. You can also get Radio Monte Carlo (105.3–105.5 FM in Milan, 104.2 FM in Genoa, 105.5 FM in Turin) which broadcasts news in English hourly between 8 am and 8 pm (sports news at 4 pm, traffic news at 8 and 9 am and 7 pm). Across the region RTL Hit Parade (102.5 FM) runs English news bulletins at 9 am, noon, 5 and 8 pm. It has a Web site at www.rtl.it.

Music-based radio stations in Milan are numerous. Radio Deejay, with Internet relay at www.deejay.it, is a great one for getting a taste of the city's clubbing scene, pick it up on 99.7 FM or 107 FM in Milan. Radio 101 (Web Site: www.radio101.it), 'Move your Body' Radio Planet (Web site: www.radioplanet.it), and Radio 105 (Web site: www.105.net) are others. You can tune into dancey Radio Capitale and its constant

chart hits between 91 FM and 93.1 FM in Milan, on 89.8 FM or 93 FM in Turin, at 93.9 FM or 96.25FM in Genoa and online at www.capital.it.

The state-run television channels are RAI-1 (which broadcasts Euronews in French at 6 am daily), RAI-2 and RAI-3, which broadcasts News 24 in English at 6 am and morning news at 8 am. A complete listing of the day's programmes are posted on its Web site at www.rai.it. Italy's main commercial stations are Canale 5, Italia 1, Rete 4 and Telemontecarlo (TMC), which broadcasts CNN nightly around 3 am. BBC World, Sky Channel, CNN and NBC Superchannel are available by satellite in top-end hotels.

VIDEO SYSTEMS

Italy uses the PAL video system (the same as Australia and the rest of Europe, except France). This system is not compatible with NTSC (used in the USA, Japan and Latin America) or Secam (used in France and other French-speaking countries). Modern video players are often multisystem and can read all three.

PHOTOGRAPHY & VIDEO

Taking photographs is frowned upon in most big-name designer shops and flash photography is forbidden at many sights, including Leonardo's *Last Supper*.

All three cities tout dozens of outlets selling and processing films, but beware of poor quality and slow processing. The FNAC stores in Milan and Genova can both turn around a *pellicola* (roll of film) in 24 hours; developing costs about L13,000/16,000 for 24/36 exposures in standard format. Tapes for video cameras, including V8, are often available at the same outlets or can be found at stores selling cameras, videos and electrical goods.

Lonely Planet's *Travel Photography: A Guide to Taking Better Pictures* is written by the internationally renowned travel photographer Richard I'Anson. It's full colour throughout, designed to take on the road and might just help you capture the perfect city snapshot.

TIME

Italy is one hour ahead of GMT/UTC, in the same time zone as France, Germany, Austria and Spain. When it's noon in Milan, it's 3 am in San Francisco, 6 am in New York and Toronto, 11 am in London, 7 pm in Perth, 9 pm in Sydney and 11 pm in Auckland.

Daylight-saving time starts on the last Sunday in March, when clocks are moved forward one hour. Clocks are put back an hour on the last Sunday in October.

Italy operates on a 24-hour clock.

ELECTRICITY

The electric current in Italy is 220V, 50Hz. Power sockets have two or three holes and do not have their own switches, plugs have two or three round pins.

WEIGHTS & MEASURES

Italy uses the metric system. Basic terms for weight include *un etto* (100g) and *un chilo* (1kg). Travellers from the USA (and often the UK) will have to cope with the change from pounds to kilograms, miles to kilometres and gallons to litres. A standard conversion table can be found on the inside back cover of this book.

Note that for numbers, Italians indicate decimals with commas and thousands with points.

LAUNDRY

Coin-operated, self-service *lavanderie* (laundrettes) are abundant in all three cities.

Milan

There are several laundrettes in the Stazione Centrale area (metro MM2/3 Centrale FS), the handiest being Lavanderia Self Service at Via Tadino 4, where it costs L7500/10,000 to wash a 7/12kg load of clothes. Another is Onda Blu, Via Paisiello 4.

The laundrette just north of Navigli at Via Savona 1 charges L6000/10,000 to wash a 6.5/16 kg load and the same again for drying.

Turin

It costs L6000/12,000 to wash 7/16kg at Lava e Asciuga, which has branches at Via

Vanchiglia 10, Piazza della Repubblica 5g and Via Sant'Anselmo 9. All open 8 am to 11 pm. East of Stazione Porta Nuova, there's a laundrette at Via Tommaso 12b.

Genoa

La Maddalena coin laundrette, Vico della Maddalena 2, opens 8 am to 8 pm. A 7kg load costs L6000. At the Porto Antico, the Essetrenta laundrette at Ponte Morosini 26 (one of the wharfs) opens 6 am to 11 pm and charges L8500/17,000 per 7/14kg machine load.

TOILETS

Public toilets are far from widespread. The quickest and easiest thing is simply to stroll into a cafe or bar – although you'll probably need to buy a coffee first.

HEALTH

Italy is a healthy place. Your main risks are sunburn, foot blisters and an upset stomach from eating and drinking too much.

No jabs are required to travel to Italy but it's wise to make sure routine vaccinations such as polio (usually administered during childhood), tetanus and diphtheria (usually administered together during childhood and updated every 10 years) are up-to-date. Citizens of EU countries are covered for emergency medical treatment in Italy on presentation of an E111 certificate, but citizens of non-EU countries should make sure they have arranged appropriate health insurance. Everyone should ensure they're healthy before travelling. If you require a particular medication take an adequate supply as it may not be available locally.

Major hospitals in all three cities are listed under Emergencies later in this chapter and indicated on maps at the back of this book. Anyone (including foreigners) who is sick can receive treatment in the casualty ward *(pronto soccorso)* or emergency room of any public hospital, where you can also get emergency dental treatment. Hospitals try to have people who speak English in casualty wards, but this is not done systematically. If necessary, the hospital will call in an interpreter.

Medical Kit Check List

Following is a list of items you should consider including in your medical kit – consult your pharmacist for brands available in your country.

- ☐ **Aspirin or paracetamol (acetaminophen in the USA)** – for pain or fever
- ☐ **Antihistamine** – for allergies, eg hay fever; to ease the itch from insect bites or stings; and to prevent motion sickness
- ☐ **Cold and flu tablets, throat lozenges and nasal decongestant**
- ☐ **Multivitamins** – consider for long trips, when dietary vitamin intake may be inadequate
- ☐ **Antibiotics** – consider including these if you're travelling well off the beaten track; see your doctor, as they must be prescribed, and carry the prescription with you
- ☐ **Loperamide or diphenoxylate** – 'blockers' for diarrhoea
- ☐ **Prochlorperazine or metaclopramide** – for nausea and vomiting
- ☐ **Rehydration mixture** – to prevent dehydration, which may occur, for example, during bouts of diarrhoea; particularly important when travelling with children
- ☐ **Insect repellent, sunscreen, lip balm and eye drops**
- ☐ **Calamine lotion, sting relief spray or aloe vera** – to ease irritation from sunburn and insect bites or stings
- ☐ **Antifungal cream or powder** – for fungal skin infections and thrush
- ☐ **Antiseptic (such as povidone-iodine)** – for cuts and grazes
- ☐ **Bandages, Band-Aids (plasters) and other wound dressings**
- ☐ **Water purification tablets or iodine**
- ☐ **Scissors, tweezers and a thermometer** – note that mercury thermometers are prohibited by airlines

Tap water is drinkable throughout Italy, although Italians themselves have taken to drinking the bottled stuff. The sign *acqua non potable* tells you that water is not drinkable (you may see the sign on trains). Water from drinking fountains is safe to drink unless there is a sign telling you otherwise.

Heat Exhaustion

Dehydration and salt deficiency can cause heat exhaustion. Take time to acclimatise to the high temperatures, drink sufficient liquids and do not do anything too physically demanding.

Salt deficiency is characterised by fatigue, lethargy, headaches, giddiness and muscle cramps; salt tablets may help, but adding extra salt to your food is better.

Prickly Heat

This is an itchy rash caused by excessive perspiration trapped under the skin. It usually strikes people who have just arrived in a hot climate. Keeping cool, bathing often, drying the skin and using a mild talcum or prickly heat powder, or resorting to air-conditioning may help.

Sunburn

You can get sunburnt surprisingly quickly, even through cloud. Use a sunscreen, hat, and barrier cream for your nose and lips. Calamine lotion or Stingose are good for mild sunburn. Make sure you protect your eyes with good quality sunglasses, particularly if you will be near water, sand or snow.

Diarrhoea

Simple things such as a change of water, food or climate can all cause a mild bout of diarrhoea, but a few rushed toilet trips with no other symptoms is not indicative of a major problem.

Dehydration is the main danger with any diarrhoea, particularly in children or the elderly, as it can occur quickly. Fluid replacement (at least equal to the volume being lost) is most important. Weak black tea with a little sugar, soda water, or soft drinks allowed to go flat and diluted 50% with clean water are all good. Keep drinking small amounts often. Stick to a bland diet as you recover.

WOMEN TRAVELLERS

Milan, Turin and Genoa are not dangerous cities for women, although those travelling alone will find themselves plagued by unwanted attention from Italian men who, as a general rule, seem to believe all women are beautiful objects in desperate need of manly attention. Most of their chat-up lines are crass, childish and so stereotypical that – depending on the tone in which they're delivered – are often downright comical (How old are you? No more than 21. What do you do? Must be a model).

Imaginative they might not be but persistent they are, and shaking off an unwanted Romeo can get very trying after a while. Ignoring them, politely telling them you have a *marito* (husband) or *fidanzato* (boyfriend), or walking away can work. If all else fails, and things start to turn aggressive, approach the nearest member of the police or *carabinieri*. On the metro in Milan, watch out for men with wandering hands – keep your back to the wall and make a very loud fuss if someone starts fondling your backside.

The same 'streetwise' rules apply as in any other city. Avoid walking alone in deserted and dark streets; look for hotels that are central and within easy walking distance of places where you can eat at night (unsafe areas for women are noted throughout this book) and don't hitchhike alone.

GAY & LESBIAN TRAVELLERS

Homosexuality is legal in Italy and well tolerated in the big cities. Italian friendships tend to involve physical contact, so the sight of two men (or women) walking down a street arm in arm is not unusual. However, overt displays of affection by homosexual couples could attract a negative response in smaller coastal towns and the more remote valleys west of Turin. Milan hosts a 10-day international gay and lesbian film festival (see Special Events later in this chapter).

Gay clubs, bars and other forms of entertainment are listed in entertainment magazines (see the Entertainment sections in the city chapters) but can be more reliably tracked down through local gay organisations. There's a useful Web site at www.gay.it/guida which regional listings of local organisations, gay bars and so on.

ArciGay and ArciLesbica are Italy's national organisations for gay men and lesbians. Local branches include Milan's Centro d'Iniziativa Gay ArciGay (☎ 02 541 22 225, e cigmilano@libero.it), via Bezzecca 3; Turin's ArciGay Maurice (☎ 011 521 11 16, e maurice@arpnet.it), Via della Basilica 3/5; and Genoa's ArciGay (☎ 010 545 02 24), Salita Salvator Viale 15r.

DISABLED TRAVELLERS

Italy is not an overly friendly place for travellers with disabilities. Some public-service providers – such as Milan's public transport company ATM (☎ 02 480 31 444, e serviziodisabili@atm-mi.it) – run a disabled information service. At the Università degli Studi di Milano, disabled students can contact the Associazione Volontari per Disabili in Università (AVDU; ☎ 02 583 52 987), Via Festa del Perdono 7.

In Turin, Consulta Persone in Difficoltà (☎ 011 319 81 45), Via San Marino 10, assists disabled travellers and publishes four excellent sightseeing itineraries (in Italian only) for disabled tourists on the Web at www.comune.torino.it/itidisab.

For information on organisations assisting disabled travellers, contact AIAS Milano (☎ 02 392 64 590, e aias@mv.itline.it), Via Mantegazza 10, a non-profit organisation which gives advice on 'holidays without barriers in Italy' and has information on the accessibility of hotels, restaurants and so on in all three cities. Details (in Italian only) are on the Web at www.aias.it.

SENIOR TRAVELLERS

Senior citizens are entitled to discounts on public transport and on admission fees to many museums (see Seniors' Cards under Visas & Documents earlier in this chapter). It is always important to ask. The minimum qualifying age is 60 or 65 years. You should also seek information in your own country on travel packages and discounts for senior travellers through senior citizens' organisations and travel agencies.

MILAN, TURIN & GENOA FOR CHILDREN

They might be cities, but there's plenty to do to keep a smile on little faces. For thrills, spills, killer whales and other ideas, see the 'Kidding Around' boxed text below.

The Milan-bound who understand some Italian should invest L19,000 in a copy *Milano dei Bambini e delle Mamme* (Milan for Children & Mothers), an annual guide listing everything from creches and schools to parenting courses and what to do with the kids. It's published by Milan-based ACTL (☎ 02 864 64 080, ⓔ info@actl.it), with a Web site at www.actl.it. Nannies, au pair agencies and nursery babysitting services are also listed in *English Yellow Pages*. Bookshops sell both.

UNIVERSITIES

Milan alone has 180,000 students spread across seven universities and higher educa-tion institutions. Some study options are listed under Courses in the respective city chapters.

Milan

The leading university, Università degli Studi di Milano (☎ 02 5 83 51) dates to 1924. It comprises eight faculties, runs 27 different degree programmes and has 60,000 students. It's particularly known for its medical and science post-graduate courses. Visit its Web site at www.unimi.it. Foreign students wanting to enrol should contact its foreign students office (☎ 02 583 52 124, ⓔ ufficio.stranieri@unimi.it, metro MM1/3 Duomo), inside the main university building at Via Festa del Perdono 7.

Others include Università Bocconi (☎ 02 583 62 007), a commercial school offering six economic- and business-focused degree courses with its administration at Via Sarfatti 25 and online at www.uni-bocconi.it;

Kidding Around

Here are some ideas on what to see and do to keep the young (and young-at-heart) smiling. Genoa's watery sights makes it hands-down the best city for kids.

Milan

Feed the pigeons on Piazza del Duomo; ride the lift to the roof of the duomo; discover the largest horse in the world or seek out other Leonardo inventions at the Museo Nazionale della Scienza e della Tecnica; sprawl out in a city park or whizz the kids around on a merry-go-round in the Giar-dini Pubblici; watch the Italian Grand Prix at Monza or a football match at one of the city stadiums; take a boat ride on Lake Maggiore or ride the funicular in Como.

Turin

Explore underground tunnels by torchlight at the Museo Civico Pietro Micca; ride the glass lift up to the rooftop terrace of the Mole Antonelliana or sit on a toilet and watch movies in its Museo Nazionale del Cinema; take a trip on the funicular railway to Superga or go for a riverside stroll along the Po (no ducks); peer at cars in the Museo dell'Automobile; teach the kids to ski, snowboard or sled in the Valle d'Aosta.

Genoa

Sail around the port or along the coast; watch seals, dolphins and sharks being fed at Acquario di Genova; enjoy a bird's eye view from Il Bigo; take a swim or a twirl around the ice rink at Porto An-tico; discover Antarctica in the Museo Nazionale dell'Antardide, maritime history in the Padiglione del Mare e della Navigazione or how to build a house in La Città dei Bambini; ride the funiculars or chug to Caselle on a narrow-gauge train; build sand castles on the beach, or head further east or west to another seaside resort or coastal village.

Università Cattolica del Sacro Cuore (☎ 02 7 23 41, e rettore@mi.unicatt.it), the Catholic place to study, with a Web site at www.unicatt.it; and Università IULM (☎ 02 89 14 11), Milan's university of modern languages at Via Filippo da Liscate 1 and online at www.iulm.it.

Turin

Università degli Studi di Torino (☎ 011 670 24 21), Via Verdi 8, was founded in 1405 and is the region's most historical university. Its current building, Palazzo dell'Università, overlooking Via Po was built between 1712 and 1730. Visit its Web site at www.unito.it.

Genoa

Università degli Studi di Genova (☎ 010 2 09 91), Via Balbi 5, has its origins in medieval colleges of law and theology run by Jesuits from the 16th century and was given university status in 1862. For information on courses visit its Web site at www.unige.it.

CULTURAL CENTRES & LIBRARIES
Milan

The British Council (☎ 02 77 22 21, e enquiry.bcmilan@britishcouncil.it, metro MM3 Monte Napoleone), Via Alessandro Manzoni 38, runs a small library (☎ 02 772 22 203) offering one-day membership for L10,000, including one-hour Internet access. Annual membership costs L110,000 (L165,000 to borrow videos too and use the Internet for an hour a day). It opens 10 am to 8 pm Tuesday to Thursday, 10 am to 6 pm Friday, and 11 am to 4 pm Saturday.

The Goethe Institut (☎ 02 77 69 171, e goethe.mailand.spr@agora.stm.it, metro M1/3 Duomo) is at Via San Paolo 10; and the Centre Culturel Français (☎ 02 485 91 911, metro MM2 San Ambrogio) is at Corso Magenta 63.

Turin

Both the British Council (☎ 011 669 95 75, e info.turin@britishcouncil.it), Via Saluzzo 60 and Germany's Goethe Institute (☎ 011

562 88 10, e goethe@inrete.it), Piazza San Carlo 206, screen films and host classical music concerts and other cultural events. The Goethe Institut also runs a library, open 10 am to noon and 3 to 6 pm Monday, Tuesday and Thursday, and 10 am to 7 pm on Wednesday. The British Council has a Web site at www.britishcouncil.it.

The well-stocked mediatheque and library at the Centre Culturel Français (☎ 011 515 75 11, e ccfturin@venturanet.it), Via Pomba 23, opens 9 am to 8 pm weekdays, and 9 am to 1 pm Saturday. Events are listed in its quarterly newsletter and its Web site, www.france-italia.it, is an excellent resource for searching out Francophone cultural events in Italy.

Genoa

The British Library (☎ 010 59 16 05, e mazcco@village.it), Via XX Settembre 2, 5th floor, is an English-language library run by the Italo-Britannica Associazione. The Goethe Institut (☎ 010 839 87 75, e gegoetz@ge.itline.it) is at Via Peschiera 35. You can visit them online at www.goethezentrumgenua.it.

DANGERS & ANNOYANCES

The most likely danger you'll encounter is the swift and slippery fingers of a pick-pocket. Milan's main shopping streets, buses and trains to the airports, Stazione Centrale and the immediate area surrounding the train station are prime haunts for pickpockets and thieves. Bag-snatching is not a common occurrence, but it pays to wear the strap of your bag or camera across your body and facing the side away from the road. Motorcycle bandits have been known to operate in Genoa's *caruggi* (old-town alleys).

As in all cities, there are certain streets in Milan, Turin and Genoa that should be avoided at night, particularly for solo travellers of either sex. In all three cities, avoid the streets around the central train stations – around Milan's Stazione Centrale, east and south of Turin's Stazione Porta Nuova and in Genoa's Prè district near Stazione Principe. Come dark, the dimly lit streets and alleys of Genoa's old town and Porto Antico (Old Port) area are the stomping ground for the city's prostitutes and drug dealers, and can be downright spooky. Avoid travelling on the Milan metro alone late at night and always sit in a carriage with other people.

Parked cars, particularly those with foreign number plates or rental-company stickers are prime targets for thieves. *Never* leave valuables in your car. On the road, city traffic can be dangerous for the unprepared tourist. Many roads that appear to be one-way have lanes for buses travelling in the opposite direction – always look both ways before stepping onto the road.

EMERGENCIES

There's a list of pharmacies for all three cities online at www.farmacie.it. Most open 9 am to 1 pm and 3 to 7.30 pm.

Milan

The questura (☎ 02 6 22 61) is at Via Fatebenefratelli 11. Some staff speak English, but foreigners will receive better attention at the Uffico Stranieri (Foreigners' Office; ☎ 02 6 22 61, metro MM3 Turati), Via Montebello 26. It opens 8.30 am to 12.30 pm Monday, Tuesday and Thursday to Saturday.

The Ospedale Maggiore Policlinico (hospital; ☎ 02 5 50 31), Via Francesco Sforza 35, has an emergency unit. Milan Clinic (☎ 02 760 16 047, e info@milanclinic .com, metro MM1 San Babila), Via Cerva 25; and International Health Center (☎ 02 720 04 080, metro MM1/3 Duomo), Via San Paolo 15, are private clinics with English-speaking doctors.

Pharmacies pin a list of those open all night in their window; alternatively call

☎ 166 114 470. The pharmacy inside Galleria Carrozze at Stazione Centrale (☎ 02 669 07 35, metro MM2/3 Centrale FS) opens 24 hours. Another at Via Boccaccio 26 (☎ 02 469 52 81, metro MM1 Conciliazione) opens 9 pm to 8.30 am. In the centre, Farmacia Carlo Erba (☎ 02 87 86 68, metro MM1/3 Duomo), Piazza del Duomo 21, opens 9 pm to 8.30 am, plus 3 to 7 pm Monday, and 9.30 am to 1.30 pm and 3 to 7 pm Tuesday to Saturday.

Turin

The questura (☎ 011 5 58 81) is at Corso Vinzaglio 10 and there's a municipal police station adjoining Stazione Porta Nuova at Via Saachi 1b.

The Ospedale Mauriziano Umberto I (hospital; ☎ 011 5 08 01) is at Largo Turati 62. The pharmacy inside Stazione Porta Nuova opens 7 am to 7.30 pm. Farmacia Boniscontro, Corso Vittorio Emanuele II 66, opens 3 pm to 12.30 pm weekdays. Historic Restente, Piazza Carignano 2, dates from 1833.

Genoa

The questura (☎ 010 5 36 61) is on Via Armando Diaz.

The Ospedale San Martino (hospital; ☎ 010 55 51), Largo Rosanna Benci 10, is east of the town centre. All-night pharmacies opening 7.30 pm to 8.30 am include Ghersi (☎ 010 54 16 61) at Corso Buenos Aires 18a and Pescetto at Via Balbi 31.

LEGAL MATTERS

For the average tourist, there's little chance of brushing with the law except if you're robbed or pickpocketed. Should you need to report a crime, call the *carabinieri* (black uniform with red stripe and cars to match) for non-violent thefts and incidents that don't endanger life and the police (powder-blue trousers with fuchsia stripe, navy-blue jacket and light-blue cars with 'polizia' written on the side) for everything else.

If you're caught with drugs that the police determine are for your personal use, you'll be let off with a warning and the drugs will be confiscated. If it's determined that you

Help!	
Ambulance	☎ 118
Fire	☎ 115
Police	☎ 113
Carabinieri	☎ 112
Highway Rescue	☎ 116

intend selling them, you risk prison. Should you happen to be detained by the police, Italy touts some antiterrorism laws which can make life difficult for you: you can be held for 48 hours without a magistrate being informed and you can be interrogated without the presence of a lawyer. It is difficult to obtain bail and you can be held legally for up to three years without a trial.

The legal limit for blood alcohol level is 0.08% and random breath tests do occur.

BUSINESS HOURS

Shops open from 9 or 10 am to around 1 pm and 3.30 to 7.30 pm (or 4 to 8 pm) Monday to Saturday; many are closed Monday morning. In Milan and Turin, larger shops and department stores open Sunday afternoon and until 10 pm some evenings. Many supermarkets operate 'nonstop' from 9 am to 7.30 pm Monday to Saturday.

The opening hours of museums, galleries and archaeological sites vary, although many close on Monday or Tuesday. Banks open from 8.30 am to 1.30 pm and 3.30 to 4.30 pm (although hours can vary) weekdays only. Bureaux de change open 24 hours in all three cities.

Bars (in the Italian sense, coffee and sandwich places) and cafes generally open from 7.30 am to 8 pm, although many turn into pub-style drinking-and-meeting places after 8 pm. Clubs and discos might open around 10 pm, but often there'll be no-one there until around midnight; in Milan the scene stays busy until 3 or 4 am.

Many businesses and shops close for at least a part of August when Italians abandon the city for cooler coastal or mountain air, leaving the cities to a gaggle of enraged tourists, gobsmacked that restaurants and shops dare to shut.

PUBLIC HOLIDAYS

In addition to the national public holidays listed below, Milan, Turin and Genoa each celebrate the feasts of their patron saints in eye-catching fashion – with the Feast of St John the Baptist on 24 June in Turin and Genoa, and the Feast of St Ambrose on 7 December in Milan.

New Year's Day 1 January
Epiphany 6 January
Easter Monday March/April
Liberation Day 25 April
Labour Day 1 May
Feast of the Assumption (Ferragosto)
15 August
All Saints' Day November
Feast of the Immaculate Conception
8 December
Christmas Day 25 December
Feast of Santo Stefano 26 December

SPECIAL EVENTS

The cities' calendars burst with cultural events ranging from colourful traditional celebrations, with a religious and/or historical flavour, through to festivals of the performing arts, including opera, music and theatre. Milan's La Scala is among Europe's most important opera seasons. Europe's four big fashion events of the year strut down Milan's catwalk in January, February, June and September (see Fashion under Arts in the Facts About the Cities chapter).

Genoa hosted the G8 summit in July 2001 and will take another bow on the European stage as a European City of Culture in 2004. Turin is host to the 2006 Winter Olympics.

January
Fiera di Sant'Orso – Century-old fair of St Orso when artisans sell their crafts on the streets of Aosta, Valle d'Aosta.

February
Flormart – Miflor – Two-day international flower and garden show, with a second in mid-September, held in Milan's Fiera di Milano.
Eurochocolate – Five-day chocolate festival with chocolate street parties, the world's largest chocolate bars, chocolate tasting and tours, Turin. Details are online at www.eurochocolate .torino.it.

March
Feast of St Joseph – Italy's naval opens its doors to visitors to mark the festival of the town's patron saint on 19 March. Held in La Spezia (near Genoa).
Milano Internazionale Antiquariato – Four-day international antique show, held in the Fiera di Milano, Milan.

Automotor – International exhibition concerning everything to do with cars, held in Lingotto Fiere, Turin.

Turin Marathon – Details are online at www.turinmarathon.it.

April

International Gay & Lesbian Film Festival – Week-long festival with screenings at Turin's Teatro Nuova (L10,000 per show); programmes (☎ 011 534 48 88, @ info@turinglfilmfestival.com) are online at www.turinglfilmfestival.com.

Feast of St George – Street celebrations on 23 April to mark the city's patron saint, held in San Giorgio, Genoa.

Euroflora – Genoa's largest international flower fair is held for 10 days every five years in the Fiera di Genova. It was last held in April 2001.

Salone Internazionale del Mobile – One of Europe's biggest furniture fairs packing out the city for five days in early April, immediately followed by the big Expo Food fair in the Fiera di Milano, Milan.

BIG Torino – Biennial of Emerging Artists; held every two years in Turin with the next to take place in 2002.

May

Mille Miglia – The famous road race which sees classic cars motor from Brescia, near Milan, to Rome and back again.

Regatta of Ancient Maritime Republics – Every four years since 1956, boats from the four ancient maritime republics of Genoa, Amalfi, Pisa and Venice row into Porto Antico (Old Port). It was last held in 2000 in Genoa.

Sagra del Pesce – Hundreds of fish are fried in 3m-wide pans on the 2nd Sunday to celebrate this atmospheric fish festival held in Camogli.

Marc di Primavera – Spring trade fair held in Fiera di Genova, Genoa.

Festa della Focaccia – Held in Genoa on the 4th Sunday to honour Liguria's bread; a feista of focaccia with every topping imaginable.

Fiera del Libro Torino – Five-day book fair held in Lingotto Fiere, Turin.

June

Antiqua – One-week antique fair luring collectors Europe-wide to Genoa's Fiera di Genova.

International Gay & Lesbian Milan Film Festival – Five-day film festival screening films from around the world. Programmes are online at www.cinemagaylesbico.com.

Medieval Day – Life in a medieval marquisate is recreated with stalls, costumes and processions through Saluzzo's old streets (2nd Sunday).

Giorni d'Estate – Summer Days in Turin, with street dances, open-air concerts and historical processions on the banks of the River Po, held in Turin from June to September.

Festivita Patronale di San Giovanni Battista – Feast of St John the Baptist sees celebrations fill the streets in Turin and Genoa.

July

Festival Internazionale del Balletto – International ballet festival dances through Genoa for 10 days.

September

Pellegringgi delle Casacce – Religious procession of crucifixes through the old streets in Voltri, Genoa.

Concorso Internazionale di Violino – International violin festival, luring some of the world's top virtuosi to the Teatro Carlo Felice in Genoa.

Douja d'Or – Ten-day wine festival held in Asti, south of Turin.

Festival delle Sagre – Open-air food festival, held on the 2nd Sunday in Asti, south of Turin.

Il Palio – Some 21 madcap jockeys race their horses around central Piazza Alfieri on the 3rd Sunday of the month in Asti, south of Turin.

Italian Grand Prix – Tears around the Monza autodrome, outside Milan, every September.

October & November

Truffle Fairs – Held in mid-October in Alba and throughout November in Asti, south of Turin.

Salone Nautico Internazionale – International boat show, held for one week in mid-October in the Fiera di Genova, Genoa.

Festa della Zucca – Pumpkin festival celebrated with creative culinary dishes concocted from pumpkins on the 2nd and 3rd weekends in November, Genoa.

Musica – Ranging from ethnic sounds to jazz and pop, this five-day music fair is held in Lingotto Fiere (Turin).

Torino Film Festival – Prestigious week-long film festival, with full programme details (☎ 011 562 33 09, email info@torinofilmfst.org) at www.torinofilmfest.org.

December

Mercato di Sant'Ambrigio – Milan's biggest feast day, celebrated every year on 7 December, is marked with religious celebrations and traditional fairs around the Fiera di Milano (metro MM1 Amendola Fiera). La Scala marks the occasion by opening its opera season on this day.

DOING BUSINESS

Milan has a substantial international business community. More than a third of Italy's 1630-odd multinational companies are based in the city, which boasts a per capita GDP of 22,000 euros (equal to that of London and almost as high as Amsterdam's). Networking opportunities are rife and there's innumerable organisations whose sole purpose is to help Anglophones integrate into the local business community.

The Italian Stock Exchange (☎ 02 72 42 61, ⓔ info@borsaitalia.it) is in Milan at Piazza Affari 6. Its Web site (in English too) at www.borsaitalia.it is an invaluable information source for economic indicators, news and daily market round-ups.

Work Permits

EU citizens don't require any permit to work or start a business in Italy but non-EU citizens wishing to work in Italy need a *permesso di lavoro* (work permit). If you intend to work for an Italian company and will be paid in lire, the company must organise the permesso and forward it to the Italian embassy or consulate in your country – only then will you be issued with an appropriate visa. Non-EU citizens intending to work for non-Italian companies, be paid in foreign currency or go freelance, must organise the visa and permesso in their country of residence through an Italian embassy or consulate. This process takes months, so look into it early.

In any case, it is advisable to seek detailed information from an Italian embassy or consulate on the exact requirements before attempting to organise a legitimate job in Italy. Advice should also be sought from the following organisations, all of which provide support and assistance to those hoping to break into – or those already in – the local business community.

Networking

Milan Milan's Camera di Commercio, Industria e Agricoltura (Chamber of Commerce, Industry & Agriculture; ☎ 800 26 82 20 toll-free, 02 8 51 51 51), Via Meravigli 12, opens 9 am to 1.30 pm Monday, 9 am to 3.30 pm Tuesday to Thursday, and 9 am to 12.30 pm Friday. It has a Web site at www.mi.camcom.it.

For city data and economic information, try the Chamber of Commerce's Centro Informazione Economia (Economic Information Centre; ☎ 02 851 55 368, ⓔ piazza .affari@mi.camcom.it), Via Camperio 1. A Euro Info Centre (☎ 02 851 55 243/4, ⓔ eic@mi.camcom.it), which can resolve any euro-related problems that you or your business encounter, is also here.

The British Chamber of Commerce for Italy (☎ 02 87 77 98, 02 87 69 81, ⓔ bcci@britchamitaly.com, metro MM1 Cairoli), Via Camperio 9, helps members network, provides business support and stocks information on trade fairs, taxation, business start-ups and more. Membership details are online at www.britchamitaly.com. The British Consulate's commercial desk (☎ 02 720 20 153) issues advice 9.15 am to 12.15 pm and 2.30 to 4.30 pm weekdays.

English-speaking women working in Milan can join the Professional Women's Association of Milan (☎ 02 204 04 613, ⓔ pwa@pwa-milan.org). Updated information on the twice-monthly meetings and 'networking dinners' is online at www.pwa-milan.org.

Business services to suit your every need, from English-speaking accountants and advocates to consultants and catering services, are listed in *English Yellow Pages*.

Turin While its mammoth headquarters on Via Francesco da Paola enjoy a facelift (expected to take several years), Turin's Camera di Commercio Industria Artigianato e Agricoltura (Chamber of Commerce, Industry & Agriculture; ☎ 011 5 71 61) is split across eight different sites. The most useful is its branch at Via Pomba 23, home to its statistics department (☎ 011 571 67 41), library and research centre. It opens 9 am to noon and 2.30 to 3.45 pm Monday to Thursday, and 9 am to 12.15 pm Friday.

Genoa The Camera di Commercio (Chamber of Commerce; ☎ 010 2 70 41, 010 270 43 73/5), Via Garibaldi 6, opens to visitors

8.30 am to noon weekdays. It stocks reams of documentation in English, including company lists, economic data and information on doing business in the city.

The Agenzia Regionale in Liguria (☎ 010 5 30 82), inside Palazzo Ducale on Piazza de Ferrari, handles regional development. More details are online at www.regione .liguria.it.

Trade Fair, Exhibition & Conference Centres

Milan Milan's trade fair, exhibition and conference centre, Fiera di Milano (☎ 02 4 99 71, ℮ fieramilano@fieramilano.it, metro MM1 Amendola Fiera & Lotto-Fiera 2), Larga Domodossola 1, covers a vast area of 375,000 sq m. Comprising 26 pavilions and 30-plus entrances, it's built around Piazzale Italia, the central core where the Fiera Service Centre (☎ 02 499 77 641) is. During exhibitions, free shuttle buses marked 'Circolare Fiera' encircle the complex.

With the exception of July and August, there's almost always a fair taking place at the Fiera di Milano – it hosts some 80 events per year. Exhibition calendars can be requested by faxing 02 499 77 963 or by email on ℮ info.fierami@fieramilano.it. There's also a listing on the Fiera's Web site at www.fieramilano.com.

Some trade fairs and exhibitions spill over into the Padiglione Sud, south of the city in Lacchiarella.

Turin Lingotto Fiere (☎ 011 664 41 11, ℮ info@lingottofiere.it), Via Nizza 294, is Turin's former FIAT factory-turned-state of the art exhibition and conference centre. The 52,070-sq-m exhibition space hosts fairs from September to June; updated exhibition calendars are available on its Web site at www.lingottofiere.it.

In the city centre, smaller events are held at Centro Congressi Torino Incontra (☎ 011 557 68 00, ℮ contact@torinoincontra.org) at Via Nina Costa 8. You can visit them online at www.torino incontra.org.

Genoa Fiera di Genova (☎ 010 5 39 91, ℮ fierage@fiera.genova.it) overlooks the sea from its coastal perch, east of the historic port at Piazzale John F Kennedy 1. Its annual calendar of events is online at www.fiera.ge.it.

At Porto Antico, part of the cotton warehouse complex of Magazzini del Cotone has been converted into a waterside congress centre: Cotone Congressi Genova (☎ 010 248 56 11, ℮ cotonecongressi@ cotonecongressi.it), which has a Web site at www.cotonecongressi.it.

WORK

Finding work is not easy. During the ski season, you might be able to pick up some casual work in Valle d'Aosta resorts. In Milan, a possible source of work is teaching English, although competition is stiff and the pay unspectacular. In all three cities, pick up a copy of *Secondamano*, a Milan-based newspaper with local editions for Turin and Genoa. It's crammed with classifieds and advertisements; you can find some online at www.secondamano.it.

In Milan, the British Council and the Chambers of Commerce are not in the habit of employing people but might be able to point you in other directions. Likewise, the British Consulate can't find you work but can give you an information sheet on employment and residence in Milan, which includes some pointers. The latter directs job seekers to Manpower (☎ 02 706 08 324, ℮ callcenter.ovido@manpower.it), an employment agency handling temporary work for English speakers at Via d'Ovidio 8, which is online at www.manpower.it.

ACCOMMODATION

Prices for accommodation quoted in this book are intended as a guide only. There is generally a fair degree of fluctuation in hotel prices in all three cities, especially in mid-range and top-end hotels which appear to juggle their prices depending on how big the trade fair and when it's on. Rates rise by around 5% or 10% annually.

In every class of hotel, it can sometimes be worth bargaining – many will lower the rates advertised if you intend staying several nights. Mentioning the names of a few close competitors yields few results, given that hotels are almost always full.

Advance reservations are absolutely essential, particularly in Milan where hotels get disconcertingly booked up weeks in advance. Thankfully, the city does have a clutch of reputable agencies on hand to keep track of what is available where and make reservations for you (see the boxed text 'Finding a Hotel Room' in the Milan chapter). However you make your reservation, you will have to give a credit card number as confirmation; many require confirmation by fax or letter too.

There is often no difference between a pensione and an *albergo* (hotel); in fact, some hotels use both titles while many simply run with 'hotel'. However, a pensione will generally be of one to three star quality, while an albergo can be awarded up to five stars. Along the coast you might see signs reading *affittacamere* – rooms for rent by private individuals that fall outside the national star classification system.

A *camera singola* (single room) is uniformly more expensive per person in Italy than a *camera doppia* (double room with twin beds) and a *camera matrimoniale* (double room with a double bed). Tourist offices in all three cities have booklets listing alberghi and affittacamere, including prices (not always up-to-date). They likewise have lists of agencies through which you can rent accommodation on both a short- and long-term basis. Real-estate agencies in Milan and Turin are also listed in *English Yellow Pages*.

FOOD

Eating is one of Milan, Turin and Genoa's great pleasures so be adventurous. And, if you're not intimidated by eccentric waiters or indecipherable menus, you might well find yourself agreeing with locals that nowhere in the world is the food as good as in Italy – or rather in 'their' city.

Places to eat – of which there's a mind-boggling choice – fall into several categories. A *tavola calda* offers cheap, pre-prepared meat, pasta and vegetable dishes in a self-service style. A *pizzeria* serves pizza, but usually has a full menu too. An

osteria is either a wine bar offering a small selection of dishes, or a *trattoria* – a less sophisticated version of a *ristorante* (restaurant). A trattoria touting no printed menu often offers the most authentic food, with menus changing daily to accommodate what's available at the market. Many restaurants impose a cover charge of around L3000 per person and open from 12.30 to 3 pm and then from 7.30 pm. A handful of trattorie open weekdays only and don't accept credit cards.

City dwellers rarely indulge in a sit-down *colazione* (breakfast), but rather wash down a quick *cornetto* (croissant) with a *cappuccino* at the bar. Cafes, *paninerie* (sandwich bars) and *pizzerie* abound and you'll never be short of somewhere to grab a filled *panini* (bread roll) or pizza *al taglio* (by the slice). Snacks are an institution with bars laying out an astonishing array of hors d'œuvres from 5 pm onwards – free for those who order an aperitif.

Unlike much of rural Italy, *pranzo* (lunch) and *cena* (dinner) assume equal importance in Milan, Turin and Genoa. Both meals form an integral element of many people's working day – a vital opportunity for networking and wooing potential clients. For those out to impress, the Italian Full Monty consists of *antipasto* (starter), *primo piatto* (first course, comprising pasta or *risotto*), *secondo piatto* (second course of meat or fish), followed by *insalata* (salad) or *contorno* (vegetable side dish), fruit or *dolce* (dessert), and a shot of *caffè* (always espresso). Those with a watch or wallet to watch are better opting for a speedier (and better-value) lunchtime menu or *menu del giorno* (menu of the day) which includes a first and second course, maybe dessert and a 25cl jug of house wine or 50cl bottle of mineral water for a fixed price (from L25,000/60,000 in mid-range/top-end places). Many upmarket restaurants serve *degustazione* platters – a prime opportunity to sample several regional dishes.

Milan

The city has a strong provincial cuisine. *Polenta* (a cornmeal porridge slightly similar to American grits) is served with almost everything, and *risotto* – traditionally scented with saffron (hence its bold yellow colour) and bone marrow to become *risotto alla milanese* – dominates the first course of most menus. A wilder variation originating from Pavia, south of Milan, where one-third of Italy's rice is produced, is *risotto con le rane* (risotto peppered with small frogs). Another first course, one of the oldest in Mamma Milano's recipe book, is *minestrone alla genovese*, a vegetable soup with rice, potatoes, bacon bits and red kidney beans.

Pizzoccheri is buckwheat pasta with cabbage, potatoes and melted bitto cheese, typical to Milan and surrounding Lombardy. Another unusual dish is *torta di zucca*, pumpkin pie stuffed with sweet almond biscuits, eggs, apple and parmesan.

Bone marrow is a key feature of Milan's quintessential second course too – *ossobuco* (literally 'bone hole'), sliced veal shanks stewed with vegetables and onions and topped with *gremolata* (chopped parsley, garlic and lemon). Pigs' skins, trotters and ribs are braised in wine with vegetables to create *cassoeula*, a stew-like concoction commonly served with polenta.

Fritto misto alla milanese is another meaty dish, comprising fried slices of bone marrow, liver and lung. Tripe is thinly sliced and boiled with beans to make Milanese *busecca*. Should such tummy treats not appeal, you can always opt for a *cotoletta alla milanese*, a breaded and fried veal cutlet offering few surprises.

Dolci (desserts) include *torta di tagliatelle*, a cake made with egg pasta and almonds, and *polenta e ösei*, little sponge cakes with jam, covered with yellow icing and topped with chocolate birds and more jam. *Torta meneghina*, a traditional Milanese sponge cake, often soaked in Grand Marnier and baked, is another a heart-warming dessert. On All Saints' Day, sweet chestnuts are boiled with cream and white wine to make *busechina*. Milan's sweetest culinary pleasure is *panettone* (literally 'little loaf'), a light fruit loaf traditionally baked as a Milanese dessert and known worldwide as Italian Christmas cake. The lofty heights of Lombardian cathedrals are said to have inspired its unusual dome shape.

Cheeses typical to Milan and Lombardy include *gorgonzola*, a pungent blue cheese originating in northern Lombardy and ranging in taste from *piccante* (aged and sharp) to *dolce* (sweet and young); and *mascarpone*, a sinfully soft and cream-like Lombardian 'cheese' which is used in numerous desserts, including *tiramisù* (sponge cake soaked in coffee, mascarpone and cocoa) and *torta paradiso* (a soft cake from Pavia).

Turin

Turin's cuisine is heavily influenced by neighbouring France, while the massive migration of southern Italians to the city brought traditions of cooking unmatched anywhere else in the north. This, coupled with its great chocolate tradition and *tartufi bianchi* (white truffles) – considered 'perfection' by truffle connoisseurs – makes visiting Turin especially sweet.

If Pavia and its surrounds produce one-third of Italy's rice, then the remaining two-thirds come from here. *Risotto alla piemontese* is Piedmont's most quintessential dish, cooked up from rice, butter, white wine and truffles; the 'red' variation touts tomato sauce. Another irresistible first course is *trifulin*, truffle-filled ravioli in a creamy mushroom sauce. Typical only to Turin, *calhiettes tradizionali* is a mix of grated potatoes, minced lard, meat and onion, mixed with eggs and flour to make a lunchtime 'omelette' or 'patty'.

Game birds and animals, including pheasant, quail and chamois, commonly appear as second courses on most menus. Pheasant in particular often comes with *fonduta*, a truffle-free version of *fondua* – a fried 'fondue' mix of melted fontina cheese, butter and egg yolks on toast, topped with thin slices of truffle. Fontina cheese is a curious cross between Gouda and Brie and is liberally used in the cuisine of Valle d'Aosta, west of Turin, where traditional dishes include *valpellineuntze* (a thick soup of cabbage, bread, beef broth and fontina) and *gnocchi alla bava* (potato dumplings with tomato, fontina, cream and truffles.

Carbonada con polenta is another thick soup, traditionally made with the meat of the chamois, although beef is now generally used. *Mocetta* (dried beef) is popular. Mild Bra and mouldy Castelmagno are other alpine cheeses made here.

The plains south of Turin produce some of Italy's best red wines including Barolo, the secret behind *brasato al Barolo*: beef from the region marinated in an aged Barolo red, spiced, and slowly braised for hours with tomatoes, celery, onions, carrots and what's left of the marinade. Alba white truffles and lovely little *lumache* (snails) come from the same Piedmontese pocket.

Typical desserts to be tasted include that old Savoy favourite *panna cotta*, a thick creamy dish not unlike creme caramel; and *torta tradizionale valdese alla crema*, simple cream cake baked to celebrate Turinese feasts and holidays. *Bonèt*, a sweet egg pudding with milk, sugar, macaroon, coffee and fortified Marsala wine, is another dessert typical to Piedmont. Marsala is also used in *zabaglione*, a calorie overload of whipped eggs, marsala and sugar – dunk *amaretti* (sweet almond biscuits) in the creamy mix for a sweet gastronomic orgasm.

Genoa

The taste of the Mediterranean – fresh herbs, olive oil and seafood – comes to life in Genoa and along its seaside shores. *Pesto genovese*, pesto to the rest of the world, is a delicious uncooked pasta sauce of fresh basil, garlic, olive oil, pine kernels and cheese, ground together with a pestle and mortar. The cheese used, a ewe's milk cheese called *pecorino*, is the only cheese unique to these parts, given the region's coastal non-cow grazing terrain. *Minestrone alla genovese* is pretty much the same as the Milanese soup, with the exception that the Genoese top it off with a dollop of pesto.

Salsa di noci, another type of pesto, is made from ground nuts and is best sampled wrapped around a plate of tagliatelle or *trenette*, a distinctive long flat pasta from Liguria of which there's a wholemeal variation too *(trenette avvantaggiae)*. *Pansotti in salsa di nocci* is ravioli stuffed with *prebog-*

gion (a mix of wild Ligurian herbs) and dressed in a thick and creamy hazelnut sauce. Other typical ways to eat Italy's quintessential dish is with *crema di porrodori secchi* (sun-dried tomato sauce) or *crema di rucola* (creamed rocket, best served with gnocchi).

Traditional Ligurian pies include *torta pasqualina* made with spinach, ricotta cheese and eggs; *torta baciocca* with potatoes, parmesan cheese, eggs and parsley;

Coffee & Chocolate

bicerin – a mix of coffee, hot chocolate, milk and whipped cream found only in Turin

caffè americano – large black weakish coffee, served already watered down or with a jug of hot water

caffè freddo – long glass of cold black coffee

caffè lungo – literally 'long coffee', usually translating as a slightly diluted espresso

cappuccino (or '*cappuccio*') – coffee with hot, frothy milk and often topped with a sprinkling of powdered cocoa; generally luke-warmish and only drunk by Italians with breakfast and in the morning

cappuccino senza schiuma – cappuccino without the froth

corretto – espresso with a dash of grappa or another spirit

doppio espresso – 'double' the amount of a regular espresso

espresso – small shot of very strong black coffee

latte macchiato – milk with a spot of coffee

macchiato – espresso with a small amount of milk

JANE SMITH

As Sweet as Heaven

Never will you sip a wine so lip-lickingly sweet as Cinque Terre's *Sciacchetrà* – a dessert wine which is golden in colour and bottled in black opaque glass.

Production of this legendary 'wine of the gods' – as the Romans dubbed the amber nectar – is limited. Its steeply terraced vineyards cover an exclusive six-hectare pocket and yield no more than 10,000L per year. Bosco, Albarola and Vermentino grapes are raisined (dried) to make the Sciacchetrà DOC wine, aged for at least a year before bottling and sold for around L40,000. For a sweet taste of heaven itself, dunk *cantuccini* (dry almond biscuits) in it.

Mounting fears that Sciacchetrà producers are a dying breed were confirmed in early 2001 when Riomaggiore's local council pledged to give parcels of land to producers who would tend the vines and care for the crumbling stone walls. Bra-based Slow Food – Italy's great defender of gastronomic tradition – bought up 20,000 sq m and promptly handed it over to the world's only remaining Sciacchetrà producers – of which there are just three.

and *torta pasqualina*, a traditional Easter pie made with 33 sheets of pastry sandwiched together with layers of chard, ricotta and parmesan. Another common vegetable to the Liguria region is aubergine (eggplant) – which can be stuffed with a mix of eggs, cheese, marjoram, garlic and breadcrumbs, and then baked to make *melanzane ripiene*. *Preivi* are vegetables – often cabbage leaves – stuffed with cheese, eggs, garlic and parsley; while *ravioli di magro* is ravioli stuffed with fish, artichokes or another veggie.

Fish forms the mainstay of many second courses. *Burrida* (fish stew) can be cooked with *triglie* (red mullet), although *stoccafisso* (stockfish) was traditionally used by Genoese sailors on long voyages. *Burrida di pesce alla ligure* is fish stew with anchovies, wild mushrooms, garlic, celery and carrot. *Stoccafisso a brandacujun* is a creamy stock-

fish dish and *stoccafisso accomodato* is stockfish cooked in a pot with anchovies and served with potatoes and pine kernels. *Stoccafisso alla genovese* on a menu can mean any one of these or another variation. Other fish dishes include *bianchetti* (tiny fried anchovies, sardines or whitebait) and *boghe in scabescio* (floured fish marinated in vinegar with onions, sage, parsley and fried).

Cima alla genovese is a popular meat dish – veal breast stuffed with nuts and vegetables, bound with egg and breadcrumbs, boiled and served in slices. If you order *coniglio alla ligure*, you'll end up with a rabbit on your plate, albeit carefully cooked with pine kernels and olives.

No trip to Genoa is complete without sampling what has to be its most basic yet tastiest culinary treats – *focaccia* (flat bread topped with cheese, vegetables or anything else the chef fancies) and *farinata* (thin flat bread made from chickpea flour and served piping hot from a wood-fired oven).

DRINKS

Piedmont produces some excellent wines, most notably Barolo and Barbaresco which rank among Italy's best reds. Other wines which are easy to find in the region include Asti's sparkling whites produced south of Turin, and the dry and fruity reds and *rosatos* (rosé) of Valle d'Aosta – a tiny wine-producing valley north-west of the city which lays claim to Europe's highest classified vineyard in Morgex. Along the Genoese coast, try to lay your hands on local vintages such as Cinque Terre's renowned whites and dessert wines *Morasca, Chiaretto del Faro* and the heavenly, sweet *sciacchetrà* (see the boxed text 'As Sweet as Heaven'). Plenty of places to taste and buy these wines are listed in the relevant city chapters.

As for that all-essential aperitif Italians might take a palate-cleansing Campari bitter (straight), Campari soda (mixed with soda water) or a vermouth (a wine-based drink with herbs) such as Cinzano or Martini Bianco – all of which have been manufactured in northern Italy since the late 19th century. Cinzano started out in Turin in 1757 as a humble shop selling 'house' aperitifs concocted from 20 or so herbs, and distils 80% of all its products in the south of the city; while Martini & Rossi took root in Turin in 1863.

After dinner, sink a shot of *grappa*, a very strong, clear brew made from grapes, or *amaro*, a dark liqueur prepared from herbs. If you prefer a sweeter liqueur, try the almond-flavoured *amaretto* or the sweet aniseed *sambuca*. On the coast, Cinque Terre's abundance of fragrant lemons are turned into *limoncino*, a liqueur guaranteed to make the heart race.

Getting There & Away

AIR
Flights to Milan cover the world with an astonishing frequency, making it easy to fly in to Europe's design capital at the drop of a hat. Fares to Milan, particularly from the UK and Continental Europe, can get pricey but super-cheap flights to Turin and Genoa can usually be scooped up. If you are bound for Milan and on a budget, consider flying into either Turin or Genoa and catching a train.

Airports & Airlines
The region is well-served by airports and airlines: flights to Milan land at either Linate r Malpensa airports, Linate being substantially closer to the centre than in-the-sticks Malpensa. Turin and Genoa are served by Caselle and Cristoforo Colombo airports respectively. All airports are well-connected to public transport to the city centres; see To/From the Airports under Getting Around in the individual city chapters.

Many European and international airlines compete with Alitalia (the national carrier).

Buying Tickets
World aviation has never been so competitive – nor has it ever been such a mind-boggling minefield of carriers and fares. Discounts are widespread and the few travellers likely to pay full fare are those flying in 1st or business class. With careful planning, flexibility as to when you travel and a beady eye for short-lived promotional offers, economy-class passengers can almost always manage some sort of discount. The Internet is the most useful resource for checking air fares: many travel agencies and airlines have Web sites.

Many airlines sell discounted tickets direct to the customer, and it's worth contacting them anyway for information on routes and timetables. However, airlines occasionally release discounted tickets to travel agencies and specialist discount agencies – often the best deal around – so it's worth checking these too.

The exception to this rule is the welcome breed of 'no-frills' carriers, which mostly sell direct to travellers. Unlike 'full service' airlines, these no-frills airlines often make one-way tickets available at around half the return fare, making it easy to stitch together an open-jaw itinerary – whereby you fly into one city and out of another – at a cost substantially less than those available with regular airlines.

All these no-frills airlines encourage punters to book on the Internet. Full-service airlines can also offer some excellent fares to Web surfers, sometimes selling seats by auction or simply cutting prices to reflect the reduced cost of electronic selling.

Ticketless travel, whereby your reservation details are contained within an airline computer, is another big feature of no-frills carriers. On straightforward city breaks and

Warning

The information in this chapter is particularly vulnerable to change. Prices for international travel are volatile, routes are introduced and cancelled, schedules change, special deals come and go, and rules and visa requirements are amended. Airlines and governments seem to take a perverse pleasure in making price structures and regulations as complicated as possible. You should check directly with the airline or a travel agent to make sure you understand how a fare (and ticket you may buy) works. In addition, the travel industry is highly competitive and there are many lurks and perks.

The upshot of this is that you should get opinions, quotes and advice from as many airlines and travel agents as possible before you part with your hard-earned cash. The details given in this chapter should be regarded as pointers and are not a substitute for your own careful, up-to-date research.

Bickering Over Hot Air

From the passenger perspective, there seems little rhyme or reason as to where flights land in Milan – much to the delight of Europe's major airlines who have spent months bickering over hot air.

Airlines got embroiled in the fight in April 2000 after Italy announced that Milan's smaller, older and substantially-closer-to-town Linate airport would be reserved for flights to Rome – a route conveniently dominated by Alitalia. The European Union (EU) – the empire in the whole affair – banged that one straight on the head, only for the Italian government to suggest limiting Linate to flight routes carrying three million passengers or more a year. Given that Milan-Rome would have been the only route to notch up that magic number, the EU stopped that one in its tracks too.

The latest agreement, rubber-stamped by the EU in December 2000, allows a daily round trip between Linate and European capital cities, and two round trips for airports with annual passenger turnovers of 40 million or more.

A US$1.2 billion project (1994–8) saw Malpensa transformed from an insignificant airport handling cargo flights to a sparkling state-of-the-art hub, handling 16 million passengers in 1999. Traffic at Linate fell by 50% (from 13.6 million in 1998 to 6.6 million in 1999) after Malpensa opened to commercial traffic in October 1998.

short return journeys – exactly the types of trips these carriers cater to – the absence of a ticket can simply be one less thing to worry about. When flying complicated itineraries with full-service airlines, however, there's still no substitute for the good old paper version, especially for trips that might require a sudden change of route halfway through.

Travellers with Specific Needs

If warned early enough, airlines can often make special arrangements, such as wheelchair assistance or vegetarian meals, for travellers with specific needs. Children under two years travel for 10% of the standard fare (or free on some airlines) as long as they don't occupy a seat. They don't get a baggage allowance. 'Skycots', baby food and nappies should be provided by the airline if requested in advance. Children aged between two and 12 can usually occupy a seat for half to two-thirds of the full fare, and do get a baggage allowance.

The disability-friendly Web site, www.everybody.co.uk, has an airline directory that provides information on the facilities offered by various airlines.

Other Parts of Italy

Alitalia operates flights between Milan's Malpensa and Turin (two hours, three or four flights daily) and between Milan's Malpensa and Genoa (45 minutes, four daily); there are no direct flights between Turin and Genoa. The leading carriers on domestic routes from Milan, Turin and Genoa to other cities in Italy are Meridiana and Minerva. Smaller airlines include Rome-based Italair, the partly Lufthansa-owned Air Dolomiti (Web site: www.airdolomiti.it), and Air One (Web site: www.flyairone.it).

In Milan, domestic flights use both airports. At the time of writing, there were three to six Alitalia flights between Malpensa and Bologna, Florence (in conjunction with Azzurra Air), Pisa, Trieste, Venice and Verona; and flights between both airports and Cagliari (at least hourly), Catania, Palermo (both three to five daily) and Naples (up to nine daily). With the exception of a couple of early morning and evening flights, all Alitalia flights to Rome use Linate airport, much to the disgust of its competitive carriers (see the 'Bickering Over Hot Air' boxed text). Cagliari and Catania are also served by once- or twice-daily Meridiana flights from Linate and Malpensa airports. Meridiana also flies once or twice daily to Palermo (Linate only) and Olbia (both airports).

From Turin, Alitalia flies four times weekly to Alghero and four times daily to

Air Travel Glossary

Alliances Many of the world's leading airlines are now intimately involved with each other, sharing everything from reservations systems and check-in to aircraft and frequent flyer schemes. Opponents say that alliances restrict competition. Whatever the arguments, there is no doubt that big alliances are the way of the future.

Cancelling or Changing Tickets If you have to cancel or change a ticket, you need to contact the original travel agent who sold you the ticket. Airlines only issue refunds to the purchaser of a ticket – usually the travel agent who bought the ticket on your behalf. There are often heavy penalties involved; insurance can sometimes be taken out against these penalties.

Courier Fares Businesses often need to send urgent documents or freight securely and quickly. Courier companies hire people to accompany the package through customs and, in return, offer a discount ticket which is sometimes a bargain. However, you may have to surrender all your baggage allowance and take only carry-on luggage.

Fares Airlines traditionally offer 1st class (coded F), business class (coded J) and economy class (coded Y) tickets. These days there are so many promotional and discounted fares available that few passengers pay full fare.

Lost Tickets If you lose your airline ticket an airline will usually treat it like a travellers cheque and, after enquiries, issue you with another one. Legally, however, an airline is entitled to treat it like cash and if you lose it then it's gone forever. Take good care of your tickets.

Onward Tickets An entry requirement for many countries is that you have a ticket out of the country. If you're unsure of your next move, the easiest solution is to buy the cheapest onward ticket to a neighbouring country or a ticket from a reliable airline which can later be refunded if you do not use it.

Open-Jaw Tickets These are return tickets where you fly out to one place but return from another. If available, this can save you backtracking to your arrival point.

Overbooking Since every flight has some passengers who fail to show up, airlines often book more passengers than they have seats. Usually excess passengers make up for the no-shows, but occasionally somebody gets 'bumped' onto the next available flight. Guess who it is most likely to be? The passengers who check in late. If you are 'bumped' you are normally offered some form of compensation.

Reconfirmation Some airlines require you to reconfirm your flight at least 72 hours prior to departure. Check your travel documents to see if this is the case.

Restrictions Discounted tickets often have various restrictions on them – such as needing to be paid for in advance and incurring a penalty to be altered or cancelled. Others may have restrictions on the minimum and maximum period you must be away.

Round-the-World Tickets RTW tickets give you a limited period (usually a year) in which to circumnavigate the globe. You can go anywhere the carrying airlines go, as long as you don't backtrack. The number of stopovers or total number of separate flights is decided before you set off and they usually cost a bit more than a basic return flight.

Ticketless Travel Airlines are gradually waking up to the realisation that paper tickets are unnecessary encumbrances. On simple one-way or return trips, reservations details can be held on computer, and the passenger merely shows ID to claim his or her seat.

Transferred Tickets Airline tickets cannot be transferred from one person to another. Travellers sometimes try to sell the return half of their ticket, but officials can ask you to prove that you are the person named on the ticket. On an international flight tickets are always compared with passports.

Naples. Cagliari, Catania and Palermo are served by frequent flights to/from Turin (Alitalia and Meridiana) and Genoa (Air Dolomiti, Meridiana or Italair). There are also weekly flights from Genoa to/from Naples and Trieste with Alitalia.

You can find updated timetables and buy tickets for Alitalia at www.alitalia.it and Meridiana at www.meridiana.it. Schedules for Air Dolomiti (☎ 800 01 33 66 toll-free within Italy) can be viewed online at www.airdolomiti but electronic bookings have to be made via the Lufthansa Web site at www.lufthansa.it. Sample fares with Alitalia at the time of writing include Genoa-Milan (L212,000/426,300) and Turin-Milan (L199,000/413,000). Sample single fares with Meridiana are Milan-Catania/Cagliari/Palermo (L405,000/315,000/390,000) and Turin-Cagliari (L330,000).

For flight information at Malpensa or Linate airports, log into the Web site of the Società Esercizi Aeroportuali (SEA), which manages both Milan airports. The site, www.sea-aeroportimilano.it, features real-time arrival/departure schedules.

The UK & Ireland

With the advent of no-frills airlines such as Ryanair, Buzz, Go and Virgin Express, fares between the UK and Italy have been slashed. These airlines operate on a first-come-first-served basis, meaning that the earlier you book your ticket, the cheaper the fare will be.

At the time of writing, Dublin-based Ryanair (☎ 01-609 7881 in Ireland, ☎ 0870 156 9569 in the UK, ☎ 199 11 41 14 in Italy) was advertising special promotional return fares from London Stansted to Turin/Genoa for UK£19/10 and regular lead-in fares (minimum two nights' or Saturday night stay) for UK£63.90/63.40. Tickets bought at promotional and lead-in rates cannot be refunded or changed. A fully flexible, same-day return (booked as little as one day in advance) can cost up to UK£283.80/213.40. Flights booked online at www.ryanair.com generally cost a little less than telephone bookings. Also, the cheapest promotional fares are not always available at call centres. You can book up to 11 months in

advance. Ryanair currently has two flights daily to Turin and one/two daily to Genoa from London Stansted.

At the time of writing, Buzz (☎ 0870 240 7070 in the UK, ☎ 02 696 82 222 in Italy, e askbuzz@buzzaway.com), the no-frills airline of KLM, has single/return London Stansted-Milan Linate 'done-deal' (minimum stay of two nights or a Saturday night) fares for UK£45/90. A fully-flexible single/return, changeable up to 30 minutes before take-off, cost UK£130/260. Buzz operates three flights daily between Stansted and Milan (twice daily at weekends). Advertised fares (which include airport taxes) are the same price on the Web and at call centres – but telephone customers have to pay a UK£3 booking fee. Buzz's Web site is at www.buzzaway.com. Tickets can be booked up to six months in advance.

The British Airways cheapie, Go (☎ 0870 607 6543 in the UK, ☎ 147 88 77 66 in Italy), flies twice daily between London Stansted and Malpensa, and once daily to/from Linate. Fares for both airports are the same. At the time of writing, the cheapest advertised return fare is its 'super saver' UK£80 (including a Saturday night stay, booked at least five days in advance and flying on off-peak days), including taxes. The same restrictions apply to the 'saver' UK£110 return fare, except that it doesn't have to be booked in advance. A fully flexible return costs UK£245. As with Buzz, Web surfers don't have to pay the UK£3 credit-card charge that telephone customers do, making it cheaper to book via the Internet. Go is online at www.go-fly.com.

The last in the budget bunch, Virgin Express (☎ 020-7744 0004 in the UK, ☎ 02 482 96 000 in Milan, ☎ 800 09 70 97 for the rest of Italy) was advertising flights between London Heathrow and Milan Linate – via Brussels – from UK£89.80 return, including departure taxes. Virgin Express has several fare levels: promotional, discounted and economy tickets can't be changed or refunded, but fully-flexible ones (£178.80) can. Flights are once or twice daily. Its Web site is at www.virgin-express.com.

British Airways (BA) has flights into

Genoa from London Gatwick (starting at UK£167 return, including Saturday night stay), and to Milan's Malpensa from Birmingham, Glasgow and Manchester. Alitalia's London Heathrow-Milan flights use both Malpensa and Linate (from UK£146 with Saturday night stay).

Alitalia flies once daily to Turin from Gatwick and operates four flights weekly between Dublin and Milan.

BA and British Midland both do student deals: BA's London-Milan return youth fare available to under-26s and students aged up to 34 was UK£103 (UK£177 in peak season) at the time of writing; British Midland had a UK£105 (UK£163 peak) equivalent.

Shop around for the cheapest tickets – it can pay to go via Frankfurt or another hub: at the time of research BA's direct return Manchester-Milan fare cost UK£146 (valid for one month, including Saturday night), while Lufthansa' had a return Manchester-Frankfurt-Milan fare going for UK£113.

Continental Europe

Air travel between Milan, Turin and Genoa and other continental European cities is worth considering if you are pushed for time. Short hops can be expensive, but good deals are available from some major routes.

Milan has flights two or three times daily to most other European cities, the cheapest fares often being available in early spring and late autumn. No-frills Virgin Express (see The UK & Ireland section earlier) has a daily flight between Brussels and Linate. Turin has direct daily flights to Amsterdam; Barcelona and Madrid; Brussels; Cologne, Dusseldorf, Frankfurt, Munich and Stuttgart; Clermont-Ferrand, Lyons, Marseille and Paris; Luxembourg and Zurich. Genoa-bound services are less frequent: once a week in summer from Dusseldorf, three times daily from Paris with Air France, and four times daily from Zurich with Swiss Air.

Across continental Europe many airlines have ties with STA Travel (a student discount travel agency), where cheap tickets can be purchased and STA-issued tickets altered (usually for a US$25 fee). Outlets include: STA Travel (☎ 030-311 0950, fax 313 0948),

Goethestrasse 73, 10625 Berlin; and Passaggi (☎ 06 474 09 23, fax 06 482 74 36), Stazione Termini FS, Galleria di Tesla, Rome. In Belgium, Connections (☎ 02-550 01 00), part of the usit Group, has several offices, including one at 19–21 rue du Midi, Brussels. Have a look at the Web site at www.connections.be. In Switzerland, SSR Voyages (☎ 01-297 11 11), with a Web site at www.ssr.ch, specialises in student, youth and budget fares. In Zurich, there is a branch at Leonhardstrasse 10, and there are branches in most major Swiss cities. In the Netherlands, NBBS Reizen is the official student travel agency. A branch can be found in Amsterdam (☎ 020-624 5071) at Schilphoweg 101, 2300 AJ Leiden. In Spain, try Barcelo Viajs (☎ 91 559 1819) at Princesa 3, Madrid 28228. In France, usit Connect Voyages (☎ 01 42 44 14 00) at 14 rue de Vaugirard, 75006 Paris and OTU Voyages (☎ 01 40 29 12 12) at 39 ave Georges-Bernanos, 75005 Paris, specialise in student and young person fares. Both have branches across the country.

The USA & Canada

The flight options across the North Atlantic, the world's busiest long-haul air corridor, are bewildering. The *New York Times, Los Angeles Times, Chicago Tribune* and *San Francisco Chronicle* all have weekly travel sections where you can find travel agents' ads galore. Council Travel (☎ 800-226 8624 toll-free), with a Web site at www.council travel.com, and STA (☎ 800-777 0112 toll-free), with a Web site at www.statravel .com, have offices in major cities. Canada's best bargain-hunting agency is Travel CUTS (☎ 888-835 2887 toll-free), which has offices in major Canadian cities and a Web site at www.travelcuts.com.

Alitalia flies daily to Malpensa from Boston, Chicago, New York and San Francisco; a return fare from the East Coast starts at US$328 return (including a Saturday night stay, valid for 30 days, non-refundable and nonchangeable).

Continental Airlines, American Airlines, Northwest Airlines and Delta Airlines are transatlantic airlines flying into Malpensa. Volare Airlines flies into Linate.

Australia & New Zealand

Saturday's travel sections in the *Sydney Morning Herald* and Melbourne's *The Age* contain ads offering cheap fares to Europe. One of Australasia's best discount-air fare shops is Flight Centre (☎ 131 600 Australia-wide), with a Web site at www.flightcentre .com.au and an office (☎ 03-9650 2899) at 19 Bourke St, Melbourne. STA Travel (☎ 131 776 Australia-wide) has a Web site at www.statravel.com.au and offices in Sydney (☎ 02-9212 1255) and Auckland (☎ 09-309 0458). Both agents have branch offices throughout Australia and New Zealand. Trailfinders, with a Web site at www.trailfinders.com, has branches in Sydney (☎ 02-9247 7666), Brisbane (☎ 07-3229 0887) and Cairns (☎ 07-4041 1199).

Airlines such as Thai, Malaysian, Qantas and Singapore all have frequent promotional fares; check daily newspapers for details.

Airline Offices

Airline offices in Milan, Turin & Genoa are:

Air France
(☎ 02 748 66 463) Malpensa airport; (☎ 848 88 44 66 within Italy, ☎ 02 77 38 21, metro MM3 Monte Napoleone) Piazza Cavour 2, 20121 Milan; (☎ 010 59 14 47) Via Roma 8, 16121 Genoa

Alitalia
(☎ 02 748 65 194 passenger information, ☎ 02 748 65 250 luggage information, ☎ 02 748 65 120 domestic flights, ☎ 02 748 65 190 international flights) Malpensa airport; (☎ 147 86 56 42 international flights, ☎ 147 86 56 41 national flights, metro MM3 Missori) Via Albricci 2, 20122 Milan; (☎ 011 567 83 38) Turin airport; (☎ 010 5 49 37) Via XXII Ottobre 12, 16121 Genoa
Web site: www.alitalia.it

American Airlines
(☎ 02 748 66 371) Malpensa airport; (☎ 02 679 14 400, metro MM3 Repubblica) Via Vittor Pisani 19, 20124 Milan
Web site: www.aa.com

Austrian Airlines
(☎ 02 864 61 200, metro MM1/3 Duomo) Piazza Armandi Diaz 5, 20123 Milan

British Airways
(☎ 02 748 66 596) Malpensa airport; (☎ 147 81 22 66 toll-free, metro MM3 Missori) Corso Italia 8, 20122 Milan

Delta Air Lines
(☎ 02 585 81 122/3) Malpensa airport; (☎ 167 86 41 14 toll-free) Viale Monte di Pietà 21, 20121 Milan

Iberia
(☎ 02 748 66 431) Malpensa airport; (☎ 02 72 01 02 60, metro MM3 Missori) Via Albricci 8, 20122 Milan

Lufthansa
(☎ 02 748 62 420) Malpensa airport; (☎ 02 806 63 025, metro MM3 Missori) Via Larga 23, 20122 Milan; (☎ 010 58 37 25) Via Pionieri e Aviatori, 16154 Genoa
Web site www.lufthansa.it

Meridiana
(☎ 02 748 66 565) Malpensa airport; (☎ 02 584 17 333, @ tariffe.orari@meridiana.it, metro MM3 Missori) Via Albricci 7, 20122 Milan; (☎ 011 567 80 32) Turin airport
Web site: www.meridiana.it

SAS
(☎ 02 748 66 442) Malpensa airport; (☎ 02 720 00 193, metro MM3 Missori) Via Albricci 7, 20122 Milan

BUS

You'd be daft to take the bus between Milan, Turin, Genoa and Italy's other big cities – take the train.

Eurolines

Eurolines, a consortium of national coach operators, is the main international carrier connecting Milan, Turin and Genoa to the UK, Continental Europe, Scandinavia and North Africa. Routes and Eurolines-affiliated companies can be found on its Web site at www.eurolines.it. The London office (☎ 0870 514 3219) at 52 Grosvenor Gardens, London SW1W 0AU, is online at www.eurolines.co.uk.

On most routes, those aged under 25 or over 60 qualify for a 10 to 20% discount and those aged four to 12 qualify for a 50% discount; a return ticket costs much more than two one-way tickets. Milan is included on the Eurolines Pass allowing unlimited travel between up to 30 European cities. Passes valid for 30/60 days cost UK£175/219 (UK£139/175 for those aged under 26 and seniors); add another UK£60 to UK£70 for travel from June to the end of August.

Sample adult/youth fares for single journeys to Milan or Turin are UK£79/70 from London, which takes 13½ hours, and FF440/FF395 from Paris, which takes 11¼ hours. From Amsterdam to Milan/Turin (22½/20¼ hours) it costs f160/190 (f145/170 for those aged under 26) and a single Genoa-Warsaw (30¼ hours) fare is L180,000 (10% less for those aged 13 to 25).

Milan Bus stations are scattered across the city. Buses to many national and international points, operated by national and regional companies, leave from and arrive at Piazza Castello, in front of Castello Sforzesco (metro MM2 Cairoli).

Autostradale Viaggi (☎ 02 80 11 61), open 6.30 am to 9.30 pm daily, sells tickets for destinations in Italy. Next door, Eurolines (☎ 02 720 01 304, 055 35 71 10, e posta@eurolines.it) opens 9 am to 1 pm and 2 to 6 pm Monday to Saturday, and 7.15 to 9 am, 12.30 to 3 pm and 6 to 7.30 pm Sunday.

Turin Most international, national and regional buses terminate at Turin's main bus station (☎ 011 433 25 25), Corso Inghilterra 1–3. Eurolines buses and buses to Milan arrive/depart from here. Some regional buses use the smaller bus station at the intersection of Via Nizza and Corso Marconi.

Genoa Buses from/to international cities arrive/depart on Piazza della Vittoria, as do limited inter-regional services and buses for other points in Liguria. Tickets for most services, including Eurolines buses, are sold at Pesci Viaggi e Turismo (☎ 010 56 49 36, fax 010 58 09 19, e pesciros@tin.it), a travel agency at Piazza della Vittoria 94r.

TRAIN

Train is by far the speediest, easiest and most comfortable means of travelling between Italian cities and to Italy from continental Europe.

Italy's national rail network is the partly privatised Ferrovie dello Stato (FS), with an excellent Web site at www.fs-on-line.com. It's served by *regionale* (Reg) or *interregionale* (IR) trains that stop at all stations, and the faster Intercity (IC), Espressi (EX) and Eurostar Italia (ES) that only stop at

Tunnelling through the Alps

An ambitious engineering project will see Turin linked by high-speed rail with Lyons in neighbouring France by 2015. Partly funded by the European Bank for Reconstruction & Development (EBRD), the US$10 billion deal signed in early 2001 will bore a 52km-long tunnel beneath Valle di Susa, west of Turin. Preliminary tests should be completed by 2006, by which time the Italian and French governments will have opted for one of two proposals – a rail tunnel, or parallel rail and road tunnels.

North of Milan in Switzerland, construction work will kick off in 2002 on Europe's longest rail tunnel (58km) linking Bodio, 40km north of the Italian border, with Erstfeld near Zurich. The project will slash travelling time between Milan and Zurich from 5¼ to 3¾ hours.

JANE SMITH

major cities. Tickets – including those bought internationally – must be validated *before* boarding the train: punch them in the yellow machines installed at the entrances to train platforms. Non-validated tickets risk a fine.

A complete listing of train schedules, plus reservations information and supplements, is published in the *Thomas Cook European Timetable*. It is updated monthly and available from Thomas Cook offices worldwide and on the Web at www.thomas cookpublishing.com.

In Italy, invest L7500 in a copy of *Pozzorario Italia*, which is published twice a year (June and September). It includes detailed timetables for both national and international trains to/from Italy. Bookshops and news kiosks sell it; ask for an *orario dei treni*.

The FS posts a fully searchable electronic timetable (with fares) on its Web site at http://orario.fs-on-line.com. Tickets for IC, EX and ES trains can be bought online.

Other Parts of Italy

Rail travel in Italy is cheap when compared to the rest of western Europe. Three to five people travelling together pay 30% less; children aged four to 12 get a 50% discount and those aged under four travel for free. FS adult discount passes available for travel within Italy include the Carta Verde (L45,000) which gives travellers aged 12 to 26 a 30/20% discount on 1st/2nd-class rail travel; the Carta d'Argento (same price) which is the equivalent for those aged 60 and over; and the Carta Prima (L50,000), available to everyone and commanding a 30% discount on 1st-class travel. All these passes are valid for one year.

Two other useful passes are the Italy Rail- card and Italy Flexi Rail, both available in Italy and in the UK from Rail Choice (☎ 020-8659 7300, ℮ sales@rail-choice.com), with a Web site at www. railchoice .co.uk. The Italy Railcard is valid for eight, 15, 21 or 30 days and is available in 1st or 2nd class. An eight day pass costs UK£188/128 in 1st/2nd class. The Italy Flexi Rail pass is valid for four, eight or 12

days of travel within one month, the four-day pass costing UK£142/96 in 1st/2nd class.

Those who have been resident in Europe for at least six months can buy the Euro Domino Pass, valid in Italy for three to eight days in a one-month period. A three-day pass for 1st-/2nd-class travel costs UK£127/87 and a youth equivalent (which is for those aged 12 to 25), valid in 2nd class only, costs UK£65. Passes are available from student travel agencies, European train stations, and Rail Europe (0870 584 8848 in the UK, ☎ 0990 848 848 from elsewhere, ℮ europrail@eurail.on.ca), 179 Piccadilly, London W1V 0BA. Information is available online at the Rail Europe Web site at www.raileurope.com.

On overnight trips to and within Italy, it's worth paying that little bit extra for a *cuccetta* (sleeping berth, commonly known as a couchette), which costs L54,200 for a bed in a four-berth 2nd-class compartment and L38,700 in a six-berth equivalent. You can take your bicycle in the baggage compartment on specified trains for L10,000 (L7000 on the regionale and inter-regionale services).

Milan Although there are several train stations in Milan, most travellers only use two or three – the main station, Stazione Centrale (☎ 02 637 12 016, metro MM2/3 Centrale FS), Piazza Duca d'Aosta, from where trains run to all major cities in Italy and throughout Europe; and Stazione Nord (also called Stazione Cadorna, metro MM1/2 Cadorna Triennale), Piazza Luigi Cadorna, the hub for express trains to Malpensa airport and services to Como. Rail services to/from many towns northwest of Milan are more frequent from Stazione Porta Garibaldi (metro MM2 Garibaldi FS), Piazza Sigmund Freud.

The FS information office (☎ 1478 8 80 88) at Stazione Centrale opens 7 am to 9 pm daily. The left luggage opens midnight to 1.35 pm and 2 pm to midnight daily. There is also a special Eurostar booking office here (☎ 02 669 81 013) where you can buy tickets from 7 am to 9 pm daily.

There are frequent trains between Milan and Turin 1½ to 1¾ hours). Tickets in 1st/2nd class cost L32,200/24,400 on an IC train and L24,300/15,300 on an IR train. For the journey between Milan and Genoa (1½ to 1¾ hours), 1st/2nd class tickets cost L35,100/24,900 on an IC train and L24,300/15,300 on an IR train.

Other services (single fares quoted) include to Venice (L37,100/23,900 by IC/IR train, three/3½ hours), Florence (L53,700/42,000 by ES/IC train, 2¾/3½ hours), Rome (L87,200/73,900 by ES/IC train, 4½/5¾ hours) and Naples (L105,300/93,900 by ES/IC train, 6½/8 hours).

Turin The main train station is Stazione Porta Nuova (☎ 011 669 04 45), Piazza Carlo Felice. Its information office (☎ 1478 8 80 88) opens 7 am to 9 pm daily; expect to queue for at least 15 minutes. International ticket sales and ticket reimbursements are handled by window Nos 1, 3 and 4. The left-luggage counter (☎ 011 665 36 61), which is opposite the tracks, opens 4.30 to 2.30 am (L5000/10,000 per 12/24 hours). Make reservations and buy tickets for ES trains at the Eurostar office (☎ 011 669 02 46), open 7.30 am to 8 pm daily.

Regular trains connect Turin with Milan (see that section earlier), Genoa (L24,900/15,300 by IC/IR train, 1½/1¾ hours) and Rome (L78,300, seven hours by IC). Second class single fares are quoted. Most trains also stop at Stazione Porta Susa, a smaller station to the north-west at Piazza XVIII Dicembre.

Genoa The two central train stations in Genoa are Stazione Principe (☎ 010 274 21 50) on Piazza Acquaverde and Stazione Brignole (☎ 010 54 30 70) on Piazza Giuseppe Verdi. It makes little difference which of the two you choose, with the exception of trips along the coast; westwards, there are more departures from Stazione Principe than Brignole.

The information offices (☎ 1478 8 80 88) at both stations open 7 am to 9 pm daily. At Stazione Brignole, train tickets for international destinations are only sold at win-

dow Nos 2 and 3, while window No 8 handles ticket reimbursements. The left-luggage lockers (signposted 'deposito bagagli'), in the waiting room, are accessible 24 hours and cost L4000/5000 per day for a small/medium locker. There is a Eurostar office (☎ 010 58 23 70) at both stations, open 7.30 am to 8 pm daily.

Genoa is linked by train to Turin and Milan (see those sections earlier) and by IC trains (second class single fares quoted) with Rome (L61,200, 5½ hours) and Naples (L83,100, 7½ hours).

Continental Europe

Milan, Turin and Genoa are well placed for travellers seeking international rail connections. It is recommended that for long trips you book seats in advance, particularly if you're travelling at the weekend or during holiday periods, otherwise you could find yourself standing in the corridor for the entire journey; reservations are obligatory for many ES trains. In the UK, the Italian Railway office (☎ 020-7724 0011) in London is more than happy to answer rail-related queries by telephone.

There are northbound trains from Milan to Switzerland and Germany, with nippy Cisalpino trains speeding up to 200km/h from Milan to major Swiss destinations. The lines are: Florence-Milan-Zurich, Venice-Milan-Geneva, Milan-Bern-Basel and Milan-Zurich-Stuttgart (Germany).

Another route links Milan with the Netherlands. The Amsterdam-Milan Overnight Express departs at 5.55 pm and arrives in Milan at 7.50 am the next morning. Northbound, the train pulls out of Milan's Stazione Centrale at 8.05 pm and arrives in Amsterdam at 10.37 am. An adult one-way 2nd-class ticket to Milan costs around f550.

Training it west, there are plenty of direct trains from Genoa into France and from Turin to France and Spain. The adult one-way, 2nd-class fare from Nice along the coast to Genoa (direct or with a change of train in Ventimiglia) is 134FF and the scenic journey takes three hours. From Paris there are two direct trains daily to Milan (612FF, seven hours), via Lyons and Turin. There are many more trains between Lyons and Turin (266FF, four hours). From Spain, the adult one-way, 2nd-class fare on the three-times weekly overnight train from Barcelona via Turin and Milan costs 14,500 ptas (17,800 ptas with couchette). It departs at 8.38 pm and arrives in Milan at 9 am.

CAR & MOTORCYCLE

Roads in Italy are not for sauntering and certainly not those leading to and around Milan, Turin and Genoa where the traffic is nothing short of hellish. The Italian attitude to driving bears little similarity to the English concept of traffic in ordered lanes (a normal two-lane road in Italy is likely to carry three or four lanes of traffic), and most motorists are speed fiends who spend serious amounts of road time up the backsides of more 'casual' motorists who drive at what would be deemed a 'normal pace' elsewhere. Once you arrive in a city, follow the *centro* (centre) signs – often no more than a black circle surrounded by three concentric black rings.

Disregarding the nutters on it, Italy's road network is not bad. Milan is the major junction of Italy's *autostrade* (motorways), including the Autostrada del Sole (A1 & A3) to Naples and Reggio di Calabria in southern Italy; the A4, (also known as the Milan-Turin), west to Turin; the Serenissima, east to Verona and Venice; the hair-raising A7, south to Genoa; and the A8 and A9, north to the lakes and the Swiss border. The city is also a hub for smaller national roads, including the S7 (Via Emilia), which runs south through Emilia-Romagna, and the S11, which runs east-west from Brescia to Turin.

All of these roads meet the Milan ring road, known as the Tangenziale Est (east) and the Tangenziale Ovest (west). From here, follow the signs into the city centre. The aforementioned A4 is an extremely busy road on which numerous accidents hold up traffic for hours. From October to April, rain, snow and that infamous Milanese fog render all roads in the area horribly hazardous.

The A5 linking Turin with the Mont Blanc Tunnel (Traforo Monte Bianco) in the west of Valle d'Aosta and France (Chamonix) is a major road-freight thoroughfare. Since the closure of the tunnel in 1997 following a fire which killed 39 people, traffic travelling between France and Italy has been redirected to the A32 – linking Turin with the Fréjus Tunnel (Traforo Frejus) at the western end of Valle di Susa and Modane (France). This will remain the only road link between the two countries until the Mont Blanc Tunnel reopens in September 2001.

The A12 connects Genoa with Livorno in Tuscany and with the A11 for Florence, and the A10 to Savona and the French border. Drivers who hate tolls and are in no hurry should also consider taking the S1, and heading in either direction along the coast, or the northbound S35 to Turin.

Tolls, Speed Limits & Petrol

Motorway tolls are levied by the Società Autostrade (☎ 06 436 32 121). Its Web site is at www.autostrade.it. Depending on the size of your car, it will cost approximately L51,000/23,500/19,000 from Rome/Venice/Bologna to Milan; and L10,500/13,000 from Milan to Turin/Genoa. Driving on state ('S' or 'SS' on maps) and provincial ('P' or 'SP' on maps) roads is free.

Cars pay FF159/198 (L47,000/58,000) for a single/return trip through the 12.9m-long Fréjus Tunnel. For more information call ☎ 04 79 20 26 00 in France, ☎ 122 90 90 11 in Italy, send an e-mail to ✉ info@tunnnel dufrejus.com or check out the Web site at www.tunneldufrejus.com. The speed limit through the tunnel is 70km/h. For information on the Mont Blanc Tunnel, call ☎ 0165 8 94 21, fax 0165 8 95 48, send an email to ✉ tmb@courmayeur.valdigne.com, or contact the APT tourist office in Courmayeur (see Excursions in the Turin chapter).

Speed limits, unless indicated otherwise, are 130km/h for cars of 1100cc or more, 110km/h for smaller cars and for motorcycles under 350cc on motorways; 110km/h on main, non-urban highways; 90km/h on secondary, non-urban highways; and 50km/h in built-up areas.

Petrol *(benzina)* prices are steep – about L2180 per litre for unleaded *(senza piombo)*, L2265 for Super and L1885 for diesel *(gasolio)*.

Rental

In cities, having a car is a pain in the neck. You might, however, want to rent a car to explore the surrounds; from Milan and Genoa most excursions are easily done by train, but sights around Turin are less accessible by pubic transport. Rental agencies are listed under Car & Motorcycle under Getting Around in each city chapter. Expect to pay from about L136,000/200,000/275,000 for a two-/three-/four-day weekend, including 200/300/400km, then L300/km. Weekday rates are substantially more expensive.

It's easy to hire a small motorcycle such as a scooter (Vespa) or moped in Genoa (see that chapter for details) but practically impossible in Milan and Turin. Agencies generally don't rent motorcycles to those aged under 18 and require a sizeable deposit. Insist on a helmet (required by law despite Genoa's bounty of bare-headed riders) if you want to stay alive.

Organisations

If you break down in Italy and are a member of a recognised national motoring organisation such as Germany's ADAC, Spain's RCE or the UK's AA, the Automobile Club Italiano (ACI; ☎ 80 30 00 toll-free, ☎ 116 emergency assistance) will come to your aid (free towing of your vehicle for the first 30km, then L1300/km). Motorists who aren't members of any affiliated club, pay a minimum call-out fee of L168,000, plus the cost of towing and any other charges incurred. The ACI has offices in Milan, Turin and Genoa. See Car & Motorcycle under Getting Around in the respective chapters for details.

HITCHING

Hitching is never entirely safe in any country in the world, and we don't recommend it. Travellers who decide to hitch should understand that they are taking a small but potentially serious risk. People who do choose to hitch will be safer if they travel in pairs and let someone know where they are planning to go.

BOAT

Tickets and reservations for ferry services to/from Genoa are available from ferry operators and travel agencies, both abroad and in the three cities covered by this book. In Milan, ferry-operator ticket offices are clustered around Piazza Armandi Diaz (metro MM1/3 Duomo).

Genoa's port, officially known as the Stazione Marittima Porto di Genova (☎ 010 241 25 34, ☎ info@smpg.it), with a Web site under construction at www.smpg.it, is a huge sprawling complex split between several sites. Cruise ships arrive at the cruise terminal *(terminal crociere)*, in Genoa's 1930s maritime station on Ponte dei Mille, a short walk from Genoa's Porto Antico and city centre. Ferry passengers arrive at the modern passenger terminal *(terminal traghetti)*, wedged further west between Ponte Colombo and Ponte Assereto. The main entrance, with its cubist facade carved from white marble, is on Calata Chiappella. By car, exit at 'Genova Ouest'. The port has a Web site at www.porto.genova.it. For information by telephone call its 24-hour service on ☎ 166 152 39 393.

Genoa is an important embarkation point for ferries to Spain, Sicily, Sardinia, Corsica, Elba and Tunisia. Most maritime activity is June to September only. Unless noted otherwise, ferry-operator contact details listed below are for ticketing desks at Genoa's passenger terminal. Fares are for a single fare in low season plus car/motorcycle.

Corsica Marittima (☎ 010 58 95 95, ☎ info@corsica-marittima.com) c/o GSA/Cemar, Via XX Settembre 2–10. A subsidiary of SNCM, this company sails to Bastia in Corsica (L35,000 plus L92,000/75,000 per car/motorcycle, six hours, twice daily from April to September).
Web site: www.corsica-marittima.com
Grandi Navi Veloci (☎ 010 2 54 65) passenger terminal; (☎ 010 58 93 31, ☎ infopax@grimaldi.it) Via Fieschi 17, Genoa; (☎ 02 890

12 281, fax 02 890 10 184, 📧 gnv-milano@ grimaldi.it), Piazza Armandi Diaz 6, Milan. Luxury ferries to the Sardinian ports of Olbia (L84,000, plus L148,000/91,000 per car/motorcycle, 10 hours, once daily from mid-June to mid-September) and Porto Torres (same fares, 11 hours, once daily); to Palermo in Sicily (L84,000, plus L148,000/91,000 per car/motorcycle, 11 hours, once daily); and Barcelona in Spain (L116,000, plus L162,000/100,000 per car/motorcycle, 18 hours, three-times weekly). The company (Grimaldi Group) also organises cruises to/from Genoa.

Web sites: www.gnv.it, www.grimaldi.it

Moby Lines (☎ 010 254 15 13) passenger terminal; (☎ 02 86 52 46/31) Via Larga 26, Milan. Ferries to/from Bastia in Corsica (L30,000, plus L70,000/66,000 per car/motorcycle, 6½ hours, two to seven weekly April to September) and Sardinia via Corsica (178km/two hours) overland between Bastia and Bonifacio. The Bonifacio-Santa Teresa crossing costs L20,000 if you already have a return Genoa-Corsica ticket; it takes 50 minutes and runs April to October. There are also ferries to Olbia (L77,300 plus L124,600/71,200 per car/motorcycle, nine hours, three to seven daily).

Web site: www.mobylines.it

SNCM Ferryterranée (☎ 010 58 95 95) c/o GSA/Cemar, Via XX Settembre 2–10. Boats to/from Tunisia, weekly from late June to late September.

Web site: www.sncm.fr

Tirrenia (☎ 800 82 40 79 toll-free, ☎ 010 2 69 81, 199 123 199). Year-round ferries or high-speed boats to Sardinia, twice weekly to four times daily, to Porto Torres (six or 13 hours), Olbia (six or 13½ hours), Arbatax (7½ hours) and Cagliari (eight or 28 hours), with onward connections to Sicily. Single fares start at L50,500/L117,100 per deck passenger/car.

Web site: www.tirrenia.it

Tris (☎ 010 576 24 11, 📧 infotickets@tris.it), passenger terminal. Ferries to Sardinia run to Porto Torres (L54,000, plus L114,000/36,000 per car/motorcycle, and Palau (L57,000, plus L139,000/46,000 per car/motorcycle).

Web site: www.tris.traghetti.com

ORGANISED TOURS

Oodles of companies in the UK offer bog-standard package tours to Milan, Genoa and Turin's Alpine terrain, comprising transport plus accommodation. They shouldn't be overlooked, especially for city breaks and short stays, as they can be good value for money. Prices fluctuate dramatically however depending on the season, the day of the week and how many stars a particular hotel has. Italian state tourist boards abroad (☎ 020-7408 1254 in the UK, 📧 enit lond@globalnet.co.uk) can supply you with a list of tour operators. Magic of Italy (☎ 020-8741 1983, ☎ 0870 027 0500), with a Web site at www.magictravelgroup .co.uk, and Alitalia's subsidiary, Italiatour (☎ 01883-621900), with a Web site at www .italiatour.com, are a couple of large London-based Italian specialists offering a wide range of tours and city breaks. Sestante CIT (known as CIT or Citalia outside Italy), with offices worldwide (☎ 020-8686 0677 in the UK) also organises tours.

Among the numerous city breaks and tours with a twist, you could consider:

Ace Study Tours (☎ 01223-835 055, fax 837 394, 📧 ace@study-tours.org) Babraham, Cambridge, CB2 4AP – week-long tours with themes such as the historical 'Lombardy – Under the Visconti & the Sforzas' trip (covering Milan and Pavia) or the 'Italian Lakes, Villas & Gardens' discovery holiday around Lakes Maggiore and Como.
Web site: www.study-tours.org

Arblaster & Clarke (☎ 01730-893 344, fax 892 888, 📧 websales@winetours.co.uk) Clarke House, Farnham Road, West Liss, Hampshire GU33 6JQ – wine and gourmet tours, including Gourmet Northern Italy.
Web site: www.arblasterandclarke.com

Grand Touring Club (☎ 01449-737 774, fax 737 400, 📧 classicevents@grandtouringclub.co.uk) Model Farm, Rattlesden, Bury St Edmunds, Suffolk IP30 0SY – self-drive hire of classic cars and tours taking in Brescia's Mille Miglia.
Web site: www.grandtouringclub.co.uk

JMB Travel (☎ 01905-830 099, fax 830 191, 📧 info@jmb-travel.co.uk) Suite Four, High Tree House, 4 Cromwell Road, Powick, Worcester WR2 4QJ – specialises in opera and music-festival city breaks and holidays, including two-/three-night trips to Milan from UK£889/979, including accommodation in a multi-starred city-centre hotel and a night at the opera at La Scala; and two-/three-night breaks in Turin from UK£436/485, taking in an opera at Teatro Regio.
Web site: www.jmb-travel.co.uk

Martin Randall Travel (☎ 020-8742 3355, fax 8742 7766, 📧 info@martinrandall.co.uk)

10 Barley Mow Passage, London W4 4PH – long-established specialist in art, architecture, archaeology and music holidays, with weekend trips to Genoa, Leonardo's Last Supper, the Courts of Northern Italy and opera tours. Web site: www.martinrandall.com

Travel for the Arts (☎ 020-7483 4466, fax 7586 0639, ⓔ enquiries@travelforthearts.co.uk) 117 Regent's Park Road, London NW1 8UR – expensive opera a la carte tours, designed around a night of opera at Milan's La Scala. Web site: at www.travelforthearts.com

Milan

- postcode 20121, 20122, 20123
- pop 1.6 million
- elevation 107m

Milan (Milano in Italian) is synonymous with style. Smart and slick at work and play, the Milanese run their busy metropolis with efficiency and aplomb: it is Italy's economic engine room, the powerhouse of world design and Paris' archrival on the catwalk. The city wrenched Europe's International Fashion Shows away from Florence in the 1980s and has long mocked Rome for losing out on the country's stock market. One could, quite frankly, say this baby's selfish, cold, heartless and haughty – all adjectives piled on the city by bewildered travellers caught up in the Milanese's mad dash of life.

Milan is strictly for city-lovers. Shopping, whether of the window variety or, for those who can afford it, the real thing, is of almost religious significance. Every big name, from Dior, Givenchy and Chanel to home-grown design houses such as Dolce & Gabbana, Armani and Prada, has its flagship store here. Dozens more individual designers – from Puccini's granddaughter to Gianni Bloggio – kick-start their careers here. Out of the city's legendary 'golden quad', there are factory stores for shopping on the cheap and a clutch of abandoned warehouses awaiting makeovers by world-renowned architects: Rodolfo Dordoni, Tadao Ando and David Chipperfield.

Theatre and cinema flourish in this oasis of sophistication. The city is top of most international music tour programmes, and its clubbing scene is hot and busy. World tenor Luciano Pavarotti has sung no less than 140 times at La Scala, Milan's opera house where Verdi premiered *Otello* (1887) and the curtain rose on Puccini's *Madame Butterfly* (1904). Plenty of classical music concerts are held in the city's collection of Romanesque churches – such as the 13th-century Basilica di San Marco, where Verdi first performed his *Requiem* (1874).

Food is another of Milan's joys. Histori-cal cafes where eminent composers sunk espresso shots are plentiful, and immigrants from the rest of Italy and abroad have introduced a surprisingly eclectic cuisine. It's not quite London or New York but in precious few other Italian cities can you find Korean, African or Malaysian specialities side by side with Sicilian, Tuscan and Lombard dishes. Mouldy gorgonzola cheese originates from near Milan – as does sweet *panettone*, the quintessential Christmas cake said to be modelled on the great lofty domes of many a Lombardy *duomo* (cathedral). Milan's, incidentally, is the fourth largest church in the world.

Though substantially smaller than Italy's ancient imperial capital, Milan is home to most of the country's major corporations and boasts the nation's largest concentration of industry. English is very much a first language in its substantial international community, rubbing off on daily city life insomuch as you'll find it on the back of public-transport tickets and on many street signs.

Within the Italian community, Milan's business and political leaders have long railed against the inefficient and corrupt government in Rome and subsidies directed to the south. The staunchly right-wing Lega Nord (Northern League), Umberto Bossi's separatist party spawned by this sense of protest in the late 1980s, continues to enjoy strong support in both Milan and its surrounds. In the 2001 elections, the city's tough mayor, Gabriele Albertini, of Silvio Berlusconi's right-wing Forza Italia party, is expected to pit his political muscle against left-wing newcomer, Nobel prize winner and writer Dario Fo.

A contentious issue at the forefront of local politics is how to tackle white-collar crime in the form of money laundering, drugs and arms rackets, and the age-old tradition of bribery and kickbacks – all alive and well in Italy's financial heartland according to international observers.

Milan's smog is almost as legendary as London's. Should you be fortunate enough to see the sun, note that a dark pair of sultry sunglasses are an essential fashion accessory any time of year. Despite many Milanese talking endlessly of escaping Milan and moving to the country, most are staunchly proud of their city and few leave – except in August when city dwellers depart en masse to escape the stifling heat. And you'd do well to stay away then too.

Getting Around

ORIENTATION

Milan is a sprawling metropolis but most of its attractions are concentrated in the centre between the duomo and Castello Sforzesco. The duomo is an unmistakable focal point for your explorations and sits plump in the geographic centre of the city, around which three concentric 'rings' radiate: the Cerchia dei Navigli 'inner ring' traces the path of the city's medieval walls to embrace Milan's historical centre and most of its main sights; the larger Viali swoops around Castello Sforzesco, where 16th-century walls once stood; and the ring road around the city centre, the Circonvallazione Esterna, forms the third ring which only motorists get to suffer.

The city is serviced by an efficient underground railway, the Metropolitana Milanese (MM); where relevant, MM stations are given in brackets after entries for places of interest. All the main metro stations appear on the Milan map.

Buses to/from many national and international points depart from and arrive at the station on Piazza Castello.

Apart from the historical centre around the duomo, the main areas of interest for tourists are Brera, immediately north of the duomo, which encompasses many galleries and fashionable shopping streets, and Navigli to the south.

Exiting Stazione Centrale, you emerge onto Piazza Duca d'Aosta (cleaned up over the years but still not an ideal place to hang out at night). A good orientation point is the Pirelli building, a slender skyscraper to your right as you leave the train station. Some of the better hotels are clustered here. To the south-east of Stazione Centrale, Via Vitruvio leads to the main area for budget hotels. It meets Piazza Lima at the intersection of Corso Buenos Aires and becomes Via Plinio.

To get from Piazza Duca d'Aosta to the city centre, walk south-westwards along Via Pisani, through the enormous park-lined Piazza della Repubblica, and along Via Filippo Turati to Piazza Cavour. From here, take Via Alessandro Manzoni, which runs off the south-western side of the piazza. This takes you through the exclusive Monte Napoleone fashion district and on to Piazza della Scala with its opera house. From there, an arcade in the glass-domed Galleria Vittorio Emanuele II leads to Piazza del Duomo.

Most car rental companies, ferry operators (see the Getting There & Away chapter) and travel agencies have offices immediately south of the duomo between Piazza Armandi Diaz and Via Albricci.

Express trains to/from Malpensa airport use Stazione Nord (also known as Stazione Cadorna), the train station immediately south of Castello Sforzesco in the north-west of the 'inner ring' (making it more central than its Centrale counterpart). Trains serving Lake Como also use Stazione Nord, easily accessed via metro MM1/2 Cadorna Triennale. Many rail services to/from destinations north of Milan – including Bergamo and Stresa on Lake Maggiore – use Stazione Porta Garibaldi, just north of the Viali and accessible via metro MM2 Garibaldi FS. Some trains to/from Pavia also stop here as well as at Stazione Centrale.

Milan's trade fair and exhibition venues are well served by public transport. Metro MM1 Amendola Fiera is a two-minute walk eastwards along Viale Ezio to the main entrance to Fiera Campionaria, north-west of the centre on Piazzale Giulio Cesare. Its southern annexe, Padiglione Sud, south of the city in Lacchiarella, is served by regular shuttlebuses from outside MM1 Amendola Fiera and MM2 Romolo metro

The *carabinieri* have matching black and red cars.

Police making a parade of themselves in Milan.

Invest in some stock at Via Calvi market.

A snippet of Milans's flower and glory

The spiralling sculpture at Piazzale Luigi Cadorna

Sun-dried tomatoes for that gourmet touch

Surveying peaceful Piazza Mercanti, Milan

Ornate fountain at Castello Sforzesco, Milan

Losing one's head at Milan's Duomo

Before taking flight, inspect this stairwell in Brera.

The illustrious Pinacoteca Di Brera art gallery

stations, and Linate airport. Approaching Milan by car, both sites are heavily signposted from the Tangenziale Ovest and Tangenziale Est (west and east ring roads).

MALPENSA & LINATE AIRPORTS

Milan has two airports. The bulk of European and other international flights use one of two terminals at Malpensa airport, some 50km north-west of the city. Visit online at www.malpensa.com. Most (but not all) domestic and a handful of European flights use Linate, about 7km east of the city centre. Its Web site is at www.sea-aeroportimilano.it.

For flight information for both airports call ☎ 02 748 52 200. For a computerised information service on flight departures only call ☎ 02 585 83 497. For information on shuttlebuses from Linate to Padiglione Sud, call the fairground's airport information desk (☎ 02 738 24 32).

TO/FROM MALPENSA AIRPORT
Milan

The Malpensa Express train links Stazione Nord (Stazione Cadorna) with Malpensa airport. During big trade fairs, trains in both directions stop at Stazione Bullona, a five-minute walk north of Fiera di Milano.

At Stazione Nord, trains depart from platform 1 every 50 and 20 minutes past the hour between 5.50 am and 9.20 pm. Additional buses depart at 5 am and 9.20, 10.20 and 11.10 pm from the stop outside the station on Via Leopardi. Journey time is 40 minutes (50 minutes by bus) and a one-way/return ticket costs L15,000/20,000 (children aged four to 12, L8000/10,000). Monthly passes are also available. Train tickets are sold in the ticket and information office (☎ 02 277 63), open 5.40 am to 8.20 pm opposite platform 1. Bus drivers sell tickets on board. Tickets cover use of the Passante Ferroviario (see Public Transport later in this chapter). Updated schedules are posted on the Internet at www.malpensa express.com.

The airport is also served by the Malpensa Shuttle coaches (☎ 02 585 8 32 02, 02 585 8 31 85), departing from Piazza Luigi di Savoia, outside Stazione Centrale, every 20 minutes between 4.30 am and 10.30 pm. The journey takes 50 minutes to one hour and a one-way ticket costs L8000 (children aged two to 12, L4000). Buy tickets from the ticket office behind the bus stop. Buses stop at both terminals; during trade fairs some buses stop at the Fiera. Updated information and schedules are online at www .airpullman.com.

The same company also operates eight to 10 shuttle buses daily between Malpensa and Linate airports. Journey time is one to 1¼ hours between Linate and Malpensa's terminal 1/2 and a one-way fare costs L15,000 (children aged two to 12, L7500).

A taxi from Malpensa airport to Milan city centre will probably cost about L150,000.

Turin

Autostradale (☎ 011 433 25 25, e auto stradale@apm.it) operates buses between Turin's main bus station, west of the city centre at Corso Inghilterra 1–3, and terminals 1 and 2 of Malpensa airport. There are three daily buses in both directions (two hours) and a one-way ticket costs L30,000 (free for children less than 1m in height). At Malpensa, tickets are sold at Agenzia Air Pullman (terminal 1 ☎ 02 585 81 064, terminal 2 ☎ 02 585 83 202).

Alitalia operates a bus service – intended for those flying with Alitalia – from Turin's Stazione Porta Nuova to Malpensa. Details are listed under To/From the Airports in the Getting Around section of the Turin chapter.

Genoa

There are two buses daily between Genoa and Malpensa (departures from Piazza della Vittoria and Stazione Principe). Journey time is three hours (L30,000).

TO/FROM LINATE AIRPORT

From Milan's Piazza Luigi di Savoia, in front of Stazione Centrale, Società Trasporti Aeroporti Milanesi (STAM; ☎ 02 748 52 757) runs buses to/from Linate airport approximately every 30 minutes between 5.40 am and 9.35 pm. Journey time is 25 minutes and a one-way ticket, sold on board by the driver, costs L5000.

You can also get local ATM bus No 73 from Piazza San Babila (corner of Corso Europa) for L1500. The journey takes 20 minutes and buses depart approximately every 10 to 15 minutes between 5.30 am and 8 pm.

For information on direct bus links between Linate and Malpensa airports, see To/From Malpensa Airport earlier in this chapter.

A taxi from Linate airport to Milan city centre should cost no more than L30,000.

PUBLIC TRANSPORT

Anyone accustomed to the underground systems in London or Paris will find Milan's MM (metro), built in the 1960s, a doddle by comparison. The lines are numbered, colour coded (red MM1, green MM2, yellow MM3 and blue Passante Ferroviario) and run from about 6 am to midnight. The network is run by Azienda Trasporti Milanesi (ATM; ☎ 800 016 857 toll-free, ⓔ info@atm-mi.it), Milan's public transport company which also operates the city's equally efficient fleet of ATM buses and trams. The 120 routes are detailed on ATM's Web site at www.atm-mi.it.

A one-way public transport ticket costs L1500 and is valid for one metro ride or up to 1¼ hours travel on buses and trams. A cheaper BI4 (four-journey integrated ticket) costs L6000 and allows four metro trips or 75-minute bus/tram journeys, and a book of 10 tickets costs L14,000. Unlimited one/two-day tickets for bus, tram and MM are also available for L5000/9000 Sunday and holidays, the one-day pass only covers travel for the entire family (up to two adults and two kids).

Passes aimed at daily travellers include a 2x6 weekly pass (L11,000) valid for two journeys per day over six days, a regular weekly pass (L35,000 for the first pass, then L20,000 thereafter) allowing unlimited weekly travel on all ATM public transport routes, and a monthly pass (L90,000, then L75,000).

Tickets are available from automatic vending machines at MM stations and from authorised tobacconists and newsstands.

Passes can only be bought at the ATM office (☎ 02 48 03 11, ⓔ abbonamenti@atmmi.it, metro MM1 Cairoli, MM1/2 Cadorna Triennale), Via Ricasoli 2, open 8.45 am to 12.45 pm and 2 to 3.45 pm; or at the underground ATM offices in MM1/3 Duomo and MM2/3 Centrale FS, MM1/2 Loreto, MM2 Romolo and MM1/2 Cadorna Triennale stations. All underground offices open 7.45 am to 7.15 pm Monday to Saturday. The Duomo office distributes free public transport maps.

CAR & MOTORCYCLE

Entering central Milan by car is a horrible hassle and best avoided if at all possible. Once in, having masterminded the system of one-way streets designed with the sole intention of keeping you out, you risk sitting in noisy traffic jams with an irritating rash of horn-honking motorists. Your best bet by far is to dump your vehicle in one of the out-of-town car parks (see Parking later in this section) and ride the metro into town.

Motoring information, road maps and guides are provided by the Automobile Club Italia (ACI; ☎ 02 774 51, fax 02 78 18 44, ⓔ info@acimi.it), Corso Venezia 43, open 8.30 am to 12.45 pm and 2.15 to 5 pm weekdays. The club's branch office (☎ 02 31 65 13), near the Fiera at Corso Sempione 41, opens 8.30 am to 12.30 pm and 2 to 5.30 pm weekdays. The ACI's Web address is www.aci.it. If you have the misfortune to break down, call ☎ 116.

There are 24-hour petrol stations throughout the city, including on the corner of Via della Moscova and Bastoni di Porta Volta, and near Porta Genova at the southern end of Viale Papiniano.

Car Rental

All the major rental companies have offices at both airports and at Stazione Centrale, including:

Avis
  (☎ 02 585 84 81) Malpensa airport
  (☎ 02 71 72 14) Linate airport
  (☎ 02 669 02 80) Stazione Centrale

(☎ 02 86 34 94, 02 890 10 645) Piazza Armandi Diaz 6

Europcar
(☎ 02 585 81 142) Malpensa airport
(☎ 02 761 10 258) Linate airport
(☎ 02 864 63 454) Piazza Armandi Diaz 6

Hertz
(☎ 02 585 81 137) Malpensa airport
(☎ 02 702 00 256) Linate airport
(☎ 02 669 00 61) Stazione Centrale
(☎ 02 720 04 562) Via Gonzaga 5

Italy by Car (Thrifty)
(☎ 02 585 81 176) Malpensa airport
(☎ 02 761 10 234) Linate airport
(☎ 02 670 31 51) Via Vittor Pisani 13

Maggiore (National)
(☎ 02 585 81 133) Malpensa airport
(☎ 02 71 72 10) Linate airport
(☎ 02 669 09 34) Stazione Centrale

Parking

ATM operates a clutch of large out-of-town car parks, conveniently located at either end of all three metro lines and easily accessible for motorists arriving in Milan by *autostrada* (motorway). Parking here is cheaper than in central Milan: most car parks charge L2000/3000 for four/eight hours and L4000 for more than eight hours, although a handful are cheaper (L1000/3000 for up to/over four hours). If you have a regular or 2x6 weekly ATM pass (see Public Transport earlier in this chapter), you can buy a six-day parking pass costing L12,000 (L9000 in some cheaper car parks). Approaching Milan from Turin, exit the A4 at Milan Viale Certosa and park in the Lampugnano multi-storey car park (metro MM1); coming from Genoa on the A1, take the Milan Piazzale Corvetto exit and abandon your vehicle in the Rogoredo car park, Via Cassinis 74 (metro MM3).

Central Milan is dotted with expensive car parks (look for signs with a white P on a blue background); the subterranean one beneath Stazione Centrale opens 24 hours. Parking is limited to two hours in areas marked with a blue line (a yellow line indicates residents' parking only) and payable (L2500 per hour or a flat fee of L5000 after 8 pm) by SostaMilano card. These so-called 'scratch-and-park' cards (whereby you scratch off the date and hour

then display it on your dashboard) are sold at ATM offices, tobacconists and by parking attendants. Electronic versions are also available.

At least once a fortnight the streets are cleaned, meaning you have to shift your car between midnight and 6 am. Warning signs reading *divieto di sosta* are usually displayed the day before this operation takes places. Illegally parked cars attract fines and can be towed away.

TAXI

Don't bother trying to hail taxis as they generally won't stop. Head for taxi ranks (there are 112 throughout the city, marked with a yellow line on the road) which have telephones. You can order a taxi by calling Autoradiotaxi (☎ 02 85 85), Radio Taxi (☎ 02 67 67, 02 83 83) or Radio Taxidata (☎ 02 53 53).

ORGANISED TOURS

The Autostradale bus company (☎ 02 339 10 794) runs a three-hour bus tour of the city; da Vinci's *Last Supper* and Cimitero Monumentale are among the sights included. Tours depart at 9.30 am from Tuesday to Sunday (except the last two weeks in August) from in front of the APT office on Piazza del Duomo (corner of Via Marconi). Tickets costing a rather extravagant L60,000 include admission fees (children aged under 12, free). Information and tickets are available from the APT tourist office.

Better value, perhaps, is ATM's Ciao Milano tourist tram (☎ 02 720 02 584 for information and reservations), a vintage piece from the 1920s that runs twice daily (three times daily at the weekend), April to October, past the main points of interest. Tickets valid for one day cost L30,000 and are sold at the tourist office. Once aboard the tram, you can get off and get back on as you please; stops include Piazza Castello, Via Torino (for Piazza del Duomo), Chiesa di Santa Maria delle Grazie, Porta Venezia, Piazza Repubblica and Via Alessandro Manzoni (for the Monte Napoleone fashion district).

Things to See & Do

Highlights

- Admire Leonardo's masterpiece in the Cenacolo Vinciano; see what the *Last Supper* would have looked like in stone at the Cimitero Monumentale

- Explore Milan's impressive navel: visit the *duomo* (cathedral) and its unforgettable rooftop terrace

- Visit the Museo Teatrale alla Scala and peek in at the city's famous opera house – score a ticket if you can

- Shop like a millionaire in the legendary Quadrilatero d'Oro

- Wash the city dust right out of your hair in Italy's lake district, a train-hop north of Milan

SUGGESTED ITINERARIES

Depending on your length of stay you might want to see and do the following in Milan:

Half-Day
Visit the duomo and scale its 165 steps for a rooftop panorama of its statues, spires and the sprawling city; then stroll through Galleria Vittorio Emanuele II to view La Scala. Spend any time left in the golden quad.

One Day
Spend longer exploring Piazza del Duomo and Piazza della Scala, visiting one of the Palazzo Reale museums or Museo Teatrale alla Scala. In the afternoon take your pick of Castello Sforzesco, the Brera district (Pinacoteca di Brera) or Sant'Ambrogio (Leonardo's *Last Supper* and Basilica di Sant'Ambrogio).

Two Days
Centre your second day around seeing that 'big' sight you skipped the first; or skip it altogether and shop (see the special section 'Shopping in Milan'). Alternatively, explore Navigli or spend longer wandering around Brera.

DUOMO TO BRERA

Milan's impressive navel, **Piazza del Duomo** (metro MM1/3 Duomo), has the atmosphere of London's Piccadilly Circus, though the statue of Eros hardly compares with Milan's most visible monument – the duomo. The city's central meeting place since medieval times, it was from palaces on this piazza that archbishops meted out justice until the 13th century, and the powerful Visconti dukes thereafter.

The square remains Milan's social, geographic (and pigeon) centre. It gained its monumental appearance between 1865 and 1873 when architect Giuseppe Mengoni enlarged it, running elegant porticoed promenades down its northern and southern sides. **Palazzo della Veneronda** (1841–53), an eclectic 19th-century palace pierced by a small church, fills its eastern side, from where **Galleria Pattari**, a short covered walkway, links Piazza del Duomo with Via Pattari. Around the corner, **Corso Vittorio Emanuele II** – Milan's main pedestrian street crammed with designer fashion shops – struts off eastwards.

Beware birdseed sellers who flog seeds to unsuspecting tourists (the camcorder-wielding variety are particular targets) by popping seed in their pockets, prompting pigeons to dive-bomb the victim – and the victim to buy seed to avoid being dive-bombed again. Cunning.

Duomo

Milan's stunning cathedral – 158m long and 33m wide – is the world's fourth largest church. A first glimpse of this late-Gothic wonder is certainly memorable, with its marble facade shaped into pinnacles, statues and pillars, the whole lot held together by a web of flying buttresses. Some 135 spires – built between 1397 and 1812 – and 3200-odd statues have somehow been crammed onto the roof and into the facade. The central spire, soaring 108m into the sky, dates to 1774 and is capped by a gilded 4m-tall copper statue of the **Madonnina** (literally 'our little Madonna'), the traditional protector of the city. The surrounding forest of spires, statuary and pinnacles distracts observers from an interesting omission – Milan's duomo has no bell tower.

Said to stand on the site of a pagan

Roman temple, the duomo was commissioned in 1386 by Gian Galeazzo Visconti. Several architects later and a push from Napoleon in 1805 brought the mammoth project to completion in 1813. Its facade is carved from creamy Candoglia marble and its 12,000 sq m interior shelters a nave and four aisles, adorned with 15th-century stained-glass windows on the right and later copies on the left. A congregation of 40,000 can fit inside.

High above the altar is a nail said to have come from Christ's cross and publicly displayed once a year on the second Sunday in September. Originally lowered using a device made by Leonardo da Vinci called the *nigola*, the nail is now retrieved by more modern means. Since 1491 the nigola has been stored near the roof on the right-hand side as you enter the duomo through the brass doors (note the marks of bombs that fell during WWII) at the main entrance off Piazza del Duomo. Inside, a stairwell leads to an early Christian **baptistry**, built around AD 378 and said to predate the Gothic church. It can be visited 10 am to noon and 3 to 5 pm Tuesday to Sunday. Admission is free.

From the northern side of the duomo, a staircase leads to the **roof terrace** from where the best panorama of the city and surrounds unfolds. Don't miss Milan's memorable skyscraper, **Torre Velasca**, a 20-storey building topped by a six-storey protruding block. A classic late 1950s design by Studio BBPR, this building deserves a look.

Scaling the 165 (some say 158) narrow steps of the spiral (L4000) is a physical and observational (on humanity) exercise, with Italians muttering 'Mamma Mia' in between gasps for air and curses at having to walk so far, Brits complaining about filing up/down on the 'wrong' side, and Japanese viewing the entire proceedings through a video-camera lens. The *ascensore* (lift; L9000), accessed by the same entrance, is less fun but kinder on the thigh muscles. Lift and staircase both open 9 am to 4.30 pm.

Palazzos Arcivescovile & Reale

The southern side of Piazza del Duomo, opposite the side entrance to the cathedral, is

dominated by **Palazzo Arcivescovile** and **Palazzo Reale**, the traditional seats of Milan's ecclesiastical and civil rulers from the 11th and 12th centuries. The archbishop of Milan first moved into his Archbishop's Palace in 1170.

Milan's neoclassical Royal Palace (☎ 02 439 11 119; MM1/3 Duomo) was remodelled to its current appearance, as part of Piermarini's redevelopment of the cathedral square, in 1778. It served as the seat of the Milan city council in the 11th century and as the private residence of the Visconti family from the 12th century. Following the gruesome murder in 1412 of Giovanni Visconti on the steps of **Chiesa di San Gottardo in Corte** (1330–36) – the palace chapel immediately behind it on Via Pecorari – the ducal seat was shifted to the less penetrable Castello Sforzesco (see that section later in this chapter). The palace was heavily bombed during WWII, although the chapel – including its beautiful brick bell tower nicknamed the 'campanile del duomo' (cathedral's bell tower) – survived unscathed.

Works by Italian futurists and lesser-known 20th-century Italian artists can be viewed in the **Civico Museo d'Arte Contemporanea**, the modern art museum inside the palace. It opens 9.30 am to 5.30 pm Tuesday to Sunday (to 10.30 pm Thursday). Admission costs L15,000 (students L10,000; children aged under six, free). Guided tours (L10,000) in Italian depart from the main entrance at 4 pm Wednesday, 9 pm Thursday and 11 am and 4 pm weekends.

In the palace's left wing is the **Museo del Duomo** (☎ 02 86 03 58), with a rich collection of sculptures and ecclesiastical treasures dating from the 14th to 19th centuries. Dedicated to six centuries of cathedral history, the museum opens 9.30 am to 12.30 pm and 3 to 6 pm. Admission costs L10,000 (students L2000, children aged 12 to 18, L5000). A combination ticket for the cathedral museum and rooftop-terrace lift costs L12,000.

Galleria Vittorio Emanuele II

Known as *il salotto di Milano* (Milan's drawing room) thanks to its elegant cafes such as Savini and Il Salotto, the Galleria Vittorio Emanuele II (metro MM1/3 Duomo), along with the duomo, is Milan's crowning glory. Virtually destroyed in the 1943 bombing raids and rebuilt afterwards, its cruciform walkways lead 196m northwards off Piazza del Duomo to Piazza della Scala and 105m in an east–west axis.

One of the first buildings in Europe to employ iron and glass as structural elements, the magnificent covered gallery (1864–78) was designed by Giuseppe Mengoni, who unfortunately died before the project was complete (1878); he allegedly fell off scaffolding on the site. Although named after Italy's first king, it was originally dedicated to Franz Joseph of Austria when the plan to build it first cropped up in 1859. The four (delightfully photogenic) mosaics around the central octagon represent Europe, Africa, Asia and North America. Smear the sole of your shoe across the bull for good luck.

Piazza della Scala

Strolling through Galleria Vittorio Emanuele II you emerge in front of a 19th-century **statue** of **Leonardo da Vinci** (1872) and, to the left, Milan's legendary opera house, **La Scala** (MM1/3 Duomo), on Piazza della Scala. Officially called **Teatro alla Scala**, the fabulous playhouse opened on 3 August 1778 with Salieri's opera *Europa Riconsciuta* and was the venue for innumerable operatic first nights throughout the 19th and early 20th centuries. Practically destroyed during WWII, it was rebuilt and reopened in 1946 under the baton of Arturo Toscanini, who returned from New York after a 15-year absence. For the full story, see the boxed text 'La Scala' in the Facts about the Cities chapter.

Adjoining the theatre is the **Museo Teatrale alla Scala** (☎ 02 85 15 58 31/13, ⓔ scala@energy.it), Via Filodrammatici 2 (entrance on Piazza della Scala). Curiosities include death masks for Wagner and Puccini, Toscanini's baton and a musical score signed by the maestro, as well as tiny snuff boxes, spy glasses and portraits of La Scala soloists such as Ernesto Cavallini and Maria

Callas. Piano recitals are occasionally hosted at the museum, using the grand Steinway & Sons piano which belonged to Hungarian composer Franz Liszt. The rest of the museum's musical instrument collection is a short walk southwards on Piazza Mercanti (see that section later).

Most days, when there's no rehearsal on (☎ 02 88 79 473 to check in advance), the museum runs guided tours of the opera house – or rather, of one box, from which you can peep across at the distinctive C-shaped auditorium. It opens 9 am to 12.30 pm and 2 to 5.30 pm daily (Monday to Saturday only between 1 November and 30 April). Admission costs L6000 (children aged 12 to 18, L3000). The instrument collection can be visited 9 am to noon and 2 to 5 pm weekdays only; you will only be let in if you have an 'invitation' (free) from the Piazza della Scala museum; ask for one at the ticket desk when leaving.

Opposite La Scala on the square's eastern side is **Palazzo Marino**, built between Piazza della Scala and Piazza San Fedele in 1558 by Galeazzo Alessi and a masterpiece of 16th-century residential architecture. Milan's municipal council has sat here since 1859 and one room, the Sala dell'Alessi, can be visited (free). Ironically, the most impressive building on the square – easily dwarfing La Scala – is **Palazzo della Banca Commerciale Italiana** (1907), on the northern side. It's still a bank today.

Piazza Mercanti

Via Santa Margherita runs parallel with Galleria Vittorio Emanuele II creating a second link between Piazza del Duomo and Piazza della Scala. From 1176, when the *comune* (Milan city council) scored its freedom in Legnano until the Viscontis took over in the 13th century, the free city of Milan was governed from Piazza Mercanti (metro MM1/3 Duomo), an old medieval market place and charming pedestrian square at Via Santa Margherita's southern foot (north-western corner of Piazza del Duomo).

Palazzo della Regione (1233), with its decorative red-brick vaults, served as the town hall and seat of power during the 13th century. The building opposite, **Palazzo Affari al Giureconsulti** (1823), was Milan's stock exchange in the 19th century and now houses the Chamber of Commerce and the musical-instrument collection of the Museo Teatrale alla Scala (see Piazza della Scala earlier).

Pinacoteca Ambrosiana

From Piazza Mercanti, make a short detour southwards along Via Cesare Cantù to Piazza Pio XI and the **Pinacoteca Ambrosiana** (☎ 02 80 69 21, e info@ambrosiana.it, metro MM1 Cordusio), Piazza Pio XI 2, with a Web site at www.ambrosiana.it. This is one of Milan's finest galleries and contains Italy's first real still life, Caravaggio's *Canestra di Frutta* (Fruit Basket; 1596), as well as works by Tiepolo, Titian and Raphael. Also on show is Leonardo da Vinci's *Musico* (Musician).

The building was actually set up by Cardinal Federico Borromeo in 1609 as a much-admired fine public library. One of the first in Europe, its role in life was to collate documentation to assist the cardinal in his mission to unravel the mysteries of the Bible. Nine years later it was followed by the gallery, whose collection was donated by the cardinal. That collection continued to grow in the following centuries – to 35,000 manuscripts, over 700,000 printed works and a large collection of Leonardo manuscripts, spread across 24 rooms today. The gallery opens 10 am to 5.30 pm Tuesday to Sunday. Admission costs L12,000 (those aged over 65 and under 18, free).

Behind the gallery on Piazza San Sepolcro is red-brick **Chiesa di San Sepolcro**, begun in 1030 and featuring a Romanesque crypt. It was dedicated to the Holy Sepulchre during the Second Crusade. The forum of Roman Mediolanum (Milan) stood between this square and Piazza Pio XI – a small section of it has been uncovered in Pinacoteca Ambrosiana's library. The Fascist party met in 1919 in **Palazzo Castini**, a palace built in the 18th century on the site of Roman thermal baths. Few other Roman relics remain: those that survived were either blown to bits by WWII bombs or built on. Neoclassi-

cal **Palazzo della Borso** (Milan's stock exchange), constructed in 1931 on Piazza degli Affari – the site of a Roman amphitheatre dating to about AD 1 – is a classic example.

Along Via Alessandro Manzoni

A quick backtrack to Piazza della Scala brings you to the foot of one of Milan's most glamorous streets, Via Alessandro Manzoni, studded with neoclassical *palazzi* (palaces/mansions), of which there are some 60 scattered about the city centre – a far cry from the several hundred still standing at the end of the 19th century, but still impressive.

Walking north-eastwards, the first stop is **Museo Poldi-Pezzoli** (☎ 02 80 15 15, e museopoldipezzoli@tiscalinet.it, metro MM3 Monte Napoleone), the mansion-museum at No 12. The original room layout is retained, making it a pleasure to wander around the two floors of this old mansion, filled with collections of jewellery, porcelain, sundials, tapestries, ancient armaments, period furniture and paintings. On the 1st floor are works by Tiepolo, Botticelli, Giovanni and Jacopo Bellini, Piero della Francesca, Mantegna, Crivelli, Lorenzo Lotto, Il Pinturicchio, Filippo Lippi and others. The rich collection was bequeathed to the city in 1881 by nobleman and collector Giacomo Poldi-Pezzoli. The mansion opens 9.30 am to 12.30 pm and 2.30 to 6 pm Tuesday to Sunday. Admission costs L10,000 (those aged 12 to 18, L5000).

Another mansion, **Palazzo Manzoni** (☎ 02 864 60 403, e manzoni@energy.it, metro MM3 Monte Napoleone), is tucked down Via Morone, the street running along the southern side of the Museo Poldi-Pezzoli. Milanese writer Alessandro Manzoni (1785–1873) lived here from 1813 until his death (following which Verdi composed *Requiem* as a tribute to his great friend). Surly doormen guide you through the two dimly lit rooms – Manzoni's study, with an outstanding painted ceiling and the notary of his friend Tommaso Gropssi, showcases a series of B&W photographs. Admission is free.

For many visitors to Milan, the street's most startling building is the pre-WWII **Assicurazioni Generali building** (metro

MILAN

MM3 Monte Napoleone), Via Alessandro Manzoni 31, constructed in 1937 with statues on its outer facade designed by the patron saints of Milan, Venice and Trieste. A bold architectural project in 2000 converted it into the spectacular **Emporio Armani**. The flagship store, with its stunning interior, is a sight to see even for those not into designer shopping. See the special section 'Shopping in Milan' for more details.

Wrenching yourself away from Armani's glittering window displays, continue northwards past Paul Smith at No 30 and monumental **Palazzo Borromeo d'Adda** (1764 –1839) at No 39 to the red brick arches of **Archi di Porta Nuova** (metro MM3 Monte Napoleone), built between 1810 and 1813 on the site of the northern city gate (1171). In the late 13th century, the ditch surrounding the medieval city was replaced by fortifying walls, around which lay a ring of canals (which have since disappeared). This old medieval boundary – delineated east and west of Archi di Porta Nuova by Via Senato, Via Fatebenefratelli and their respective continuations – forms the innermost of Milan's three concentric circles today. This inner circle is known as 'Cerchia dei Navigli'.

Quadrilatero d'Oro

Remaining within the 'city walls', walk eastwards along Via della Spiga to reach Milan's famous 'golden quad' – the place to shop for designer fashion in Europe. Its streets – **Via della Spiga** (north), **Via Sant' Andrea** (east), **Via Monte Napoleone** (south), where Gucci opened its first Milan shop in 1951, and the northern section of Via Alessandro Manzoni (west) – are encrusted with designer boutiques and jewellery shops of Tiffany & Co standing. Interspersed within these gems is a generous sprinkling of neoclassical palazzi and the illustrious **Caffè Cova** (see the boxed text 'Historical Cafes' later in this chapter), where European high society has quaffed cappuccino and cocktails since 1950.

For a peep at how the city's wealthy lived in the 19th century, visit **Museo Bagatti Valesecchi** (☎ 02 760 06 132, 02 760 14 857, ⓔ info@museobagattivalsecchi.org, metro

MM1 San Babila, MM3 Monte Napoleone), in a sumptuous palace in the heart of the golden quad at Via Santo Spirito 10 (entrance on Via del Gèsu). Built for the Bagatti Valsecchi brothers between 1878 and 1887, the mansion-museum is crowded with art, furniture and numerous other authentic treasures from the duchy's golden era. It opens 1 to 5 pm Tuesday to Sunday. Admission costs L10,000 (L5000 Wednesday).

Armani and Kenzo flutter their eye-lashes at **Palazzo Morando Attendolo Bolognini**, a block east at Via Sant'Andrea 6. The **Museo di Storia Contemporanea** (☎ 02 760 06 245, ⓔ contempo@energy.it, metro MM1 San Babila, MM3 Monte Napoleone), dedicated to interwar Milanese history, is on the ground floor of the 18th-century palace; and the **Museo di Milano** (☎ as above, ⓔ milano@energy.it), with its collection of 18th- and 19th-century paintings of Milan, is on the 1st. Both open 10 am to 6 pm Tuesday to Sunday. Admission costs L14,000 (those aged 11 to 18, L10,000).

A short stroll southwards along Via Bagutta, past **Trattoria Bagutta** at No 12a (see Places to Eat later in this chapter), where Milan's artists and literati met in the post-WWII period, takes you out of the Quadrilatero d'Oro and onto **Piazza San Babila** (metro MM1 San Babila), a fountain-adorned square guarded by the lion of **Colonna del Leone** (1626) and 11th-century **Chiesa di San Babila**. The church was constructed on the site of a paleo-Christian church (dating to AD 46), botchily rebuilt in 1575 and between 1853 and 1906. Several more designer boutiques and palazzi languish on Corso Europa, linked by covered shopping galleries to **Corso Vittorio Emanuele II**, Milan's main pedestrian shopping street which struts westwards from Piazza San Babila to Piazza del Duomo.

BRERA

Hip Brera – immediately west of Via Alessandro Manzoni within the central city 'ring' – is Milan's Montmartre. Several young up-and-coming designers have shops here, alternative cafes and bars abound and there's a wealth of art treasures to be discovered in the city's leading art gallery. The quarter gained its bohemian touch in 1776 when Maria Theresa of Austria founded the Accademia di Belle Arti on **Via Brera** – a street which, together with cobbled **Via Fiori Chiari** at its northern end, is considered one of Milan's trendiest streets. Verdi premiered his *Requiem* in the **Basilica di San Marco** (1254), on Brera's northernmost fringe.

Museo di Risorgimento

From the north-western end of Via Monte Napoleone, cross Via Alessandro Manzoni and continue westwards along Via Borgonuovo to the Museo di Risorgimento (☎ 02 884 64 176, risorgi@energy.it, metro MM1 San Babila, MM1/3 Monte Napoleone), inside a neoclassical palace at No 23, focusing on Italian history up to 1870 with lots of Napoleonic memorabilia. The museum opens 9 am to 5.30 pm Tuesday to Sunday. Admission is free. Its library, which can be visited 9 am to 4.30 pm weekdays, contains a fine collection of Risorgimento manuscripts and documents.

Palazzo di Brera

Maria Theresa's **Accademia di Belle Arti** and the illustrious **Pinacoteca di Brera** art gallery (☎ 02 894 21 146, e info@amicidi breca.milano.it; MM2 Lanza), Via Brera 28, are both inside Palazzo di Brera: a Baroque palace built in 1651 for the wealthy Jesuit order and adopted by the Austrians in 1773 after kicking out the monks. Napoleon stands in the centre of an elegant interior courtyard, around which the sprawling complex is wrapped.

Pinacoteca di Brera, one of Italy's largest art museums, contains an extensive treasury of paintings that has continued to grow since the gallery was inaugurated in the early 19th century. Andrea Mantegna's masterpiece *The Dead Christ*, actually painted by Mantegna (1430–1506) for his own tomb in Mantua, is one of the better known works on display. One of the largest pieces – a monumental 347cm by 770cm – is Gentile Bellini's *St Mark Preaching in Alexandria*, started by the Venice-born painter in 1504

and finished after his death three years later by brother Giovanni (who later painted the *Madonna and Child* masterpiece in 1510). Also represented are several Lombard artists: Giovanni di Milano from Caversaccio near Como (1346–69); Milan-born Gaudenzio Ferrari (born 1546); and Caravaggio (1571–1610), alongside side Raphael (look for his *Marriage of the Virgin* altarpiece of 1540), Tiepolo, Rembrandt, Goya, van Dyck, El Greco, Picasso, Braque and others.

The gallery opens 8.30 am to 7.15 pm Tuesday to Sunday. Admission costs L8000 (those aged 18 to 25, L400; those aged over 65 and under 18, free). Two-hour guided tours (L8000) in Italian only depart at 3 pm Saturday, and 10 am and 3 pm Sunday. Anglophones can rent an audioguide at the ticket desk for L7000 (L10,000 for two people). The bookshop sells several informative guides, such as 336-page *The Brera Gallery* (Touring Club of Italy; L38,000) and the cheaper *Brera* (Electa, L15,000).

NORTH TO STAZIONE CENTRALE

Instead of bearing west from Via Alessandro Manzoni into Brera, you can continue north through the Archi di Porta Nuova to **Piazza Cavour** (metro MM3 Monte Napoleone), a secessionist square the 'other side' of Milan's medieval walls. In the 1940s, **Palazzo dell'Informazione** (1938–42), the huge building housing the Poliform furniture shop on the square's north-eastern side, housed the offices of the Fascist newspaper *Il Popolo d'Italia.*

It was outside his office at Via Palestro 20 that Maurizio Gucci was shot in 1995. Two years previously, a Sicilian Mafia terrorist bomb exploded outside Via Palestro 14, killing five people and destroying the **Padiglione d'Arte Contemporanea** (PAC; ☎ 02 760 09 085, e segreteria@pac-milano .org, metro MM1 Palestro), a 1950s contemporary art space since rebuilt. Next door at No 16 is the **Civica Galleria d'Arte Moderna** (GAM; ☎ 02 760 02 819, metro MM1 Palestro, MM3 Turati), displaying predominantly 19th-century works of art. It is housed in neoclassical **Villa Reale** (1790), the popular wedding reception venue for wealthy Milanese, where Napoleon lived for a short time. Both museums open 9.30 am to 5.30 pm Tuesday to Sunday. Admission to GAM is free but the PAC commands a L10,000 admission fee.

Immediately opposite lays late-18th-century **Giardini Pubblici** (see Parks later in this chapter), with a small **Museo del Cinema** on its western fringe, a green-domed 1930s **Planetarium** (☎ 02 295 31 181, metro MM1 Porta Venezia & Palestro) on its northern fringe, and a copper-coloured building (1888–93) filled with stuffed animals, skeletons, rocks, dinosaur eggs, and so on, to form a fusty **Museo Civico di Storia Naturale** (☎ 02 884 63 298), Corso Venezia 55. The collection dates to 1838 and can be viewed 9 am to 6 pm (6.30 pm weekends). Admission is free.

At the park's easternmost corner, the northern end of Corso Venezia, is **Porta Venezia** (metro MM1 Venezia). The sturdy gate was built between 1826 and 1828 to replace Porta Orientale, one of six gates intersecting new city walls raised by the Spanish after 1549. These walls embraced a much larger area than their predecessors and form what is called 'Viali' today – the middle of the three concentric circles surrounding Milan.

Viali's westward path leads along Bastoni di Porta Venezia and its continuation, Bastoni di Porta Nuova, to Venezia's sister gates **Porta Nuova** (metro MM2/3 Repubblica) and **Porta Garibaldi** (metro MM2 Garibaldi FS & Moscova), the latter still touting its 19th-century toll houses. Midway between Venezia and Nuova you reach **Piazza della Repubblica** (metro MM2/3 Repubblica), a truly enormous square laid out in the 1930s after the city's first central train station, built here in 1864, was shifted about 800m north. **Hotel Principe di Savoia**, on the square's western side, is among Milan's most historic hotels.

Milan's grandiose **Stazione Centrale** (metro MM2/3 Centrale FS), with its iron-and-glass roof and immense 200m-long front facade (1927–31) ornately sculpted with a menagerie of winged creatures, is a classic of

the Fascist era. Debate still rages about **Alba di Milano** (2001), an extraordinary 'beam of light' designed by British architect Ian Ritchie, in front of the station on Piazza Duca d'Aosta. The innovative sculpture is made from optical-glass fibre and stainless-steel wire which conducts waves of light in the dark. Commissioned to mark the third millennium, it apparently symbolises Milan's world fame as designer and innovator.

Gio Pirelli's **skyscraper** (metro MM2/3 Centrale FS) was equally controversial when unveiled in 1960. It stands 127m tall directly opposite the central train station, on the western side of Piazza Duca d'Aosta, and houses Lombardy regional council.

AROUND CASTELLO SFORZESCO

From the early 15th century until Spanish domination, the Duchy of Milan was ruled by the Viscontis and Sforzas from Castello Sforzesco which, until 1549, stood outside the city walls. The leafy area (see Parks later in this chapter) north-west of the castle was not landscaped until the late 1890s, although chariots raced around a neoclassical arena built here as early as 1806. Military parades, originally held here, later marched northwards to **Sempione** – the quarter of town north of Parco Sempione, dominated by Milan's renowned Fiera di Milano (trade fair and exhibition centre).

Heading southwards, Piazzale Luigi Cadorna (metro MM1/2 Cadorna Triennale) is dominated by Stazione Nord, the city's northern train station. In front is **Ago, Filo e Nodo** (2000), a sculpture of 'Needle, Thread & Knot' by Swedish-Dutch duo Claes Oldenburg and Coosje van Bruggen. Beyond the obvious, the bright piece of Pop Art has something to do with Malpensa trains and planes taking-off.

Pedestrian Via Dante (1890) links Castello Sforzesco with the city heart by way of Piazza Cordusio and Via Orefici. Straddling the western limits of the central circle is Sant'Ambrogio, one of Milan's most sacred quarters which grew up around the mausoleum of the city's patron saint (see Basilica di Sant'Ambrogio later in this chapter).

Castello Sforzesco

This Renaissance-style castle (metro MM1/2 Cadorna Triennale, MM1 Cairoli, M2 Lanza), originally a Visconti fortress, was entirely remodelled by Francesco Sforza in the 15th century, with Leonardo da Vinci aiding in designing the defences. The Spanish used it for military purposes, embedding it within their new city walls, and today it is home to some excellent art museums, open 9.30 am to 5.30 pm Tuesday to Sunday. Admission is free.

A vast collection of Lombard sculptures from early Christian times to the 17th century is displayed in the **Museo d'Arte Antica**, including a fresco by Leonardo da Vinci and Michelangelo's *Pietà Rondanini*. Other collections include an applied arts display and a decent picture gallery, featuring works by Bellini, Tiepolo, Mantegna, Correggio, Titian and a van Dyck, in the **Pinacoteca e Raccolte d'Arte**. There's also a museum devoted to prehistoric and ancient Egyptian artefacts. Perhaps most enchanting is the collection of musical instruments in the **Museo degli Strumenti Musicali**. Don't miss the hurdy-gurdy designed for a woman to play in the 18th century and the pochette, a pocket-size violin used by dancing instructors from the 17th to early 20th centuries.

Civico Museo Archeologico & Palazzo delle Stelline

Trace the path that the lumbering Spanish Viali once wove southwards along Via Carducci to Largo d'Ancona, then bear east along Corso Magenta to the Civico Museo Archeologico (☎ 02 864 50 011, metro MM1/2 Cadorna Triennale) at No 15. The archaeogical museum features substantial Roman, Greek, Etruscan, Gandhara (ancient north-west Indian) and medieval sections and is housed in one wing of Monastero Maggiore, a 9th-century Benedictine convent rebuilt in the 1500s. Adjoining it is **Chiesa di San Maurizio** containing fabulous 16th-century frescoes by Bernardino Luini. A concert here is well worth attending (see Classical Music later in this chapter).

The museum opens 9.30 am to 5.30 pm Tuesday to Sunday and admission is free. Captions are in Italian but the museum sells an informative English-language brochure (L2000) explaining what's what and mapping out an archaeological itinerary around town. The church can be visited 9 am to noon and 4 to 5.30 pm Tuesday to Sunday. Mass (Greek-Byzantine rite) is at 6 pm weekdays and 10.30 am Sunday.

Backtracking to Largo d'Ancona, Corso Magenta runs westwards to **Palazzo delle**

Cimitero Monumentale

Graves cover a vast expanse of 250,000 sq m at Milan's Monumental Cemetery, opened in 1866 to stop the random burial of corpses across the city. Graves remained modest until 1895 when families were allotted permanent plots, following which gravestones and shrines exploded out of all proportion as families sought to create the most enviable grave.

In 1936, Jesus and his disciples featured in Leonardo's *Last Supper* were recreated in stone (to exact 3-D proportions and with the same facial expressions) to decorate the tomb of distillery magnate Davide Campari (1867–1936). The same artist, Giannino Castiglioni (1884–1971), also designed the moving bronze sculpture (life-size) of an unknown couple lying beneath a sheet on their deathbed – literally.

Each year on All Saints' Day (1 November), Milanese pour into the cemetery to lay flowers and light candles on the thousands of graves. Only Milan's richest and most famous are buried here today. The cemetery (☎ 800 915 586) opens 8.30 am to 5.30 pm Tuesday to Sunday (free). Guided tours (L10,000) in Italian only depart at 10.15 am on Sunday; advance booking only (☎ 02 66 04 61 05). The cemetery bookshop sells the excellent, 206-page *The Monumental Cemetery of Milan* (L20,000).

Stelline at No 59. Once a school for orphans in the 17th century, it's been transformed into a congress centre, three-star hotel and offices for the European Commission and other embassies. Andy Warhol and Daniel Spoerri are among those to have had their work displayed in the Galleria Refettorio delle Stelline (refectory), which hosts temporary contemporary art exhibitions.

The Last Supper

Leonardo da Vinci's mural depicting the Last Supper decorates one wall of the Cenacolo Vinciano, the refectory adjoining **Chiesa di Santa Maria delle Grazie** (metro MM1/2 Cadorna Triennale, MM1 Conciliazione), Corso Magenta. The complex was built for the Dominicans between 1463 and 1483 and is as much admired for its striking Renaissance dome, added in 1492 alongside a new cloister and sacristy, as for the incredible masterpiece it shelters. Mass is celebrated in the church at 7.30, 8.30 and 9.30 am and 6.30 pm.

Frescoes depicting the Last Supper of Christ and his later crucifixion were frequently painted in Dominican refectories in the 15th century. Painted between 1494 and 1498, Leonardo's work is unusual as it's believed to capture the moment when Jesus uttered, 'One of you will betray me'. The word *cenacolo* means refectory, the place where Christ and the 12 Apostles celebrated the Last Supper, and is also used to refer to any mural depicting this scene. The northern wall painting was butchered by the Dominicans in 1652 when they raised the refectory floor by 1m, prompting them to chop off a lower section of the scene – along with Jesus' feet. The Crucifixion (1495) on the southern wall was painted by Giovanni Donato Montorfano. Miraculously, both friezes survived WWII – unlike the refectory's vaulted ceiling and western wall (still windowless today) which were both destroyed.

Getting to see the *Last Supper* is a medieval test of faith, with groups of 25 being sluiced through every 15 minutes. The real hitch, however, is that you have to book ahead by phone – at least three or four days in advance usually if you want to guarantee

a ticket. When you eventually get through, an operator will allot you a visiting time and a reservation number which you present, 30 minutes before your visit, at the ticket desk of the Cenacolo Vinciano. Admission costs L12,000 (EU citizens aged 18 to 25, L6000; those aged over 65 and under 18, free), plus L2000 booking fee. Turn up late and you risk your ticket being sold to someone else.

You can buy English-language audio guides, costing L5000/8000 for one/two people, at the ticket desk. Guided tours (15 minutes) in English cost an extra L6000 and depart at 11.15 am and 3.30 pm Tuesday to Friday, and at 10.15 am and 3.30 pm weekends. Again, places must be booked in advance. Telephone lines operate 9 am to 6 pm weekdays and 9 am to 2 pm Saturday. From Italy call ☎ 02 894 21 146 (☎ 39 02 894 21 146 from abroad). The Cenacolo Vinciano opens 8.30 am to 7.30 pm Tuesday to Sunday (11.30 pm Saturday).

If God's on your side, you can just turn up at the Cenacolo Vinciano and snag a cancellation or unfilled place for a tour that day. If this happens, you'll be allocated a time, made to pay on the spot (minus L2000 booking fee) and told to come back 10 minutes before the scheduled visit starts.

Museo Nazionale della Scienza e della Tecnica

Leonardo did far more than paint as the fascinating displays at one of the world's largest technical museums, the Museo Nazionale della Scienza e della Tecnica (☎ 02 48 55 51, ✉ museo@musescienza .org, metro MM2 Sant'Ambrogio), Via San Vittore 21, attest.

The museum occupies a 12th-century monastery. It opens 9.30 am to 5 pm Tuesday to Friday, and 9.30 am to 6.30 pm weekends. Admission costs L12,000 (children aged under three, free). At weekends, 'Nonno & Bambino' tickets (L13,000) are available; they include admission for an adult aged over 60 and a child aged up to 12.

From the National Science & Technical Museum it is an easy walk westwards to the increasingly trendy area around Via Savona (see the Ticinese to Navigli section).

MILAN

Basilica di Sant'Ambrogio

A short stroll eastwards along Via San Vittore, brings you to the Romanesque **Basilica di Sant'Ambrogio** – dedicated to Milan's patron saint, Saint Ambrose, and dominating the piazza of the same name. Founded in the 4th century by Ambrose, bishop of Milan (for more details see the boxed text 'A Saint of the World' in the Facts about the Cities chapter), the red-brick complex has been repaired, rebuilt and restored several times since and is a bit of a hotchpotch of styles. The shorter of the church's two bell towers dates to the 9th century, as does the remarkable ciborium under the dome inside. It is believed that at least parts of the columns inside date back to the time of Saint Ambrose. The saint himself is buried in the crypt. The attached **museum** (☎ 02 864 50 895), closed for renovation until the end of 2001, houses relics dating from the earliest days of the basilica's existence. It usually opens 10 am to noon and 3 to 5 pm Monday and Wednesday to Sunday (afternoons only at weekends). Museum admission costs L5000.

Petrarca (Petrarch) lived in a house opposite the church when visiting Milan in 1353. Behind it is the **Università Cattolica del Sacro Cuore**, Milan's Catholic university. To the north, a footpath leads from elongated Piazza Sant'Ambrogio to **Tempio della Vittoria** (1927–30), a marble temple honouring soldiers killed during WWI. Walking around the ossuary in its basement is unsettling. An eternal flame to the unknown soldier burns in front of the temple, open 8.30 am to noon and 1 to 5 pm Tuesday to Sunday.

TICINESE TO NAVIGLI

Ticinese, south-west of the medieval centre, was the city's traditional working class quarter. It gains its name from the River Ticino that flows into Milan westwards along the Naviglio Grande – the largest canal built here in the 12th century. Navigable from 1272, the waterway quickly became a vital trade route for barges carrying goods north from Milan. When the duomo was built, it was along the Naviglio Grande's murky waters that its marble arrived. From the 17th century, barges docked at Darsena –

The World's Largest Horse

Leonardo da Vinci designed the world's largest equestrian statue in the 15th century but it was not until 1999 that his four-legged idea was raised. It stands in all its horsy glory at Piazzale dello Sport 6 (metro MM1 Lotto), west of the racetrack in the San Siro district. From the metro station, walk 1.5km south-westwards along Viale Frederico Caprilli.

---

the dock immediately west of Piazza XXIV Maggio where the canal ends. In medieval times, an inner ring of canals (since filled in) linked it closer to the city.

This canalside area has been rejuvenated enormously in recent years and, as with so many quasi-industrial heartlands, has re-emerged as a hip and trendy place to be. Some of the city's most authentic trattorie and liveliest bars are along **Ripa di Porta Ticinese** and **Alzaia Naviglio Grande** – the tow paths running either side of the canal. A little north, around **Via Savona**, designers have moved in.

Porta Ticinese

Approaching the quarter along Corso di Porta Ticinese, you pass Chiesa di San Lorenzo Maggiore (MM3 Missori), Piazza Vetra, an early Christian church built between 355 and 372, remodelled in the 13th century and given its essentially Renaissance look in 1894. In front of the lovely basilica is an impressive line-up of 16 towering Roman columns, Milan's most explicit Roman remains and, as such, an unexpected delight. The 9m-tall columns formed part of a 3rd-century temple and were moved here in the 5th century. On the square is a statue of Constantine, the emperor behind the Edit of Milan (AD 313) allowing Christianity to be practised.

The burnt red arch of **Porta Ticinese**, the gate immediately south of the basilica on the intersection of Corso di Porta Ticinese and Via de Amicis, served as the southern-most entrance to medieval Milan. In the 13th century, a canal lapped around its outer edge. The current structure was rebuilt between 1861 and 1865. Confusingly, a short walk farther south brings you to Piazza XXIV Maggio and another **Porta Ticinese**. It was built by the Spanish.

Peering across at the busy intersection and market place is **Chiesa di Sant'Eustorgio**, Piazza Sant'Eustorgio, built in the 9th century and altered in the 11th. It features a 15th-century Cappella Portinari (Chapel of St Peter Martyr) and a baptistry designed by Donato Bramante.

Città delle Culture

A block north of Naviglio Grande, across the railway tracks into Stazione Porta Genova, a monstrous factory complex is to become a state-of-the-art Città delle Culture (City of Cultures). The 17,870 sq m complex, to be designed by British architect David Chipperfield, will house a **Museo Archeologici e Preistorici** featuring Etruscan, Greco-Roman and Middle Eastern treasures and a **Centro delle Culture** displaying a bounty of world ethnographical exhibits (from Milan, India, Japan and China). Chipperfield will demolish the old factory canteen at Via Tortona 22 and 33–5 and build a new construction from scratch – expected to be at the cutting edge of contemporary architecture. This will home a **Centre of Non-European Cultures**. TV studios, a cinema school, puppet workshops, a library and film archive, bookshops and a couple of bars and restaurants will also star in the city's new city. Check with the tourist office for up-to-date details.

PARKS

Central Milan has two green spaces where Sunday strollers can stroll in peace: Parco Sempione (metro MM1 Cairoli), immediately north-west of Castello Sforzesco; and the Giardini Pubblici (metro MM1 Palestro), on the north-eastern fringe of the historic centre.

Vast **Parco Sempione** (1894) is adorned with neoclassical Arca della Pace, a sadly neglected arena (inaugurated by Napoleon in 1806 and where an audience of 30,000 watched horses gallop around the oval track), and the rather ugly Palazzo dell'Arte

(see Theatre later in this chapter). The park opens 6.30 am to 8 pm (9 pm in March, April and October; 10 pm in May; and 11.30 pm June to September).

The more manicured **Giardini Pubblici** (1784), with its statues and benches overlooking the elegant Museo Civico di Storia Naturale (see the North to Stazione Centrale section earlier in this chapter), is more attractive. Jogging tracks – packed at weekends – encircle the gardens and there's old-fashioned roundabouts and other things to amuse kids at its western end. The park gates open 6.30 am to 8 pm (to 9 pm March, April and October, 9.30 pm June to August, and 10 pm in May).

ACTIVITIES

An excellent starting point for action-seekers is Milano Sport (☎ 02 80 14 66, fax 02 80 14 60), Piazza Armandi Diaz 1a, which has information on Milan's wealth of activities. Details on everything from swimming pools and cycling tracks to rock 'n' roll, mambo and shiatsu sessions are listed in its free pocket guide *Corsi*, published annually. Milano Sport opens 10 am to 7 pm weekdays.

Canoeing and kayaking clubs row row row their kayaks and canoes along the Naviglio Grande canal in Navigli; the tourist office should have a list.

Expats yearning for an innings can always contact Milan Cricket Club (☎ 02 264 12 123, [e] stevetrow@yahoo.com); the predominantly Anglophone club bats April to October.

Swimming

The glass-covered pool (☎ 02 469 52 78, metro MM2 Sant'Agostino) at Via Montevideo 11 in the middle of Parco Solari, a small park just north of Navigli, opens 10 am to 9.20 pm weekdays, and 12.30 pm to 5 pm Saturday, May to July (shorter hours in winter). The *piscina* (pool) is closed in August. The Bacone (☎ 02 294 00 393, metro MM2 Sant'Agostino), Via Piccini 8, is one of a dozen or so public pools to organise aqua-aerobics, kids' swimming classes, life-saving and other activities.

Large outdoor complexes equipped with pools, slides and other watery amusements include the playful Lido (☎ 02 392 6 61 00, metro MM1 Lotto), just east of the Fiera di Milano on Piazzale Lorenzo Lotto, and Aquatica (☎ 02 482 00 134), Via Airaghi 61, way west of the centre next to Città di Milano camping and the Tangenziale Ovest (west ring road). To get here, go to MM1 De Angeli station and take bus No 72 to the park. Both open June to September.

Rollerblading & Skating
There is a rollerblading rink inside the Lido complex (see Swimming earlier). The ice-skating rink in Palazzo del Chiaccio (☎ 02 73 98), Via Piranesi 14, immediately east of Stazione Porta Vittoria, opens until 11.30 pm, 12.30 or 1 am Wednesday to Saturday and throws boppy discos on ice most Saturday evenings (usually from 9.30 pm).

COURSES
If you can understand some Italian, invest L19,000 in a copy of *Milano Corsi*, an annual guide listing over 200 different courses ranging from hat- and shoe-making to Web design and learning Italian. It is published by Milan-based ACTL (☎ 02 864 64 080, @ info@actl.it), with a Web site at www.actl.it, and is sold in bookshops.

The city's scores of language schools are listed in the annually published *English Yellow Pages* (see under Books in the Facts for the Visitor chapter). The tourist office has a list of design schools.

The University of Milan (☎ 02 5 83 52, fax 02 583 06 830, metro MM1/3 Duomo), Via Festa del Perdono 7, accepts international students. Degree courses are exclusively in Italian and students have to provide certified proof of an advanced level of Italian. Visit online at www.unim.it.

Language
International House (☎ 02 527 91 24, 02 805 78 25, fax 02 556 00 324, @ ihmilan@tin.it, metro MM3 Missori), Piazza Erculea 9, offers intensive two- and four-week Italian-language courses that include 15 or 20 hours per week of group tuition (L500,000 for a two-week course/30 hours tuition). It also runs a 10-week part-time course (L720,000/ 40 hours of group tuition) and private tutoring (L65,000 per hour). Self-catering accommodation or B&B with a host family can be arranged. Students must pay L100,000 to enrol. See its Web site at www.international house.com for detailed course information.

Linguadue (☎ 02 295 91 972, fax 02 295 19 973, @ info@linguadue.com, metro MM1 Lima), Corso Buenos Aires 43, runs standard, semi- and super-intensive courses. Standard one-month courses comprising 20 hours of group tuition per week cost L1,040,000 (L260,000 for a fifth week). Super-intensive one-month courses include 30 hours per week (mix of private/group tutoring) and cost L3,680,000. Individual tuition in general or business Italian starts at L700,000 for 10 hours.

Other schools with teaching centres in downtown Milan include Panton Italian for Foreigners (☎ 02 46 21 85, @ panton@ tin.it, metro MM1/2 Cadorna Triennale), attached to Milan's English-language bookshop at Via Boccaccio 45.

International teaching specialists Berlitz (☎ 02 869 00 31, fax 02 80 93 95) has language centres at Via Larga 8 (metro MM1/3 Duomo) and Via Mercadante 17 (metro MM1/2 Loreto). You can also try Gruppo Oxford (☎ 02 669 87 180, fax 02 670 75 710, @ info@oxford.it, metro MM1 Goria), Via Campanini 7, with a Web site at www.oxford.it; and Istituto Dante Alighieri (☎ 02 720 11 310, fax 02 720 11 557, @ ici dante@tin.it. metro MM1/2 Cadorna Triennale), Piazzale Luigi Cadorna 9.

Food & Wine
International House (see under Language earlier) runs a two-week Italian-cookery and wine course. It includes two afternoons of tuition per week (when students learn how to cook two traditional Italian dishes – which they then eat) and costs L200,000. Courses are run by Italian chefs – in Italian.

Design
The Istituto Europeo di Design (☎ 02 579 69 51, fax 02 550 12 613, metro MM1 San Babila), Via Amatore Sciesa 4, runs intensive one-month summer courses in photography,

interior design, fashion design and graphic advertising. It also runs full-time three-year courses.

Aspiring jewellers can learn the art of crafting gold at Scuola Orafa Ambrosiana di Luca Solari (☎/fax 02 294 050 05, 🇪 info@scuolaorafaambrosiana.com, metro MM1 Porta Venezia & Lima), a goldsmith school at Via Alessandro Tadino 30. A 'hobby' goldsmith course comprising 50 hours' individual tuition (three hours per day) costs L1,350,000. Advanced courses in enamel work and waxing are also available. Details are posted on the school's Web site at www.scuolaorafaambrosiana.com.

If you can't beat 'em, join 'em. Fashion has arrived at the universities. The Università Bocconi (☎ 02 583 62 018), Via Sarfatti 25, offers a fashion and design component in its MBA course (in Italian). Visit online at www.uni-bocconi.it. Aspiring McQueens can also try the Università Cattolica (☎ 02 7 23 41), Largo Gemelli 1, which offers various six month postgraduate courses.

The Instituto Superiore di Architettura e Design (ISAD; ☎ 02 552 10 700, fax 02 569 94 494, 🇪 isad@planet.it, metro MM3 Porta Romana), Via della Commenda 37, runs a range of inspirational two-year courses in interior, garden and furniture design. Shorter courses in designing spaces for the disabled (two weeks) and furniture restoration (60 hours) are also available. See www.isad.it for more information.

Opera

International House (see under Language earlier) runs two-week courses in Italian opera history (from the 17th to 20th century). Courses costs L300,000 and include three afternoons of group tuition per week. Lessons are in Italian.

Places to Stay

Milan's hotels are notorious for being among Italy's most expensive and the priciest in Europe after London, Paris and Rome. In short, this is because the city does not have enough beds to go round. Finding a room (let

alone a cheap one) is, quite simply, a mission and a half. If there's a trade fair on, you have few hopes of scoring a bed for the night – unless, of course, your highly efficient clued-in PA booked you a room several months in advance. Hotels get heavily booked up in every price range.

When you have found a room several dozen telephone calls later, the chances are it will probably be much more expensive than you anticipated...but you'll still take it! An immediate saving can be made by avoiding the city during trade fairs (almost all the time) when already obscenely high prices shoot even further through the roof. Most mid-range and top-end hotels tout a price scale rather than fixed rate, meaning you can negotiate.

The APT office occasionally makes recommendations but never takes bookings (see the boxed text 'Finding a Hotel Room'); the Stazione Centrale office can be more helpful in this respect and will occasionally call around if things are tight. Both offices distribute *Milano Hotels*, a free 130-page listings guide to Milan's 350-odd hotels, *residenze turistico alberghiere* (self-catering residences available to rent on a weekly or monthly basis) and *campeggi* (camp sites). It is published annually.

Both offices also stock lists of private rooms, student accommodation, religious institutions and boarding houses that can be rented by the month.

PLACES TO STAY – BUDGET

Milan's cheapest one- and two-star joints slumber around Stazione Centrale. As in any other capital city, quality varies. 'Cheap' in Milan translates as no less than L60,000/95,000 for a single/double with kitsch beige 1970s furnishings and a shared bathroom in the corridor.

Camping

Città di Milano (☎ 02 482 00 134, fax 02 482 02 999, Via Airaghi 61) is a fair distance from the centre. Take the metro to MM1 De Angeli station, west of the city centre, then bus No 72 from Piazza de Angeli to the Di Vittorio

Finding a Hotel Room

Two agencies, recommended by the tourist office, can tell you what accommodation is available where and make advance reservations for free. They are generally geared to the fatter wallet, touting only a handful of selected one- and two-star hotels in their computer system compared to an exhaustive range of three- and four-star hotels. A swift phone call to these agencies quickly reveals if a trade fair is on (and how big it is).

Centro Prenotazioni Hotel Italia (CPHI)

(☎ 800 015 772 toll-free in Italy or 02 295 31 605 from abroad, ⓔ info@chphi.it) – Reservations for one- to five-star hotels, starting at L90,000/140,000 for singles/doubles and peaking at L600,000. Reservations are free, but it needs a credit-card number as a guarantee; upon arrival in Milan, you pay the hotel directly. Telephone lines open 9 am to 8 pm Monday to Saturday, and 9 am to 5 pm Sunday.
Web site: www.cphi.it

In Italia: Centro Servizi a Prenotazioni Alberghiere

(☎ 800 008 777 toll-free in Italy or 02 272 01 330 from abroad, ⓔ info@initalia.it) – Reservations for one- to five-star hotels all over Italy, starting at L100,000/150,000 for singles/doubles in Milan. Reservations are free but a credit-card number is required. The agency opens 9 am to 7 pm Monday to Saturday.
Web site: www.initalia.it

stop, from where it is a 400m walk to the camp site. It costs L12,000/10,000/3000 per person/tent/car. Campers must telephone in advance. By car, leave the Tangenziale Ovest at San Siro-Via Novara. The site opens February to November.

Otherwise, the nearest camp site is *Autodromo* (☎ 039 38 77 71), some 22km north of the city in Monza (see Spectator Sports later in this chapter). It charges similar rates and opens April to September.

Hostels

Milan's only HI hostel, *Ostello Piero Rotta* (☎ 02 392 67 095, fax 02 330 00 191, Viale Angelo Salmoiraghi 1), charges L26,000 for B&B. Take the metro in the direction of MM1 Molino Dorino and get off at QT8 (the name of the station and surrounding area), from where it is a two-minute walk southwards along Viale Angelo Salmoiraghi. The hostel is a short walk from the Lido water park (see Swimming earlier in this chapter).

Protezione della Giovane (☎ 02 290 00 164, Corso Garibaldi 123, metro MM2 Moscova & Lanza) accommodates women aged between 16 and 25. Beds start at L40,000. Staff only speak Italian.

Hotels – Duomo to Brera

Surprisingly, Milan's city centre has some interesting options which, although top of the budget range, offer an unbeatable location and comfort – one level up from rock-bottom – in renovated rooms which have seen a lick of paint in recent years.

Within spitting distance of Piazza del Duomo is highly recommended *Hotel Speronari* (☎ 02 864 61 125, fax 02 700 31 78, Via Speronari 4, metro MM1/3 Duomo), tucked in a shop-lined side street of busy Via Turino. Comfortable singles/doubles/triples with shower cost L100,000/150,000/230,000 and basic, bathroom-less equivalents clock in at L80,000/110,000/160,000. Its handful of doubles with shower and toilet cost from L160,000 to L180,000 per night. Reserve weeks in advance to guarantee a room .

Another cheap and central deal can be found at *Hotel Nuovo* (☎ 02 864 64 444, fax 02 864 60 542, Piazza Beccaria 6, metro MM1/3 Duomo, MM1 San Babila), just off Corso Vittorio Emanuele II. Strangely flashy from the outside, this new one-star pad touts plain singles without/with bath for L60,000/100,000 and equivalent doubles for L80,000/130,000.

Heading southwards from Piazza del Duomo along Via Mazzini and its continuation, Corso Italia, you hit the little-known *Hotel Ullrich (☎ 02 864 59 156, fax 02 80 45 35, Corso Italia 6, metro MM3 Missori)*, a family-run *pensione* on the 6th floor of a well-kept old building. Singles/doubles with shared bathroom cost L60,000/100,000. From the interior courtyard, head up the left staircase marked 'scala A'.

Hotels – North to Stazione Centrale

This is the patch to find Milan's rock-bottom options. Some hotels around the train station do not take bookings. Many – although cheap – double quietly (and sometimes not so quietly) as brothels. You could easily sleep in one of these places and be blissfully ignorant – or you could be less fortunate.

One-star *Hotel Valley (☎ 02 669 27 77, fax 02 669 87 552, Via Soperga 19, metro MM2/3 Centrale FS, MM3 Caiazzo)* is not in the greatest of spots but the rooms are reasonable and the staff friendly. Singles/doubles with bathroom, TV and phone cost L120,000/150,000. Singles/doubles with shower and washbasin (shared toilet in the corridor) cost L70,000/130,000 but they get booked up quickly. Reception opens 24 hours; buzz the buzzer to get in.

East of Corso Buenos Aires, single-starred *Hotel del Sole (☎ 02 295 12 971, fax 02 295 13 689, Via Gaspare Spontini, 6 metro MM1 Lima)* sports adequate singles/doubles/triples for L60,000/90,000/L130,000 (L90,000/130,000/150,000 with bathroom). The bizarre staircase and mirrored walls are memorable highlights.

Distinctly dodgy but dirt-cheap *Albergo Nettuno (☎ 02 294 04 481, fax 02 295 23 819, Via Alessandro Tadino 27, metro MM2/3 Centrale FS, MM1 Porta Venezia)* has rock-bottom rooms a 10-minute walk south-east of Stazione Centrale. Rest your weary head here for a mere L60,000/80,000 for a single/double (L90,000/120,000 with bathroom).

A few blocks south, one-star *Hotel Brianza (☎ 02 294 04 819, 02 295 27 243, fax 02 295 31 145, e hbrianza@tiscalinet.it, Via Panfilo Castaldi 16, metro MM1 Piazza Venezia, MM2/3 Repubblica)*, astride the corner of Via Lazzaretto, has equally depressing but inexpensive rooms costing L100,000/120,000 for one/two people.

On the same street, *Hotel Porta Venezia (☎ 02 294 14 227, fax 02 202 49 397, Via Panfilo Castaldi 26, metro MM1 Piazza Venezia, MM2/3 Repubblica)* is ideal for lovers of Chinese food, given the distinct culinary smell that fills its shabby reception. Single/double rooms with shared facilities are unbeatably cheap at L65,000/100,000.

Down near Piazza della Repubblica, renovated *Hotel Casa Mia (☎ 02 657 52 49, fax 02 655 22 28, Viale Vittorio Veneto 30, metro MM2/3 Repubblica)* has something of a family atmosphere and is a charming spot for the price. Two-star singles/doubles cost L90,000/140,000 at weekends, L110,000/160,000 on weekdays, and L140,000/200,000 during trade fairs. Rates do not appear to be fixed however, so try to bargain.

Hotel Verona (☎ 02 669 83 091, fax 02 669 87 236, Via Carlo Tenca 12, metro MM2/3 Repubblica) is also close to Piazza della Repubblica. Singles/doubles cost L100,000/160,000 including TV and breakfast. Again, you can bargain the price down depending on the time of year and the day of the week you stay.

One-star *Hotel Kennedy (☎ 02 294 00 934, fax 02 294 01 253, Viale Tunisia 6, metro MM2/3 Repubblica)* has acceptable singles/doubles with shared bathroom for L70,000/90,000, and doubles only with private bathroom costing L130,000. All rooms are on the 6th floor. Three floors down, on the 3rd floor of the same building, *Hotel San Tomaso (☎/fax 02 295 14 747)* touts friendly English-speaking staff and basic singles/doubles costing L65,000/105,000 (L70,000/120,000 with shower), and doubles with toilet and shower for L150,000.

There is a crowd of budget and mid-range places along Via Napo Torriani. *Hotel Brasil* (☎ *02 749 24 82, Via Modena 20, metro MM1 Porta Venezia)* is not a bad place, although a bit of a walk from the closest metro station. Rooms are clean and of a reasonable size. Bare-bone singles/doubles kick off at L70,000/90,000 (L85,000/100,000 with shower, and L110,00/130,000 with shower and toilet).

Hotels – Around Castello Sforzesco

Albergo Commercio (☎ *02 864 63 880, Via Mercato 1, metro MM1 Cairoli)* offers singles/doubles with shower for L70,000/ 90,000 but it's often full. From Piazza Cordusio, walk northwards up Via Broletto, which later becomes Via Vetero and then Via Mercato. The entrance to the hotel is around the corner on Via delle Erbe.

PLACES TO STAY – MID-RANGE

Mid-range options abound in Milan. Unless stipulated otherwise, breakfast is included in the prices listed below.

Hotels – Duomo to Brera

Neon-lit *Hotel Rio* (☎ *02 87 41 14, fax 02 86 56 89, Via Mazzini 8, metro MM1/3 Duomo)*, just off Piazza del Duoma, is a small but friendly affair. Three-star singles/doubles/triples start at L150,000/ 230,000/290,000 (July, August and non-fair weekends) and peak at L170,000/ 250,000/330,000 (during trade fairs, which is most of the year).

Equally close to the cathedral spires is *Hotel Casa Svizzera* (☎ *02 869 22 46, fax 02 720 04 690, Via San Raffaele 3, metro MM1/3 Duomo)*, opposite a charming little church. Singles/doubles peak at L280,000/350,000 but can be bargained down (generally at weekends).

Midway along Via Torino, *Hotel Gritti* (☎ *02 80 10 56, fax 02 890 10 999,* e *hotel .gritti@iol.it, Piazza Santa Maria Beltrade 4, metro MM1/3 Duomo, MM1 Cordusio)* has rooms overlooking a quiet(ish) square cost-

ing upwards of L160,000/230,000/330,000 for a single/double/triple.

Ideal for shopping fiends is *Hotel Manzoni* (☎ *02 760 05 700, fax 02 78 42 12,* e *hotel.manzoni@tin.it, Via Santo Spirito 20, metro MM3 Monte Napoleone)*, a great place to drop, deep in the heart of shopping land. Comfortable singles/doubles cost L230,000/330,000 – fair or no fair.

Hotels – Around Castello Sforzesco

Midway between the Duomo and Castello Sforzesco is *Albergo Vecchia Milano* (☎ *02 87 50 42, 02 87 59 71, Via Borromei 4, metro MM1 Cordusio)*, near Piazza Borromeo. This good, if slightly expensive, two-star place has sunny yellow walls, wooden period furnishings and singles/doubles with bathroom for L140,000/200,000. Prices are higher when there's a trade fair or festival on.

Hotel London (☎ *02 720 20 166, fax 02 805 70 37, Via Rovello 3, metro MM1 Cairoli)*, off Via Dante, looks swanky but charges reasonable rates. Singles/doubles cost L140,000/210,000 with shared bathroom (L160,000/250,000 with shower and toilet). Rates drop by L10,000 per night when there's no exhibition on. Breakfast costs an extra L15,000 and you can ask for a 10% discount if you pay your hotel bill in hard cash.

In a quiet alley close to the castle is highly recommended *Hotel Cairoli* (☎ *02 80 13 71, fax 02 720 02 243, Via Porlezza 4, metro MM1 Cairoli & Cordusio)*, just off Via Camperio. Three-star rooms cost L170,000/265,000 with breakfast (20% discount if no trade fair or festival is on).

Three-star *Hotel King* (☎ *02 87 44 32, fax 02 890 10 798,* e *info@hotelkingmilano .com, Corso Magenta 19, metro MM1/2 Cadorna Triennale)*, a stone's throw from the archaeology museum, is a pleasant enough pad with singles/doubles setting punters back by L150,000/220,000 (up to L248,000/350,000 at peak times) per night.

PLACES TO STAY – TOP END

Get ready to blow mega bucks in these pricey but pleasing pads, best suited to a corporate bank account (or any, for that matter, other

MILAN

than your own) or the strictly loaded. Prices fluctuate wildly and generally reflect the size or prestige of whatever fair is on in town – expect to pay top whack, for example, during April's furniture fair. Rates are lowest in December, January, July and August.

Hotels – Duomo to Brera

One of the best-value places in this price range and well worth a nibble is *Hotel Spadari* (☎ 02 720 02 371, fax 02 86 11 84, [e] reservation@spadarihotel.com, Via Spadari 11, metro MM1/3 Duomo), a modern hotel for rich foodies with taste – given its exclusive location next door to Peck. Singles/doubles cost upwards of L348,000/388,000.

Hotel Galileo (☎ 02 7 74 31, fax 02 760 20 584, [e] galileo@milanhotel.it, Corso Europa 9, metro MM1 San Babila) charges upwards of L360,000/460,000 for its moderate singles/doubles, while charming *Hotel Ambasciatori* (☎ 02 760 20 241, fax 02 78 27 00, [e] ambasciatorhotel.it, Galleria del Corso 3, metro MM1 San Babila), snug inside a glass-topped mall, has splendidly refurbished singles/doubles from L366,000/489,000.

Four-star *Grand Hotel Plaza* (☎ 02 85 55, fax 02 86 72 40, Piazza Armandi Diaz 3, metro MM1/3 Duomo) is a classic example of Milan's rash of top-end hotels, ugly outside but proffering an oasis of red leather, peace and luxury once past the costumed doorman. Singles/doubles cost L310,000/410,000.

An equally grim facade shields *Jolly Hotel President* (☎ 02 77 461, fax 02 78 34 49, [e] milano_president@jollyhotels.it, Largo Augusto 10, metro MM1/3 Duomo), immediately south of Armani on Via Durini. Prices for double rooms range from L502,000 to L592,000 depending what's on when, where.

Off busy Via Larga, immediately south of Piazza del Duomo, looms *Hotel Brunelleschi* (☎ 02 8 84 31, fax 02 80 49 24, Via Baracchini 12, metro MM3 Missori), a concrete monster with a dramatically theatrical reception. Single/double rooms cost a monstrous L395,000/500,000 at peak times. Use of a mobile phone (excluding calls) is one of the perks thrown in.

A heady cocktail of marble, mirror and stained glass greets guests at *Hotel Sir Edward* (☎ 02 87 78 77, fax 02 87 78 44, Via Mazzini 4, metro MM1/3 Duomo), where singles/doubles with whirlpool baths command L380,000/480,000.

Beautiful doubles slink in at L475,000 (up to L600,000 on trade-fair weekdays) at nearby *Star Hotel Rosa* (☎ 02 88 31, fax 02 805 79 64, Via Pattari 5, metro MM1/3 Duomo); while designer chairs by Italian designer Branzi sit upright in reception at five-star *Grand Hotel Duomo* (☎ 02 864 62 027, fax 02 864 50 454, [e] grandduomo@hotmail.com, Via San Raffaele 1, metro MM1/3 Duomo). Doubles dressed top-to-toe in contemporary design furniture kick off at L440,000 (L515,000 in high season).

Bathrooms clad in Italian marble are among the trademarks of four-star *Hotel de la Ville* (☎ 02 86 76 51, fax 02 86 66 09, Via Hoepli 6, metro MM1/3 Duomo), a large hotel which has long lured a glamorous set. Catwalk stars pay L380,000/510,000 for a single/double to stay here.

Fabulous *Carlton Hotel Baglioni* (☎ 02 7 70 77, fax 02 78 33 00, [e] carlton.milano @baglionihotels.com, Via Senato 5, metro MM3 Monte Napoleone, MM1 Palestro) is one of Milan's 11 five-star hotels. It resides in a neat townhouse, spitting distance from Via della Spiga's design boutiques. Price is absolutely irrelevant for the money-is-no-option clientele that it lures.

Hotels – North to Stazione Centrale

Two of Milan's oldest and priciest hotels languish (with a few uniformed guards loitering outside) near the central train station. Historic *Hotel Principe di Savoia* (☎ 02 623 05 555, fax 02 65 37 99, [e] reso47 principedisavoia@luxurycollection.com, Piazza della Repubblica 17, metro MM2/3 Repubblica) has an extravagant, stained-glass and chandelier interior that has to be seen to be believed. Its 490 sq m presidential suite – strictly for lira millionaires – has its own sauna, jacuzzi and swimming pool. Humbler singles/doubles start at L509,000/709,000.

Peering across the station, **Excelsior Hotel Gallia** *(☎ 02 6 78 51, fax 02 667 13 239, e reservations@excelsiorgallia.it, Piazza Duca d'Aosta 9, metro MM2/3 Centrale FS)* is inside a lovely Art Nouveau building which – since 1932 – has hosted distinguished guests such as Ernest Hemingway and Maria Callas. A stroll back into early 20th-century splendour, this Royal Meridien chain hotel charges from L500,000/600,000 today for elegant singles/doubles. It has a Web site at www.excelsiorgallia.it.

Hotels – Around Castello Sforzesco

The Radisson SAS' **Bonaparte Hotel** *(☎ 02 8 56 01, fax 02 869 36 01, Via Cusani 13, metro MM1 Cairoli)* charges at least L395,000/445,000 for basic singles/doubles.

Places to Eat

Italians say Lombard cuisine is designed for people who do not have time to waste – because they're always in a hurry for work. Result? Most streets in the historic centre, especially around the duomo and north towards Stazione Centrale, are riddled with sandwich bars and fast-food outlets – great for eaters on a tight budget. At the other end of the scale, you can blow a small fortune on dining, should that be your desire.

Please see under Food in the Facts for the Visitor chapter for details of Milan's cuisine.

PLACES TO EAT – BUDGET
Restaurants

Nowhere can beat the cost:quality ratio dished up by **Trattoria da Pino** *(☎ 02 760 00 532, Via Cerva 14, metro MM1/3 Duomo, MM1 San Babila)*, a fabulous authentic and unpretentious trattoria, where strangers dine at shared tables. The place, tucked down a quiet side street, gets packed by noon with Milanese workers. Its L21,000 lunchtime menu is built solely from hearty home-made cooking and has a 25cl jug of wine (or 50cl of mineral water) thrown in.

In the Monte Napoleone district, shoppers on the move can indulge in a quick and cheap bowl of home-made pasta standing up at the traditional Italian delicatessen **Armandola** *(☎ 02 760 21 657, Via della Spiga 50, metro MM3 Monte Napoleone)*, at the north-western end of the street. Pick the right day and the fresh white Alba truffles it sells might just end up (at a price) on your plate. Balsamic vinegar is its other house speciality (see Self-Catering later in this chapter for more details).

Tucked nearby is **Brek** *(Piazza Cavour, metro MM3 Monte Napoleone)*, overlooking Porta Nuova. The canteen-style restaurant dishes up respectable food with speed from 11.30 am to 3.30 pm and 6.30 to 10.30 pm. A tummy-filling plate of spaghetti costs L5000. The chain has less picturesque outlets at Corso Italia 3 and Piazzetta Giordano.

Ciao *(Corso Buenos Aires 7, metro MM1 Lima, MM1/2 Loreto)* is another chain (other outlets on Corso Europa, Via Dante 5 and Piazza del Duomo) where you can refuel on quality fodder for less than L15,000. Pasta/mains average L6000/7000.

Around the station, quick snacks can be munched sitting down or standing up at **Spontini Bar** *(Corso Buenos Aires 60, metro MM2/3 Centrale FS)*, accessible from Via Spontini and **Spontini Pizzeria** next door.

An easy stroll south of Castello Sforzesco is **The Break** *(Via Camperio 11, metro MM1 Cairoli)*, another canteen-style goody known for its cheap dining. Buy a L50,000/100,000/200,000 chip card and you get a 5/10/15% discount.

Navigli touts a number of eateries. For good, cheap Greek snacks and meals, you can't beat **Ghireria Greca** *(Ripa di Porta Ticinese 13, metro MM2 Porta Genova FS)*. On the other side of the canal overlooking the water is **Brellin** *(☎ 02 581 01 351, Alzaia Naviglio Grande 14, metro MM2 Porta Genova FS)*, the place to lunch after browsing in the surrounding antique shops. Enjoy all-day Sunday brunch in a flower-filled garden.

Pizzerias

Milan is riddled with pizzerias. On the Internet, www.pizza.it lists 100-plus places where you can dig your teeth into an authentic margherita or quattro stagione.

MILAN

The first Milanese pizza was cooked up at **Ristorante di Gennaro** (☎ 02 805 34 54, Via Santa Radegonda 14, metro MM1/3 Duomo), handily placed near Galleria Vittorio Emanuele II. Next door at No 16, one of Milan's oldest fast-food outlets, **Luini** (☎ 02 864 61 917), sells panzerotti (pizza dough stuffed with tomatoes, garlic and mozzarella) – ideal for pizza-seekers wanting to save thousands of lira or munch on the move.

The other hot choice around Piazza del Duomo is **Premiata Pizzeria** (☎ 02 894 06 075, Via de Amicis 24, metro MM1/3 Duomo), run by the legendary pizza kings who also keep the crowds coming at their original outlet (☎ 02 894 00 648, Alzaia Naviglio Grande 2, metro MM2 Porta Genova FS) in the Navigli district. You can leave full at either for L20,000. Also in Navigli, funky **Be Bop** (☎ 02 837 69 72, Viale Col di Lana 4, metro MM2 Porta Genova FS) is known for its soya-flour pizza dough.

Pizzeria **Transatlantico** (☎ 02 295 26 098, Via Marcello Malpighi 3, metro MM1 Porta Venezia), close to the Museo Civico di Storia Naturale and its surrounding public gardens, is inside an attractive Art Nouveau building and has the bonus of staying open until 1 am.

Minimalist decor and a buoyant, well-dressed crowd (who clearly have no problem with cash- or wine-flow) add a dash of carefree panache to **Paper Moon** (☎ 02 760 22 297, Via Bagutta 1, metro MM1 San Babila), a chic pizzeria that serves much more than Italy's quintessential dish. Count on paying L35,000 for a full meal, excluding drinks.

East of Stazione Centrale, the menu at **Geppo Pizza Big** (☎ 02 284 65 48, Viale Brianza 30, metro MM2 Caiazzo & Loreto), with nearly a 100 pizza varieties, is as big as its name. Big is one of Milan's tastiest and cheapest pizzerias – pay about L15,000 for a full meal. **Rino Vecchia Napoli** (☎ 02 261 90 56, Via Chavez 5), way north of the centre, is another 'must' for any Milanese pizza nut. Despite its way-off location, advance reservations are absolutely essential.

Cafes – Duomo to Brera

A short stroll southwards from Piazza del Duomo, **Caffè Torino** (Via Torino 49, metro

MM1/3 Duomo) makes for a tasty sandwich and coffee stop for Via Torino shoppers. Well-stuffed panini (filled rolls), oozing imagination, average L7000.

A good alternative north of the square is **Bar Biffino** (Via Andegari 15, metro MM1/3 Duomo, MM3 Monte Napoleone), a friendly spot to grab a panino (L7000) and extra-creamy cappuccino (L2300) between sights. Doubling as a tobacconists (entrance on Via Alessandro Manzoni), Biffino lacks the pretension and inflated prices of the busy cafes around La Scala.

Nearby **Caffè Verdi**, next to La Scala on Via Verdi, charges an outrageous L6000 for a cappuccino alone – hardly justifiable despite its ornate interior strewn with musical scores and other operatic memorabilia.

On pedestrian Corso Vittorio Emanuele II (metro MM1/3 Duomo), shoppers can pull in for a pricey pitstop at **Antica Cremeria San Carlo al Corso** or **Bar Haiti**, two terrace cafes next to Basilica di San Carlo al Corso. No free table in the sun? Duck through the passageway to historic **Caffè San Carlo** or take cover in **Coast to Coast Cafe** (☎ 02 760 24 475), open until 2 am inside Galleria de Cristoforis.

The glass-roofed cafe on the 1st floor of **Peck** (see the special section 'Shopping in Milan'), Milan's finest food store, has what can only be the softest chairs to sink into in town. This is where older fur-clad Milanese sip espresso in china cups, served by dapper young men in black jackets. Predictably, service is both impeccable and flattering. Another elegant choice in this upmarket quarter is **Caffè Spadari**, with a delicious range of cakes and pastries on the corner of Via Spadari and Via Cantú. If there's no spare table, cross the street to **Rachelli** (☎ 02 869 36 14), another cafe in the same league.

It might have a boring name but **Bar Centro** (☎ 02 760 01 415, Corso Giacomo Matteotti 3, metro MM1 San Babila) sports a refreshingly eclectic decor and dare-devil terrace on the porticoed pavement. Mingle here with a cocktail- and cappuccino-quaffing crowd. Farther north is the trendy **Sunflower Bar** (☎ 02 760 22 754, Via

Pietro Verri, 8 metro MM1 San Babila), another haunt of the fashion-conscious, which likewise has an outside terrace beneath arches. A filled panini sitting down costs L8000.

Continuing northwards to the Monte Napoleone shopping district, *Rêve Café (☎ 02 760 01 505, Via della Spiga 42, metro MM3 Monte Napoleone)*, next-door neighbour to flamboyant Anna Molinari at Via della Spiga 44, is a bold affair with red, blue and green walls luring a young crowd.

Another fashionable option for those who back the minimalist horse is one of two cafes inside *Emporio Armani (Via Alessandro Manzoni 31, metro MM3 Monte Napoleone)*, Armani's fashion emporium. First/second courses – without labels – cost

L20,000/25,000 and there's a healthy choice of salads (L16,000 to L28,000) for the calorie-conscious. It opens noon to 7.30 pm Monday to Saturday.

Cafes – Ticinese to Navigli

Things hot up around Navigli, a happening part of town crammed with cafes and bars to revel in. *Caffè Cucchi (☎ 02 894 09 793, Corso Genova 1, metro MM2 Porta Genova FS)*, at the northern end of the street, is a fine place for piazza- and people-watching over breakfast, lunch or an evening aperitif accompanied by a meal-size pick of tasty snacks. Head farther south-west and you'll come across *Rococó Caffè*, a cool bistro on the corner of Via Casale and the Alzaia Naviglio Grande.

Historical Cafes

The following institutions are fabulous places at any time of day, be it for a breakfast-time *cornetto* (croissant or pastry) dunked in cappuccino froth or an early evening aperitif in the company of lavish hors d'oeuvres.

In addition to the choice few reviewed, you could try *Biffi (☎ 02 480 06 702, Corso Magenta 87)* or *Ambrosiano*, which basks in the shadow of the cathedral astride the corner of Piazza del Duomo and Corso Vittoria Emanuele II.

Cova
(☎ 02 760 05 578, Via Monte Napoleone 8, metro MM3 Monte Napoleone) Founded in 1817 by a soldier in Napoleon's army who set up shop in front of La Scala, this elegant and expensive tearoom and chocolate shop has languished in the heart of the Monte Napoleone shopping district since 1950 (the original was destroyed during WWII). Sit amid a wealthy mix of Milanese and Japanese tourists and sip tea, eat *panettone* or lunch on a cheese platter and strawberries.

Marchesi
(☎ 02 87 67 30, Via Santa Maria alla Porta 11a, metro MM1 Cordusio) The legendary cafe has been in the cake and coffee business since 1824. Its heavily wood-panelled interior shelters luscious displays of chess and draught boards made from chocolate.

Il Salotto
(Galleria Vittorio Emanuele II, metro MM1/3 Duomo) Marketed as a typical Milanese spot, the 'drawing room' is generally filled with tourists and harassed waiters. An outrageous L7000 for a cappuccino sitting down is the price you pay for the historic, chandelier-lit interior and glass-covered winter terrace.

Taveggia
(☎ 02 760 21 257, Via Visconti di Modrone 2, metro MM1 San Babila, MM3 Duomo) With its dozen or so cornetto types, juicy fruit tarts and cakes, this traditional bar and pasticceria dating to 1910 makes a grand breakfast choice. Open 7.30 am to 8.30 pm.

Zucca
(☎ 02 864 64 435, Galleria Vittorio Emanuele II 21, metro MM1/3 Duomo) Milan's most historic cafe overlooking Piazza Duomo, with an Art Deco mosaic interior unveiled at the same time as the covered shopping gallery. Don't be confused by the 'Campari' sign outside; that was its original name.

Several fun places to seek refreshment line Via Savona (metro MM2 Porta Genova FS), the street running parallel to the Naviglio Grande canal two blocks south. *Papagayo Cafe (Via Savona 20)*, *Mai Dire Bar (☎ 02 837 31 73, Via Savona 11)* and *Al Panino (☎ 02 894 20 192, Via Savona 1b)* are great places to enjoy lazy lunches with friends. Spartan *Ciriboga (☎ 034 781 55 693, Via Savona 10)* oozes a natural charm with its healthy L15,000 lunch deal and not-to-be-missed fruity creations such as *ravioli al vapore di anatra mandarino e castagne* (steamed ravioli filled with duck, mandarin and chestnuts; L13,000) and banana muffins.

Cafes – Elsewhere

Where there's shops, there's cafes. Corso Buenos Aires (metro MM1 Lima) is lined with cheap places to grab a quick bite. *Pattini & Marinoni* at No 53 sells bread and pizza by the slice for about L3000.

West of Piazza del Duomo, Via Dante (metro MM1 Cordusio or Cairoli) is bespeckled with places to down espresso shots. *Caffè Sforzesco* at No 7 serves a good-value *menu del giono* (menu of the day) on a terrace opposite Piccolo Teatro.

Gelaterie

A classic place is *Viel*, Corso Buenos Aires 15, a favourite late-night haunt for young Milanese. The *gelati* are good and the *frullati di frutta* (fruit shakes), better. It opens 8 to 2 am Wednesday to Monday.

Fast Food

Autogrill, on the northern side of Piazza del Duomo, houses Burger King, Spizzico and Ciao, all open 7 to 2 am.

McDonald's has numerous outlets around town, including at Via Torino 47 (open 10.30 or 11 am to 10 pm); Piazza del Duomo (open 10 am to midnight); corner of Corso Europa and Via Borgogna; corner of Via San Marco and Via della Moscva; and Piazza Cordusi (open 10 am to midnight).

There are several fast-food outlets, including *Spizzico* and *Burger King* on Corso Buenos Aires.

Self-Catering

Bakers, chocolate-makers, confectioners, specialist wine shops and Peck – the Harrods of Milan – are listed in the special section 'Shopping in Milan'. There is a fresh-produce *market* at weekends at Via Benedetto Marcello and a daily morning market on Piazza XXIV Maggio, the giant intersection at the eastern end of Ripa di Porta Ticinese.

Via Speronari (metro MM1/3 Duomo), just off Piazza del Duomo, is the best street in the centre to shop for bread, cakes, salami, cheese, fruit and wine. *Il Bread & Breakfast* at No 6 sells a crowd-luring range of pizza slices and focaccia as well as cakes, bread and fresh pasta. Hunks of Parmigiano reggiano (L28,900 per kg) are sold on the fresh cheese counter at *Superfresco Standa*, a five-minute walk away at Via Palla 2a (entrance next to FNAC on Via Torino). Panini, pizza slices and ready-made salads are sold in the supermarket entrance; everything else is downstairs. It opens 8.30 am to 8 pm Monday to Saturday.

Super Sconto, on Via Panfilo Castaldi, just off Corso Buenos Aires, is another handy supermarket for picking up supplies. The *Supercentrale* supermarket located inside Stazione Centrale opens from 5.30 am to midnight.

In the fashion district, *Armandola (☎ 02 760 21 657, Via della Spiga 50, metro MM3 Monte Napoleone*; see Restaurants earlier in this section) is a charming *salumeria* (salami shop) and *rosticceria* (roast meat shop) rolled into one, selling unusual salamis, cold meats, caviar and truffles (fresh in season and conserved the rest of the year). It's also the place to buy *aceto balsamico* (balsamic vinegar) aged for up to 25 years in juniper wood barrels. Nearby *Il Salumaio (Via Monte Napoleone 12, metro MM3 Monte Napoleone)*, another Milanese institution, is an equally sensational delicatessen.

Chocolate-chip cookies, brownies and cheesecakes are stacked high inside *California Bakery*, which has outlets at Via Solferino 12 (MM2 Moscova) and on the corner of Corso Magenta and Via Carducci (metro MM1/2 Cadorna Triennale). Both sell healthy breakfast/lunch packs (L7000/16,000) and an imaginative array of New Yorker bagels.

PLACES TO EAT – MID-RANGE

In these mid-range places, antipasti/pasti kick in around the L18,000/20,000 mark and main courses average L25,000. Advance bookings are not essential – but are advised.

Restaurants – Duomo to Brera

A handful of hip places to eat line cobbled Via Fiori Chiari (metro MM3 Monte Napoleone, MM1 Cairoli), a charming pedestrianised street speckled with pavement terraces in summer. *Orient Express* at No 8 is a rather chic spot for a post antique-browsing drink or, on Sunday, brunch (if you can get in). The place resembles a train but prices are less than on its Vienna-bound equivalent. First/second courses here average L25,000/30,000.

Equally arty is *L'Innominato* (☎ 02 869 98 865, Via Fiori Chiari 20), recommended for its traditional *risotto giallo* (saffron-spiced risotto) with porcini mushrooms (L18,000) and meaty Milanese cutlets (L28,000).

Heading north, *La Latteria di Via San Marco* (☎ 02 659 76 53, Via San Marco 24, metro MM2 Moscova) is a fabulous little *cremeria* which draws its shutters at weekends. Monday to Friday it cooks up traditional home-cooked cuisine to a polenta-loving crowd. At the crossroads, bear eastwards along Via Montebello to reach *Il Verdi* (☎ 02 659 07 97, Piazza Mirabello 5, metro MM3 Turati), an old and glamorous favourite where many a model has munched on one of its infamous 'mega salads'.

Milanese rail workers clearly eat well if standards set by tasty *Osteria del Treno* (☎ 02 670 04 79, Via San Gregorio 46, metro MM2/3 Repubblica), inside the Circolo Cooperativo Ferrovieri (railway cooperative), are anything to go by. Anyone can dine here. It doesn't accept credit cards and its house paté is yum.

Restaurants – Around Castello Sforzesco

Charmingly old-fashioned *Antica Osteria Milanese* (☎ 02 86 13 67, Via Camperio 11, metro MM1/2 Cadorna Triennale) is a traditional frill-free trattoria that fills up with suits (predominantly male) every lunchtime. Antipasti/pasta dishes average about L20,000 and mains cost upwards of L25,000. Don't miss the *meneghina alla griglia al Grand Marnier* (L8000), Milanese sponge cake soaked in liqueur and baked.

Honey strudel (L10,000) is a good enough reason as any to dine at *Osteria Borromei*, very close to Albergo Vecchia Milano on Via Borromei (metro MM1 Cordusio). This homely place has a lovely vine-covered terrace and a quiet mellow courtyard. It opens weekdays only and serves antipasti/first/second courses for L18,000/18,000/28,000.

Near Cimetero Monumentale is a trio of trendy eating places which double as drinking spots too (all open until 2 or 3 pm). Original *ATM* (☎ 02 655 23 65, Bastoni di Porta Volta 15, metro MM2 Moscova), sandwiched between speeding cars on a traffic island, was an old ATM terminal until Milanese glamour queens transformed the ungainly glass-and-steel bunker into a chic place for 20- to 30-somethings. The mirrored doors in the squat-and-pee Turkish-style toilet do absolutely nothing to increase its size.

Bahnhof (☎ 02 290 01 511, Via Giuseppe Ferrari, metro MM2 Moscova), in the pits overlooking the railtracks leading into Stazione Porta Garibaldi, is one of Milan's top places to see and be seen. It touts a minimalist, stainless-steel interior and moderately priced food worthy of the hike.

Looking for the best grub in all of Wyoming? Try *Honky Tonks* (☎ 02 345 25 62, Via Fratelli Induno 10, metro MM2 Moscova), a US-inspired 1940s diner three minutes north of Jackson on the 26/89/189.

Restaurants – North to Stazione Centrale

For southern-Italian feasting, wrap your mouth around the goodies in the *Tipica Osteria Pugliese* (Via Tadino 5, metro MM1

Porta Venezia). The self-serve antipasti are enough to make you drop the main courses.

You can have a taste of Africa at *Ristorante Mar Rosso (Via Panfilo Castaldi 42, metro MM1 Porta Venezia)*, which specialises in Eritrean food. A walk through the back streets reveals other little restaurants too.

Particularly recommended for its Tuscan dishes is *Il Faro* (☎ *02 284 68 38, Piazzale San Materno 8, metro MM1/2 Loreto)*, a short walk north-east of the metro station. One stop farther east is *Ristorante Cuccuma (metro MM2 Piola)*, on the corner of Via Pacini and Via Fossati. The eccentrically lit Neapolitan place offers excellent seafood and pizzas, often accompanied by sentimental Italian hits.

Heading west towards Stazione Porta Garibaldi and Corso Como you'll find the area haunted at night by a certain Milanese high-society crew, all seemingly in search of the most expensive drink. You can find a couple of good places here. For about L50,000, you too can munch where Ho Chi Minh once sampled the best of Lombard food, at *Antica Trattoria della Pesa* (☎ *02 655 57 41, Via Pasubio 10, metro MM2 Moscova)*.

Restaurants – Ticinese to Navigli

Options abound in this area, renowned for its innovative cuisine cooked up by a mixed bag of chefs. Ode to two wheels *Le Biciclette* (☎ *02 839 41 77, Via Torti 1, metro MM2 Sant'Ambrogio)*, in a converted bicycle workshop, cooks up imaginative Italian cuisine and is a popular brunch and bar spot too. It opens noon to 2 am.

One outstanding spot, where a full meal with wine could come to as much as L60,000, is *Osteria dell'Operetta* (☎ *02 837 51 20, Corso di Porta Ticinese 70, metro MM2 Porta Genova FS)*.

Trendies also flock to *Trattoria Toscana* (☎ *02 894 06 292)*, with an interior garden (heated in winter) at No 58 on the same street. Again, you'll pay about L60,000.

Attempt to order anything less than the full-blown four-course dining experience at *Ponte Rosso* (☎ *02 837 31 32, Ripa di Porta Ticinese 23, metro MM2 Porta Genova FS)* and you'll be severely frowned at. Apple

strudel with pine kernels and cinnamon, pears cooked in sweet wine and an aromatic choice of cold meats are among its simple dishes. The traditional trattoria is run by a wine and balsamic vinegar connoisseur (whose extraordinary collection of cork screws, cocktail shakers and so on, adorns the walls).

Other notable places on this canal-side stretch are *Al Pont de Fer* (☎ *02 894 06 277, Ripa di Ticinese 55, metro MM2 Porta Genova FS)*, where you can sip wine and discover ecstasy with a sublime slice of caramel and honey *torta*; and *Le Vigne* (☎ *02 837 56 17, Ripa di Ticinese 61, metro MM2 Porta Genova FS)*, where those seeking nothing more than a feast of local cheese and wine are heartily welcomed. Both places have impressive wine lists.

Cheese fiends can also follow the canal further down to a string of enticing restaurants. Among them, *Osteria dei Formaggi Asso di Fiori* (☎ *02 894 09 415, Alzaia Naviglio Grande 54, metro MM2 Porta Genova FS)* is a good choice – meals are made with a whole range of Italian cheeses. There are other choices further down the street.

Yet another traditional spot to dine on original cooking is *Posto di Conversazione* (☎ *02 58 10 66 46, Alzaia Naviglio Grande 6, metro MM2 Porta Genova FS)*, an atmospheric *osteria* where you can sample veal cutlet with cheese fondue, followed by plum pie and walnut ice cream.

A few blocks north of the Naviglio Grande canal, near Parco Solari and the National Science & Technical Museum, is *Trattoria all'Antica* (☎ *02 837 28 49, Via Montevideo 4, MM2 Sant'Agostino)*, a simple spot known for its home-made gnocchi (L18,000) dressed in a variety of tasty sauces. Most gnocchi variations require at least two people; if you're dining solo ask what dishes your neighbours are eating.

PLACES TO EAT – TOP END

For gourmets with a bottomless pocket, there are several Milanese institutions where the rich, famous and wannabes have been frequenting for years. Most are placed right in the city-centre spotlight.

Stunning views of the cathedral spires

seriously risk distracting diners (not the place for a romantic dinner for two) at contemporary *Bistrot (☎ 02 87 71 20, Via San Raffaele 2, metro MM1/3 Duomo)*, the culinary temple of world-renowned Milanese chef Gualtiero Marchesi, topped with a glass ceiling on the top floor of Piazza del Duomo's Rinascente department store. The lunchtime/evening menus are not bad value at L60,000/90,000.

Elegant *Savini (☎ 02 79 55 28)*, inside Galleria Vittorio Emanuele II, has lured punters seeking an unforgettable gastronomic experience since 1867. Almost as old and equally as popular with the fashion set is *La Bice (☎ 02 79 55 28, Via Borgospesso 12, metro MM1/3 Duomo)*, a tartancarpeted pad dating to 1926. Antipasti average L22,000 and fish/meat mains will set you back L35,000 or more. Splurgers seeking an L80,000 bite of heaven can plump for truffles.

After the last curtain has fallen at La Scala, head for *Biffi Scala & Toulà (☎ 02 86 66 51, Via Filodrammatici 2, metro MM1/3 Duomo)*, a well-established haunt where hungry opera buffs have dashed for decades. It opens until 10.30 pm.

If your mouth is watering and money is no object, you could try *Ristorante Peck (☎ 02 87 67 74, Via Victor Hugo 4, metro MM1/3 Duomo)*, run by the same team as its namesake food store. Main courses start at L35,000.

Another longstanding favourite – in converted horse stables of all things (albeit those of a palace) – is *Bœucc (☎ 02 760 20 224, Piazza Belgioioso 2, metro MM1/3 Duomo, MM1 San Babila)*, where you can lunch for L70,000. Its summer terrace is a hot spot with a chi-chi, shade-wearing set.

Nearby *Don Lisander (☎ 02 760 20 130, Via Alessandro Manzoni 12a, metro MM3 Monte Napoleone)* dishes up a pricey Milanese risotto and a host of Tuscan dishes. Again, it's expensive, with antipasti/pasti/mains costing upwards of L22,000/24,000/38,000. Tables bask in its elegant tree-topped courtyard in summer.

The third in a trio of memorable summer terraces is *Al Mercante (☎ 02 805 21 98,*

Piazza Mercanti 17, metro MM1 Cordusio), wrapped around a Renaissance palace.

In the 1990s, Maurizio Gucci allegedly wined and dined the then-glamorous Patrizia at *Santa Lucia (☎ 02 760 23 155, Via San Pietro all'Orto 5, metro MM3 Monte Napoleone)*, a place which continues to attract a newsworthy clientele.

On Brera's southern fringe, *Il Coriandolo (☎ 02 869 32 73, Via dell'Orso 1, metro MM3 Monte Napoleone)* is an elegant spot with an ornately moulded ceiling and a delicious *risotto alla vecchia maniera Milanese* (old Milanese risotto) for L16,000. Fish/meat dishes average L35,000.

A short walk east of the historical centre and nearest metro station, *Giannino (☎ 02 551 95 582, Via Amatore Sciesa 8, metro MM1 San Babila)*, dating to the 1900s, is a good place to sample traditional Milanese dishes such as *cotoletta alla Milanese* or *ossobuco* (veal shank).

North towards Stazione Centrale, Gualtiero Marchesi is also the driving force behind *Terrazza (☎ 02 760 01 186, Via Palestro 8, metro MM1 Palestro)*, again up high on the top floor of the Centro Svizzera (Swiss Centre) building. Its interior design is as striking as at Bistrot, as are its views, this time overlooking public gardens.

Entertainment

Milan has some of Italy's top clubs, several cinemas screening English-language films and a fabulous year-round cultural calendar, topped off by La Scala's opera season which opens with a splendid splash each year on December 7 – the city's patron saint's day (Sant'Ambrogia). The season for theatre and concerts opens in October.

An essential reference for any culture buff is *Milano Mese*, a free monthly entertainment guide published by the APT office. Its listings are in English and cover everything from exhibitions, trade fairs and markets to classical music concerts, theatre, sports events and cinema schedules. Daily newspapers also run entertainment listings (in Italian).

ASA ANDERSSON

Mix with Milan's high society and quaff a cocktail or three

For some clue as to what's happening in the club scene, *Corriere della Sera* (Web site: www.corriere.it) has a reasonable supplement, *ViviMilano*, published every Wednesday and available at newsstands and on the Internet at www.vivimilano.it; while *La Repubblica* (Web site: www.repubblica.it) reaches the counters on Thursday with *Tutto Milano*. Both papers include cinema listings.

BARS

There are two areas in particular to search for a drink, some music and the madding crowd – Brera and Navigli. Otherwise, good bars are sprinkled at distant intervals across the city.

Many places listed under Cafes and Restaurants in the Places to Eat section earlier double as popular bars come dusk: Navigli's Le Biciclette and ATM, Bahnhof and Honky Tonks, north of Castello Sforzesco near Cimitero Monumentale, are all actively worth seeking out after dark. Most chic and trendy bars, including these, stay open until 2 or 3 am.

Duomo to Brera

Brera is the stamping ground for many trendy Milanese who mill through its narrow lanes and swirl in and out of watering holes, where a beer can cost anything from L8000 to L20,000 – depending on the bar,

the music (or lack of) and, of course, the venue.

A clutch of smoke-filled bars loiter around cobbled Via Fiori Chiari (metro MM2 Lanza, MM3 Monte Napoleone), including ***Bodhran Pub*** (*☎ 02 890 11 355)*, a linger-over-a-pint sort of place at No 21.

Popular joints with a mixed bag of revellers are big hip ***Biblos*** (*☎ 02 805 18 60,* **ⓔ** *biblosbiblos@hotmail.com, Via Madonnina 17)* and ***L'Écurie*** (*☎ 02 80 44 03, Via Madonnina 3)*, a music bar with a friendly crowd and lots of salads and pizza named after Corsican towns. The Stable opens until 2 am Thursday to Saturday (until 9.30 pm Monday to Wednesday).

A funky old favourite on the fringe of this quarter is ***Le Trottoir*** (*☎ 02 80 10 02, Corso Garibaldi 1)*, another French-inspired place (literally 'The Pavement') wedged on the corner of Via Tivoli. Aspiring artists hang their wild art on the wacky walls on the ground floor, a small stage hosts alternative bands (often jazz) and food is served upstairs.

Less rough on the wallet but by far the most legendary joint in this quarter is ***Jamaica*** (*☎ 02 87 67 23, Via Brera 32, metro MM3 Monte Napoleone)*, where artists and intellectuals have lamented the world's woes since 1921. Its pavement terrace is the best for lapping up Brera street life (open 9 to 2 am).

Ticinese to Navigli

For an alternative to Brera's bars, head south for Navigli along Corso di Porta Ticinese and make ***Iron Cafe*** (*☎ 02 835 83 09, Corso di Porta Ticinese 60, metro MM2 Porta Genova)* your first port of call. Roughly cut from concrete and iron, the industrial designed bar screens the latest in music videos on a wall-size screen.

At the southern foot of Corso di Porta Ticinese is ***Le Café Viarenna*** (*☎ 02 839 22 11, Piazza XXIV Maggio 4, metro MM2 Porta Genova)*, a music bar which throbs with happy punters from 7 pm to 2 am daily. It also serves food (L7000/10,000 for a first/second course). Neighbouring ***Loco Bar*** gets equally packed.

One pleasant bar you could start with (if

you like Guinness) is **Black Friars** (☎ *02 581 06 130, Corso di Porta Ticinese 16, metro MM2 Porta Genova)*, an Ireland-inspired pub. The sun shines from the floor of **Tasca** *(Corso di Porta Ticinese 17)*, a cool and sedate tapas and wine bar a little north. Industrial **Colonial Café** *(Via de Amicis 12, metro MM2 Porta Genova)* is a newer affair with light-and-airy cane furnishings and a bar that gets packed at weekends. It opens 11 am to 2 am.

Delving into the heart of Navigli, **Fanfüla** (☎ *02 894 06 749, Ripa di Porta Ticinese 37, metro MM2 Porta Genova)* is a *paninoteca* (sandwich shop), *birreria* (beer bar) and *enoteca* (wine bar) rolled into one. Its slightly grungy feel makes a nice change. *Musica dal vivo* (live music) tops off weekend sessions.

Another focal point for busy nightlife is Via Cardinale Ascanio Sforza, which runs along the Naviglio Pavese canal. Several bars float along this stretch of canal (see Jazz later in this chapter).

North of Castello Sforzesco

In the hip area around Via Garibaldi, **Radetzky** (☎ *02 657 26 45, Corso Garibaldi 105, metro MM2 Moscova)* is reminiscent of a Parisian cafe with its air of traditional elegance, table-cluttered pavement terrace and breakfast-friendly opening time (from 7.30 am).

A hot spot in this area, on the select crawl of many a Milanese model, is chic **Makia** (☎ *02 33 60 40 12, Corso Sempione 28, metro MM1 Pagano)*. This is an ultra-modern drinks and food bar with furnishings reflecting the very latest in contemporary design. The headquarters of RAI television are a flick-of-the-hair away, making it a drawcard with Milan's hobnobbing TV set.

Elsewhere

A short walk south of Castello Sforzesco, upmarket **Bar Magenta** (☎ *02 805 38 08, Via Carducci, 13 metro MM2 Sant'Ambrogio)* is a traditional meeting place for both seekers of that quintessential aperitif and more adventurous Milanese night owls. It opens until 3 am.

East of the city-centre ring near Stazione Porta Vittoria, you'll find **L'Atlantique** (☎ *02 551 93 925, Viale Umbria 42)*, a hip bar which was very much *alla moda* at the time of writing. Interior design is hi-tech and Sunday brunch is served from 12.30 pm. The bar opens until 4 am.

For Brazilian sounds, try out **Pau Brasil** (☎ *02 295 15 816, Via Melzo 24, metro MM1 Porta Venezia)*, a trendy ethnic place just north-east of the gardens around Museo Civico di Storia Naturale.

On the southern fringe of Milan's central 'ring' lies studenty **Coquetel** (☎ *02 836 06 88, Via Vetere 14)*, an ideal summer hangout given its green 'n' grassy location overlooking Parco delle Basiliche (open until 2 am). Punters are allowed to play football. The closest metro is MM1 Cordusio, a good 20-minute walk away.

Grab pub grub at Scottish **Rob Roy** (☎ *02 720 10 849,* e *robroy@robroy.it, Piazza Armandi Diaz 5, metro MM1/3 Duomo)*. Brits bask on the terrace of **Victory** *(Via Borgogna)* and in front of TV at **English Pub** *(Via Valpetrosa, metro MM1/3 Duomo)*, a football pub off Via Torino.

Matches involving a Milanese side can often be watched at **Ronchino's** (☎ *034 755 15 807, Via Maurilio 8, metro MM1 Cordusio)*, an unpretentious enoteca tucked down another narrow street off Via Torino. It dishes up *musica dal vivo* (live music) Thursday to Saturday.

Aussies exchange travellers' tales down under at the **Kooka Bar** (☎ *02 541 22 507, Piazzale Libia 3, metro MM3 Porta Romana)*, an Australian sports bar with TV screen, cocktails and happy hour from 8 pm.

CLUBS

Milan boasts dozens and dozens of places to dance the night away, although the 'scene' for Milanese social butterflies tends to revolve very much around a clutch of 10 or so clubs. They generally open until 3 or 4 am. Among the most central is **La Banque** (☎ *02 869 96 565, Via Porrone 6, metro MM1 Cordusio)*, with a ground-floor restaurant and a throbbing dance floor safely ensconced in an underground cellar. Its ground floor used to be a bank before. Admission costs L30,000 and includes a drink. Behind Stazione Centrale, *Tunnel (Via Sammartini 30, metro MM2/3 Centrale FS)* is another subterranean place known for its cutting-edge repertoire of rising Milanese and Italian bands.

In Brera, brick meets steel at *Heaven (☎ 02 864 62 575, Via Fiori Chiari 17, metro MM2 Lanza)*, Brera's biggest club with dance floor and face control. Heading north, *Shocking (Bastioni di Porta Nuova 12, metro MM2 Moscova, MM3 Repubblica)* – the height of fashion – pulls different crowds with thematic changes in music each evening. It opens 10.30 pm to 3 am Tuesday to Saturday. Likewise, there's face control at the door.

Alcatraz (☎ 02 690 16 352, Via Valtellina 25, metro MM2 Garibaldi FS), an excellent venue for live concerts, is farther north again near Cimitero Monumentale. On Friday and Saturday nights, it is transformed into one of Milan's biggest clubs. Glamorous *Hollywood (☎ 02 655 55 74, 02 659 89 96 from 11.30 pm, Corso Como 15, metro MM2 Garibaldi FS)* is another big club to try in the neighbourhood – it's usually heaving with models (or wannabe models waiting to be spotted).

East of Milan's 'inner circle', mainstream *Plastic (☎ 02 73 39 96, Viale Umbria 120, metro MM3 Lodi TIBB)* has lured a punkier crowd for years. Its bouncers are very big. Admission costs upwards of L15,000 (depending on night and event).

A fair hike south-east of the city centre is *I Magazzini Generali (☎ 02 552 11 313, Via Pietrasanta 14)*, another thumping space, used for live bands and disco jivers. Admission costs L30,000 (free Wednesday). It is hiply housed in a converted warehouse and opens 10 pm to 3 am.

Nearby *Propaganda, (☎ 02 583 10 682, Via Gian Carlo Castelbarco 11)* and *Rolling Stone (☎ 02 73 31 72, Corso XXII Marzo 32)* are other venues to watch out for. Propaganda charges L25,000 (including one drink) to get in on Saturday (less on other evenings).

GAY & LESBIAN VENUES

Several mainstream clubs such as *Hollywood* and *Plastic* host weekly gay nights (in Plastic-speak, 'man2man' nights). *After Line (☎ 02 669 21 30, Via Sammartini 25, metro MM2/3 Centrale FS)*, behind Stazione Centrale, is one of the biggest gay venues.

For an update on 'in' clubs of the moment where it's safe to be 'out', contact Arci Gay/Centro d'Iniziativa Gay (☎ 02 581 00 399), Via Torricelli 19. Several gay venues only let you in if you hold an ArciGay membership card (see Gay & Lesbian Travellers in the Facts for the Visitor chapter).

POP & ROCK

Milan is included in many bands' world tours and has seen a healthy round of stars pass through, including Peter Gabriel, Red Hot Chili Peppers, Michael Jackson and Spice Girls to name but a few. On the Italian band circuit, Milan lures all the big names – Vasco Rossi, Claudio Baglioni, Zucchero and Milan's very own Paolo Conte – as well as younger stars such as Bologna's Luna Pop.

Ticket offices (see the boxed text 'Where to Buy Tickets') distribute printed lists of what bands are playing when and where. Venues vary enormously and range from mainstream discos such as *Alcatraz*, *Magazzini Generali*, *Propaganda* and *Rolling Stone* (see Clubs earlier in this section) to theatres such as *Teatro Smeraldo (☎ 02 290 06 767, Piazza XXV Aprile 10, metro MM2 Garibaldi FS)*.

The biggest gigs are held at *Palavobis (☎ 02 334 00 551, Viale Sant'Elia 33, metro MM1 Lampugnano)*, near the Stadio San Siro; and *Filaforum di Assago (☎ 02 48 85 71)*, further out of town; Elton John and Eric Clapton are among the big names to have played here recently. To get there, take the MM2 line to Romolo and pick up a shuttle bus put on for concerts.

JAZZ

The Milan Jazz Festival rocks through the city in November, the highlight of the jampacked, year-round calendar of jazz festivals. The tourist office has details. *Teatro Manzoni* (see Theatres later in this section) hosts

MILAN

Where to Buy Tickets

Biglietteria (ticket offices) sell tickets for theatre performances, rock concerts, football matches and other sporting events (*annullato* means 'cancelled' and *esaurito* means 'sold out'). Tickets cost anything from L45,000 for bands such as The Corrs or Thin Lizzy to L78,000/110,000 for a hot seat at a Paolo Conte/Elton John concert.

FNAC (☎ 02 87 80 04, ⓔ fnac@ticketweb.it), Via Palla 2 (entrance on Via Torino), distributes a free monthly list of happening concerts, events and matches (football, volleyball, basketball). You can collect tickets reserved electronically with Ticketweb (see below) here too. The shop opens 9.30 am to 8 pm Monday to Saturday (9 pm Thursday).

On Piazza del Duomo, La Prevendita (☎ 02 720 03 370), in Virgin Megastore in the Duomo Centre, sells tickets from 10 am to midnight. Box Tickets (☎ 02 79 55 02), in Messaggerie Musicali in Galleria del Corso 2 (entrance on Corso Vittorio Emanuele II), is another to try.

On the Internet, theatre and concert listings and tickets are available through Milan-based Ticket One (☎ 840 052 720 toll-free or ☎ 02 39 22 61, ⓔ info@ticketone.it) with a Web site at www.ticketone.it; or Ticket Web (☎ 02 760 09 131) at www.ticketweb.it. Electronic agency Milano Concerti (☎ 02 487 02 726 infoline, ⓔ info@milanoconcerti.it) at www.milanoconcerti.it, handles tickets for international rock concerts (Spice Girls, Bowie, Claudio Baglioni et al).

elegant jazz soirees at weekends, as does rough-cut *Le Trottoir* in a converted tobacconists (see Bars earlier in this chapter).

Milan's temple of jazz, *Capolinea (Via Lodovico il Moro 119)* lies in the heart of Navigli's deep south. It has been an institution with jazz fiends since the 1950s.

Le Scimmie (☎ 02 894 02 874, Via Cardinale Ascanio Sforza 49, metro MM2 Porta Genova FS) is the other place to go hang (rather, sway) to the sound of a sax. Its inside a canal barge, again in Navigli on one of its liveliest night-time streets (a 10-minute walk from the metro station). A beer costs L10,000, concerts kick off at 10.30 pm and food is served until 2 am.

Jazz Café (☎ 02 336 04 039, Corso Sempione 8, metro MM1 Conciliazione) captures the elegance of the 1920s jazz age with its period furnishings, young cocktail-quaffing crowd and occasional weekend brunches washed down with the jazzy dulcet of a sax-led ensemble. It opens until 3 am Monday to Saturday.

CLASSICAL MUSIC

Milan enjoys a fat calendar of classical music concerts in addition to the symphonic performances at legendary La Scala (see Opera & Ballet later in this chapter). The

Conservatorio Giuseppe Verdi (☎ 02 762 11 101, Via del Conservatorio 12, metro MM1 San Babila), with a Web site at www.verdi2001.com, and *Auditorium di Milano (☎ 02 833 89 201, ⓔ info@orchestrasinfonica.milano.it, Corso San Gottardo 42a, metro MM2 Porta Genova)*, near Porta Ticinese, are the most prestigious venues. It has a Web site at www.orchestrasinfonica.milano.it.

Among the most atmospheric are the concerts held in *Chiesa di San Maurizio (Corso Magenta 15, metro MM1/2 Cadorna Triennale)*, inside Monastero Maggiore next to the Civico Museo Archeologico. Most concerts are Baroque or Renaissance performances by small classical ensembles, organised by I Concerti del Quartetto (☎ 02 760 05 500, ⓔ sanmaurizio@quartetto-milano.it, Via Durini 24). The APT tourist office sells tickets.

Occasional concerts are held in a handful of other churches around the city, including historic *Basilica di Sant'Ambrogio* (see Things to See & Do earlier in this chapter). Both the tourist office and *Milano Mese* have schedules.

CINEMAS

On Monday, English-language films are screened at *Anteo (☎ 02 659 77 32, Via*

Milazzo 9, metro MM2 Moscova), a lively cinema complex, where you can also flick through books in its specialist cinema bookshop and dine in its tasty 1st-floor *Osteria del Cinema (☎ 02 290 11 475)* before or after the flicks. On Tuesday take your sweetheart to *Pilnius (☎ 02 295 31 103, Viale Abruzzi 28–30, MM1 Lima)* and on Thursday head for *Mexico (☎ 02 489 51 802, Via Savona 57, MM2 Porta Genova).* Tickets for all three cinemas cost L10,000 (those aged under 18, L7000) and you can buy a 10-film subscription for L60,000. For programme information call ☎ 02 657 10 93; Anteo is online at www.anteospaziocinema.com.

Other cinemas occasionally show *lingua originale* (original language) films, including historic *Odeon (☎ 02 87 45 47, Via San Radegonda 8),* just off Piazza del Duomo. Its plush interior alone makes a trip to the flicks here well worth it, even if the film showing is in Italian.

THEATRE

As in any major European capital, Milan's theatre scene stages everything from classical to avant-garde productions and revolves around 50 or so highly active theatres. Check *Milano Mese,* the newspapers and at the APT tourist office to find out what's showing where.

Theatres in the centre enjoying a high profile include *Teatro Piccolo (☎ 02 723 33 222, Via Rovello 2, metro MM1 Cordusio),* Milan's leading theatre, where national companies perform predominantly classical works. Its box office on the corner of Via Dante opens 10 am to 6.45 pm. *Teatro Lirico (☎ 02 72 33 31, metro MM1/3 Duomo, Via Larga 14, MM3 Missori)* also acts as a stage for Piccolo.

In the heart of the Monte Napoleone district, *Teatro Manzoni (☎ 02 760 20 543,* e *teatromanzoni@athena2000.it, Via Alessandro Manzoni 42, MM3 Monte Napoleone)* is the other big name in the Milanese theatre circuit. Details of its Sunday-lunchtime jazz and classical music concerts (L15,000) are posted online at www.teatromanzoni.it.

Teatro Carcano (☎ 02 551 81 377, Corso di Porta Romana 63 MM3 Crocette) with a Web site at www.teatrocarcano.com; and *Teatro Filodrammatici (☎ 02 869 36 59,* e *filodrammatici@tiscalinet.it, Via Filodrammatici 1, metro MM1/3 Duomo),* off Piazza della Scala, are two older theatres which play host to visiting companies.

Teatro dell'Arte (☎ 02 890 11 644, e *info@teatrocrt.org, metro MM1/2 Cadorna Triennale),* part of the Centro di Ricerca per il Teatro (CRT) inside Palazzo dell'Arte, an ungainly block built between 1922 and 1933 on the fringe of leafy Parco Sempione, is another name to look for.

The curtain rises on puppet shows, funny and serious for kids and adults alike, at *Teatro delle Marionette (☎ 02 469 44 40, Via degli Olivetani 3, metro MM2 Sant' Ambrogio).* Milan's puppet theatre hosts shows at 10 am weekdays, 4 pm Saturday, and 3 and 5.30 pm Sunday. Tickets cost L20,000 (those aged up to 25, L14,000).

OPERA & BALLET

The opera season at Teatro alla Scala, known across the world as La Scala (see the boxed text 'La Scala' in the Facts About the Cities chapter), runs from 7 December through to July. With the exception of the last two weeks in July and all of August, theatre, ballet and concerts are staged here year-round.

Scoring tickets to the opera requires enormous luck and/or perseverance. Performances sell out several months before, making booking *well* in advance absolutely vital. For all the opera classics – *Carmen, La Traviata* and so on – tickets are snapped up within minutes of going on sale, making the chances of getting a ticket in advance dishearteningly slim. Your only hope may be the 200 'standing-room' tickets (actually balcony seats with restricted view, making it necessary to stand to see but giving you the option to bob your bum down between arias). These go on sale at the entrance to the Museo Teatrale alla Scala 30 minutes before the scheduled starting time and can cost as little as L10,000. Even this is far more complicated than first appears however: opera buffs turn up as early as 6 am on the day of the performance to queue.

An inspired performance by Duomo characters

Dolci ~ Biscotti ~ Pranzi

Milan delivers the goods.

5 ORTICA

1737

Will you tramp the streets or take a tram?

Tranquil Lake Como, just half an hour from Milan

The largest of the Italian Gothic cathedrals, consecrated in 1418: the Duomo of Milan

JON DAVISON

Just one of the Duomo's 164 stained-glass windows, decorated and animated by some 3600 figures

NEIL SETCHFIELD

In addition to standing-room tickets, 'last-minute tickets' – any remaining unsold tickets – are sold (for 50% of the full-price ticket) from noon on the day of the performance. Given all performances are sold out months before, however, the chances of ever landing a ticket this way are pretty remote.

The box office (☎ 02 720 03 744), sign-posted 'biglietteria' in the portico in Via Filodrammatici on the left-hand side of the building, opens from noon to 6 pm daily and until 15 minutes after curtain's up on performance nights. You can check what performances are on and how many tickets (usually zero across the board) and which seats (thus, not applicable) are still available on the computer terminal, embedded in the wall next to the entrance. Tickets may also be purchased online at www.lascala.milano.it.

Opera, ballets, musicals and other large-scale productions are also staged at Milan's 1924 *Teatro Nazionale (☎ 02 480 07 700, Piazza Piemonte 20, metro MM1 Wagner)*. Sister theatre *Teatro Smeraldo (☎ 02 290 17 020, Piazza XXV Aprile 10, metro MM2 Garibaldi FS)* is a venue for modern dance performances. Both sell tickets online via their respective Web sites at www.teatro nazionale.com and www.smeraldo.it.

SPECTATOR SPORTS
The Italian Grand Prix tears around the Monza autodrome, several kilometres out of town along Viale Monza from Piazzale Loreto, every September. See under Spectator Sports in the Facts for the Visitor chapter.

Milan's two football clubs, AC Milan and FC Internazionale (known simply as Inter), play on alternate Sundays during the football season at the San Siro stadium, also called Meazza (after Giuseppe Meazza, one of the greats of Italian football). Tram No 24 and bus Nos 95, 49 and 72 run there, or you can take the metro and get off at MM1 Lotto metro station, from where a free shuttle bus runs to the stadium. Tickets are available at the stadium or, for AC Milan matches, from Milan Point (☎ 02 79 64 81), Via San Pietro all'Orto 8, or branches of the

Cariplo bank. Buy tickets for Inter matches at Banca Popolare di Milano branches, or call ☎ 02 770 01. Tickets cost from L25,000 to L65,000 – or more for big matches. More footie details are also included in the Facts for the Visitor chapter.

Excursions

The hard-working people of Milan might well have built Italy's economic and fashion capital into a businesslike place, which more closely resembles the great cities of northern Europe than the wilder south, but silly they're not. Well placed in the heart of Lombardy, their financial metropolis offers numerous escape routes. An enchanting string of lakes – all an easy train ride away – lie north of Milan, while its eastern and southern realms are peppered with affluent towns, such as Bergamo, Brescia, Cremona and Pavia, that preserve an enchanting character all of their own.

LAKE MAGGIORE
The most captivating of the lakes, Maggiore (Lago Maggiore, also called Lago Verbano) is stunning in parts, although its shores are flatter and less spectacular than some of its pre-Alpine counterparts.

Fed principally by the Rivers Ticino and Tresa, Lago Maggiore is about 65km long. As the main resort on the lake's western shore, **Stresa** (pop 4885, elevation 200m), 80km north-west of Milan, gets thronged with British and German tourists in summer who flock here to dip their toes in Maggiore's less-than-crystal-clear jade waters and catch a boat to one of the tiny **Borromeen Islands** (Isole Borromee). The smallest, Bella, was named after Charles III's wife, the *bella* Isabella, in the 17th century and has courted a host of famous holiday-makers – Wagner, Stendhal, Byron and Goethe among them.

Stresa's IAT office (☎ 032 33 01 50), Via Pietro Canonica 8, has information on lake-side walks and accommodation. It opens 10 am to 12.30 pm and 3 to 6.30 pm week-days, and 10 am to 12.30 pm Saturday.

Things to See & Do

From Stresa, you can take a cable car westwards to the summit of Monte Mottarone (1491m), the highest peak in the vicinity. Modest skiing possibilities are an added attraction to the views and the nearby **Parco del Mottarone** offers pleasant walking opportunities. The cable car (☎ 032 33 03 99) usually runs every 20 minutes between 9 am and 5 pm, or you can drive up through the park (L7000 per car for use of a private road). **Villa Pallavicino**, a huge garden with a zoo where the animals roam relatively freely, offers superb views of the lake and the surrounding mountains (L11,000).

The four Borromeen Islands – Bella, Pescatori (or Superiore), Madre and San Giovanni – lie immediately north of Stresa and form Maggiore's most beautiful corner. The main drawcard is **Palazzo Borromeo**, a sumptuous 17th-century palace built for the Borromeo family on Bella Island. Its interior is filled with works by Giovanni Tiepolo and Anthony van Dyck, Flemish tapestries and Canova sculptures, and its gardens are magnificent. The palace can be visited April to October.

Isola Madre, by contrast, provides fertile ground for Italy's tallest palm trees.

Getting There & Away

Stresa lies on the Domodossola–Milan train line. Trains arrive/depart from Milan's Stazione Centrale or Stazione Porta Garibaldi. Journey time is one to 1¼ hours (about 12 daily, L13,400).

By car, the A8 autostrada connects Milan with Varese, south-east of Lago Maggiore. Exit at Legnano for the S33 road, which passes the lake's western shore to Stresa. The A8/A26 from Milan has an exit for Lago Maggiore, via Arona.

Ferries and hydrofoils around the lake are operated by Navigazione Lago Maggiore (☎ 0322 23 32 00), connecting Stresa with numerous villages around the lake as well as the islands (five to 20 minutes) and Locarno in Switzerland (1½ hours). A variety of day tickets are available for unlimited trips – a circular ticket for the three islands costs L15,000 (children aged four to 11,

L8000) – although many unhurried visitors opt for single-trip tickets costing L8800 (children aged four to 11, L4400). Services are reduced in low season.

A good trip to take is a circular excursion from Stresa to Domodossola, from where you get a charming little train to Locarno (take your passport) and a ferry back to Stresa (L46,000; children aged four to 11, L23,000).

LAKE COMO

Marie Henri Beyle first set foot on the shores of Lake Como (Lago di Como) as a 17-year-old conscript under Napoleon. Years later, as Stendhal, he wrote in *La Chartreuse de Parme* (1839) that the blue-green waters of the lake and the grandeur of the Alps made it the most beautiful place in the world. Pliny the Elder and Pliny the Younger were born here but are not known to have gushed about the area to the same degree as Stendhal. In any case, many people would no doubt consider Como's other famous son as having achieved quite a deal more for the world: Alessandro Volta, born in 1745, came up with, well, the battery.

The town of Como, 50km north of Milan, is the main access town to Lake Como, sitting at the foot of the immense body of water which sprawls another 51km north to create an upside-down 'Y' shape. On the last Saturday of the month, its streets are filled with a huge antiques market – a fabulous excuse for a day trip here. Boating is the other big thing to do. Ferries yo-yo year-round between Como and the fairytale lakeside villages around the lakeshore: Must-sees include **Villa d'Este** at Cernobbio, a monumental 16th-century villa that is now a hotel (see Places to Stay & Eat later in this section); **Isola Comacina**, the lake's sole island, where Lombard kings took refuge from invaders; and **Villa Carlotta** near Tremezzo, with its magnificent gardens. Pretty **Bellagio**, the 'pearl' of the lake 30km north of Como, sits plump on the point where the western and eastern arms of the 'Y' split.

Bathers wanting to wash the city dust out of their hair should note that Lake Como's waters are murky. Swimming, though permitted in parts, is inadvisable.

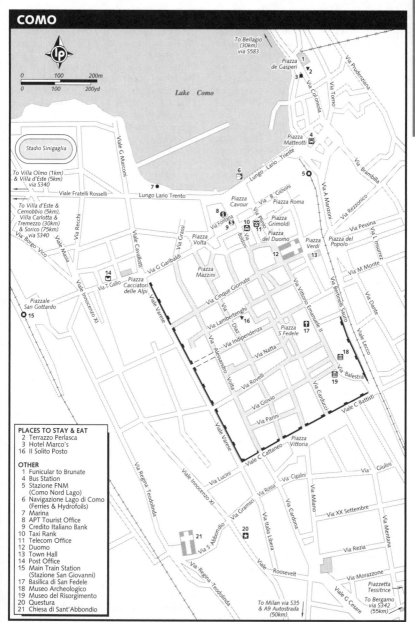

COMO

To Bellagio
(30km)
via S583

Piazza
de Gasperi

Lake Como

Stadio Sinigaglia

To Villa Olmo (1km)
& Villa d'Este (5km)
via S340

To Villa d'Este &
Cernobbio (5km),
Villa Carlotta &
Tremezzo (30km)
& Sorico (75km)
via S340

Lungo Lario Trento

Lungo Lario Trieste

Piazza
Matteotti

Piazza
Cavour

Piazza Roma

Piazza
Grimoldi

Piazza
del Duomo

Piazza
Verdi

Piazza del
Popolo

Piazza
Volta

Piazza
Mazzini

Piazza
Cacciatori
delle Alpi

Piazzale
San Gottardo

Piazza
S Fedele

Piazza
Vittoria

Piazza
Tessitrice

To Milan via S35
& A9 Autostrada
(50km)

To Bergamo
via S342
(55km)

PLACES TO STAY & EAT
2   Terrazzo Perlasca
3   Hotel Marco's
16 Il Solito Posto

OTHER
1   Funicular to Brunate
4   Bus Station
5   Stazione FNM
    (Como Nord Lago)
6   Navigazione Lago di Como
    (Ferries & Hydrofoils)
7   Marina
8   APT Tourist Office
9   Credito Italiano Bank
10 Taxi Rank
11 Telecom Office
12 Duomo
13 Town Hall
14 Post Office
15 Main Train Station
    (Stazione San Giovanni)
17 Basilica di San Fedele
18 Museo Archeologico
19 Museo del Risorgimento
20 Questura
21 Chiesa di Sant'Abbondio

Orientation & Information

The APT office (☎ 031 26 97 12, e apt info@lakecomo.org), on Como's main town square overlooking Lake Como at Piazza Cavour 17, is a 600m walk from the main train station (Stazione San Giovanni). It opens 9 am to 1 pm and 2.30 to 6 pm (closed Sunday in winter). Visit its Web site at www.lakecomo.com.

Boats depart a little way along the shore from the piazza, and it's only a short walk along Lungo Lario Trieste from Stazione Ferrovia Nord Milano (FNM), a smaller train station running frequent shuttles to/ from Milan.

Things to See & Do

From Piazza Cavour, walk along arcaded Via Plinio to Piazza del Duomo and Como's marble-faced **duomo**, built and repeatedly altered from the 14th to the 18th centuries. The cathedral combines elements of Baroque, Gothic, Romanesque and Renaissance design and is crowned with a high octagonal dome. Next to it is the polychromatic **town hall**, altered in 1435 to make way for the cathedral.

The **Basilica di San Fedele**, Via Vittorio Emanuele II, named after the saint who brought Christianity to the Como region, went up in the 6th century but has had numerous facelifts since. On the same street, Palazzo Giovio houses the **Museo Archeologico**, with important prehistoric and Roman remains, and Palazzo Olginati is home to the **Museo del Risorgimento**, with mementoes from Garibaldi's period – he actually stayed in this building for a time. Both open Tuesday to Sunday.

Above the lakeside town, **Brunate** peers down on Como and its watery surrounds from a 720m-high perch. A funicular whisks walkers and lake-gazers up from the funicular station on Piazza de Gasperi (L41007200 one-way/return). Walking trails also scale the hill – reckon on at least two hours hiking up. The APT office has information on other walks in the area, including a 50km trail from **Cernobbio**, 5km north of Como, to **Sorico** on the lake's northern tip.

Places to Stay & Eat

In Como, lakeside *Villa Olmo (☎ 031 57 38 00, Via Bellinzona 6)* is 1km from the main train station; bus Nos 1, 6, 11 and 14 stop 20m short of the hostel. B&B costs L24,000. The hostel opens March to November.

At the other extreme, Cernobbio's regal *Villa d'Este (☎ 031 34 81, e info@villdeste .it, Via Regina 40)* is ideal for those with a bottomless bank and a taste for queenly pleasures. Singles/doubles cost L570,000/ 890,000 (L765,000/1,150,000 high season).

Back in Como, Joe Bloggs won't come to any harm checking into *Hotel Marco's (☎ 031 30 36 28, Via Coloniola 43)*, with well-kept rooms costing about L120,000/ 170,000.

Sandwich bars and self-service restaurants are abundant in Como's pedestrian grid. One notch up, *Il Solito Posto (☎ 031 27 13 52, Via Lambertenghi 9)* is a reliable lunch spot; as is *Terrazzo Perlasca (☎ 30 39 36, Piazza de Gaspari 8)* at the foot of the funicular and dishing up nice water views.

Getting There & Away

Trains from Milan's Stazione Centrale arrive at Como's main train station (listed on timetables as Stazione San Giovanni). Journey times is 35 minutes and trains run hourly from about 7.15 am to 9.30 pm. Trains from Milan's Stazione Nord (Stazione Cadorna) are more frequent (one hour, about every 30 minutes) and arrive at Como's Stazione FNM (the last stop, listed as Como Nord Lago) – timed to link with ferries.

Navigazione Lago di Como (☎ 031 57 92 11), Piazza Cavour, operates ferries year-round to numerous spots across the lake, including Cernobbio (L2400 one-way, eight minutes), Isola Comacina (L9000, 1¼ hours), Tremezzo (L11,100, 1½ hours) and Bellagio (L11,100, 1¾ hours, or 45 minutes by hydrofoil). Day tickets allowing unlimited trips are also available.

BERGAMO

postcode 24100 • pop 118,300
• elevation 249m

Virtually two cities, Bergamo's walled hilltop upper town *(città alta)* – from where

MILAN

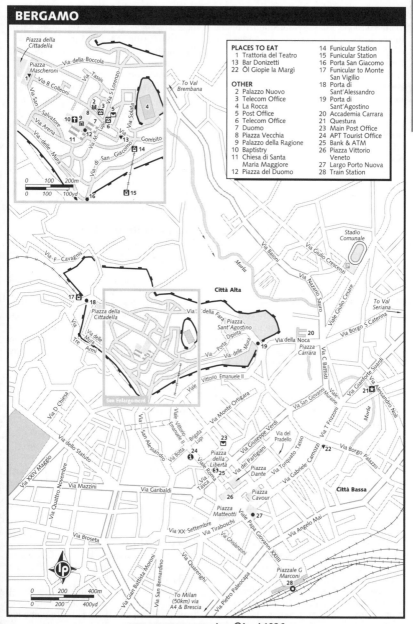

BERGAMO

PLACES TO EAT
1 Trattoria del Teatro
13 Bar Donizetti
22 Öl Giopie la Margì

OTHER
2 Palazzo Nuovo
3 Telecom Office
4 La Rocca
5 Post Office
6 Telecom Office
7 Duomo
8 Piazza Vecchia
9 Palazzo della Ragione
10 Baptistry
11 Chiesa di Santa Maria Maggiore
12 Piazza del Duomo
14 Funicular Station
15 Funicular Station
16 Porta San Giacomo
17 Funicular to Monte San Vigilio
18 Porta di Sant'Alessandro
19 Porta di Sant'Agostino
20 Accademia Carrara
21 Questura
23 Main Post Office
24 APT Tourist Office
25 Bank & ATM
26 Piazza Vittorio Veneto
27 Largo Porto Nuova
28 Train Station

euro currency converter €1 = L1936

Milan's skyscrapers 50km south-west are visible on a clear day – is surrounded by the lower town *(città bassa)*, the sprawling modern counterpart to this magnificent former outpost of the Venetian empire. Although long dominated by outsiders, Bergamo has retained a strong sense of local identity, best expressed in the Bergamaschi's local dialect – all but incomprehensible to visitors. The old city's wealth of medieval, Renaissance and Baroque architecture, coupled with tempting cuisine, are reasons to take a day-trip here.

Information

In the lower town, the APT office (☎ 035 21 31 85) is at Viale Vittorio Emanuele II 20, the road swinging east around the old-town walls to enter the città alta at Porta di Sant' Agostino. Its upper, old-town equivalent, Vicolo Aquila Nera 2 (☎ 035 23 27 30), opens 9 am to 12.30 pm and 2 to 5.30 pm.

Things to See & Do

Piazza Vecchia – medieval Bergamo's heart – is hard to miss. Whichever way you enter the walled hill-top town (a funicular covers the last leg of the climb from the lower town), you'll soon find yourself in this gracious square. Imposing **Palazzo della Ragione**, built in the 12th century but largely reconstructed four centuries later, fills its southern side. Next to it, **Torre Civica** still tolls the 10 pm curfew. Climb to the top for wonderful views; it opens March to September daily and weekends year-round.

The core of Bergamo's spiritual life, **Piazza del Duomo**, lies immediately behind. Bizarrely, its modest Baroque **duomo** plays second fiddle to neighbouring **Chiesa di Santa Maria Maggiore** (1137), an imposing Romanesque church whose weather-worn exterior hides a lavish Baroque interior. Its octagonal **baptistry** (1340) was originally built inside but was shifted outside in the 19th century. The gaudy **Capella Colleoni** (1470–76) is an extravagant addition to the church and named after its architect.

Stroll downhill along Via B Colleoni and Via Gombito, past **Torre Gombito**, a 12th-century tower, and turn left to **La Rocca**,

Bergamo's 14th-century fortress. Views from here are splendid – but even more splendid from the top of **Monte San Vigilio**, linked by another funicular from Porta di Sant' Alessandro.

Through Porta di Sant'Agostino, cobbled Via della Noca leads to **Accademia Carrara**, an art gallery dating to 1780 and containing an impressive range of Italian masters, particularly of the Venetian school. Look out for an early *St Sebastian* by Raphael and for works by Botticelli, Canaletto, Lorenzo Lotto, Andrea Mantegna, Giovanni Tiepolo and Titian. It opens 9.30 am to 12.30 pm and 2.30 to 5.30 pm Wednesday to Monday. Admission costs L5000 (those aged over 60 and under 18, free).

Places to Stay & Eat

Bergamo is an easy day trip from Milan – what hotels there are fill up distressingly quickly.

Culinary pleasures to sample for lunch include *casonsei* (ravioli stuffed with meat) accompanied by a fine red Valcalepio from the region and *polenta e ösei* (little sponge cakes with jam, covered with yellow icing and topped with chocolate birds and more jam). Try them at *Trattoria del Teatro (☎ 035 23 88 62, Piazza Mascheroni 3)* or the lower town's more touristy *Öl Giopì e la Margì (☎ 035 24 92 06, Via Borgo Palazzo 27)* where handsome young Bergamaschi run around in local costume (closed August).

Typical Lombardian wine and cheese, including the region's very own gorgonzola, can be sampled at *Bar Donizetti (☎ 035 24 26 61, Via Gombito 17)*, a down-to-earth *enoteca* (wine bar) completely devoid of any pretension. Pavement cafes abound around Piazza Vecchia and under Via Gombito's porticoes.

Getting There & Away

From the train station on Piazza G Marconi there are trains to/from Milan's Stazione Porta Garibaldi (a handful from Stazione Centrale too). Journey time is between 50 minutes and one hour (at least hourly between 5.30 am and 10.30 pm). Bergamo has

MILAN

direct rail links with Brescia (45 minutes) and Cremona (1½ hours) too.

To reach Bergamo by car from Milan, take the A4 autostrada or S11. On entering Bergamo note that the 'centro' signs refer to the città bassa. Follow the 'città alta' signs for the old city. Bus No 1 connects the train station with the funicular to the upper town.

BRESCIA
postcode 25100 • pop 200,000
• elevation 149m

When the Romans took control of Brescia (the name derives from a word meaning 'hill') in 225 BC, the Gallic town already had hundreds of years of obscure history behind it. Charlemagne and his successors were in the driver's seat in the 9th century, followed for 1000 years by a parade of outside rulers. During the 1848 and 1849 revolutions in Europe, Brescia was dubbed 'The Lioness' for its 10-day anti-Austrian uprising – an unsuccessful prelude to its participation in the movement towards Italian unification a decade later.

Although a little rough around the edges, this provincial capital and arms-production centre 50km south-east of Bergamo and

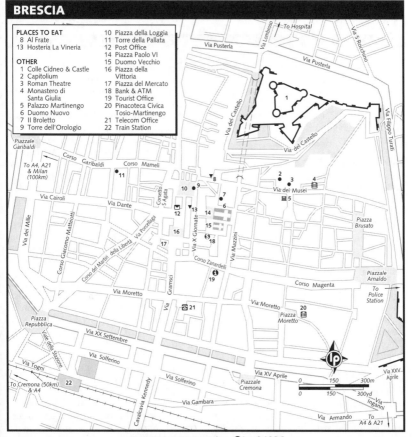

BRESCIA

PLACES TO EAT	10 Piazza della Loggia
8 Al Frate	11 Torre della Pallata
13 Hosteria La Vineria	12 Post Office
	14 Piazza Paolo VI
OTHER	15 Duomo Vecchio
1 Colle Cidneo & Castle	16 Piazza della
2 Capitolium	Vittoria
3 Roman Theatre	17 Piazza del Mercato
4 Monastero di	18 Bank & ATM
Santa Giulia	19 Tourist Office
5 Palazzo Martinengo	20 Pinacoteca Civica
6 Duomo Nuovo	Tosio-Martinengo
7 Il Broletto	21 Telecom Office
9 Torre dell'Orologio	22 Train Station

Cremona

Cremona (pop 81,000) jealously maintains its centuries-old status as premier exponent of the delicate art of making the perfect string instrument. All the great violin-making dynasties started here – Amati, Guarneri and Stradivari – and there's plenty of opportunity to get better acquainted with the craft; ask at the APT office (☎ 0372 232 33), Piazza del Comune 5, for a list of workshops.

In Cremona's rust-red heart, there's a small violin collection of Amatis, Guarneris and a 1715 Stradivari in **Palazzo Comunale**, Piazza del Comune. Items from the Stradivari workshop are displayed in the **Museo Stradivariano**, Via Palestro 17. Never is there a more melodious time to visit than during the International String Instrument Expo every third October; the next is in 2003.

Cremona is an easy day trip by train from Milan's Stazione Centrale, via Treviglio (L9900, two hours, seven to 12 daily). By car, follow the S415 (Paullo exit); the A21 takes you to Brescia, where it joins with the A4.

JANE SMITH

100km east of Milan, is worth a trip for its Roman relics and ecclesiastical treasures. The APT office (☎ 030 4 34 18/10, **e** aptbs@feriani.com), Corso Zanardelli 38, with a Web site at www.bresciaholiday.com, opens 9 am to 12.30 pm and 3 to 6 pm weekdays, and 9 am to 12.30 pm Saturday.

Things to See & Do

Brescia's historic centre is dominated by **Colle Cidneo**, topped by a rambling **castle** that's been the core of the city defences for centuries. Its main round tower, **Torre Mirabella**, was built by the Viscontis in the 13th century. One of Italy's most extensive collections of weapons can be seen in the castle's **Museo dell'Armi Antiche**, while its neighbour, the **Museo del Risorgimento**, deals with Italian unification history. The grounds around the castle walls – a smoochers' hang-out – can be freely wandered.

At the foot of the castle on Via dei Musei are the remains of the **Capitolium**, a Roman temple built in AD 73, and a modest **Roman theatre**. More intriguing is **Monastero di Santa Giulia** (☎ 030 297 78 34), Via dei Musei 81b, in which the city museum, open 9.30 am to 5.30 pm Tuesday to Sunday, is housed. The star piece of its collection is the 8th-century Croce di Desiderio, a Lombard cross encrusted with hundreds of jewels.

Admission costs L10,000 (those aged over 65 and under 16, L7000).

Heading west, Brescia's central square, **Piazza Paolo VI**, is dominated by the uniquely shaped **Duomo Vecchio**, an 11th-century Romanesque basilica built over a 6th-century circular structure and dwarfed by its neighbour, the Renaissance **Duomo Nuovo**. To its north-west is Piazza della Loggia, with its squat 16th-century **loggia** (lodge) in which Palladio had a hand, and **Torre dell'Orologio**. The tower's exquisite astrological timepiece (1544) is modelled on the one in Venice's Piazza San Marco. South-westwards lies the **Piazza della Vittoria**: laid out by Piacentini in 1932 and dating to the Fascist era, its a perfect example of the period's monumentalism.

On Piazza Moretto, the **Pinacoteca Civica Tosio-Martinengo** features works by artists of the Brescian school as well as by Raphael.

Places to Eat

Corso Mameli and Via dei Musei are Brescia's 'happening' eating and drinking streets, with plenty of restaurants, cafes and bars to sample *risotto*, or one of the city's many traditional beef dishes, accompanied by a bottle of fine regional wine from Botticino, Lugana and Riviera del Garda. *Hosteria La Viniera (Via X Giornate 4)*, which doubles as an *enoteca*, is a good place to indulge in *degustazione* (tasting).

If you have L50,000-plus in your wallet head for *Al Frate* (✆ *030 375 14 69, Via dei Musei 25)*, a charming place serving well-presented regional dishes – it's often full.

Getting There & Away

The train station is a 10-minute walk from the city centre. Brescia (one hour) is on the Milan–Verona–Venice railway line; trains from Milan's Stazione Centrale run almost hourly between 6 am and 10.15 pm. Other services include to/from Bergamo and Cremona (both 45 minutes).

By car, the A4 and S11 head to Milan and the A21 and S45 head to Cremona.

PAVIA

postcode 27100 • pop 85,000
• elevation 77m

Originally the Roman Ticinum, Pavia later rivalled Milan as the capital of the Lombard kings until the 11th century. The city became a pawn of power politics as the Renaissance dawned, being occupied by Spain in the early 16th century, Austria in the 18th century and France from 1796 until 1859.

Today this thriving industrial and agricultural centre, 40km south on the banks of the River Ticino, is virtually a satellite of Milan. Christopher Columbus was among the notable graduates to attend Pavia's prestigious **university** on Corso Strada Nuova, while self-taught physicist Alessandro Volta, who discovered the electric volt, lectured here. Don't believe any tale you might be told about Columbus' ashes being held in a safe in the director's office – the Genoese adventurer is buried in Spain.

Things to see in town include the forbidding **Castello Visconti** (1360) with its two massive towers (of the original four) watching over the northern end of the medieval city; the 14th- to 19th-century **duomo** topped by the third largest dome in Italy (and a bell

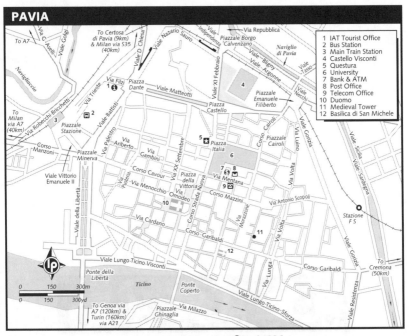

PAVIA

1	IAT Tourist Office
2	Bus Station
3	Main Train Station
4	Castello Visconti
5	Questura
6	University
7	Bank & ATM
8	Post Office
9	Telecom Office
10	Duomo
11	Medieval Tower
12	Basilica di San Michele

tower which toppled over in 1989, killing four people); and Romanesque **Basilica di San Michele** (1090) where Barbarossa was crowned Holy Roman emperor in 1155.

Pavia's big must-see is **Certosa di Pavia** (1396), a splendid Carthusian monastery 9km north of the centre. It was founded by the Visconti family and was among the most lavish buildings produced during the Italian Renaissance. Its Gothic interior shelters a giant sculpture made in 1409 from hippopotamus teeth, including 66 small bas-reliefs and 94 statuettes. Behind the 122 arches of the larger cloisters are 24 cells, one for each monk. Several are among the open to the public. Admission is free.

The IAT office (☎ 0382 2 21 56), Via Filzi 22, produces a decent map and information brochure. To get here from Piazzale Minerva, across from the train station at the western edge of the centre, walk north-east along Viale Battisti for about 400m.

Risotto peppered with small frogs *(risotto con le rane)* is Pavia's culinary speciality.

Getting There & Away

Eight daily trains run from Milan's Stazione Centrale or Stazione Porta Garibaldi to Certosa di Pavia (35 minutes) and Pavia (40 minutes).

By car, take the A7 autostrada from Milan and exit at the Bereguardo or Gropello C turn-off. To stop at Certosa di Pavia en route, take the S35 instead and turn off at Torre del Mangano; the charterhouse is well signposted from here.

SHOPPING IN MILAN

Anything that money can buy can be snapped up in Milan which, alongside Paris and London, ranks as one of Europe's greatest places to shop. As well as tasty food and wine shops, the city is known for its fashion boutiques – everything from the fabulous and fanciful to the frighteningly hideous – and design shops where rare and original pieces can be found: furniture is its main draw, although designers in this centre of innovation turn their hand to automobiles, paper and other design too.

Milan's historical Quadrilatero d'Oro (Golden Quad) embraces most upmarket and exclusive fashion boutiques, although there are plenty of affordable shops selling clothing, footwear and accessories behind the duomo around Corso Vittorio Emanuele II; between Piazza della Scala and Piazza San Babila; and around Via Torino, Corso XXII Marzo and Corso Buenos Aires. In the 1960s Giorgio Armani dressed the windows of La Rinascente, the city's only real department store, on the northern side of Piazza del Duomo (open 9 am to 10 pm Monday to Saturday, and 10 am to 9 pm Sunday).

Markets fill the waterfronts around the canals, notably on Viale Papiniano on Tuesday and Saturday mornings. There is a flea market at Viale Gabriele d'Annunzio on Saturday and a decent antique market in Brera at Via Fiori Chiari every third Saturday of the month. Milan's version of Portobello Road, a huge market where you can buy just about anything is held on the last Sunday of each month on the Alzaia Naviglio Grande and Ripa di Porta Ticinese.

BOOKS

This city is a bookworm's delight. Bookshops are spacious, well-stocked and they welcome browsing biblophiles with seats, stools and/or sofas on the shop floor where one can read in peace. Books in English are shelved in the *stranierie* section. With the exception of Rizzoli, which opens daily, the shops listed below open 9 or 9.30 am to around 7 or 8 pm Monday to Saturday.

ASA ANDERSSON

Mainstream

Feltrinelli

(☎ 02 760 00 618, metro MM1/3 Duomo) Piazza del Duomo and Via Alessandro Manzoni 12. The branch on Piazza del Duomo is inside the Autogrill shopping complex; its second branch has a particularly wide range of newspapers and glossy magazines.

Messaggerie Musicali

(☎ 02 760 55 404, metro MM1/3 Duomo) Galleria del Corso 2. This mega media store on Corso Vittorio Emanuele II has English-language novels, travel literature, and works by Italian writers in its 2nd-floor international bookshop. There is an exhaustive array of maps and guides on the 1st floor and international press can be located on the ground floor.

Nuova Libreria Rizzoli

(☎ 02 864 61 071, metro MM1/3 Duomo) Galleria Vittorio Emanuele. If you can fight your way past the tourist hordes, you'll uncover a fabulous range of translated works by Italian writers, Italian-inspired travel literature, Italian history books and novels in English, as well as foreign newspapers and magazines. Its smaller branch, above McDonald's on the western side of Piazza del Duomo, touts a kids' play area and computer terminals where you can surf the Net for free.

Foreign

American Bookstore

(☎ 02 87 89 20, metro MM1 Cairoli) Via Manfredo Camperio 16. One of two exclusively Anglophone bookstores catering solely to English speakers.

English Bookshop

(☎ 02 469 44 68, e tmpanton@hotmail.com) Via Mascheroni 12. A well-stocked English-language bookshop with a great range of fiction, dictionaries, language-learning text books and books about Italy. Annoyingly, many titles are plastic-wrapped, making it impossible to flick through them prior to purchase.

Île de France

(☎ 02 760 01 767, metro MM1 San Babila) Via San Pietro all'Orto 10. Books in French from the city's only *libreria francese*.

Specialist

Franco Maria Ricci

(FMR; metro MM1 San Babila) Via Durini 19. Beautiful books on art and theatre (in Italian) by one of Italy's most exclusive publishing houses can be enjoyed at this small bookshop with an interior designed like a theatre. Don't miss its *Enciclopedia di Milano* or *Teatro alla Scala*, both exquisitely illustrated. It stocks rare books too. It opens 10 am to 1 pm and 2 to 7.30 pm Monday to Saturday.

Libreria dell'Automobile

(☎ 02 760 06 624) Corso Venezia 43. Pull into this motoring bookstore, stacked full of books and manuals on anything and *everything* to do with cars (including the Italian Grand Prix and FIAT); there are reams of stuff in English. It opens 2.30 to 7 pm Monday and 9.30 am to 7 pm Tuesday to Saturday.

Libreria del Mare

(☎ 02 864 64 426, e info@libreriadelmare.it, metro MM1 Cordusio) Via Broletto 28. This marine library has titles covering everything from storm tactics to superyachts, as well as navigational maps and sailing guides. It opens 9.30 am to 1 pm and 3.30 to 7.30 pm weekdays.

Libreria dello Spettacolo
(☎ 02 864 51 730, ⓔ info@libreriadellospettacolo.it, metro MM1/2 Cadorna Triennale) Via Terraggio 11. Most titles are in Italian but this theatre-, cinema- and music-book specialist is well worth a browse nonetheless. It has a Web site at www.libreriadellospettacolo.it.

Libreria di Via della Spiga
(☎ 02 760 11 819, metro MM3 Monte Napoleone) Via della Spiga 30. An excellent range of art, architecture, design and fashion titles can be enjoyed at this 'golden quad' shop, open 3 to 7 pm Monday and 10 am to 7 pm Tuesday to Saturday. Failing that, take a two-minute walk to the 1st-floor bookshop inside Emporio Armani (see Fashion later), also crammed with fashion and design titles.

Touring Club Italiano
(☎ 02 535 99 71, metro MM3 Missori) Corso Italia 10. The nearest you'll get to a travel bookshop, minus the literature, with an extensive range of guidebooks and maps.

CHILDREN'S FASHION & TOYS

La Rinascente is as good as place as any to shop for mainstream games, toys and trinkets for kids, as well as for all the paraphernalia that comes with having a kid. Nano Bleu (☎ 02 760 20 595, metro MM1 San Babila), with shops at Corso Vittorio Emanuele II 15 and Via San Pietro all'Orto 3, sells a heart-melting menagerie of cuddly toys and dolls.

Children aspiring to be the best-dressed designer kid on the block should drag their parents straight to Pinco Pallini (metro MM3 Monte Napoleone), a house for children's fashion at Via della Spiga 40.

Naj-Oleari (☎ 02 805 67 90, metro MM3 Monte Napoleone), Via Brera 8, sells fabulous designer handbags made from scrunched-up paper balls (for rich kids and adults alike), and playful and practical innovations for children.

Exquisite dolls' houses – and everything from bookshelves to pots and pans to furnish them with – are crafted in astonishing detail at Cosediunaltro Mondo (☎ 02 659 91 10, ⓔ casette@tin.it, Metro MM2 Moscova), Via Solferino 25. Its workshop also restores old dolls' houses.

DESIGN

Design shops and galleries in the world's design capital are spread throughout the city. Magazines with occasional listings to look out for in newspaper stands include *Interni*, a monthly design magazine founded in 1954 with bilingual texts in English and Italian. Others that have grown on the back of the design industry include *Abitare*, *Domus* and *Casabella*, an architectural journal.

Furniture

Original Panton chairs, Memphis' New-Design *Carlton* stack of shelves produced in Milan in 1981, and the lush-lipped *Bocca* sofa all form part of the awe-inspiring 1950–2000 collection at Galleria Mode (☎ 02 869 09 48, ⓔ info@modernmariato.it) on the corner of Corso Vittorio Emanuele II at Via San Paolo 1.

Nilufar, Via della Spiga 32, is another pricey boutique dealing exclusively in rare and/or original furniture designed between 1950 and 2000.

Area Design (☎ 02 802 99 561), Via Borromei 11, specialises in designer chairs, tables, lamps and other collector items from the 1960s, 1970s and 1980s.

Heading towards Stazione Centrale, you pass Kartell's large white space at Via Turati 1 (☎ 02 659 79 16, @ kartell@kartell.it) where you can pick up a reproduction of Ron Arad's *Bookworm* bookshelf, Philippe Starck's transparent chair and oodles of other popular plastic designs.

Further north from the centre, on the corner of Viale Crispi and Via Varese, Understate (☎ 02 626 90 435) stocks some beautiful pieces, including reproductions of Frank Gehry's *Wiggle Side Chair* first carved out of corrugated cardboard in 1972.

There are larger furniture shops with more moderately priced reproductions and pieces by lesser-known designers on Via Larga, on the corner of Corso Matteotti and Via San'Pietro all Orlo, and at Via Durini 16–18.

Accessories

Kitsch reigns at Emporio Casa at Corso Europa 2; and Koivu (☎ 02 760 22 118), Corso Europa 12, which specialises in feet-shaped weighing scales, flower-filled toilet seat covers and 'David' glow lamps that would even make Michelangelo smirk. Another place to shop for kitsch is Gong (☎ 02 87 68 78), Via Mercato 20, where bizarrely shaped soaps, pen holders and plastic jewellery reign supreme. Similar items – soap shaped like egg boxes, micro-scooters and electrical appliances – fill Moroni Gomma (☎ 02 79 62 20), Corso Matteotti 14. Alessi (☎ 02 79 57 26), Corso Matteotti 9, is directly opposite.

There's another clutch of design shops on Corso Monforte and Via Damiano, a two-minute walk east from Piazza San Babila. Light specialist Flos (☎ 02 760 01 641) displays 1950s designs by Castiglioni, and contemporary creations by Philippe Starck and Jasper Morrison et al, at its two showrooms at Corso Monforte 9 and Piazzetta Giordono 2 opposite. Artemide (☎ 02 760 06 930), Corso Monforte 19, is another well-known design house for lighting fixtures. Spectacular creations by Alberto Meda, Paolo Rizzatto and a handful of guest designers light up LucePlan (☎ 02 760 15 760), around the corner at Via San Damiano 5. Bohemian souls will find ethnic lamps at Etnie (☎ 02 83 73 098), Corso di Porta Ticinese 67.

Shop for boldly designed cutlery (silver and stainless steel) and kitchen utensils at Zani&Zani, a well-known 1970s Italian design house with a striking showroom on the corner of Via San Damiano and Corso Venezia. The latest in bathroom accessories fill DePadova (☎ 02 77 72 01), a huge space at Corso Venezia 14.

La Pharmacia della Via Durini (☎ 02 760 02 613), Via Durini 25, is crammed with exotic gems, jewels and knick-knacks from around the world. There's an equally rich collection of lacquered bowls, monumental mirrors, silk scarves and drapes at TAD (☎ 02 86 90 110), near Emporio Armani on Via Croce Rossa.

All things glass is the mainstay of Bicchiere Vetrerie di Empoli Spa, a quaint boutique at Via Monte Napoleone 14. Galleria Scaletta di Vetro (☎ 02 79 59 28), inside the pedestrian gallery opposite Teatro Manzoni, off Via Manzoni, also sells expensive bowls, vases and sculptures.

Automobile Design

Free spirits can buy their very own Vespa to love and cherish at the Piaggio Centre (☎ 02 319 61 212, ℮ andrea.ventura@piaggio.com), Corso Sempione 43, open 2.30 to 7 pm Monday; 9 am to 12.30 pm and 2.30 to 7 pm Tuesday to Friday; and 9 am to 1 pm and 2 to 6.30 pm Saturday. Its Web site is at www.piaggio.com.

Mercedes Benz, inside Galleria Emanuele II, sells wallets, key rings and other objects embossed with the Mercedes logo. A stage showcases the latest Mercedes Benz car and there's a multimedia studio with a huge screen and the latest in video technology to oggle at.

Paper Design

Paper has been made by hand at Fabriano (☎ 02 763 18 754), Via Verri 3, since 1872. Calendars, guestbooks and photograph albums all star in its superb contemporary collection. It can make paper to measure too.

Ordning & Reda (☎ 02 869 96 630, ℮ milano@ordnin-reda.com), Via Fomentini 5, specialises in Swedish paper design – agendas, diaries, eyeball-shaped mousepads – in striking primary colours.

For handmade paper embedded with flower petals, ribbons and pretty boxes shop at Papier, off Via Torino on Via Maurilio.

FASHION

Key information on Milan's world of fashion can be found in *The World Fashion Book Italia*, the industry manual published by ADG Communication (☎ 02 584 30 123, ℮ adgcomm@tin.it) and listing everything from fashion houses and photographers to modelling agencies and make-up artists. Annual and twice-yearly editions (March and October) can be subscribed to via its Web site at www.worldfashion book.com.

Select where you want to shop by how much cash you wish to spend. Window shoppers and those with a bottomless wallet can head for the golden quad: everyone else should head elsewhere.

Quadrilatero d'Oro

This is Europe's fashion Mecca, where the world's best-known designers showcase the season's creations in state-of-the-art boutiques. The legendary 'golden quad' (metro 'MM3 Monte Napoleone') is sketched out by Via della Spiga (north), Via Sant'Andrea (east), Via Monte Napoleone (south) and Via Alessandro Manzoni (west).

Big names stud traffic-free **Via della Spiga**, including: Florentine designer Robert Cavalli at No 42, whose sensuality-driven designs dress Whitney Houston; Madonna's favourite fashion house, Dolce & Gabbana (see the boxed text 'Interior Design' later in this section); and a clutch of Milan-bred couturiers (listed later in this section). New York's bejewelled Tiffany sparkles at 19a, Sergio Rossi sells shoes at No 15 and Massimo Piombo at No 34 is a small Genoese fashion house. Invest in that perfect pair of gloves from Sermoneta at No 46.

Via Borgospesso and **Via Santa Spirito** prance off southwards from here. Malhas, at Via Santa Spirito 10, showcases the ultimate in evening wear, with glittering bustiers oozing outrageous sex appeal.

Interior Design

The interior design of some shops is simply so striking that the items they sell become a mere detail.

British architect David Chipperfield came up with Dolce & Gabbana's golden-quad boutique – a minimalist affair where a peacock-blue jacket, say, hangs in splendid isolation in a glamorous white space.

Ritmo Latino's interior (☎ 02 760 04 600), inside Galleria del Toro at Corso Matteotti 22, is just so fabulous that it takes a while to fathom out what it actually sells: the shop floor is glass and there are precious rocks underneath.

Concrete meets glass in the boutique of Genoese designer Massimo Piombo (☎ 02 760 08 226), Via della Spiga 34 (second entrance on Via Senato). Real-time video clips flash across a giant screen, walls are cast from raw concrete, glitzy chandeliers light the place and clothes are hung as art installations.

Replay (☎ 02 763 10 196), Corso Vittorio Emanuele II, an easily affordable store with a fountain in its basement, a jungle of plants and denim-ware laid out to bare on stones, is the most down-to-earth of the lot.

Via Sant'Andrea unveils Armani and Kenzo (opposite the Museo di Milano), Cesare Paciotto (for shoes), Japanese pleat-maniac Issey Miyake, Chanel, Moschino, Prada, Helmut Lang and Fendi (for glitzy bags and jackets).

Via Pietro Verri, the southern continuation of Via Sant'Andrea, offers ample opportunity to off-load more cash: try John Richmond, Jil Sander, Yves St-Laurent and Berluti (at No 5), which has cobbled men's shoes since 1895. Shadeless shoppers, who'd rather melt into the Milanese crowd, can invest in that all-essential pair of Nouvelle Vague or Gigli sunglasses at Occhi Ali (☎ 02 78 19 99), a trendy 'eyewear shop' (they're not called opticians these days) at Piazza Meda 3/5. Borsalino on this street, with another shop on Piazza alla Scala, is one of Milan's oldest and most reputable milliners (see the boxed text 'Mad as a Hatter' later in this section).

Shoppers seeking shoes should strut straight to **Monte Napo** – as those who shop here refer to this exclusive street, darling: Bally, Camper, Sergio Rossi, Salvadore Ferragamo, Fausto Santini and Fratelli Rossetti are all here. Leather-lover Louis Vuitton is at No 14, next to Emilio Pucci, a Florentine fashion house best known for its sports (including stunning ski) wear. Those seeking diamonds as a best friend can try the police-guarded Cartier shop on the corner of Via Monte Napoleone and Via Gesu; or Damiani at Via Monte Napoleone 16, founded in Milan in 1924 and known worldwide for its bold and original jewellery designs. Glittering gobstoppers aside, its dramatic geometric marble facade and dazzling spots make Italy's leading diamond house impossible to miss.

The northern end of Manzoni sizes up equally well with Brit Paul

VIA
MONTE
NAPOLEONE

219

Shirts, ties and some
sharp-looking suits: if
you're into big names
then the Napoleone
fashion district will be
right up your street.

NEIL SETCHFIELD

MARTIN MOOS

Top: An impressive archway leads to Galleria Vittorio Emanuele II's glass-domed arcades.

Bottom: Versace shopfront, Via Monte Napoleone

Prada is this person's particular bag. On the tiles at the Galleria Vittorio Emanuel II, shop around for yours.

If the shoes fit, then splash out on some high-fashion Italian footwear. But if you're not out to spend, while away some hours window shopping or people watching.

Smith at No 30 and Armani's revolutionary flagship store opposite. Armani is one of a handful of fashion's Milanese maestros:

Armani
(☎ 02 760 03 234) Via Sant'Andrea 9. Descend the concrete ramp to find the basement Armani Uomo (men's collection) or head up high for Armani Donna (women's collection); note Milanese brolly etiquette in rainy weather. Armani Accessori is at Via della Spiga 19; his casual wear for both genders is at Via Durini 22; clothes for (rich) kids are at Via Durini 23; and Armani's formal *collezioni* is next door at No 25.

Emporio Armani
(☎ 02 723 18 630) Via Manzoni 31, other entrances on Via Pisoni and Via Croce Rossa. Armani's designer department store, covering 6000 sq m, made international headlines with its innovative 'democratic fashion' when it opened in October 2000. Find Sony's latest cutting-edge technologies in the basement; flowers, perfume, cafe, sushi bar, and the Armani Donna, Uomo and Accessori collections on the ground floor; and Armani Casa, jeans, books, another cafe and Nobu – the powerhouse of Japanese restaurants – on the 1st.

Mariella Burani
(☎ 02 760 03 382) Via Monte Napoleone 3. Burani is notable for her five differing collections aimed, among others, at the young 'n' trendy woman (Amuletti collection), the city woman (Selene) and the larger-sized woman (Piu'donna).

Gianfranco Ferré
Via della Spiga 11. Buy power-dressing designs by the northern Italian designer, who broke into design as an assistant at a raincoat manufacturer in Genoa and has since made enough dosh to live on the shores of Lake Maggiore.

Gucci
This Florence-founded firm has been at Via Monte Napoleone 5 since 1951. The last Gucci to rule the leatherware empire, Maurizio Gucci, was shot outside his 1st-floor office at Via Palestro 20 in 1995. His murder was later traced to his estranged wife Patrizia Reggiani, who apparently paid US$285,000 to have Gucci assassinated. She was sentenced to 26 years in prison in 1998; the last media report from her Milan prison cell was an alleged suicide attempt in November 2000.

Public since 1995, the Gucci Group notched up sales in December 2000 alone of some US$145 million, a 25% increase on the previous year. The group holds majority stakes in Yves St-Laurent, Sergio Rossi, Boucheron, Swiss watchmakers Bédat & Co (whose watches cost from US$4000 to US$30,000) and British designer Alexander McQueen. The group's gross profits rose from US$168.1 million in 1995 to US$693 million in 1998.

Krizia
(☎ 02 760 08 429) Via della Spiga 23. Fashion house named after Plato's woman- and beauty-loving character called Crizia, founded by Bergamo-born designer Mariuccia Mandelli in the 1950s. Among other treasures, it owns one of the world's most exclusive celebrity get-away spots, the K-Club hotel on Barbuda island (sailing distance from Antigua).

Missoni
Prêt-à-porter knit classics make Missoni stand tall at Via Sant'Andrea 2. Rosita Jelmini (born 1932) and Tai (born 1921), both from northern Italy, made cameras flash in 1967 when Missoni models marched down the catwalk bra-less – and wearing very thin knits. Designs are bold and multicoloured.

Gio Moretti

Via della Spiga 4. Long-standing Milanese boutique known for having the latest avant-garde designs by international fashion houses before anyone else. Try here for designs by the Nina Ricci fashion house, founded by the Turin-born designer of the same name; and creations by Puccini's Milan-born granddaughter, Elvira Biki.

Moschino

Fried eggs for blazer buttons and models dripping in irony are among the notable trademarks of Milan's wild child, Moschino, with shops at Via Sant'Andrea 12 and Via Durini 14. An art student at the Brera Academy, Franco Moschino (1950–94) illustrated Versace collections in the 1970s before launching his own in 1984. Bold political messages tag most Moschino creations – among the first to flaunt fake 'ecologically-friendly' fur on the catwalk.

Prada

This powerhouse, with shops at Via Monte Napoleone 6, Via Sant'Andrea 21 and Via della Spiga, made headlines (including within the archrival Gucci Group) when it materialised that Prada had bought 9.5% of Gucci stock. Prada started life in 1913 as a leatherware shop in Milan. Granddaughter, Miuccia Prada and husband Patrizio Bertelli run the house, known for its wearable fashions, today. Understatement is its big buzz word and Miu Miu (Miuccia's nickname) is its cheaper, more garish and fun label.

Valentino

V is for Valentino – Mario Valentino (born 1932) – whose high-society designs dress most of Hollywood. Born north of Milan, the designer moved to Paris in his teens and to Rome in the 1960s – all out of love for the fashion industry in which he made a splash with his first collection in 1962. Producing prêt-à-porter, haute-couture and lines for younger dressers, V has boutiques at Via San Spirito 3, and on the corner of Via Sant'Andrea and Via Monte Napoleone.

Versace

Despite its southern Italian origins, Versace – with boutiques at Via Monte Napoleone 11 and Via San Pietro all'Orto 10 and 11 – has its nails clawed firmly under Milan's skin. Scooping prize after prize with his sumptuous and extravagant designs, Gianni Versace (1946–97) was the industry king in the 1980s. His first Milan store opened in 1978 and he launched big-name models such as Kate Moss. *Men Without Ties*, *Do Not Disturb*, *Rock & Royalty* and *The Art of Being Yourself* are among the photographic titles Versace published before his murder outside his Miami Beach villa in 1997. Sting, Princess Diana, Elton John and Naomi Campbell attended his funeral in Milan's duomo. He is buried next to his villa on Lake Como.

Corso Vittorio Emanuele II & Around

South of the golden quad stretches Corso Vittorio Emanuele II (metro MM1/3 Duomo and MM1 San Babila), a wide pedestrian street lined head to toe with shops. Mainstreamers such as Intersport and Footlocker (sports gear), Benetton and Onyx (teen fashion), Swatch (watches), Body Shop (smelly stuff) and Replay – *the* hot spot for alternative jeans, denim skirts and other streetwear – live here, alongside more exclusive labels such as Stefanel (sexy French fashion), Furla (luxury bags), Moreschi (leather goods) and shoemakers Vergelio, Bruno Magli and Pollini.

Shop-laden galleries dart off north and south from here. Inside **Galleria Passarella**, the hot link between Corso Vittorio Emanuele II

Mad as a Hatter

Milan was Europe's leading manufacturer of ribbons, gloves, bonnets and hat straw in the 16th century, hence the word 'milliner', which originated in 1529 – the name the English gave to the Milanese haberdashers who sold such fineries.

But it was the hatters in England who turned out to be mad. The deadly quicksilver (mercury) they used to stiffen and shape felt hats made them as mad as a hatter (a phrase coined in 1839). Milliners make and sell women's hats today.

and Corso Europa, you'll find funky Zap (a mixed bag of marginally more affordable labels including Kookai, Liv Jo and Christian Lacroix) and Fiorucci Fashion Market, a large 1970s-style shop crammed with glitter-coated hair grips, comic strip t-shirts, heart-shaped cushions, fake-fur-covered filofaxes and other kitsch accessories.

Versace graces **Via San Pietro all'Orto** and Calvin Klein stands tall at Via Durini 14, a ridiculously large store neighboured by Milan's Moschino. Vito Nacci holds court in a palace at Via Durini 11, while BCBG Maxazria sports some really fun designs (and its own restaurant) at No 21. Hugo Boss overlooks Piazza San Babila at the eastern end of Corso Matteotti.

Elsewhere

Pedestrian **Via Dante** (metro MM1 Cordusio) is a good street for budget-conscious shoppers. More mainstream names such as Mephisto (shoes), Max & Co (women's fashion), Petit Bateau (cute kid's clothes) and Lush (luscious bath salts and soaps) line its length.

Via Torino (metro MM1/3 Duomo) is another safe bet for shoppers lacking cash to splash about. Reasonably priced street fashion is sold at Energie, Via Torino 19, which sports sofas to lounge on and copies of *The Face* to flick through while your mate's trying stuff on. Salmoivaghi & Vigino at No 22 sells shades.

Alternative dressers seeking a touch of youthful bohemia should shop on **Corso di Porta Ticinese** (metro MM3 Missori), linking Largo Carrobbio with Porta Ticinese near Navigli. The boutiques at Nos 46, 48, 60 and 78 (northern end of the street) are all worth a gander for their hip, Alexander McQueen-style tops, trousers and skirts stitched from a wealth of unexpected fabrics.

FOOD & DRINK

For gourmet eating head for Peck, Milan's exclusive three-storey food store at Via Spadari 7–9, with an online home delivery service at www.peck.it. Established in 1883, it is among Europe's elite gourmet outlets – if anything, more tempting than London's Harrods or Fortnum & Mason – and famous since 1920 for its home-made *ravioli*. Wandering around in here (strongly advised) will open your eyes to undreamed of culinary delights, ranging from cheeses (up to 3500 variations of

ASA ANDERSSON

Parmigiano alone) to 30 types of coffee beans, 120 tea types and numerous freshly prepared meals to take home. Take a look at the fine wines (three quarters of them Italian) which cost anything from US$10 to US$1000! Peck opens 3 to 7.30 pm Monday, and 8.45 am to 7.30 pm Tuesday to Saturday.

Sweets & Chocolates

Bananas, mushrooms, chestnuts, cobs of corn and other fruits and vegetables are crafted from marzipan with uncanny realism at Pasticceria Fratelli Freni (☎ 02 87 70 72), Via Torino 1. It has a second outlet straddling Corso Vittoria Emanuele II at Via Beccaria 3.

Wine

Peck's wine cellar (see earlier in this section for details) is impeccable. N'Ombra de Vin (☎ 02 659 96 50), Via San Marco 2, is another well-established Milanese cellar, open 4 to 7.30 pm Monday, and 8.30 am to 1 pm and 4 to 7.30 pm Tuesday to Saturday. It has a very educational Web site at www.vinoplease.it.

Parini Drogheria (☎ 02 760 02 303, ℮ parini@parinidrogheria.it), Via Monte Napoleone 22, with a Web site at www.parinidrogheria.it, has displayed evocative racks of wine, biscuits, Torrini Baci (chocolate kisses wrapped in a secret love message) and other temptations in its red-brick cellar since 1913. Equally tempting displays of similar products fill Principessa Hortensia (☎ 02 805 49 20), Via Santa Maria alla Porta 11.

Wine and olive oil are the specialities of Verdi & Pancani, a quaint shop at Corso Italia 6 that has been in business since 1898. Olea (☎ 02 720 99 330), Via dell'Orso 18, specialises in olive oil and balsamic vinegar.

MUSIC

The best bet for recordings of the great sopranas and tenors singing their heart out at Milan's fabulous opera house is, predictably, La Scala Bookstore (☎ 02 869 22 60, metro MM1/3 Duomo) which adjoins the theatre on Piazza alla Scala. As well as CDs, it stocks operatic posters and a small selection of books too, and operates a search service for rare recordings. It opens 3 to 7 pm on Monday, 10 am to 7 pm Tuesday to Saturday, and during performance intervals. It has a Web site at www.lascalabookstore.com.

Smash hits can be listened to before purchase inside multi-floored RicordiMediaStores, which has outlets at Corso Buenos Aires 33 (☎ 02 295 26 244, metro MM1 Lima) and inside Galleria Vittorio Emanuele II (☎ 02 864 60 272, metro MM1/3 Duomo). It offers online shopping through its Web site at www.ricordimediastores.it.

Turin

- postcode 10100
- pop 950,000
- elevation 287m

A gracious city of wide boulevards, elegant arcades and grand public buildings, Turin (Torino in Italian) rests in regal calm beside a pretty stretch of the River Po in the Piedmont region. Touting itself as Europe's capital of Baroque, the city – with its palatial ducal residences, porticoed squares and multitude of magnificent mansions – definitely has the air of a capital *manqué* rather than some provincial outpost. Although much of the industrial and suburban sprawl west and south of the centre is predictably awful (and, unfortunately, the only image many who've never been to the city have of it), there's actually an enormous green belt in the hills east of the river, proffering splendid views of the snow-covered Alps to the west and north.

Turin, the Savoy capital from 1559 and as such ranked among Europe's most modern and best fortified cites, was for a brief period after unification the seat of Italy's parliament. It was also the birthplace of Italian industry and remains its cradle. Giants such as FIAT (Fabbrica Italiana di Automobili Torino) lured hundreds of thousands of impoverished southern Italians to Turin and housed them in vast company-built and -owned suburbs such as Mirafiori to the south. FIAT's owner, the Agnelli family – which also happens to own Juventus football club, Turin's local newspaper and a large chunk of the national daily *Corriere della Sera* – is one of Italy's most powerful establishment forces. But Turin itself is a left-wing bastion. Industrial unrest on FIAT's factory floors spawned the Italian Communist Party under the leadership of Antonio Gramsci and, in the 1970s, the left-wing terrorist group called the Brigate Rosse (Red Brigades).

There's far more to Turin than FIAT cars however – which is where its fabulous element of surprise kicks in. Often 'written off' as 'industrial', most people turn up in Turin with zero expectations of the city and leave avid fans of the place. The most precious of its oddball collection of world-famous products is the Holy Shroud, the linen in which Christ's body was supposedly wrapped after his crucifixion. Generally kept under wraps, the cloth lures thousands of pilgrims to the city every few years when the Pope and Archbishop of Turin decide to pull the Shroud out for public veneration; 2000 was the last such occasion.

Turin's tastiest product is chocolate (which maybe explains those old-fashioned weighing scales chained to columns beneath the porticoes on many central squares and streets). Gold-wrapped Ferrero Rocher chocolates and Nutella – inspired by Turin's hazelnutty *gianduia* cream – are made here, and master chocolate-makers and confectioners such as Peyrano and Leone still craft their sweet products by hand. Lavazza coffee, likewise roasted in Turin, Martini & Rossi, Cinzano, sparkling Asti and Italy's great velvet reds of Barbaresco and Barolo are other naughty-but-nice culinary pleasures that await visitors.

Most Turinese claim their city is an hour away from anywhere – it is almost true. Cosmopolitan Milan and the Genoese seaside are both short train journeys away, while some of Europe's most glamorous ski pistes and greatest peaks – Mont Blanc (Monte Bianco) just across the border in neighbouring France and the Matterhorn (Monte Cervino) in neighbouring Switzerland – are spitting distance west. The generous sprinkling of Alpine resorts and villages in-between will host the Winter Olympics in 2006.

Getting Around

ORIENTATION

Stazione Porta Nuova, the central train station built by Mazzucchetti in 1865, is the main point of arrival. Trams and buses from in front connect it with the historic centre, which is quite spread out. Busy Corso

Vittorio Emanuele II is the main east-west route and Via Roma links the station (south) with Piazza Castello (north). Piazza Carlo Felice, the square in front of the train station, and Via Nizza which continues south past it, is the main axis of Turin's seedier side of life and can be dodgy at night.

The Mole Antonelliana dominates the horizon to the east, near Via Po (the student area), Piazza Vittorio Veneto and the mighty River Po. Across the water on its right (eastern) bank is the quarter of Borgo Po and hills. Some of Turin's great palaces, the Lingotto Fiere congress centre and industrial plants sprawl south of the city centre.

CASELLE AIRPORT

Turin is served by Caselle international airport (☎ 011 300 06 11), 16km north-west of the city centre. Flight schedules are posted on its Web site at www.turin-airport.com.

TO/FROM THE AIRPORTS

The Società Autotrasporti della Dalmazia e Montenegro (SADEM; ☎ 011 300 01 66, e sadembus@tin.it) runs buses from Stazione Porta Nuova (40 minutes) and Stazione Porta Susa (30 minutes) to the airport, departing every 30 minutes between 5.15 am and 10.30 pm (6.30 am and 11.30 pm from the airport). A single ticket costs L6000 (L7000 on board). Its Web site at www.sadem .it includes up-to-date schedules.

At Stazione Porta Nuova, tickets are sold at Caffè Cervino, the unmarked bar at Corso Vittorio Emanuele II 57 (close to the corner of Via Sacchi); look for the sign in its window reading 'Biglietteria SADEM Aeroporto Caselle'. Buses use the stop on the corner of Corso Vittorio Emanuele II and Via Sacchi. At Stazione Porta Susa, Bar Milleluci at Piazza XVIII Dicembre 5, sells tickets. At Caselle airport, tickets are available at the kiosk (signposted 'bus tickets') next to the ATM in the arrivals hall or from the automatic dispenser inside the main entrance. Buses to/from Caselle airport stop in front of the arrivals hall (domestic flights exit).

Buses for Milan's Malpensa airport leave from the main bus station, west of the centre on Corso Inghilterra (see To/From Malpensa

Airport in the Milan chapter for full details). Additionally, Alitalia operates a Volobus service from Stazione Porta Nuova to Malpensa (two hours, twice daily). A one-way ticket is an extortionate L200,000 and seats must be reserved in advance (☎ 1478 6 56 41 in Rome). The service is free for Alitalia passengers who can even check in their luggage at Alitalia's Stazione Porta Nuova office (☎ 011 669 02 46) before hopping aboard.

SADEM (see earlier) runs one bus daily to/from Caselle airport and Aosta (1½ hours) year round. An updated schedule is posted on SADEM's Web site at www.sadem.it.

PUBLIC TRANSPORT

The city's dense network of buses, trams and a funicular is run by Azienda Torinese Mobilità (ATM; ☎ 800 01 91 52 toll-free, e atm@atm.torino.it), with a Web site at www.comune.torino.it/atm. Tickets are sold at its information booth at Stazione Porta Nuova, open from 7.15 am to 7 pm Monday to Saturday and 10 am to 4.30 pm Sunday.

Tickets are also sold at tobacconists. There are automatic ticket dispensers at both the train stations and at larger bus and tram stops. To validate your ticket, punch it in the orange machines on board buses, trams and the funicular. An urban ticket valid for 90 minutes costs L1500 (10-ticket carnet L14,500) and a four-hour *biglietto shopping* (valid 9 am to 8 pm) is available for L3000. An all-day pass costs L5000.

Journeys within the outer suburbs require a suburban ticket (L1500, valid for 60 minutes); those between the centre and suburbia (to Rivoli or Stupingi for example) require an urban-suburban ticket (L2400, valid 70 minutes).

Services generally run 6 am to midnight.

CAR & MOTORCYCLE

Driving in Turin is chaotic (and a nerve-racking experience for non-speed fiends). Everything is comparative however and if you've arrived fresh from Milan, for example, you'll find Turin's marginally more genteel motorists a joy to engage in road combat with. Parking your car will most likely present the greatest challenge (see that section below).

Motoring information, road maps and guides are provided by the Automobile Club Torino (ACT; ☎ 011 5 77 91), Via San Francesco da Paola 20a, open 8.30 am to 1 pm and 2 to 5 pm weekdays. The automobile club is online (in Italian only) at www.acitorino.it.

There are 24-hour petrol stations on the corner of Corso Vittorio Emanuele II and Corso Massimo d'Azeglio; on Corso Inghilterra; and on Piazza Borromini on the other side of the river.

Car Rental

ACT (☎ 011 562 35 14, 011 577 92 71), at Via San Francesco da Paola 20a, rents cars at competitive rates. Other rental companies include:

Avis (☎ 011 470 15 28) Caselle airport; (☎ 011 669 98 00) Stazione Porta Nuova; (☎ 011 50 08 52) Corso Filippo Turati 37
Europcar (☎ 011 567 81 65) Caselle airport; (☎ 011 650 20 66) Stazione Porta Nuova
Hertz (☎ 011 567 81 66) Caselle airport; (☎ 011 669 91 58) Stazione Porta Nuova
Italy by Car (Thrifty) (☎ 011 567 80 96) Caselle airport
Maggiore (National) (☎ 011 470 19 29) Caselle airport; (☎ 011 650 30 13) Stazione Porta Nuova

Parking

Parking is a nightmare. Thankfully, however, the Turinese don't give a damn who parks where, meaning it's quite acceptable to abandon your vehicle in the middle of certain streets (literally) or on the pavement. Street parking (in official spaces) costs L1600 per hour.

The APT office doles out a free brochure entitled 'Moving Round the City' which maps out Turin's most central car parks (generally L2000 per hour or L22,000 per day). These include ones on Piazza Solferino, Corso Umberto I and Corso Galileo Ferraris; near the river on Piazza Vittorio Veneto; and within walking distance of Stazione Porta Nuova at the southern end of Via Roma and on Piazza Bodini.

TAXI

Call ☎ 011 57 37/0 or ☎ 011 33 99 for a cab.

BICYCLE

Some streets tout a separate cycle lane for two-wheelers and several cycling routes are signposted across the city.

You can hire a bicycle at the left-luggage desk (signposted 'deposito bagagli'), opposite the tracks at Stazione Porta Nuova, from 6 am to midnight. Rental costs L5000/7000/12,000 for six/12/24 hours.

BOAT

ATM also runs Navigazione sul Po (☎ 800 019 15 12 toll-free) which operates boat trips on the River Po. Boats depart from Imbarco Murazzi, Via Murazzi del Po 65. Return trips include to Borgo Medioevale (L4000), Italia 61 (L8000) and Moncalieri (mid-June to the end of September only, L10,000). Departures are six times daily (weekends only in May, and three times daily on Sunday and holidays, October to April).

ATM's Torino Pass (L15,000), valid for one day, covers one boat ride, a return trip on the Sassi-Superga funicular and unlimited use of buses and trams.

ORGANISED TOURS

Ask about ATM's trips by Touristibus (which, so the brochure says, 'lead and pet you'). At the time of writing, a two-hour city tour departed at 2.30 pm daily and three-hour excursions to either Agliè or Moncalieri departed at 2.30 pm Friday and Saturday. Tickets cost L12,000 (children aged under 12 years L10,000) and are also valid for the day on public transport. Buses depart from the stop on the Via Po side of Piazza Castello.

ATM also runs shuttlebuses (navette turistiche) to/from Rivoli, Venaria Reale and La Mandria, departing three to five times at weekends and holidays. Tickets, sold at ATM offices and tourist offices, cost L5000 (those aged over 65 and under 18, L4000; those aged under 14, free) and get you reduced admission fees at the palaces.

The Centro Guide Torino (☎/fax 010 562 41 00, ✉ centroguideto@tiscalinet.it), Via Peyron Amedeo 8a, organises thematic city tours (historical cafes, palaces of Savoy, etc) in Italian only. Tours depart at weekends and cost L15,000 (those aged eight to 18, L8000). Reservations can be made at the APT office on Piazza Castello. Guide Turistiche per Il Piemonte (☎ 011 812 94 65), Via delle Rosine 15, is another company that organises Italian-only city tours; again, the APT office has details.

Things to See & Do

Highlights

- Explore 18th-century tunnels beneath the city at the Museo Civico Pietro Micca

- Savour Turin's *caffè* society over a cup of *bicerin* in an old-fashioned cafe

- Watch old Italian movies or ride to the roof in a panoramic glass lift at the Museo Nazionale del Cinema

- Ride the funicular to the Basilica di Superga for some stunning views

- See how the Savoy kings lived at palatial Palazzo Reale

- Take a gastronomic trip south of Turin: taste Barolo wines, sample snails and see a psychedelic church amid vineyards

SUGGESTED ITINERARIES

Half-Day
Depending on your interests, either take in Piazza Castello's Palazzo Reale and Palazzo Madama, then stroll along Via Roma to a historic cafe; or head along trendy Via Po to the Mole Antonelliana and its Museo Nazionale del Cinema.

One Day
Spend the morning discovering Piazza Castello's sights, lunch in 19th-century splendour (at Baratti & Milano for example), then head along Via Po and across the river in the afternoon.

Two Days
Take your pick of Turin's museums and galleries on day one; then head out of town to Superga, Rivoli and/or Stupingi the following day.

PIAZZA CASTELLO

It is the vast squares and elegant boulevards that lend Turin its air of reserved majesty. Fittingly, there is no better place to start exploring the city than Piazza Castello, its grandest square in the heart of the historic centre and housing a wealth of museums, theatres and cafes in its porticoed promenades.

Essentially Baroque, the piazza was laid out from the 14th century to serve as the seat of dynastic power for the House of Savoy. When distinguished architects such as Filippo Juvarra (1678–1736) were taken on by the Savoys in the 17th and 18th centuries to transform Turin into one of Europe's great capitals, it was to Piazza Castello they turned. Aristocratic palaces were built and the fashionable thoroughfare of **Via Roma** – Turin's most fashionable catwalk since 1615 – was laid.

In the square's north-western corner is **Chiesa di San Lorenzo** (1666–80), designed by architect Guarino Guarini. Its rich interior compensates for its sparse facade.

Palazzo Madama
It was around **Porta Praetoria**, the eastern entrance to the Roman city of Augusta Taurinorum, that Piazza Castello sprung up. In the 13th century the two towers of the Roman gate were incorporated into a castle, the red-brick facade of which today forms the eastern wall of Palazzo Madama. This part-medieval, part-Baroque 'castle' dominating the square served as the residence of Madama Reale Maria Cristina, the widow of Vittorio Amedeo I, in the 17th century. It gained its magnificent western facade by Filippo Juvarra in 1718–21 and later served as a prison, military barracks, a royal cellar and seat of the subalpine senate (1848) and supreme court (1869).

Today the palazzo houses the **Museo Civico d'Arte Antica** (Civic Museum of Ancient Art; ☎ 011 442 99 11), closed until mid-2001 when restoration work should be complete. Some 30,000 paintings by 15th- to 18th-century masters are in its collection.

Palazzo Reale

Statues of Roman deities Castor and Pollux guard the entrance to the Royal Palace (☎ 011 436 14 55), residence of the House of the Savoy until 1865. The austere, apricot-coloured building was erected for Carlo Emanuele II around 1646, although its sumptuous interior of chandeliers and Chinese vases, gilded furnishings and coffered ceilings dates from the 17th to 19th centuries.

Particularly notable is the **Scala delle Forbici** (literally 'staircase of scissors'), a series of central ramps linking the entrance hall to the private apartments. The staircase (1720–21) was designed by Filippo Juvarra in anticipation of the arrival of Carlo Emanuele III's new bride, Anna Christina of Bavaria. It was considered a feat of modern engineering at the time, much to the joy of the Turinese architect who sculpted an ornamental pair of scissors in stone (supposedly to cut off the tongues of his critics) on his controversial creation.

Guided tours of the palace (in Italian only) whisk visitors through several rooms, including the dining room with its original parquetry floor (1732); the Chinese Room with its black lacquer panelling; Daniel's Gallery, used as the ballroom in the 18th century and named after the Viennese artist who painted its magnificent vaults (1688–92); and the so-called Machine Room where the queen's hand-cranked elevator arrived.

The Savoys stored their arms in the **Armeria Reale** (Royal Armoury; ☎ 011 518 43 58), tucked beneath the porticoes in the palace's eastern wing. Its collection of daggers, guns and other weapons is said to be among Europe's best. In the adjoining **Biblioteca Reale** (Royal Library; ☎ 011 54 38 55), dating to 1831, there are 200,000 volumes, 5000 16th-century books, several thousand manuscripts and a self-portrait scribbled in crayon by Leonardo da Vinci. Behind the wing are the **Giardino Reale** (see the boxed text 'Romantic Strolls').

Palazzo Reale and the Armeria Reale open 8.30 am to 7.30 pm Tuesday to Sunday. Admission to each costs L8000 (those aged 18 to 25, L4000; those aged over 65 and under 18, free). Visiting the gardens and library is free.

Archivio di Stato & Teatro Regio

Under the porticoes in Piazza Castello's north-eastern corner you'll find a couple of historic cafes, the **Archivio di Stato** (1730–34), the **Prefecture** (1733–57) and **Teatro Regio** (1740), and the **Nuova Regio** (built in 1943 on a former military academy site). These public buildings formed part of the *zona di comando* (command zone) – a complex linked to Palazzo Reale by a system of galleries and passageways allowing the Savoys to pass from one to another without sticking a small toe outside. Although it was the brainchild of Amedeo di Castellamonte (1673), the project did not kick off until 1714 and took 100 years to complete.

The **Archivio di Stato** (State Archives; ☎ 011 54 03 82, Ⓔ astoarchivio@multix.it), the first 'zone' building to be designed by Javarra, can be visited by guided tour at 9.30, 10.30 and 11.30 am on Monday and Thursday. Tours are free. The archives, split between here and a converted hospital (1817) at Via Piave 21, contain documentation from 13 centuries stored on 70km of shelves.

Duomo di San Giovanni

Linked to Piazza Castello by a covered walkway is the marble facade of Duomo di San Giovanni, Turin's only remaining piece of Renaissance architecture, on Piazza San Giovanni. It was built (1491–98) on the site of three 14th-century basilicas and shelters the **Shroud of Turin** (see the boxed text 'The Holy Shroud' under History in the Facts

TURIN

about the Cities chapter), a decent copy of which can be viewed in front of the altar. The adjoining **Cappella della Santa Sindone** (1668–94), rightful home since 1694 to the cloth in which Christ's body was supposedly wrapped after his crucifixion, has been closed for restoration since 1997 when it was severely damaged by fire. The Romanesque **bell tower**, standing alone to the left of the cathedral (1720–23), was designed by Juvarra.

Augusta Taurinorum

Just to the north of the cathedral you can see the remains of a 1st-century **Roman amphitheatre** and **Porta Palatina**, the red-brick remains of a Roman-era gate almost identical to its counterpart that stood on Piazza Castello. The forum of the Roman city probably stood a few blocks south on Piazza Palazzo di Città. The southern boundary of the castrum bordered Via Santa Teresa.

A bounty of archaeological finds from the ancient city of Augusta Taurinorum can be viewed in the **Museo d'Antichità** (☎ 011 521 22 51), Via XX Settembre 88c, a trip down 7000 years of memory lane to the earliest Pianura Padana (Po plain) settlements. The vast collection is in the former orangeries of Palazzo Reale, open 8.30 am to 7.30 pm Tuesday to Sunday. Admission costs L8000 (those aged 18 to 25, L4000; those aged over 65 and under 18, free).

PIAZZA CARIGNANO TO PIAZZA SOLFERINO

A wealth of palaces stud this aristocratic quarter which sprung up south of the historic centre in the 18th century.

Piazza Carignano sits a block south of Piazza Castello. Its western side is flanked by Teatro Carignano where Vittorio Alfieri's *Cleopatra* was premiered in 1775, and its southern side is blessed by **Chiesa di San Filippo Neri** (1714). Vittorio Emanuele II, Italy's first king, was born in **Palazzo Carignano** (1679–85), the palace on the square's eastern side. It was here that the Chamber of Deputies of the Kingdom of Sardinia met (1848–60) and where Italy's first parliament sat between 1861

and 1864 (until the capital was moved to Florence). Risorgimento architect, Camillo Benso di Cavour, was born and died in the neighbourhood at Via Lagrange 25, and Nietzsche stayed at Via Carlo Alberto 6 when in town in 1888.

Surrealist Dali and 'wrapping' fiends Christo & Jeanne Claude (who famously 'wrapped' the following's floors and staircases) are among those to have starred in the modern-art gallery inside 17th-century **Palazzo Bricherasio** (☎ 011 517 16 60), Via Lagrange 20. Those interested in modern art should make a short detour to **Galleria Civica d'Arte Moderna e Contemporanea** (☎ 011 562 99 11, ✉ gam@commune .torino.it), Turin's excellent contemporary art museum, further south at Via Magenta 31. Works of art by 19th- and 20th-century artists such as Renoir, Courbet, Klee and Chagall can be viewed whilst sitting down on Philippe Starck chairs. It opens 9 am to 7 pm Tuesday to Sunday. Admission costs L10,000 (reduced, L5000; first Friday of the month, free to everyone).

Museo Nazionale del Risorgimento Italiano

The short-lived parliament forms part of the excellent National Museum of the Italian Risorgimento (☎ 011 562 11 47), Via Accademia delle Scienze 5, with extensive displays of arms, paintings and documents tracing the turbulent century from the 1848 revolts to WWII (Italian captions only). It opens 9 am to 7 pm Tuesday to Sunday. Admission costs L8000 (those aged over 65 and under 25, L5000; those aged under 10, free).

Museo Egizio & Galleria Sabauda

In the 18th century young nobles studied at the **Palazzo dell'Accademia delle Scienze** (1679), a Jesuit college built from red brick at Via Accademia delle Scienze 6. The monumental edifice, the facade of which dates to 1787, was meant to stretch the whole way north to Piazza Castello. Since 1824 it has housed Turin's **Museo Egizio** (☎ 011 561 77 76, ✉ egizio@multix.it), a museum of ancient Egyptian art ranked second only to those in London and Cairo. Its mammoth collection originates from a bunch of antiquities Carlo Felice of Savoy purchased from a French consul in Egypt in 1824. Among its wealth of recreated tombs is that of pharaoh architect Kha and wife Merit; the contents displayed (unearthed in 1906) were buried with them and are believed to date to 1400 BC.

The royal art collection has been displayed in **Galleria Sabauda** (☎ 011 561 83 91), a showcase of 14th- to 19th-century Piedmontese, Italian and Flemish masters in the same building as the Egyptian Museum, since 1865. Catalogued by dynasty, it is easy to see exactly what each king bagged.

Both museums open 8.30 am to 7.30 pm Tuesday to Sunday. Admission to Museo Egizio costs L12,000 (those aged 18 to 25, L6000; those aged over 65 and under 18, free). Admission to Galleria Sabauda costs L8000 (those aged 18 to 25, L5000; those aged over 65 and under 18, free). A combination ticket costs L15,000 (reduced L7500).

PIAZZA SAN CARLO TO PIAZZA SOLFERINO

Walking a block west, around the southern side of Palazzo dell'Accademia delle Scienze, you emerge on Piazza San Carlo (1637–60), Turin's elegant drawing room where several renowned cafes recline in the shade of the square's characteristic porticoes – of which central Turin has 18km. Traffic revolves around an equestrian **statue of Emanuele Filiberto** (1838), the Savoy duke who made Turin the capital of his duchy. Twin Baroque churches, **Chiesa di San Carlo** (1619) and **Chiesa di Santa Cristina** (1715–18) cap the southern end of the square – 170m long and 75m wide.

A stroll west along Via Vittorio Alfieri brings you to Turin's banking district. **Palazzo Lascaris di Ventimiglia** (1663–5), home to the Consiglio Regionale dei Piemonte at No 19, has a lavish courtyard worth a peek. Those game for a laugh should walk a block north to the **Museo della Marionetta** (☎ 011 53 02 38), adjoining **Chiesa di Santa Teresa** (1642) at Via Santa Teresa

5. The Puppet Museum brings the history of 17th-century puppet theatre alive with marionettes. It opens 9 am to 1 pm weekdays, and 2 to 6 pm Saturday. Puppet shows are staged at 3 pm Sunday. Admission costs L5000 (children aged three to 13, L4000). Ring the bell to enter.

Another extremely elegant promenade is **Piazza Solferino**, over to the west. From the square's northern end, **Via Pietro Micca** (1885) leads straight back to Piazza Castello.

VIA GARIBALDI & AROUND

Medieval Turin, immediately west of Piazza Castello, was fortified until the 17th century. Its main thoroughfare was **Via Garibaldi**, lined today with affordable shops, cafes and pavement terraces. A chessboard of narrow pedestrian streets – a pleasure to get lost in – borders it to the north and south: **Via Mercanti**, **Piazza delle Consolata** and **Via delle Orfane**, named after the 16th-century orphanage at No 11 on the street, are all enchanting.

With the liberation of Turin in 1563, Emanuele Filiberto graced his ducal capital with a mighty star-shaped **citadel** (1564–8). Its flamboyant history is told in the **Museo Storico Nazionale dell'Artiglieria** (☎ 011 562 92 23), inside the keep (all that remains of the citadel) on the corner of Corso Galileo Ferraris and Via Cernaia. The museum opens from 9 am to 12.30 pm and 2 to 4.15 pm Monday to Thursday, and 9 to 11.45 am Friday. Admission is free.

Farther west, the modern face of Turin smirks with mischievous delight from its sky-high perch, a 1960s skyscraper housing RAI TV, at Via Cernaia 23.

Museo della Sindone

The Museum of the Shroud (☎ 011 436 58 32, ⓔ sindone@tin.it), Via San Domenico 28, does little to unravel the mystery of the Holy Shroud, despite informative displays and unexpected 'shroud' paraphernalia such as the first camera used to photograph the cloth (1898), the first colour photograph of it (1969), and test tubes used to store traces of human blood removed from the shroud in 1978. More information is included in the boxed text 'The Holy Shroud' under History in the Facts about the Cities chapter.

The museum can be visited by guided tour (in Italian) from 9 am to noon and 3 to 7 pm daily; ask for an English-language audioguide to avoid confusion. Admission costs L10,000 (those aged over 65 and under 13, L8000).

Museo Civico Pietro Micca

The might of Turin's citadel was tested in 1706 when the French besieged the Savoy capital, the drama of which is vividly captured in this fascinating museum named after the legendary hero of the four-month siege (see the boxed text 'The Pietro Micca Staircase'). Detailed captions in English outline French attacks on other fortresses in the Duchy of Savoy and there's a scale model of Turin before the Battle of Turin (1706). The highlight is a guided tour by torchlight of a 300m section of the defensive tunnels running beneath the city.

The museum (☎ 011 54 63 17), Via Guicciardini 7a, opens 9 am to 7 pm Tuesday to Sunday. Guided tours of the subterranean galleries run several times daily; at other times guides (Italian- and French-speaking only) will show you around if they have nothing better to do. Admission costs L5000 (free between 1 and 7 pm Sunday).

VIA PO TO BORGO PO

Turin's hip young scene, revolving around the city's university, can be freely enjoyed in the cafes and *trattorie* around **Via Po**, an arcaded street connecting Piazza Castello with the river, via Piazza Vittorio Veneto. It was known as one of Europe's widest and most beautiful streets in the 18th century and became home to the royal university, **Palazzo dell'Universita** (1712–30) at No 17, under Vittorio Alberto II.

The lumbering dome of **Grand Madre di Dio** in **Borgo Po** peeps across the length of Via Po. The church, built on the right (eastern) bank of the Po, was part of a 19th-century project that landscaped the waterside areas either side of the river. The steps leading up to the church were the steps which Michael Caine famously careered down in his mini in *The Italian Job* (see Films in the Facts for the Visitor chapter).

Ai Murazzi is an arcaded promenade stretching along the Po between Ponte Vittorio Emanuele I and Ponte Umberto I. The stone vaults embedded in the riverside embankments – used as wash- and dye-houses in the 1860s – are the hip venue for a clutch of underground bars and clubs (see Entertainment later in this chapter).

Museo Nazionale del Cinema

Considered by many to be Turin's most remarkable sight is the **Mole Antonelliana**, a couple of blocks north of Via Po at Via Montebello 20. Intended as a synagogue when it was started in 1863, this extraordinary structure – at 167m tall the world's highest traditional brick building – comes as something

---

The Pietro Micca Staircase

Some 10,000 men fought inside the citadel to their city when French and Spanish troops besieged Turin (1706) during the War of the Spanish Succession (1701–13). The enemy's meanest means of attack was underground – digging out tunnels to penetrate the citadel without anyone seeing. It was the task of the miners to ferret out the next attackers and lay explosives in their path.

Many of these subterranean galleries still exist 14m beneath the city. An estimated 15km run under the Museo Civico Pietro Micca – including the Pietro Micca staircase. This was built to link a lower and higher level of tunnels and was blown up on 28 August 1706 by Turin's war hero, Pietro Micca, to stave off attack. The explosion killed Pietro Micca and his mining comrades within a 40m radius; a crucifix adorned with fresh flowers testifies this.

The Pietro Micca staircase, as it came to be known, was only unearthed in 1958.

---

of a shock when you first see it from the surrounding narrow streets. Capped by an aluminium spire, it is a display of engineering as an art form (in a similar vein perhaps to the Eiffel Tower) and quite a spectral sight when lit up at night.

Since 2000 it has housed the equally riveting **Museo Nazionale del Cinema** (☎ 011 812 56 58), split across five floors and taking visitors on a fascinating interactive tour of cinematic history – from its birth through to the film production process and the movies that were made. Love, death, horror and Turin are among the themes illustrated with movie clips in 10 chapels – each better than a film set – in the Temple Hall; in the 'love' chapel you lie on a bed of red heart-shaped cushions to watch the movies, and in the 'humour' one you walk through an American fridge and sit on a toilet. In case you're still bored, 35mm films are screened in the Temple Hall and a wackier show of images is projected on its domed ceiling every 10 minutes or so. A breathtaking **Ascensore Panoramico** (Panoramic Lift) silently whisks you up in 59 seconds to the Mole's roof terrace.

The National Museum of Cinema opens 10 am to 8 pm Tuesday to Sunday (until 11 pm Saturday). Allow at least two hours to visit. Admission costs L10,000 (those aged 10 to 18, L8000; those aged under 10, free) and the lift costs L7000 (reduced L5000). A combined ticket costs L13,000 (reduced L10,000).

Borgo Po

On clear days a super silhouette of Basilica di Superga (see the 'Super Superga' boxed text) on the hillside can be enjoyed from **Ponte Vittorio Emanuele I** (1810–15), the stone bridge linking Piazza Vittorio Veneto with Borgo Po. The neoclassical **Chiesa di Gran Madre di Dio** (1818–31) here, set on an axis with Piazza Castello, was built to commemorate the return of Vittorio Emanuele I from exile in 1814. It was undergoing a L2 billion facelift in early 2001 and was closed.

From Piazza Gran Madre di Dio, a road spirals up **Monte dei Cappuccini** (284m), a hill used as a defensive outpost since Roman times. Carlo Emanuele I destroyed its medi-

Super Superga

In 1706, Vittorio Amedeo I promised to build a basilica to honour the Virgin Mary if Turin was saved from besieging French and Spanish armies. The city was indeed saved so architect Filippo Juvarra built the Basilica di Superga on a hill across the River Po to the north-east of central Turin. It became the final resting place of the Savoys, whose lavish tombs make interesting viewing. In 1949, the plane carrying the entire Turin football team crashed into the basilica in thick fog. The tomb of the team lies at the church's rear.

Take tram No 15 from Piazza Vittorio Veneto to the Sassi-Superga stop on Corso Casale, then walk 20m to Stazione Sassi, the funicular station (☎ 800 01 91 52 toll-free) at Strada Communale di Superga 4 (corner of Corso Casale). From here, a funicular chugs uphill about every 30 minutes between 9 am and 8 pm, Wednesday to Monday (between 9 am and 2 pm on Sunday). The journey time is 20 minutes and a single/return ticket costs L3000/6000 (L5000/8000 on weekends). If the line is closed (Tuesday and during bad weather), take bus No 79 from the stop on Strada Communale di Superga.

If you have a vehicle, the drive up through the thickly wooded Pino Torinese helps give the lie to the belief that Turin is little more than a polluted, industrial town.

eval fortification in 1583 to build **Chiesa e Conventa di Santa Maria**. From the terrace in front there's sweeping views of Turin and the western Alps.

One wing of the 17th-century convent now shelters the **Museo Nazionale della Montagna** (☎ 011 660 41 04, @ posta@ museomontagna.org), founded by the Club Alpino Italiano (CAI) in 1877. Exhibits focus on Alpine flora and fauna, as well as man's meddling with the mountain range and his attempts to scale the world's great peaks. The National Mountain Museum opens 9 am to 7 pm daily. Admission costs L10,000 (those aged over 65 and 10 to 18, L7000; children aged under 10, free).

From here, **Parco Valentino** is an easy walk away (see the boxed text 'Romantic Strolls').

PIAZZA CAVOUR TO PIAZZA CARLO EMANUELE II

Back on the left bank, a short stroll west along **Via Giovanni Giolitti** takes you past the bench-clad squares of Piazza Maria Teresa and Piazza Cavour to the **Museo Regionale di Scienze Naturale** (☎ 011 432 30 80, @ redazione.mrsn@regione.piemonte .it), Via Giovanni Giolitti 36. The Museum of Natural Science, several floors of which are closed for renovation until 2005, lives in the eastern wing of a 17th-century hospital. An Alaskan brown bear greets those who dare enter the animal-stuffed building, open 10 am to 6 pm Wednesday to Monday. Admission costs L5000. Part of Turin university occupies the hospital's western wing on Via Accademia Albertina.

A block north is **Piazza Carlo Emanuele II**, a square laid out with noble palaces and churches between 1675 and 1684. Daughters of the aristocracy studied at the convent and **Chiesa di Santa Croce Juvarra** (1718–30) on the square's southern side, and the brightest of the poorest attended the **Collegio delle Province** (1737) next door but one. Someone filthy rich resided at **Palazzo Coardi di Carpeneto** (1680), a palace at No 17 with a heavily embellished 18th-century stuccoed facade and ornate interior courtyard.

SOUTH ALONG THE PO

Walking south along the River Po, you come to **Castello del Valentino** (1621–42), a mock French-style chateau where Maria Cristina and Vittorio Amedeo I held their courtly frolics. It is closed to the public but it houses the architectural faculty of Turin polytechnic so you can wander around. The French-style park around it (see the boxed text 'Romantic Strolls') opened in 1856 and is among Italy's most celebrated – particularly by rollerbladers, cyclists and smooching young romancers. Equally admired are the **Orto Botanico** (☎ 011 670 74 47), Viale Mattioli 25, botanical gardens dating to 1729 and tended by green-fingered university profs.

The gardens can be visited from 9 am to 1 pm and 3 to 7 pm at weekends, April to September. Admission costs L5000 (those aged over 60 and under 10, L3000).

Farther south is Disney-style **Borgo e Rocco Medioevale** (☎ 011 443 17 01, @ borgo.medioevale@comune.torino.it), a 'medieval' fortress and village built for the Italian General Exhibition in 1884. The fortress opens 9 am to 7 pm Tuesday to Sunday. Admission costs L5000 (those aged over 65 and 18 to 25, L3000). Strolling the village 'streets' is free.

The first FIAT races into gear at **Museo dell'Automobile** (☎ 011 67 76 66), Corso Unità d'Italia 40 (south along Via Nizza). Among the museum's 400 masterpieces is the Isotta Franchini driven by Gloria Swanson in the film *Sunset Boulevard*. The museum opens 10 am to 6.30 pm Tuesday to Sunday. Admission costs L10,000 (those aged over 65 and under 15, L7000). Take bus No 34 from Stazione Porta Nuova.

Farther south still along Via Nizza is **Lingotto Fiere**, Turin's congress centre and exhibition hall. Until 1982 FIAT cars were manufactured in this former factory, constructed in 1912–23 and transformed into the architectural icon it is today by Renzo Piano (see the boxed text 'Renzo Piano' in the Facts about the Cities chapter). The distinctive ball of blue glass sheltering a conference room at the top of the building was Piano's creation, although Lingotto's crowning glory remains the **track** (1919) on its flat roof on which FIAT tested its cars. The track can be visited 8.30 am to 7.30 pm Tuesday to Friday and Sunday. Admission is free.

FIAT still churns out cars from its plant built in 1935–8 in the suburb of Mirafiori. Underground tunnels, built as air-raid shelters, allegedly link the monstrous complex.

Palazzina di Caccia di Stupingi

A visit to the Savoys' sprawling hunting lodge, in manicured grounds beyond Mirafiori, is a must. The Juvarra creation, a rococo delight, was designed for Vittorio Amedeo II in 1729. It is slowly being restored with FIAT money and many parts of the building are in original condition.

Pieces of art and furniture from the Savoys' collection of 17th- and 18th-century palaces are displayed in the **Museo di Arte e Ammobiliamento Storia** (Museum of Art and Furnishing; ☎ 011 358 12 20, e pstorico@mauriziano.it), open 10 am to 6 pm Tuesday to Sunday. Admission costs L10,000.

Take bus No 4 from Via San Secondo (near Stazione Porta Nuova) or along its southbound route from Piazza della Repubblica to Piazza Caio Mario, then bus No 41 to the palace (L2400).

ACTIVITIES

Turin's biggest playground is the surrounding mountains where Turinese dash to at weekends to walk, ski, climb, mountain bike, paraglide, etc. See Excursions later in this chapter for details.

Before donning walking boots, walkers might want to contact the CAI (☎ 011 54 60 31, e cai.torino@iol.it), Via Barbaroux 1. The club dating to 1863 has information on guided hikes and *rifugi* (mountain huts) in Valle di Susi and Valle d'Aosta (see Excursions later in this chapter). Its office opens 2.30 to 6.30 pm weekdays.

The Piscina Stadio Comunale Corso (☎ 011 442 17 07), Corso Galileo Ferraris 294, is one of the municipal's indoor swimming pools. Admission costs L6600 and 10-ticket carnets (L55,800) are available. Call first to check when it's open to the public.

COURSES

Learn Italian at the Oxford Centre which has centres at Via Barletta 45 (☎ 011 35 93 53), Via Bertola 47a (☎ 011 562 15 98) and Corso Dante 64 (☎ 011 663 15 33) and a Web site at www.oxfordcentre.it. Cultural Lab Lingua e Cultura (☎ 011 817 34 43, ☎/fax 011 817 34 39, e iclab@tin.it), Via Giovanni Giolitti 29, and Regency School (☎ 011 562 74 56), Via Arcivescovado 7, online at www.regency.it, are other schools. The APT office has a complete list. Francophones can study Italian at the Centre Culturel Français (see Cultural Centres under Information in the Facts for the Visitor chapter).

Romantic Strolls

Turin boasts a clutch of lovely parks and promenades just made for walking hand-in-hand. These include the **Giardino Reale** (Royal Gardens), landscaped in 1697–8 by André le Nôtre who also laid out the royal gardens at Versailles; the pretty green squares of **Piazza Cavour** and **Piazza Maria Teresa**; and waterfront **Parco Valentino**, the city's largest park, with kiss-me-quick pavilions and Parisian-inspired beds. All the promenades running along the River Po entice young lovers (and a menagerie of dogs, drunks, kids, babies and grannies), as do the Alpine vistas visible from terraces on Monte dei Cappuccini and Basilica di Superga.

Places to Stay

Accommodation in Turin is not cheap – but not expensive either when compared to Milan. Finding a bed to lie your head, in either a rock-bottom budget joint or a five-star palace, is relatively easy but seeking out a decent budget-to-mid-range place to stay midweek can be difficult. Cheaper places tout fixed rates, irrespective of the day, but many upmarket pads drop their prices by 10 to 15% Friday and Saturday night.

The APT office can tell you what is available where and make a reservation (for free) for you. It stocks comprehensive lists of places to stay around Turin for motorists seeking somewhere out of town.

PLACES TO STAY – BUDGET

Many budget places are ensconced on the 2nd, 3rd or 4th floor of an ageing building serviced by a rattling iron-cage style lift, or simply no lift at all. Most can only be accessed via an intercom on street level into which you yell. Check what time reception stays open until as many shut up shop at about 11 pm; few issue front door keys to night owls.

Several readers have written to complain of sporadic low water pressure (read: less than a pathetic dribble out of the shower head, making showering impossible) in some of these budget hotels. Many demand prepayment upon arrival, don't accept credit cards and don't serve breakfast.

Camping
Villa Rey (☎/fax 011 819 01 17, Strada Val San Martino Superiore 27) is about 3km east in the hills. It charges L7000/9000/2000 per person/tent/car and opens March to October. Take bus No 61 from in front of Stazione Porta Nuova to the end of the line, then bus No 54 from the corner of Corso Casale and Corso Gabetti to the site.

Hostels
Ostello Torino (☎ 011 660 29 39, fax 660 44 45, Via Alby 1), also east of the River Po, can be reached from Stazione Porta Nuova by bus No 52 Monday to Saturday and bus No 64 on Sunday and holidays. Ask the driver where to get off. B&B costs L24,000 from mid-October to mid-April and L22,000 the rest of the year. A meal costs L15,000.

Hotels – Around Piazza Castello
Little traffic passes by quiet *Albergo Canelli (☎ 011 54 60 78, 011 53 71 66, Via San Dalmazzo 5b)*, an ageing place off Via Garibaldi on the fringe of cobbled Turin. Bare but serviceable singles/doubles start at L25,000/35,000.

Nearby *Albergo Kariba (☎ 011 53 48 56, Via San Francesco d'Assisi 4)* charges L40,000/60,000/90,000 for singles/doubles/triples. Digs are marginally more comfortable but equally kitsch.

Albergo Duoma (☎ 011 436 03 47, Via Milano 18), on the 2nd floor of a spartan building near Repubblica market, has 10 rooms with shared bathroom costing L85,000 for one or two. Buzz the buzzer to enter.

No wonder the monumental statues tucked behind the twin churches of Piazza San Carlo frown: they stare at *Hotel Nazionale Torino (☎ 011 561 12 80, fax 011 53 89 89, Piazza CLN 254)*, an ugly concrete block. Singles/doubles warranting neither complaint nor exultation cost L135,000/190,000, including breakfast (15% discount at weekends).

Hotels – Around Stazione Porta Nuova
Cheapies abound around the train station. The clutch of one- and two-star joints in the less salubrious streets south-east of the station are best avoided by women travelling solo. Breakfast costs extra at these places.

Hotel Nizza (☎/fax 011 669 05 16, Via Nizza 9) is in a porticoed promenade on the 2nd floor of a shady street. Singles/doubles cost L70,000/100,000. Nearby *Albergo Paradiso (☎ 011 669 86 78, Via Berthollet 3)* is far from paradise but has dirt-cheap rooms costing L50,000/70,000 for one/two. There are a handful more cheap ('n dodgy) joints on Via Galliari.

Albergo Sila (☎ 011 54 40 86, Piazza Carlo Felice 80) touts clean and relatively modern rooms costing L80,000/100,000 per single/double with shared toilet (L120,000 with bathroom). It's on the 3rd floor.

Neighbouring neon-lit *Hotel Roma (☎ 011 561 27 72, fax 011 562 81 37, ℮ hotel.roma@tin.it, Piazza Carlo Felice 60)* is a solid budget to mid-range choice. 'Tourist' singles/doubles go for L80,000/115,000, 'economy' singles/doubles/triples are L118,000/151,000/161,000 and renovated rooms for one/two/three cost L139,000/172,000/189,000 (15% cheaper Friday and Saturday nights).

Large *Hotel Bologna (☎ 011 562 02 90, fax 011 562 01 93, Corso Vittorio Emanuele II 60)* is in a similar class but often full. Its scant handful of singles with shared bathroom cost L55,000 and more comfortable singles/doubles go for L100,000/150,000, including breakfast.

A couple of blocks north of the train station is *Hotel Campo di Marte (☎ 011 54 53 61, 011 53 06 50, Via XX Settembre 7)*, a 1st-floor hotel at the top of a dank staircase. Clean but rock-bottom singles/doubles go for L70,000/90,000. Walk east and you hit *Albergo Versilia (☎ 011 65 76 78, Via Sant'Anselmo 4)*, a basic place with a picturesque location opposite a synagogue. Count on L60,000/80,000 for a single/double here.

At the top end of this range are *Albergo Magenta (☎ 011 54 26 49, fax 011 54 47 55, Corso Vittorio Emanuele II 67)*, a small 2nd-

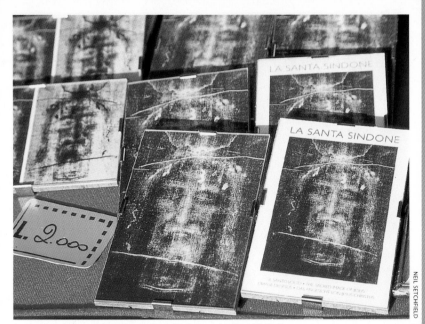

A selection of shrewd Shroud paraphernalia that can be found in Turin

The renowned chandelier-lit Caffè Torino, Piazza San Carlo, Turin

You'll probably take a shine to Via Roma, Turin.

The Mole (as the Turinese affectionately call it)

Launched in Turin in 1957: the Fiat Nuovo 500

Chiesa di San Lorenzo's remarkable dome

Making an impressive entrance at Palazzo Reale

floor hotel with pleasing rooms for one/two costing L90,000/120,000; and *Hotel Montevecchio* (☎ *011 562 00 23, fax 011 562 30 47, Via Montevecchio 13)*, a family-run place in a residential area with singles/doubles costing L110,000/140,000.

PLACES TO STAY – MID-RANGE

Unless otherwise stipulated, breakfast is included in the prices listed.

Hotels – Around Piazza Castello

Three-star *Hotel Venezia* (☎ *011 562 33 84, fax 011 562 37 27, Via XX Settembre 70)* is a chichi spot with two white china dogs that greet guests at the entrance. Graceful singles/doubles cost L150,000/200,000. In the same league, *Le Petit Hotel* (☎ *011 561 26 26, fax 011 562 28 07,* @ *lepetithotel@ satnet.it, Via San Francesco d'Assisi 21)* has rooms costing L160,000/210,000.

Just off grand and leafy Corso Umberto I is Via Brofferio, home to two good mid-range places, both undergoing facade facelifts at the time of writing and offering plenty of street parking: *Hotel Artuá* (☎ *011 517 53 01, fax 011 517 51 41, Via Brofferio 1)*, part of the reputable Logis d'Italia chain; and *Albergo Solferino Artuá* (☎ *011 561 34 44, fax 011 562 22 41, Via Brofferio 3)*. Both reside on the 4th floor of a grandiose townhouse. Singles/doubles cost L145,000/160,000.

Teetering on the edge of top end is *Hotel Chelsea* (☎ *011 436 01 00, fax 011 436 31 41, Via XX Settembre 79)* which touts a flower-filled terrace restaurant and comfortable L170,000/210,000 singles/doubles.

Mozart and Verdi were among the more distinguished guests to have slept at *Hotel Dogana Vecchia* (☎ *011 436 67 52, fax 011 436 71 94, Via Corte d'Appello 4)*. Singles/doubles cost L180,000/220,000. If you get lucky, it may have a few cheaper rooms available without private bathroom.

Hotels – Around Stazione Porta Nuova

Such good-value it could almost pass as budget is *Albergo Astoria* (☎ *011 562 06 53, fax 011 562 58 66,* @ *astoriah@tin.it, Via XX Settembre 4)* where comfortable

singles/doubles cost L120,000/150,000. Marble columns add a grand touch.

Stylish *Hotel Genio* (☎ *011 650 57 71, fax 011 650 82 64,* @ *hotel.genio@hotel res.it, Corso Vittorio Emanuele II 47)*, tucked under the porticoes, has a pool of umbrellas at the ready for guests when it rains. Singles/doubles start at L170,00/ 200,000. Its nearby sister, also part of the Best Western chain, *Hotel Gran Mogol* (☎ *011 561 21 20, fax 011 562 31 60,* @ *hotel.genio@hotelres.it, Via Guarini 2)* charges similar rates. Best Western has two more three-star pads west of the station around Corso Stati Unii. Check out Best Western's Web site at www.bestwestern.it.

Hotels – Elsewhere

Hotel Dock & Milano (☎ *011 562 26 22, fax 011 54 59 39,* @ *info@dockmilano.com, Via Cernaia 46)* is handily placed near Stazione Porta Susa. Three-star singles/doubles cost L160,000/200,000.

Late-night revellers seeking a bed for the night in the River Po area could check into *Hotel Lo Scudiero* (☎ *011 839 93 52, fax 011 839 32 60, Corso Casale 89)*, a decent three-star place open 24 hours. Singles/doubles/triples/quads cost from L100,000/ 120,000/150,000/200,000.

PLACES TO STAY – TOP END

Grand Hotel Sitea (☎ *011 517 01 71, fax 54 80 90,* @ *sitea@thi.it, Via Carlo Alberto 35)*, where the Juventus football team is apparently put up when in town, is an oasis of calm and sophistication sandwiched between Piazza San Carlo and Piazza Carlo Emanuele II. Singles/doubles cost L320,000/430,000.

Turin Palace Hotel (☎ *011 562 55 11, fax 011 561 21 87,* @ *palace@thi.it, Via Sacchi 8)* opened in 1872 and is the city's last word in late-19th-century luxury. Regal singles/doubles cost L295,000/365,000 (L190,000/ 250,000 weekends).

Its modern counterpart, *Star Hotel Majestic* (☎ *011 53 91 53, fax 011 53 49 63, Corso Vittorio Emanuele II 54)*, lures an international conference set with its stereotypical rooms costing L270,000/350,000 (L205,000 at weekends).

TURIN

Places to Eat

The area around Via Po is great for cheaper restaurants full of students. Via Garibaldi also hosts a number of cheerful spots for a bite to eat. Please see under Food in the Facts for the Visitor chapter for details of Turin's food.

PLACES TO EAT – BUDGET
Restaurants

In the old-town *Pastis*, at the northern end of Via Sant'Agostino on Piazza Emanuele Filiberto, is a tapas bar with a bold interior where you can eat cheaply (L6000 per tapas plate). Next door, French-inspired *Free Vélo* hosts good-value theme evenings which tend to revolve around eating as much as you can for a fixed price.

A reliable vegetarian option near Stazione Porta Nuova is *Kashimir* (☎ 011 562 73 91, Via Gioberti 4), an Indian and Pakistani place which cooks up decent veggie dishes (from L10,000 to L14,000) and serves a L12,000 lunch menu. If you're into crepes, duck beneath the arcades of Vittorio Emanuele to *Il Vicola* (Via Gioberti 3), a sweet and savoury pancake house. Don't miss the one smothered in Turinese Nutella (L10,000).

East of the train station, *Ristorante Self-Service* (Via Accademia Albertina 33) is a canteen-type place with a tummy-filling L10,000 menu, including a first and second course, vegetable side dish, fruit and dessert. *Intermezzo Self-Service* (Via Saluzzo 52) dishes up first/second courses for L3500/5500 and a L10,000 lunchtime deal which includes 25cl of wine. *Lunch & Eat* (Via Giovanni Giolitti 16) is another self-service place with a cheap munchable menu.

Lucky Nugget Saloon (Corso Vittorio Emanuele II 21) is a large music restaurant-cum-bar with a self-service food bar for the budget-conscious.

For a real change, *Kirkuk Kafè* (☎ 011 53 06 57, Via Carlo Alberto 24d) serves up Kurdish, Turkish, Iraqi and Iranian food. Call to book as it's popular, cheap (about L20,000 for a meal) and tiny.

Pizzerias Ask any Turinese where to eat pizza and the answer is always the same: Mamma Mia! Once a tiny place with just three tables, jam-packed *Mamma Mia* (☎ 011 88 83 09, Corso San Maurizio 32) touts numerous tables inside and out today. Geographically named pizzas (Turin, Genoa, England, Italy etc) cost from L9500 to L15,000 and antipasti/pasta starts at L8000/10,000. Mamma Mia has a second outlet at Via Parini 9.

Another top pizza pad is *Gennaro Esposito* (☎ 011 53 59 05, Via Passalacqua 1g), a bright and cheerful joint open until midnight Monday to Saturday. It cooks up 26 types of pizza (the one with mozzarella, gorgonzola and pears is a juicy choice) and several different *focaccia*. Pizzas/focaccia average L15,500/11,000.

The third in the legendary trio *Fratelli La Cozza* (☎ 011 85 99 00, ℮ ciro@lacozza .com, Corso Regio Parco 39) is famed as much for its owner who makes everyone laugh – Turinese comic TV presenter Piero Chiambretti – as for its delicious Napoli-inspired pizzas.

Less exciting but busy *Cernaia 3* (☎ 011 54 90 81, Via Cernaia 3) is a spacious place split across two floors. A portion of *farinata* (thick chickpea-flour pancakes, salted and oiled) costs L4000 and it has 68 pizza types costing from L6000 to L16,000 (plus between L1500 and L5000 for one of 50 extra toppings).

Cafes

Cafe culture has been an integral part of Turinese life since the city's *Risorgimento* days (see the boxed text 'Caffè Society' later). There's somewhere to dive in for an espresso on almost every street corner and there are covered cafe terraces, just made for lingering over longer cappuccinos, on many of the porticoed promenades, including on Piazza Castello and Piazza San Carlo, Via Roma and Via Po.

Neuv Caval 'd Brôns (☎ 011 54 53 54, ℮ ross@cavalbrons.it, Piazza San Carlo 157) is a lavish place with a vaulted trompe l'oeil ceiling and oodles of finger-licking cakes and pastries. Its imaginative and well-stuffed panini (from L4000/3500 to eat in/take away) are a winner with hungry tourists.

Near the river, Piazza Vittorio Veneto lures a more lounging, student set. Notable choices include **Antonelli** (☎ 011 817 25 44, Piazza Vittorio Veneto 1) where an in-crowd sips hot chocolate (so thick you can spoon it) or an aperitivo della casa while soaking up the sun's late afternoon rays on its spacious terrace; **Caffè Elena** (☎ 011 812 33 41, Piazza Vittorio Veneto 5), which also has tables outside; and **Caffè Flora** at No 24, which offers nice Po views from its riverside perch.

In the cobbled maze west of Piazza Castello, **Olsen** (☎ 011 436 15 73, Via Sant'Agostino 4) cooks up home-made strudels, muffins, banoffee pie and cherry clafoutis, ensuring that this informal, down-to-earth spot is always packed. Vegetarian paella is often among its choice of hot dishes. There are more cafes along pedestrian Via Garibaldi.

Heading south, **Norman**, on the corner of Via Pietro Micca and Via Bellezia, is a chandelier-lit place with a L30,000 lunchtime buffet and main dishes from L12,000. In summer, its tables spill out beneath the arcade.

Gelaterie Dating from 1884, **Pepino** (☎ 011 54 20 09, Piazza Carignano 8) is the oldest of Turin's gelaterie (ice-cream parlours). Expect to pay at least L11,000 for the privilege of sitting, either inside or on its outside terrace. Its mandarino reale is royally served inside an orange. **Gelateria Fiorio**, part of Caffè Fiorio (see the boxed text 'Caffè Society') is Turin's other ice-cream legend.

Miretti (☎ 011 53 36 87, Corso Giuseppe Matteotti 5) is another Turinese favourite, open 7 to 1.30 or 2 am Tuesday to Sunday. A cone to eat on the move costs L2500 (L500 per extra ball) and flavours include yoghurt, peach, nougat, chestnut and minty After Eight.

Sparkling **Gatsby** (☎ 011 562 25 456, Via Soleri 2) is the swish modern spot to go suck ice. Do as the Turinese do: lick chocolate or noisette in winter and a fruity flavour in summer.

Fast Food

Busy **La Focacceria** (Via Sant'Agostino 6) is Liguria's answer to fast food. Farinata costs L2000 a slice, focaccia with one of 13 different toppings costs as little as L1500 a slice, and there are 16 different pizza types to choose from (from L2500/25,000 for a slice/entire pizza).

The Italian version of fast food is **Brek** (☎ 800 58 22 85 toll-free, ✉ info@brek.com) which has outlets at Piazza Carlo Felice 22 (☎ 011 53 45 56) and Via Santa Teresa 23b (☎ 011 54 54 24). Expect to pay L20,000 for a full meal comprising salad, a piece of grilled meat with potatoes or pasta and veggies, fruit and dessert.

Poetically named **Mellow** has a handful of outlets sprinkled around the city, including on the corner of Via Bertola and Corso Siccardi 15 (☎ 011 562 12 82), and on the corner of Via Nizza 3 (☎ 011 669 91 74) and Via San Pio. Fork out L3500 for a hotdog, L4500 for a piece of mellow chicken or L2500/3500 for a burger.

McDonald's has Ms stuck up at Piazza Castello 59 (☎ 011 54 25 42), Stazione Porta Susa and Piazza Statutu.

Self-Catering

Near Stazione Porta Nuova, **La Baita del Fromagg** (☎ 011 562 32 24, Via Lagrange 36) is a well-stocked delicatessen selling sausages, rounds of Parmigiano reggiano (Parmesan cheese), unusual meats and fats such as lard laden in aromatic herbs, jars of white truffles, truffle butter and other conserved delicacies. Build the perfect picnic with a loaf of bread (savoury, fruit or sugar-topped) from **Gertsio** (Via Lagrange 34).

Pastificio Delfilippis (☎ 011 542 21 37, Via Lagrange 39) sells every type of pasta under the Italian sun. House specialities include tortellini stuffed with unexpected fillings such as spinach, salmon and fonduta (a type of melted cheese from Valle d'Aosta); artichokes, asparagus, eggplant and mushrooms; or ham, walnuts and gorgonzola cheese.

Near Piazza Castello, tempting food shops huddle on Via Mercanti and along the western end of Via Garibaldi. Hunks of meat hang

Caffè Society

Turin's many literary luminaries and political potentates have certainly not wanted for places to chat the day away. Perhaps partly due to Turin's legacy of French and Austrian involvement, and maybe also as a result of the indifferent weather, the city has a flourishing and chic cafe life. Centred around a handful of sumptuous 18th- and 19th-century coffee houses, it is that shot of espresso downed at the bar, that cappuccino or champagne cocktail brought to you on a silver tray or that aperitif accompanied by a complimentary banquet of hors d'oeuvres which remain the great stalwarts of traditional Turinese *caffè* society.

Al Bicerin (☎ *011 436 93 25, Piazza della Consolata 5*). Cavour, Dumas et al came here to drink *bicerin*, a heart-warming mix of coffee, spoon-thick hot chocolate, milk and whipped cream, shaken and stirred to create Al Bicerin's most famous beverage. Dating to 1763, this tiny wood-panelled cafe overlooks one of Turin's most picturesque cobbled squares (the setting for many a film set).

Baratti & Milano (☎ *011 651 30 60, Piazza Castello 27*). Elegant Baratti & Milano, with a stunning interior dating to 1858, serves coffee and cake standing up or around tables in its tea-room, and a fabulous L26,000 lunchtime menu – comprising a main course (served with pasta *and* potatoes), dessert, coffee and water or wine – in its adjoining restaurant. Crowds flock here on Sunday to buy cakes, sweets and biscuits – all beautifully boxed and ribbon-wrapped – from its old-fashioned shop counter.

Fiorio (☎ *011 817 32 25, Via Po 8*). This is another nationalist haunt favoured by Count Camillo Benso di Cavour and other pro-unification patriots who, so legend claims, frequently ate ice cream here. Fiorio still serves its own ice cream, as well as omelettes (L6000), roast beef (L12,000) and other hot lunchtime dishes. The cafe opened its doors in 1780.

Mulassano (☎ *011 54 79 90, Piazza Castello 15*). Mulassano (1907–09) is an Art Nouveau gem, richly clad with a marble floor, mirrored walls adorned with vines of grapes sculpted in wood, a coffered wood-and-leather ceiling and – to complete the pretty ensemble – four small tables. As in days gone by, the theatre mob from nearby Teatro Regio simply adore this place, darling.

in the window at *Ideal* (*Via Garibaldi 46*), a *macelleria* (butcher). **Gastronomia Florida**, next door at No 46a, sells salads, ready-made dishes, cheese, cold meats, fresh pasta and tempting fruit tarts. Shop for bread and cakes at *Lonzar*, a *pasticceria* (bakery) at No 44.

Supermarket chain **Di per Di** runs shops at Via Passalacqua 3, Via Santa Teresa 19, Via Gioberti 32 and Piazza Savoie 2, all open 8 or 8.30 am to 7.30 pm (until noon Wednesday) Monday to Saturday. Large **Metà Metà** (*Via Giovanni Giolitti 16*) opens 8.30 am to 1.30 pm and 3.30 to 7.30 pm Monday to Saturday (closed Wednesday afternoon).

PLACES TO EAT – MID-RANGE

Away from the centre, a trendy place to dine is **I Birilli** (☎ *011 819 05 67*, e *info@*

birilli.com, Strada Val San Martino 6), near Piazza Asmara on the eastern bank of the River Po. The place dates to 1929 and is owned by comic Italian showman Piero Chiambretti, a born-and-bred Turinese.

Late-night eaters should try **Caffè Rossini** (see Pubs & Bars under Entertainment later in this chapter), a historic joint with a kitchen open 10.30 to 3.30 am daily.

Restaurants – Around Piazza Castello

There are some lovely spots to savour traditional cuisine in the old-town streets west of Piazza Castello. A longtime favourite is **Tre Galline** (Three Hens; ☎ *011 436 65 53, Via Bellezia 37d*) which serves Piedmontese food at prices just a smidgen out of the

Caffè Society

Platti (☎ 011 506 90 56, 🖳 platti875@tin.it, Corso Vittorio Emanuele II 72). The original Art Nouveau interior (1870) remains firmly intact at this sweet-laden coffee and cake shop, crammed with glazed fruit-filled tarts, jars of honey-soaked almonds, walnuts and orange slices and other tempting treats to eat in or take away. Skip the terrace overlooking Corso Umberto I (noisy) and lunch inside. First/second courses average L16,000/25,000.

San Carlo (☎ 011 53 25 86, Piazza San Carlo 156). Host to a gaggle of *Risorgimento* nationalists and intellectuals in the 1840s, this sumptuous cafe dating to 1822 is where bankers and other suited folk network today. Mirrored walls, a marble floor and frescoed ceiling add a splendid touch. Fare served at the bar or one of seven tables include 28 types of coffee (a cappuccino sitting down is L4000), cocktails (from L12,000) and hot toasted snacks.

Samambaia (☎ 011 669 86 24, Via Madama Cristina 20). A feast for eyes and stomach, historic Samambaia is conveniently wedged between the River Po and the centre. A really popular lunchtime spot, its 1910 interior is chock-a-block with chocolates, cakes, cookies and other calorie-laden luxuries. Help yourself to a slice of *croccante* (honey-soaked apple tart sprinkled with flaked almonds) or *tarte tatin* (upside-down apple pie) and pay afterwards at the till.

ASA ANDERSSON

Torino (☎ 011 54 51 18, Piazza San Carlo 204). Caffè Torino has served coffee beneath its chandelier-lit, frescoed ceiling since 1903. Stand with the gaggle of Turinese at the bar or pay a fortune for silver service: L8000/12,000 for a cappuccino/bicerin sitting down, L15,000 for a salty dog or Singapore sling, or L20,000 for a champagne cocktail. Smear the sole of your shoe across the brass bull (embedded in the pavement) when leaving to ensure good luck.

TURIN

---

budget range. Try the *sottofiletto di fassone con fonduta di Castelmagno e aceto balsamico* (pheasant fillet with cheese fondue and balsamic vinegar) for L26,000.

Nearby, *I Tre Galli* (☎ 011 521 60 27, Via Sant'Agostino 25) is spacious and full of light. It serves food until 12.30 am (open until 2 am), although wine is the primary reason why most people visit this rustic joint.

For a taste of the alternative, fill up on spicy couscous and grilled meats served with flare at *Hafa Café* (☎ 011 436 70 91, Via Sant'Agostino 23c), a stylish Moroccan place. Slumber on floor cushions in its sunken 'Zen' room or sip mint tea at a table. Mains average L14,000.

Another tasty spot is *Il Bagatto* (☎ 011 436 88 87, Via Sant'Agostino 30a), a vineria (wine bar) with ochre walls, a L13,000 menu (pasta, main dish and 25cl of wine) and first/second courses from L6000/8000 (open until 2 am Tuesday to Sunday).

Heading south towards Piazza San Carlo is *Il Granaio* (☎ 011 562 10 03, Via San Francesco d'Assisi 87), a *pastificio* (pasta shop) which dishes up pasta (L9000) and sweet/savoury tarts (L4000 with salad) in the small restaurant it runs on the premises. Don't miss the melon and ham pie or Tuscan *castagnaccio* (chestnut-flour cake topped with pine kernels and rosemary).

Restaurants – Around Stazione Porta Nuova

There are several excellent places to dine around Piazza Carlo Emanuele II.

Dedicated vegetarians should try *Il Punto Verde* (☎ 011 88 55 43, Via San Massimo 17), a cheap veggie place. Any one course costs L10,000 (two-course menu L15,000).

Another trendy choice around here is *Société Lutéce* (☎ 011 88 76 44, Piazza Carlo Emanuele II 21). A definite *ciao* rather than *arrividerci* place, the bistro sports retro furnishings and serves a L25,000 weekend brunch. In summer, its pavement terrace is one of Turin's best (and least bothered by traffic).

In the same area *Caffè Guglielmo Pepe* (☎ 011 812 68 43, Via della Rocca 19) is a bastion of Turinese society. Tuna carpaccio costs L15,000, a simple *caprese* (tomato, mozzarella and basil salad) is L13,000 and first/second courses average L10,000/18,000. It has a cheaper stand-up section.

A couple of blocks east of Stazione Porta Nuova, *Dai Saletta* (☎ 011 668 78 67, Via Belfiore 37) dishes up Piedmontese fare. Must-tries include *trifulin* (truffle-filled ravioli in a creamy mushroom sauce) and *brasato al Barolo* (mouth-melting-tender meat braised in Barolo wine). Count on paying L40,000 per head, excluding wine. Advance reservations are essential.

Away from the centre but well worth the trek – if you can get a table – is *Antiche Sere* (☎ 011 385 43 47, Via Cenischia 9), a traditional trattoria where Turinese take friends and house guests when in town. You'll pay at least L50,000 per person, excluding wine. Again, reserve in advance.

PLACES TO EAT – TOP END

Fine dining can be enjoyed at *Balbo* (☎ 011 839 57 75, Via Andrea Doria 11), an exclusive spot best enjoyed on a credit card other than your own. Fish/Piedmontese *degustazione* (tasting) platters brought to you by slick dicky-bowed waiters cost L110,000.

Another legendary spot is *Restaurant del Cambio* (☎ 011 54 37 60, Piazza Carignano 2) which peers at Baroque Palazzo Carignano from its snug position next to Teatro Carignano. Antipasti/pasta averages L30,000/25,000, meat dishes start at L40,000 and there's a L100,000 *menu di tradizione* (min-

imum two people). Advance reservations and smart dress are recommended.

Near Stazione Porta Nuova, *Rendez-Vous* (☎ 011 88 76 66, Corso Vittorio Emanuele II 38) is another select spot with modern decor and refined French menus costing L38,000 and L40,000. *C'era Una Volta* (☎ 011 65 54 98, Corso Vittorio Emanuele II 41) dishes up a L45,000 menu featuring typical Piedmontese favourites. Buzz the buzzer to get through the hefty wooden door.

Japanese *Arcadia* (☎ 011 561 38 98, Galleria Subalpina 16), Turin's only sushi bar, is set inside one of Turin's glass-topped galleries off Piazza Castello. Tuck into a plate of octopus or opt for a sushi-centred L55,000 *menu giapponese* (Japanese menu).

Entertainment

Friday's edition of newspaper *La Stampa*, with a Web site at www.lastampa.it, runs an entertainment supplement entitled *Torino Sette* which lists what's on where. Its daily *Spettacoli Cronaca* includes cinema, theatre, exhibition listings, reviews and a calendar of events.

The free quarterly *Events: Torino & Surroundings* published by the APT office lists upcoming exhibitions, classical concerts, festivals, fairs and theatre events. Also worth picking up is the free 80-page *News Spettacolo*, again available at the APT office. The weekly booklet lists a couple of hundred entertainment venues, ranging from straight and gay to innocent and downright naughty. It includes cinema and theatre listings, as well as weekly events in music bars and dance clubs. Web site: www.newspettacolo.com.

The city's cultural information service, Vetrina per Torina (☎ 800 01 54 75 toll-free, ✉ vetrina@comune.torino.it), Piazza San Carlo 159, opens 11 am to 7 pm Monday to Saturday. It posts event listings on the Web site www.comune.torino.it/cultura.

Auditorium Giovanni Agnelli (☎ 011 664 45 51, ✉ congressi@lingotti.its.iz), inside the Lingotto complex at Via Nizza 206, is the main venue for pop concerts.

PUBS & BARS

Turin's drinking scene is fun, varied and caters to everyone from wine and Campari quaffers to beer slurpers and grappa shot slammers. With the exception of those on Ai Murazzi, bars tend to be spread out.

La Taverna dei Guitti (☎ *011 53 31 64,* e *guitti_lobit@libero.it, Via San Dalmazzo 1)* is a quaint old-fashioned cafe which hosts live jazz and cafe-theatre most Thursday and Friday evenings from 10 pm (open until 2 am Thursday to Tuesday).

On the old town's southern fringe, *American Stars* (☎ *011 54 89 33, Via Pietro Micca 3a)* is a 1970s-style American bar with the Blues Brothers draped across a pink cadillac bar, pinball machines and a juke box. It hosts live bands and shakes wild cocktails.

Roar Roads (☎ *011 812 01 71, Via Carlo Alberto 3)* defies categorisation. A conventional British-style bar crammed with tables, it serves grub and beer, including an odd wooden contraption rigged with eight half pints of different beer types for L30,000.

Things hot up down by the river on Ai Murazzi, the riverside promenade stretching along the Po between Ponte Vittorio Emanuele I and Ponte Umberto I. Its hot spots change all the time, although old favourites such as *Jamming* at Via Murazzi del Po 17–19 and the legendary *Giancarlo* (☎ *011 817 47 24, Via Murazzi del Po 49)* never seem to die.

Nearby *Caffè Rossini* (☎ *011 521 41 05, Corso Regina Margherita 80e)* is a historic venue which can be relied on almost any time of day (open 10.30 to 3.30 am).

Across the water, a notable *vineria* is *Cantine Rosso* (☎ *011 819 55 31, Corso Casale 79)*, a rare spot where you can sip wine in a peaceful walled garden. The bar's wine-tasting evenings and other thematic events are hugely popular.

Several music bars are clustered farther west along the same street: *Red Pub* at No 48 and *Arc Ciel* at No 44, are worth a drink en route to *Zoo Bar* (☎ *011 819 43 47,* e *zoobar@barrumba.com, Corso Casale 127)*, an industrial bar which hosts bands, DJs and cabarets; it's run by Barrumba (see Clubs later in this chapter). From Piazza

Vittorio Veneto, take bus No 61 to the Casaborgone stop.

Irish pubs, as unIrish as any Irish pub outside Ireland, include *Shamrock Inn* (☎ *011 817 49 50, Corso Vittorio Emanuele II 34)* and *Murphy's Pub* (☎ *011 689 13 13, Corso Vittorio Emanuele II 28)*, both near Stazione Porta Nuova; *Macgilllycuddy's (Via Bligny 0)*; and *The Bassoc Inn (Via Galliari 7)* which hosts live bands. English *Shakespeare*, next door to a 17th-century palace at Via Bogino 5, sports pints and pub grub.

CLUBS

Turin nightlife is said to be among Italy's best, although the scene is spread in dribs and drabs across the city. Flyers and posters advertising events can be found in the Ricordi Media Store and Rock & Folk (see CDs under Shopping later in this chapter). Both sell tickets (from L15,000 to L40,000) for concerts and DJ gigs in local clubs. Most venues have their own Web site listing upcoming events; Dinamo 2000 (www .dinamo2000.it) is a general listings site.

One of the most central places to dance is *Barrumba* (☎ *011 819 43 47,* e *ivaldo@ barrumba.com, Via San Massimo 1)*, an indie-rock club which has a Web site at www.barrumba.com.

Another favourite is *Theatró* (☎ *011 518 71 07, Via Santa Teresa 10)*, a music restaurant with a clutch of young DJs who mix tunes from 11 pm. The artsy venue is an old cinema.

In the less salubrious warren south of Porta Stazione Nuova is cutting-edge *Zip Sound Café (Via Giacosa 2)*, on the corner of Via Nizza 37. East of the station, Via Principe Tommaso also has a few happening places. Farther south, 100% house is played at *Rock City (Corso Dante 19a)*.

All genres and sounds feature at *Azimut* (☎ *011 23 24 58, Via Modena 55)*, known for its 1960s bands, and *L'Angelo* (☎ *011 28 43 59, Via Cremona 2)*. Busy clubs north-west of the centre include *Supermarket* (☎ *011 25 94 50, Via Madonna di Campagna 1)* which stages concerts every week; and *Docks Dora* (☎ *011 28 02 51, Via Valprato 68)*, the real star of Turin's music scene: Café Blue Docks sets the converted 1912 warehouse complex jiving with house and techno from 11 pm to 4 am Wednesday to Sunday. Admission is free. You'll find several other places nearby.

Other big names in the dance and music circuit are *Magazzino di Gilgamesh* (☎ 011 74 92 801, Piazza Moncensio 13b) and *Hiroshima Mon Amour* (☎ 011 317 54 27, e hma@iol.it, Via Bossoli 83), a massive club which hosts cabarets, live bands and plays everything from folk and punk to tango and techno. It has a Web site at www .hiroshimamonamour.org.

A hot Saturday-night music venue is *Palazium* (☎ 011 521 73 40, e palazium@ jumpy.it, Via Porta Palatina 23) playing hip hop, reggae, soul and garage.

GAY & LESBIAN VENUES

Caffè Leri (☎ 011 54 30 75, Corso Vittorio Emanuele II 64) and *Matisse* (Via Garibaldi 13), the birthplace of Turin's gay movement in 1970, are among the city's gay and lesbian venues. *Centralino* (Via delle Rosine 16a) is one of many discos to host a weekly gay night.

Arcigay Maurice and InformaGay (see Gay & Lesbian under Information in the Facts for the Visitor chapter) can direct you to many more gay entertainment spots, as can www.gay.it/guida/Piemonte.

CLASSICAL MUSIC

The Orchestra Filarmonica di Torino, with a Web site at www.oft.it, has its pit at the *Conservatorio Giuseppe Verdi* (☎ 011 436 06 91, 010 436 13 40, e cmverdi@tin.it, Piazza Bodoni). The Orchestra Sinfonica Nazionale della RAI performs at the *Auditorium Giovanni Agnelli* (☎ 011 664 04 58, Via Nizza 280). A season of symphonic concerts is also held in Teatro Regio (see Theatre later in this chapter). Tickets cost L30,000 to L90,000.

Music buffs in Turin for a while should consider buying a Nessun Dorma, a carnet of eight tickets (L200,000) valid for an assortment of classical music concerts held at the above-mentioned venues; Vetrina per Torina (see the introductory paragraph under Entertainment for details) sells the carnet.

CINEMAS

Monday is the night when most Turinese head for the big screen.

Near the Mole Antonelliana, *Massimo* (☎ 011 812 56 58, Via Montebello 8) offers an eclectic mix of films, mainly in English or with subtitles. One of its three screens is run by the Museo Nazionale del Cinema (see Things to See & Do earlier in this chapter) and only screens classic films from its huge film library.

Lux (☎ 011 54 12 83, Galleria San Frederico), immediately north of Piazza San Carlo, is worth a visit for its fabulous location inside Galleria San Federico (see Shopping later in this chapter), off Via Roma. Other cinemas screening foreign films in their original language include *Reposi* (☎ 011 53 14 00, Via XX Settembre 15), and *Olimpia* (☎ 011 53 24 48, Via Arsenale 3).

THEATRE, OPERA & BALLET

Turin has numerous theatres. Among its leading lights is *Teatro Regio* (Piazza Castello 215) for operas and ballets. Tickets (from L24,000 to L75,000) are sold at its box office (☎ 011 881 52 41, e biglietteria@ teatroregio.torino.it), open 10.30 am to 6 pm Tuesday to Friday, 10.30 am to 4 pm Saturday and an hour before performances start. See also the Web site at www.teatroregio .torino.it. It is sometimes possible to watch sold-out performances for free live on TV in *Teatro Piccolo Regio* (☎ 011 881 52 46, Piazza Castello 215), the theatre next door where Puccini premiered *La Bohème* in 1896.

Tickets for performances at *Teatro Stabile* (Piazza San Carlo 159) are sold at its box office (☎ 800 23 53 33 toll-free, ☎ 011 517 62 46, e info@teatrosabiletorino.it), Via Roma 49, open 10 am to 6 pm Tuesday to Saturday.

SPECTATOR SPORTS

Rival football clubs Juventus and Torino currently share Stadio delle Alpi (☎ 011 966 59 93), Strada Altessano 131, although rich Agnelli-owned Juventus plans to build a new stadium for itself in time for the 2002/2003 season and Torino aspires to return to the Filadelfia stadium. See Spectator Sports in the Facts for the Visitor chapter. Tickets for matches (L40,000 to L130,000) are sold at the Ricordi Media Store (see CDs under Shopping for details). Juventus has its club headquarters (☎ 011 6 56 31, fax 010 660 45 50) at Corso Galileo Ferraris 32 and a Web site at www.juventus.it. Torino is at Via Maria Vittoria 1 and www.toro.it/.

Shopping

WHAT TO BUY
Sweets & Chocolate
Turin's best-known confectioner, Leone at Corso Regina Margherita 242, has made sweets since 1857. Favourites include fruity bonbons inscribed with the word *allegria* (meaning 'happiness') on the outer wrapper; old-fashioned 'matchboxes' filled with tiny *pastiglie* (pastilles) in mint, mandarin and a myriad of other flavours; and its gold-wrapped *gianduiotti*, a chocolate filled with hazelnut cream unique to Turin.

Peyrano, with a shop at Corso Moncalieri 47, is Turin's most famous chocolate house. Its ornate boxes of *Dolci Momenti a Torino* (Sweet Moments in Turin) cost L62,500 per 400g; the *grappini* (chocolates with grappa) are equally addictive. Gerla, Corso Emanuele II 88, and Giordano, Piazza Carlo Felice 69, are other well-known chocolate makers.

Historic shops selling bonbons, chocolates and jellied fruits packaged so beautifully they're too good to eat include Stratta (1836) at Piazza San Carlo 191; Abrate (1866) with its lovely 1920s shop at Via Po 12a; and Avvignano (1883) at Piazza Carlo Felice 50 which sells delicious *crema di marroni* (sweet chestnut cream) and *sorrisi di Torino* (literally, 'smiles from Turin') beneath a stunning ceiling.

Dolciaria Fontanao (button-sized macaroons) and hoop-shaped *buscotti mautino* (a type of biscuit) are among the traditional Turinese offerings lavishly displayed at Caffè Burro Uova, Via San Tommaso 13.

Cheese
Buy a round of Parmigiano reggiano to take home from Borgiattino Formaggi (☎ 011 55 38 37), Corso Vinzaglio 29, an authentic *formaggeria* (cheese shop) run by the Borgiattino family since 1927. It opens 8.30 am to 1 pm and 4 to 7.30 pm Monday to Saturday.

Wine
Parola (☎ 011 54 49 39), near Stazione Porta Nuova at Corso Vittorio Emanuele II 76, is a first-rate wine cellar which stocks vintages from the last 100 years.

At Fongo Domenico (☎ 011 54 13 37), Via Mazzini 3, you can fill up your own bottle with cheap red wine for L2200 per litre. The shop sells everything from grappa to Moscovskaya vodka and runs a little bar where you can whet your whistle with a quick shot or two. It opens 9 am to 8 pm. P.I.A.N.A, Via Garibaldi 38, is another place stocking several hangovers' worth of wine, spirits and liqueurs.

WHERE TO SHOP
Turin's most prestigious shopping street is **Via Roma** which, on Saturday and Sunday afternoons, gets thronged with weekend strollers parading beneath its porticoes and peering at its window displays. Unlike most other shops in Turin, these boutiques open 3 to 7 pm on Sunday. Many more fashion shops are on parallel **Via Lagrange**; central department store La Rinascente is at No 15.

The elegance of another age is captured in the glass-topped malls of **Galleria Subalpina** (1873) linking Piazza Castello with Via Battisti; and Versace-clad **Galleria San Frederico** which runs in a T-shape between Via Roma, Via Bertola and Via Santa Teresa. Expensive art, antiques and bookshops linger in these covered shopping malls. Porticoed **Via Po**, with its pavement cafes and alternative fashion shops, attracts a younger crowd. In Turin's medieval quarter, **Via Mercanti** – with its traditional bookbinders and candlestick makers – is the street to stroll for handmade crafts and unusual souvenirs.

South of the centre at Lingotto is **I Portici**, an indoor shopping centre.

Books
An excellent range of maps and guides is sold at the Touring Club Italiano bookshop, open

TURIN

Market Day

The pandemonium of Turin's central food and clothes market fills **Piazza della Repubblica** every morning until noon. On Saturday, the area north of the square around Porta Palazzo heaves with the market stalls of **Il Balôn** where stallholders flog everything from art and antiques to ceramics, carpets and other collector items. On the second Sunday of every month it becomes **Il Gran Balôn**, an even bigger market (and Europe's biggest according to the most Turinese) – heaven for antique collectors. Whatever. It lures antique dealers from far and wide and you can buy anything from fine furniture to old-fashioned petrol pumps.

9 am to 7 pm weekdays and 9 am to 1 pm Saturday at Piazza Solferino 3b. Other shops selling a decent range include Libreria Zanaboni at Corso Vittorio Emanuele II 41 (with Lonely Planet in English) and Libreria Dante Alighieri (☎ 011 53 58 97, e info@ fogola.com) at Piazza Carlo Felice 15.

Libreria Luxemburg, Via Battisti 7, is an Anglo-American bookshop selling English-language novels, travel guides, newspapers and magazines. Librairie Française (☎ 011 83 67 72), Via Bogino 4, is the French equivalent. A fabulous choice of art, architecture and design books – many in English – are stacked high at Libreria Druetto (☎ 561 91 66, e drulib@tin.it), Via Roma 227.

Legatoria Rocchietti (☎ 011 54 42 66), in a 15th- to 16th-century house at Via Mercanti 9a, binds and restores antique books. It also makes albums of hand-crafted paper, as does Icarta (☎ 011 81 23 685), Piazza Vittorio Veneto 1, which sells books of paper embedded with dried flower petals.

CDs

Ricordi Media Store (☎ 011 562 11 56), Piazza CLN 251, is the mainstream choice for CDs of all genres (rock, pop, classical, Italian and international).

The hip choice is Rock & Folk (☎ 011 839 45 42, e rockfolk@rockandfolk.com),

with a Web site at www.rockandfolk.com and shops at Via Bogino 4 and Via Battisti 19. Its staff are young, fun and know exactly what bands are playing where.

Fashion

Most designers have a boutique on Via Roma, including Gucchi (No 49), Salvatore Ferragamo (No 108), Sergio Rossi (No 116), Marina Rinaldi (No 314), Louis Vuitton (No 320), Cartier (No 330) and Calvin Klein (Nos 12 and 354). More affordable names such as Benetton (No 48), Lacoste and Adidas (No 72), Hermes (No 120), Stefanel (No 283), Timberland (No 326) and Swatch (No 351) are also here. Dolce & Gabbana is at Via Lagrange 35.

Bolder dressers should strut down Via Po. Renni, which has a shop here, at Via Cavour 2 and Via Madama Cristina 141a, sells funky shoes, boots, bags and cutting-edge items to cover (ish) the body. Nearby, Camden Town (☎ 011 812 25 07), Via San Massimo 5, is an ode to Alexander McQueen. Tartan trousers, glitter shirts with fur cuffs and the latest in London street fashion fills the racks of this hip fashion-music store. Camden Town is a good place to ask about 'in' clubs, bars and happening events.

Heavy-duty footwear and recycled army jackets are part of Shoeco's wardrobe at Piazza Carlo Emanuele II 19. Stockings and tights for wild and sexy pins can be purchased at Calzedonia, with boutiques at Via Roma 372, Via Po 10a and Piazza Statuto 5. For hats, head to a *cappelleria* (hat shop) such as Foresto Borsalino at Piazza Carlo Felice 9 (traditional); Regge at Corso Vittorio Emanuele II 70 (felt and fur); or Imberti di Ferreso at Via XX Settembre 14 (men only).

Design

Panton chairs and remakes of other design legends sit inside Ferrero (☎ 011 54 32 98), an interior design shop at Corso Matteotti 15. Kitchenware by Alessi is among the modern 'things for the house' sold at La Casa Moderna, Corso Umberto I 14. Culti at Corso Vittorio Emanuele II 90 captures the true spirit of minimalism with its stark collection of beds, baths and bathrobes. Buy a tatami or futon to match from Natural-Mente, Via Sant'Agostino 22, or Linn Sui International, 8 Via San Quintino.

Closter (☎ 011 812 84 41, e closter@tin.it), a furniture shop at Via Mazzini 40f, sells retro stuff. Contemporary designs by Starck, Castiglioni and Pagani light up Morphiluge, a lamp shop at Via Assarotti 17.

Collectables

If you collect stamps, first-day covers or phonecards, try Bolaffi (☎ 011 557 63 00) which has dealt in the latter from its shop at Via Cavour 17 since 1891. Film posters are Jules & Jim's game, an eclectic shop at Via Bogina 19a with walls plastered with silver-screen stars.

Model FIATs, Vespas and other miniatures are the speciality of Toro Assicurazioni, Corso Umberto I 74. La Bottega (☎ 011 53 92 83), Via Assarotti 8, restores and sells antique carpets. Bianghetti, Piazza Savoie 0, makes priestly cassocks.

Excursions

Food worms (or creeps, in the case of snails) its way into almost every possible excursion that can be enjoyed from the historic Savoy capital – as does fine red Barolo wine, sparkling white Asti, Cinzano and Martini (see the boxed text 'Martini & Rossi'). A generous peppering of feisty 17th-century fortresses and the James Bond thrills 'n spills of Europe's most prestigious Alpine resorts ensures that people who don't eat or drink don't get bored.

ASTI

postcode 14100 • pop 73,300
• elevation 123m

Settled long before it was made a Roman colony in 89 BC, Asti has a rocky history. An independent city state in the 13th and 14th centuries, it was subsequently passed around between Spain, Austria, Napoleon's France and finally the Savoys, prior to unification. Since the 1850s the grapes grown on the largely flat plains around it have produced Italy's top sparkling wine – Asti

(better known, incorrectly so since 1993, as Asti Spumante).

The sweet white is best drunk young and at a chilled 6–8°C, as is its less fizzy cousin Moscato d'Asti. In town there are numerous places to taste: ***Tacaband*** (☎ 0141 53 09 99, e osteria.tacaband@tin.it, Via al Teatro Alfieri 5), next to the theatre off pedestrian Corso Alfieri, is a wine cellar where you can shop and taste (its L20,000 *antipasti in degustazione* is superb).

September sees a flurry of wine festivals, notably the 10-day **Douja d'Or** (a *douja* being a terracotta wine jug unique to Asti), followed by the **Delle Sagre** food festival on the 2nd Sunday of the month and a medieval **Palio** on the 3rd which sees 21 madcap jockeys race their horses around central Piazza Alfieri. In November the square hosts several **truffle fairs**.

Out of town, 9120 hectares of Asti vineyards are tended by 6800 wine growers, meaning ample *degustazione* opportunities. The tourist office (☎ 0141 53 03 57, e atl@axt.it) at Piazza Alfieri 29, and the Consorzio per La Tutela dell'Asti (☎ 0141 59 42 15, e consorzio@astidocg.it) at Piazza Roma 10 – the consortium which defends and promotes Asti – have lists of wineries you can visit (by appointment only).

Martini & Rossi

Martini (an alcohol salesman) and Rossi (a distillery supplier) were two men from Turin who teamed up in the 1850s to create a wine and liqueur distillery of their own in 1879. What happened after that can be discovered at the **Museo Martini di Storia dell'Enologia** (☎ 011 941 92 17), Piazzale Luigi Rossi 1, Martini's wine-making history museum about 20km south-east of Turin in Pessione. The museum, in the cellars of an 18th-century villa, can be visited between 4 and 5 pm Tuesday to Friday, and 9 am to noon and 2 to 5 pm weekends. Admission is free. One of Martini's largest production plants is also here; guided tours and tasting sessions have to be arranged in advance.

Getting There & Away

Asti is on the Turin–Alessandria–Genoa railway line and is served by regular trains (hourly) in both directions. Journey time to/from Turin is 55 minutes (1¾ hours to/from Genoa).

The A21 – dubbed the 'Autostrada dei Vini' (wine motorway) – links Turin with Asti (60km).

ALBA

postcode 12051 • pop 29,800
• elevation 172m

Solid red-brick towers rise above Alba, a medieval town 30km south of rival Asti. During WWII citizens proclaimed an independent republic for 23 days after partisans liberated it from the Germans. Some of Italy's best reds come from the hills of Le Langhe around Alba, making this wine town a tasty base for a tipple or two. Barbaresco, Barolo and La Morra – named after the surrounding pinprick villages that produce them – are the big names to look out for. The tourist office (☎ 0173 3 58 33, e info@langheroero.it), Piazza Medford 3, has a list of wine cellars in the region which can be visited. Information is online at www.langheroero.it.

Alba's best-kept secret – with the single exception of Ferrero and its Nutella factory (see Food in the Facts for the Visitor chapter) – is its white truffle crop, celebrated in mid-October with a **truffle fair**. The precious white funghi can be sampled on chic Piazza Savona, a porticoed square at the end of pedestrian Via Vittorio Emanuele II.

Cinzano

Approximately 80% of Cinzano, one of Italy's best known drinks (see Drinks in the Facts for the Visitor chapter), is concocted and bottled in the monstrous UDV plant 10km west of Alba in Cinzano, the *frazione* (small area) of hilltop Santa Vittoria d'Alba on the busy S231.

Hidden among the company's distillery and warehouses is **Villa Cinzano** (☎ 0172 47 71 11), a former hunting lodge of Carlo Alberto displaying 143 precious glasses, photographs and other artefacts chronicling the history of a company that started as a

small distilling operation in Turin's hills in 1757. Vast cellars sprawl beneath and beyond the museum, both of which can *only* be visited by a pre-arranged guided tour (minimum 20 people but sweet-speaking individuals can sometimes join groups).

Barolo

Robust, velvety, truffle-scented with orange reflections and the 'wine of kings and king of wine' are among the compliments piled onto this extraordinary red wine, produced from nebbiolo grapes cultivated on 1150 hectares of land around Barolo, 20km south-west of Alba. The village celebrates wine fairs in mid-September and October, and you can taste and buy wine in its **Enoteca Regionale** (☎ 0173 5 62 77), inside the village castle; or in the **Cantina Comunale** (☎ 0173 50 92 04), Via Carlo Alberto 2, in neighbouring La Morra, about 5km north.

No, you aren't that drunk. **Capella Sol LeWitt-David Tremlett** (☎ 0173 28 25 82), a chapel on top of a vine-covered hill between Barolo and La Morra, really is coloured like a rainbow. Built by a farmer in 1914, the ruined church (never consecrated) was restored and painted with symmetrical patterns in red, blue, green, yellow and orange by English and American artists in 1999. Milanese couturier Missoni designed a priest's cassock – also coloured like a rainbow – to match. The chapel is 1.6km south-east of La Morra along a dust track, signposted off Via Roma at the southern end of the village. It can be accessed from Barolo too.

Getting There & Away

There are a handful of buses from Turin but you really need your own wheels if you intend venturing into the vineyards.

SALUZZO

About 60km south of Turin, Saluzzo warrants a day trip and is a handy base for exploring the valleys and castles of southern Piedmont. Once a medieval stronghold, the town maintained its independence until the Savoys won it in a 1601 treaty with France. One of Saluzzo's better known sons was

Lovely Lumache

Lumache (snails) are an integral part of Langhe cuisine. And never more so than in snail-paced Cherasco, a village 23km west of Alba which claims to be Italy's snail capital.

Snails are not actually born and bred in the medieval village (the climate is chilly compared to Italy's hot south, meaning eggs take an age to incubate). Rather, the country's molluscs are marketed and sold here, with the number of snails eaten in Italy increasing four-fold since 1980 to 130,000 quintals in 1997. Just 34% of these are reared by Italy's 5500 snail breeders however – the rest are imported.

Contrary to what the French do, *la lumaca* (the snail) in this neck of the woods is never served as a starter or, for that matter, curled up in it shell. Rather, the ugly little mollusc is dished up *nudo* (nude). It can be pan-fried, roasted on a spit, dressed in an artichoke sauce or minced inside ravioli. Dishes typical to Piedmont include *lumache al barbera* (simmered in Barbera red wine and ground nuts), *lumache alla piemontese* (stewed with onions, nuts, anchovies and parsley in a tomato sauce) and *lumache di bobbio* (fried with leeks then bubbled in wine and herbs).

Cherasco touts two splendid snail-driven trattorie. In a cellar on the corner of Via San Pietro and Via Cavour, *La Lumaca* (☎ 0172 48 94 21) dishes up a L50,000 menu comprising three antipasti, starter, choice of first and second courses (both with snail options), cheese, dessert and coffee. It offers a choice of 700 regional wines and opens Wednesday to Sunday. Nearby *Osteria della Rosa Rossa* (☎ 0172 48 81 33, Via San Pietro 31) has first/second courses from L9000/12,000 and a range of snail dishes averaging L12,000. It opens Friday to Tuesday. Advance reservations are essential at both.

Cherasco tourist office (☎/fax 0172 48 93 82, 48 91 01, @ cherasco2000@tin.it), Via Vittorio Emanuele 79, has a Web site at www.cherasco2000.com. Everything you ever wanted to know about *elicoltura* (helicicolture) can be discovered at the Istituto Internazionale di Elicoltura (International Institute of Snail Breeders; ☎ 0172 48 93 82, @ ist.elicicoltura@tin.it), Via Vittorio Emanuele 32, with a Web site at www.lumache-elici.com. The village celebrates an international snail fair each year in mid-September.

JANE SMITH

General Carlo dalla Chiesa, whose implacable pursuit of the Mafia led to his assassination in 1982.

Cobbled lanes twist up to **La Castiglia**, the sombre castle of Saluzzo's medieval rulers. Commanding views over burnt-red tiled rooftops is **Torre Civica**, a restored 15th-century tower which you can climb. Pass the convent of San Giovanni on the same square and you reach the **Museo Civico di Casa Cavassa**, a 16th-century noble's residence. Both open 9 am to 12.15 pm and 2 to 5.15 pm (to 5.45 pm Sunday) Wednesday to Sunday, October to March; and 9 am to 12.15 pm and 3 to 6.15 pm (to 6.45 pm Sunday) Wednesday to Sunday, the rest of the year. Admission costs L2500/5000 for the tower/museum.

A few minutes' drive 4km south of Saluzzo is 16th-century **Castello di Manta** (☎ 0175 8 78 22) with a marvellous frescoed interior and park that can be visited 10 am to 1 pm and 2 to 5 or 6 pm Tuesday to Sunday, February to December. Admission costs L8000. The **Abbaye di Santa Maria Staffarda**, 9km north, is also worth visiting.

TURIN

The tourist office (☎ 0175 4 67 10, e iat@comune.saluzzo.cn.it), Via Torino 51a, has a range of information about the surrounding valleys.

L'Ostu du Baloss (☎ *0175 24 86 18, Via Gualtieri 38)* is a charming spot for sampling scores of different regional wines and dishes. Staff at the tourist office – unusually – are happy to make recommendations.

Getting There & Away
From the intersection of Via Nizza and Corso Marconi in Turin there are bus connections to Saluzzo (1½ hours; hourly). Phone ☎ 0175 4 37 44 for information.

By car, Saluzzo is an easy drive via the A6 (get off at the Bra exit) or S20.

VALLE DI SUSA
West of Turin and easily accessible by car, bus and train, Valle di Susa takes in the Celtic old town of **Susa** (pop 6500, elevation 503m) with its modest Roman ruins; and glamorous but overdeveloped **Sestriere** (pop 900, elevation 2033m), a ski resort conceived by Mussolini and built by the Agnelli clan of FIAT fame. There are some beautiful spots in the valley and a few pleasant mountain villages, all of which can get thronged during the ski season and at weekends when Turin escapees flee the city for fresh mountain air.

Tourist offices in Susa (☎ 0122 62 24 70), at Corso Inghilterra 39; Sestriere (☎ 0122 75 54 44), at Via Pinerolo 14; and uninteresting Oulx (☎ 0122 83 15 96), at Piazza Garambois 1b, all stock an overload of information on skiing, walking, mountain-biking and other outdoor activities in Valle di Susa.

Castello di Rivoli
Commanding a strategic position at the head of the valley 13km west of Turin, Rivoli Castle (☎ 011 956 52 22) was the preferred residence of the Savoy family from the 14th century. Used as a courtly residence during the 15th and 16th centuries, it houses a contemporary art gallery filled with daring installations today. It opens 10 am to 5 pm Tuesday to Friday and 10 am to 7 pm weekends (to 10 pm every 1st and 3rd Saturday

of the month). Admission costs L12,000 (students and those aged 10 to 14, L8000; children aged under 10, free).

Rivoli is well-served by public transport. Take ATM bus No 36 from Piazza Statuto to Rivoli bus station, then bus No 36n, or any No 36 marked 'Castello', up the hill. Journey time is about one hour (L2400).

Sacra di San Michele
Perched atop Monte Pirchiriano high above the road from Turin, this brooding Gothic-Romanesque abbey (☎ 011 93 91 30) dates to the 11th century and can be visited from 9.30 to 11.30 am and 3 to 5 pm Tuesday to Sunday. Admission costs L5000.

The closest town is **Avigliana**, 26km west from Turin and 14km south-east of the abbey. Avigliana is connected to the abbey by bus (there are about three daily). Alternatively, continue by train to Sant'Ambrogio, at the foot of the hill, and tackle the steep 90-minute walk. Check opening times with the APT office in Turin or the IAT office in Avigliana (☎/fax 011 932 86 50), Piazza del Popolo 6, before setting out.

Forte di Exilles
Worth a brief look is this forbidding fort (☎ 0122 5 82 70) overlooking the quiet village of Exilles, 70km west of Turin. The fort's medieval origins are somewhat obscure and its military role only ended in 1943. It generally opens 10.30 am to 6.30 pm Tuesday to Sunday, May to September, but check with a tourist office before making a special trip. Admission costs L10,000.

VALLE D'AOSTA
Covering a mere 3262 sq km and with a population of only 116,000, Valle d'Aosta is the smallest of the Italian regions but one of the wealthiest. The valley was part of the kingdom of Bourgogne, republican France and Napoleon's imperial France, and French is afforded equal rights with Italian (only introduced to the valley in 1861).

The valley has always been an important passageway through the Alps. Early Roman sites dot the valley – earning it the nickname 'Rome of the Alps' – as do

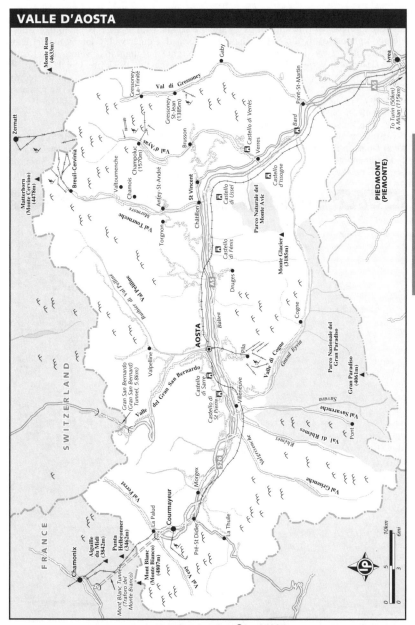

VALLE D'AOSTA

euro currency converter €1 = L1936

Romanesque and Gothic castles just waiting to be explored. Worthwhile stops – all clearly signposted off the S26 – include magnificently restored **Castello di Fénis**; sober **Castello di Verrès** which serves sentinel duty atop a rocky perch; 15th-century **Castello d'Issogne**; and the no-nonsense military outpost of **Bard**, given short shrift by Napoleon on his first campaign into Italy. The museum in **Castello di Sarre** (1710), west of Aosta, details the Savoys' royal jaunts in the valley.

The opening of the Mont Blanc Tunnel (Traforo del Monte Bianco) in 1965 con-

necting Courmayeur in the west of Valle d'Aosta with France (Chamonix) transformed a quiet valley into a major road-freight thoroughfare. Since its closure following the 1997 fire which killed 39 people, traffic (and tourism) in the region has ground to a deathly halt. The tunnel is due to reopen in September 2001.

Information

The APT offices in Aosta (☎ 0165 23 66 27, Piazza Chanoux), Courmayeur (☎ 0165 84 20 60, e apt.montebianco@psw.it, Piazzale Monte Bianco 13) and Breuil-Cervinia

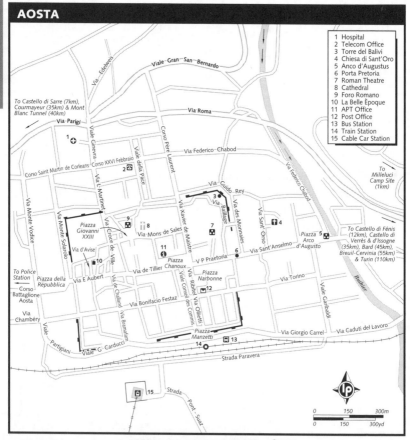

AOSTA

1	Hospital
2	Telecom Office
3	Torre del Balivi
4	Chiesa di Sant'Oro
5	Anco d'Augustus
6	Porta Pretoria
7	Roman Theatre
8	Cathedral
9	Foro Romano
10	La Belle Époque
11	APT Office
12	Post Office
13	Bus Station
14	Train Station
15	Cable Car Station

(☎ 0166 94 91 36, e breuil-cervinia@
netvallee.it, Via Carrel 29) are well-equipped
with information on the valley's castles, accommodation, etc, as well as on its mountain
of summer and winter activities.

For the latest weather forecast call Info
Meteo (☎ 0165 8 99 61). On the Web, try
www.aostavalley.com, www.montebianco
.com and www.courmayeur.net.

Things to See

Aosta's Roman ruins include **Arco d'Augusto**, between the **Porta Pretoria** – the
main gate to the Roman city – and the River
Buthier bridge at the end of Via Anselmo.
The arch bears a crucifix, added in medieval
times.

Performances are occasionally held in the
well-preserved lower section of the **Roman
theatre**, Via di Baillage, with a 22m-high
facade. The mighty **Torre del Balivi**, on the
corner of a remaining section of Roman
wall, served as a prison.

Aosta's **Cattedrale**, Piazza Giovanni
XXIII, has a neoclassical facade that belies
the impressive Gothic interior. Two 12th- to
14th-century mosaics on the floor are worth
studying.

Activities

You can do everything from mushing and
mountain biking to paragliding, ballooning
and walking your hamstrings off in Valle
d'Aosta. However, it is for skiing and
snowboarding that most people come here.
The small resorts of **Gressoney-St-Jean**
(1385m) and **Champoluc** (1570m) are the
closest to Turin (95km and 100km respectively) but **Pila** (1800m) – accessible by
cable car from Aosta (pop 39,000, 580m)
which is a speedy 113km from Turin by
autostrada or train – is the quickest and
easiest to reach.

Further afield, the valley's most glamorous resorts offer James Bond action: from
Breuil-Cervinia (2050m), 120km north of
Turin, you can ski into Switzerland (Zermatt)
and around the **Matterhorn** (Monte Cervino,
4478m). From picturesque **Courmayeur**,
150km north-west by motorway, you can
ride a cable car to Punta Helbronner (3462m)

ASA ANDERSSON

**Pretend you're James Bond in the action-
packed mountains around Turin.**

TURIN

on Europe's highest mountain **Mont Blanc**
(4807m). From here, another cable car (April
to September only) takes you on a breathtaking 5km transglacial ride across the border to the Aiguille du Midi (3842m) in
France (from where the world's highest cable
car transports you into Chamonix). The Società Guide Alpine di Courmayeur (☎ 0165
84 20 64, e guidecourma@tiscalinet.it),
next to the APT office at Piazzale Monte
Bianco 14, can guide those seeking more
daring off-piste adventures.

Numerous different ski passes are available. A simple one-day pass for Gressoney-
St-Jean/Champoluc/Pila costs L37,000/
55,000/49,000 and a three-day Skipass
Rosso covering the entire Valle d'Aosta is
L160,000. A Skipass Pool, valid for one/
three days in Breuil-Cervinia, costs L55,000/
148,000 (L66,000/180,000 including Zermatt too). In Courmayeur, a one-day pass
costs L57,000; a return La Palud-Punte Helbronner trip is L52,000.

Expect to pay at least L25,000/45,000 per
day to hire skis, boots and poles (L45,000
for boards and boots).

Places to Stay & Eat

Accommodation is expensive and difficult
to find in season. Some of the cheapest options are in Aosta where the *Milleluci*

What a Cow!

Every October thousands of Valdestans gather to watch cow fights. Known traditionally as the Bataille de Reines (Battle of the Queens), the event is organised along the lines of a beauty contest. Knockouts start in March, when locals from across the region prime their best bovines for battle, and end with the finals on the third Sunday in October, when the queen of the cows is crowned. This might seem a bit strange, but it is a tradition from the days when cows returning from mountain fields would tussle with each other. The losing cow is not injured and the match ends when one pulls away. The queen sells for millions of lire.

(☎ *0165 23 52 78)* camp site opens year-round. The site charges L10,000 per person plus L20,000 for a site. Rates stay the same year round. It's about 1km east of the centre, reachable by bus No 11. Just off Aosta's central street, **La Belle Époque** (☎ *0165 26 22 76, Via d'Avise 18)* is a hotel and pizzeria with basic singles/doubles costing upwards of L60,000/80,000.

Getting There & Away

From Turin, there are daily buses to/from Aosta (1½ to 3½ hours, seven or eight daily) and Courmayeur (2½ to 4½ hours, five daily). To get to Breuil-Cervinia, take the Aosta bus to Châtillon (30 minutes before Aosta), then a connecting bus (one hour) to Breuil-Cervinia. Buses in Turin use the Corso Inghilterra stop at Stazione Porta Susa. From Milan's Piazza Castello, there are two to four buses daily to/from Aosta (2½ hours) and Courmayeur (3½ hours).

Train is the easiest way to reach Aosta (L11,000, two to 2½ hours, more than 10 daily). Travellers to/from Milan must change trains in Chivasso. A limited train service connects Aosta with Pré-St Didier, about 5km short of Courmayeur.

By car, the A5 connects Turin with Courmayeur (and the Mont Blanc Tunnel), although the last stretch of the highway (from Morgex) is still being built. The scenic S26 runs parallel with the A5 for the entire stretch.

Genoa

- postcode 16100
- pop 640,430

Travellers who write off Genoa (Genova in Italian) as a dirty, dusty, noisy and chaotic port town (which, incidentally, is true) do the city and themselves a disservice. Once a mighty maritime republic and the birth place of Christopher Columbus (Cristoforo Colombo in Italian) in 1451, the city known as *La Superba* (literally the 'proud', 'haughty') might have lost some of its gloss over the centuries – but none of its fascination.

Genoa's story would probably have been even greater had it lent an ear to Colombus' exploration ideas; instead, Spain became a Renaissance superpower on the back of wealth discovered in the Americas. Nonetheless this did not stop Genoa from marking the 500th anniversary of the discovery of America with an Expo in 1992 which transformed the ancient Genoese harbour from city black sheep to queen bee. Genoa's best-known contemporary product, world-renowned architect Renzo Piano (born 1937), was the man behind the brilliant facelift which left Genoa with a clutch of lasting portside attractions and the confidence to stand proud once more. In 2004 the city will step back in the limelight as European City of Culture.

Founded in the 4th century BC, Genoa possibly derives its name from the Latin '*ianua*' meaning 'door'. A key Roman port, it later became a mercantile power despite being occupied by the French in 774, the Saracens in the 10th century and the Milanese in 1353. The infamous labyrinth of *caruggi* (narrow alleys), churches and palaces at the heart of the old city, near the port, bear witness to the back-stabbing dramas and intrigues of medieval Genoa, and the bickering noble dynasties which ruled it. Grimaldi, Doria, Spinola and Raggio remained family names to be feared well into the 17th century.

The Renaissance graced Genoa with an interesting collection of museums and art galleries. Reaching its peak in the 16th century under the rule of imperial admiral Andrea Doria, the city's golden age produced great works of art with masters of calibre such as Rubens, Caravaggio and van Dyck spending serious amounts of time painting landscapes of the city and portraits of the rich and powerful who ran it. Architect Galeazzo Alessi (1512–72), who designed many of the splendid buildings in the city, is regarded as highly as Andrea Palladio. Many of the sumptuous Art Nouveau and neoclassical villas along the coast date to this period.

Contemporary Genoa, with its sunny Mediterranean perch spanning Italy's most alluring strip of coastline, and gangs of easy riders who fly down old-town alleys on Vespa scooters, exudes a distinctive southern-European gregarity. Its climate is milder than cities farther north and palm trees top its clear blue skyline. And as with many a weather-beaten port, it has its seamier side which simmers away in a melting pot of visiting sailors and prostitutes (many from Africa, brought in under false pretences and condemned to years of virtual slavery to 'pay back' those who smuggled them here), delinquents and stowaways. In short, anything goes.

Inland, the city is guarded by a ring of hills, topped with defensive 17th-century forts and criss-crossed by gentle walking and mountain-bike trails. A narrow-gauge railway into the Genoese hills ensures a speedy getaway for those seeking a breath of mountain air. Westwards, a succession of busy coastal resorts forms the France-bound Riviera di Ponente with its star, sexy San Remo, being a three-hour train ride away. Heading east, the Ligurian coast – known as the Riviera di Levante – fans out into a fabled land of dramatic coves, villages and scapes with a hint of glamour thrown in: Portofino and its promontory, the protected villages of Cinque Terre, Porto Venere and the 'Gulf of Poets' are all easy day trips.

Getting Around

ORIENTATION

Genoa stretches along the Ligurian coast for some 30km and is served by 15 train stations. Central Genoa is quite compact, tucked in between two main train stations, Stazione Principe and Stazione Brignole. The main boulevard in the modern centre, Via XX Settembre, starts a short walk south-west of Brignole and spills into the city's focal point, Piazza de Ferrari.

Immediately west is the old city where most sights are. The old quarters spill west towards Porto Antico (Old Port) and around the waterfront as far north as Prè, a less salubrious street-maze near Stazione Principe. During the day, life's seamier side mixes with the fashionable set and walking around is relatively safe (and the easiest way to get around). At night the old city empties and becomes an uninviting area.

Cruise ships use the cruise terminal immediately south of Stazione Principe on Ponte dei Mille. The passenger terminal for international ferries is farther west, between Ponte Colombo and Ponte Assereto on the harbour's western side.

CRISTOFORO COLOMBO AIRPORT

The airport (☎ 010 6 01 51, ⓔ info@airport .genova.it) is at Sestri Ponente, 6km west of the city. Schedules and detailed information can be found on its Web site at www.airport .genova.it.

TO/FROM THE AIRPORTS

Airport buses (☎ 010 601 54 10), AMT's bus No 100 (also called Volabus), leave from Piazza G Verdi, in front of Stazione Brignole, every 30 minutes from 5.30 am to 11 pm (from 6.15 am to 11.45 pm from the airport to Piazza G Verdi). En route it stops at Piazza de Ferrari, Via Roma and Stazione Principe. Drivers sells tickets (L4000) and the journey time is 25 minutes.

There are also regular buses from Genoa to Milan's Malpensa airport and Nice airport in France. Buses to Malpensa (three

hours) and Nice (3¼ hours) depart twice daily from the eastern side of Piazza della Vittoria and Stazione Principe. Buy a ticket (L30,000 each) from the driver or in advance from Pesci Viaggi e Turismo (see Organised Tours later in this chapter).

PUBLIC TRANSPORT

The local public transport company, Azienda Mobilita' e Trasporti-Genova (AMT; ☎ 010 599 74 14) operates buses throughout the city. Termini include Stazione Brignole, Stazione Principe and Piazza Caricamento. The AMT information office on Piazza della Vittoria opens 6.30 am to 7 pm Monday to Saturday. Buy tickets here or from the automatic dispenser in front: a single ticket valid for 90 minutes costs L1500; a 20-ticket carnet (each ticket valid for 45 minutes) costs L26,000; and a day/month pass costs L5000/50,000. Tickets can also be used on mainline trains within the city limits (as far as Voltri and Nervi), the funiculars and lifts.

AMT bus No 33 links Stazione Brignole with Stazione Principe. To get to Porto Antico take bus No 4 from Stazione Brignole to Piazza Cavour. From Stazione Principe, bus Nos 1 to 4, 7 and 8 link Via Antonio Gramsci with Piazza Caricamento.

The 292m-long Zecca-Righi funicular, on the northern side of Largo della Zecca, climbs 1430m to link the old city with the hillside quarter of Righi. The 353m-long Sant'Anna funicular links Piazza del Portello with Castelletto. The lift (ascensore in Italian) at Piazza del Portello 18a whisks the weary-footed uphill.

Most services generally run between 6.30 or 7 am and midnight.

CAR & MOTORCYCLE

Cars and motorcycles are banned from the pedestrian old city. Automobile Club Genova (☎ 010 5 39 41, ⓔ sede@acigenova.it), Viale della Brigate Partigiane 1a, with a Web site at www.acigenova.it; and Touring Club Italiano (☎ 010 595 52 91), Palazzo Ducale 62r, are handy information sources for motorists.

There are plenty of 24-hour petrol stations

in the centre including Fina at the northern end of Via Carcassi; Agip at the southern end of Viale delle Brigate Partigiane; Shell at the southern end of Corso Torino; and Esso on Piazza Manin.

Car Rental

Avis (☎ 010 650 72 80) Cristoforo Colombo airport; (☎ 010 56 44 12) Via delle Casaccie 3

Hertz (☎ 010 651 24 22) Cristoforo Colombo airport; (☎ 010 570 26 25) Via G Casaregis 76

Maggiore (☎ 010 651 24 67) Cristoforo Colombo airport; (☎ 010 570 839 21 53) Corso Sardegna 275–81

Europcar (☎ 010 650 85 32) Cristoforo Colombo airport; (☎ 010 595 54 28) Via G Casaregis 42/1

Parking

Car parks are well signposted. At Porto Antico, Parking Acquario di Genova and neighbouring subterranean Marina Porto Antico charge L3000 per hour and open 7 am to midnight or 1 am. Marina Porto Antico offers a L60,000 weekend deal (Friday noon to Monday noon) and a 50-hour parking card (L100,000). Parcheggio Piccapietra, underneath Piazza Piccapietra, and the one on Piazza della Vittoria are other central places to park. Limited street parking is available (L3000 per hour, payable 8 am to 8 pm daily).

TAXI

Radio Taxi Genova (☎ 010 59 66) runs a 24-hour service.

BICYCLE & MOPED

Genoa sports just one known cycle-hire outlet: Nuova Centro Sportivo 2000 (☎ 010 254 12 43), at Piazza Garibaldi 18 in the old city, rents mountain and road bikes for L10,000 per day. It opens 3.30 to 7.30 pm on Monday, 9.15 am to noon and 3.30 to 7.30 pm Tuesday to Friday, and 9.15 am to noon on Saturday.

Madhatters can rent a moped to tear around the old-city alleyways, with what seems like the entire Genoese 17- to 20-something populace, from Marchald (☎ 010 31 55 04) at Via Pisacane 5r. It charges L50,000 per day (plus L150,000 deposit) to

ASA ANDERSSON

Scoot around Genoa's old-city alleyways – if your nerves are up to it...

rent a 50cc scooter (no licence required) and L70,000 per day for a 100cc equivalent (licence required). Hiring a helmet to stay alive depends on availability. Marchald opens 8.30 am to 12.30 pm and 3 to 7 pm weekdays, and 8 am to noon Saturday.

BOAT

From Genoa, the Camogli-based Cooperativa Battellieri del Golfo Paradiso (☎ 0185 77 20 91, **e** golfoparadiso@libero.it) runs ferries, June to September, along the Riviera di Levante, including to/from Camogli (L30,000 return), Portofino and San Fruttuoso (L25,000 return), Cinque Terre (L45,000) and Porto Venere (L48,000). Children aged five to 10 pay 30% less (those aged under five, free). Frequency depends on demand, although there are at least once- or twice-weekly weekend departures in June; three per week in July and September; and four to six per week in August. Boats depart from Calata Mandraccio at Porto Antico. Updated schedules and fares are posted on its Web site at www.golfoparadiso.it.

Alimar (☎ 010 25 67 75, 010 25 59 75, **e** alimarsrl@tin.it) runs Marexpress, a summertime catamaran service from Genoa to Porto Venere. Boats, depending on demand (minimum 20 people), depart at 8.30 am from Calata Zingari, near the cruise terminal, and 8.45 am from next to the aquarium daily, mid-July to mid-August. Sailing time

Whale-Spotting

There's no guarantee that you'll see one: in fact, those aboard whale-spotting excursions organised by the Cooperativo Battellieri del Porto di Genova (see Organised Tours) are advised to bring binoculars.

Trips, run in consultation with the Worldwide Fund for Nature (WWF) who plant a biologist on board, sail from Genoa into a 96,000 km sq protected zone wedged between the Côte d'Azur (France) and Tunisia. Some 12 cetacean species are known to exist here, the long-finned pilot whale and sperm whale among them. In summer, its striped dolphin population peaks at 25,000. Its whale population is estimated at 2000.

Whale-spotting expeditions depart from Genoa's Porto Antico once weekly, mid-June to mid-September (three times weekly July and August). Tickets cost L60,000 (those aged five to 12, L30,000).

is three hours and boats get back to Genoa at 7 pm. Tickets cost L45,000 (those aged five to 14, L30,000). The same catamaran also runs to/from Cinque Terre's Monterosso (L40,000, four hours).

ORGANISED TOURS

Information and tickets for boat trips are available from the ticket booths (☎ 010 248 57 10/50), next to the aquarium and skating rink at Porto Antico. Both open 9.30 am to 6.30 pm (9 am to 8 pm in summer).

Some ferries operated by the Cooperativa Battellieri del Golfo Paradiso (see Boat earlier) in July and August include sightseeing. On weekends, Alimar (see Boat earlier) operates half-day boat excursions with commentary from Genoa's aquarium to Portofino (L20,000) and San Fruttuoso (L20,000), twice on Saturday and once on Sunday. It also organises daily boat excursions around the port, hourly between 10 am and 5 pm. Tickets cost L10,000 (those aged four to 14, L7000) and tours last 45 minutes. In July and August, it also runs 30-minute night trips around the port, de-

parting from Ponte Spinola next to the aquarium at 9 pm. Updated schedules are on its Web site at www.altimar.ge.it.

The Cooperativo Battellieri del Porto di Genova (☎ 010 26 57 12, e info@battellierigenova.it), founded in 1955, runs tours of the port, departing at 10 am from next to the aquarium. Tours are 45 minutes and cost L10,000 (those aged four to 14, L7000). Between June and September, it runs boat excursions to San Fruttuoso, Portofino, Cinque Terre and Porto Venere. Departures from Calata Zingari and the aquarium are usually on Wednesday, Friday and/or weekends. Updated schedules are online at www.battellierigenova.it.

During the ski season, Pesci Viaggi e Turismo (☎ 010 56 49 36, fax 010 58 09 19, e pesciros@tin.it), Piazza della Vittoria 94r, runs bus excursions to Valle d'Aosta (see Excursions in the Turin chapter). Buses usually depart three times weekly and the journey time is about 3½ hours (leaving Genoa at 6 am and returning at 8.30 pm). A one-day return ticket costs L65,000, including ski pass. Three-/five-day trips are also possible (about L315,000/530,000, including ski pass and accommodation).

Things to See & Do

Highlights

• Get well and truly lost in Genoa's old-city *caruggi* (alleys)

• Explore Piano's Porto Antico (Old Port) – not missing the aquarium, Il Bigo and Renzo's breathtaking bubble of butterflies

• Ride a narrow-gauge railway into the Genoese hills and visit a fort

• Take a train or boat east along the coast to Cinque Terre – five of Italy's most beautiful seaside villages

• Pose, pout and visit an abbey and lighthouse in pretty pricey Portofino

GENOA

SUGGESTED ITINERARIES

Half-Day

Take a whirlwind tour of Genoa's 'must-sees': wander around Palazzo Ducale's atrium, nip into Chiesa del Gesù on Piazza Giacomo Matteotti, and bypass Cattedrale di San Lorenzo en route through the old city to Porto Antico. Pass whatever time you have left in the aquarium or one of the old-port museums.

One Day

Kick off with the half-day tour but spend longer getting lost in the old-city caruggi – not missing Castello, Piazza San Donato and Via Garibaldi – before emerging on the waterfront. Lunch in the old city and spend the afternoon discovering the port – five minutes in Il Bigo, two hours in the aquarium and 45 minutes on a boat.

Two Days

Spend the first day exploring the old city and port, then venture further afield on the second – wander through backstreets and *creuse* (cobbled lanes) to emerge up high in Righi, ride the narrow-gauge railway to Caselle, visit the monumental Cimitero Staglieno or take a boat trip along the coast.

AROUND PIAZZA DE RAFFAELE FERRARI

Piazza de Ferrari

With its star-studded cast of the Art Nouveau **Palazzo della Borsa** (former stock exchange dating between 1907 and 12), the neoclassical facade (1828) of the WWII-bombed opera house and Palazzo Ducale, Piazza de Ferrari is the focal point of central Genoa and the obvious starting place for an exploration of the city. Currently being dug up at the time of writing, the square – dedicated to a nice old duke of Galliera who gave 20 million liras to the city in 1875 to help develop the port – marks the great divide between the medieval old city and port which lie immediately to the west, and the modern city, immediately east, which sprang up in the 19th and 20th centuries. The square itself was laid out in the early 1900s.

Pinoteca dell'Accademia

This art museum, also known as Museo dell'Accademia Ligustica di Belle Arti (☎ 010 58 19 57), Largo Pertini 4, is inside arcaded Palazzo dell'Accademia Ligustica di Belle Arti, an art academy built in the 19th century on the eastern side of Piazza de Ferrari. Its collection features works by Ligurian artists from the 16th to 19th centuries. The museum opens 9 am to 1 pm Monday to Saturday. Admission costs L5000.

Palazzo Ducale

The trompe l'oeil facade of Palazzo Ducale, on the western side of Piazza de Ferrari, was painted in the 1930s. To reach the main entrance of the Ducal Palace (☎ 010 557 40 00, ✉ palazzoducale@palazzoducale.genova.it), seat of the city's rulers for six centuries, cut down the alley at the south-western corner of Piazza de Ferrari to **Piazza Giacomo Matteotti**, another large square which once served as a parade ground for the palace.

The western wing (on the left side of the square when facing the palace) is all that remains of the original medieval structure (1291). This is where the elected *doge* (city ruler) meted out justice from 1339 until the mid-16th century. Under the Republic, the most privileged prisoners – intellectuals, nobles and aristocrats – were left to rot in hell in the prisons of the red-brick **Torre Grimaldina**, raised between the 13th and 17th centuries. The red cross of Genoa's city flag flutters from its top today. Guided tours of the tower (☎ 010 557 40 00, 010 56 23 90) depart at 3, 4 and 5 pm on Sunday and cost L6000 (children aged under six, free).

The main wing was built in the 16th century, fire-damaged in 1777 and redesigned by Simone Cantoni (1736–1818) in its current neoclassical form in 1778–83. Its atrium, flanked by two porticoed courtyards, used to house the chancelleries of the Republic's magistracies, to whom people lodged their written complaints (often venomous and anonymous attacks on 'friends' and rival families) by posting slips of paper into holes dug in the atrium walls. Some are still visible.

Since November 2000 the palace has housed a **Museo del Jazz** (☎ 010 58 52 41), run by the Italian Jazz Institute (see Jazz under Entertainment later in this chapter) and tracing the colourful careers of all the jazz legends, from Louis Armstrong and Charlie Parker to Bud Powell, Eddie Condon and

GENOA

Pee Wee Russell. The Jazz Museum opens 4 to 7 pm daily and admission is free. Admission to the palace's temporary art and cultural exhibitions, open 9 am to 9 pm Tuesday to Sunday, usually costs L12,000 (children aged six to 12, L9000). An updated calendar of events is on the palace Web site at www.palazzoducale.genova.it.

Chiesa del Gesù & Cattedrale di San Lorenzo

Flanking the eastern side of Piazza Giocomo Matteotti is **Chiesa del Gesù**, also known as Chiesa di Sant'Ambrogio. Extensive renovation work on its facade should be complete by mid-2001. Its 16th-century interior is a Baroque gem and showcases masterpieces by Guido Reni and Pieter Paul Rubens.

A stone's throw west along Via San Lorenzo is the cathedral. The Genoese black-and-white striped Gothic marble facade of **Cattedrale di San Lorenzo**, fronted by twisting columns, gaudy decoration and two stone lions, is something of an amusement every time you turn a corner to see it. The cathedral was consecrated in 1118 but its two bell towers (one of which is *still* not finished) and cupola didn't go up until the 16th century. Its **Cappella del San Giovanni Battista** (1450–65) once housed relics of St John the Baptist.

Look out for **Museo del Tesoro** (☎ 010 31 12 69), the museum hidden in the cathedral sacristy which houses the *Sacro Catino*, a cup allegedly given to Solomon by the Queen of Sheba and used by Jesus at the Last Supper (how did a humble prophet/deity manage to get hold of a glass green cup like that for his evening nosh-up?). Other relics include the polished quartz platter upon which Salome is said to have received John the Baptist's head. The museum can be visited by guided tour only, 9 to 11 am and 3 to 5.30 pm Monday to Saturday. Tours costs L10,000.

OLD CITY
Via San Lorenzo

This road was laid in the mid-19th century so carriages could drive between the new city and the port. It cuts right through the city's famous caruggi – a historic maze of twisting lanes and dank blind alleys that spills in a bewildering spaghetti formation across the oldest part of Genoa. Genoese families ruling the city staked out pockets of these medieval quarters as their own, building fabulous palaces and churches for their *alberghi* (clan) and defying rival families (with death, pillage, etc) to dare set foot on their patch of land.

Intrepid pedestrians can dive head-first into this medieval labyrinth in numerous places: the best way to explore it is to just wander around. Its core is bounded (in a clockwise direction) by Porta dei Vacca, Via Cairoli, Via Garibaldi, Via XXV Aprile, and by Porta Soprana around the inland periphery. Beyond that, it straggles along the coast in both directions.

Although the area is busy in daylight, just about everything shuts at night. Exceptions are some fine eateries and the 24-hour prostitution and drug trade which are concentrated in the zone west of Via San Luca.

South of Via San Lorenzo

From Via San Lorenzo, walk south along **Via di Canneto il Curto** to **Piazza San Giorgio**, an 11th-century marketplace. The standard of the Republic – carried by the commander of expeditions during battles for good luck – was kept in **Chiesa San Giorgio**, the church with the rounded cupola on the square's eastern side. Contrasting **Chiesa San Torpete**, on its southern side, was built by merchants from Pisa in the 12th century. Farther south-east into the caruggi via Via delle Grazie and Via delle Pietre Preziose is **Torre degli Embriaci**. The 12th-century crenulated tower was built by the Embriaci family as a symbol of its position in Genoese society. By 1296 the quest to build the tallest tower had got so out of hand that the height of family towers was limited to 80 spans. Dozens were consequently decapitated. Rival families traditionally destroyed each others' towers, hence the marked absence of these towers today.

Castello Immediately east on Via Santa Maria di Castello, Basilica e Convento si Santa Maria di Castello is among Genoa's finest examples of Romanesque architecture.

GENOA

The basilica was built in the 12th century in an attempt to repopulate **Castello**, the quarter settled by the Greeks and abandoned by the Romans. The Dominican convent (1449) boasts a rich collection of archaeological treasures, manuscripts and art which can be seen as part of a guided tour (by appointment only; ☎ 010 254 95 11). Its 15th-century cloisters and loggias are worth a peek.

During the Republic, the large elongated square of **Piazza Sarzano**, dominated by the sober facade of **Chiesa San Salvatore** (now a university lecture hall), was another bustling marketplace. For decades the square spat out the skulls of Pisan prisoners captured by the Genoese fleet of San Giorgio during the Battle of Melonia (1284) and incarcerated around **Via Campopisano** – or so legend claims.... During sieges, the fortified city drew water from a well at its northeastern end. A 16th-century **rotonda** topped by a double-faced Janus (see the boxed text 'Two-Faced Genoa') marks the spot.

Behind, the **Museo di Sant'Agostino** (☎ 010 251 12 63) at Piazza Sarzano 7–9, a church museum inside a Gothic triangular cloister with a colourfully tiled bell tower, displays the best of Ligurian sacred art, including the burial monument of Margaret of Brabant, sculpted for the late wife of Henry VII of Luxemburg by Giovanni Pisano in 1311. Opening hours are 9 am to 7 pm Tuesday to Saturday, and 9 am to 12.30 pm Sunday. Admission costs L7000 (those aged over 65 and under 18, free).

Stradone di Sant'Agostino links Piazza Sarzano with **Piazza San Donato**, at the foot of Castello. In the 11th century, both the square and its timber-roofed Romanesque **Chiesa di San Donato** with its octagonal belfry, was controlled by the Sarzanos, one of three noble families in an otherwise ecclesiastical stronghold (33 of the 55 hectares inside the fortified city at this time belonged to clergy). The 16th-century palace adjoining the church was destroyed in 1650 by enemies of the Raggio family. Giovanni Paolo Raggio stabbed himself to death in prison after his plot to kill the doge during a Corpus Christi procession was rumbled. His wife gave him a knife hidden in a crucifix to commit the

Two-Faced Genoa

Genoa's mythical origins lie in two-faced Janus, the Roman God of doorways and beginnings who founded the city. He stares in two directions – towards the past with one face, and towards the future with the other.

crime. His ghost allegedly haunts the square. Sunday mass is celebrated in Chiesa di San Donato (☎ 010 246 88 69) at 10 am.

Porta Soprana & Casa di Colombo A short stroll east along Via San Donato and Salita del Prione brings you to the only remaining section of the city's 12th-century defensive walls which, in Genoa's heyday, made it virtually impregnable on the landward side. An inscription on **Porto Soprana** (1155–60), the restored easternmost gate, warns 'I am guarded by men and surrounded by extraordinary walls.... If you have come in peace, you may touch this gate but should you be seeking war, you shall be repelled, disillusioned and defeated.' The 30m-tall gate can be visited at weekends; ask at Casa di Colombo. To view the wall, duck beneath the gate and walk east along Via Colle.

Casa di Colombo (☎ 010 246 53 46), in the gate's shadow on Piazza Dante, is a much rebuilt house, said to be Colombus' birthplace, or at least the spot where his father lived. There are conflicting opinions about the authenticity of the claims (see the boxed text 'Christopher Columbus' under History in the Facts about the Cities chapter). The tiny house can be visited 9 am to noon and 2 to 6 pm at weekends. Admission is free. Behind it is **Chiostro di Sant'Andrea**, the cloister being all that remains of a Romanesque convent shut in 1794 and levelled in 1904.

From Piazza Dante, a neck-aching stretch of magnificent arcaded Art Nouveau buildings on **Via Dante** takes you back to Piazza de Ferrari.

North of Via San Lorenzo

Narrow **Salita San Matteo** links the northwestern corner of Piazza de Ferrari with

GENOA

Piazza San Matteo, a charming square filled by zebra-striped **Chiesa di San Matteo**. Founded in 1125, this was the church of the infamous Doria family who also had its aristocratic palazzo on the square. Andrea Doria's sword is preserved under the church altar and his tomb is in the crypt.

Via Banchi and its eastern continuation **Via degli Orefici** with its market stalls, cafes and cake shops; hip shop- and bar-clad **Via San Luca**; and **Via del Campo** are the main thoroughfares in this neck of the caruggi. Italy's first stock exchange (1855) opened in the 16th-century **Loggia della Mercanti** on Piazza Banchi, a busy market-place today.

A block east is **Vico dell'Amor Perfetto**, a narrow carrugio supposedly named after the brothels and houses of ill-repute to which it wiggled. Some say the Street of Perfect Love refers to the legendary love affair between French King Louis XII and one of the Spinola women. Monumental 13th-century **Chiesa Santa Maria di Vigne**, east again on Piazza delle Vigne, alludes to the vineyards that once covered the square. Criminals made the desecrated church their den in the 18th century.

Teenage prostitutes are a dime a dozen in this part of the city.

Palazzo Spinola The Spinolas were one of the Republic's most formidable and feared dynasties. Their illustrious palace is an awe-inspiring example of the splendour in which nobility lived between the 16th and 18th centuries. Genoese artists such as Valerio Castello, Lorenzo de Ferrari and Filippo Parodi are all represented in the **Galleria Nazionale** (☎ 010 270 53 00), Piazza Superiore di Pellicceria 1, housed here since 1958 when the Spinolas gave their ancestral home to the city. Pisano's *Justice* and Ruben's *Equestrian Portrait of Gio Carlo Doria* are highlights of the permanent Italian and Flemish Renaissance art collection on the 3rd and 4th floors.

The National Gallery opens 9 am to 8 pm Tuesday to Saturday, and 2 am to 8 pm Sunday. Admission costs L8000 (those aged 18 to 25, L4000; those aged over 65 and under

18, free). A combined ticket to Palazzo Spinola and Palazzo Reale costs L12,000 (those aged 18 to 25, L6000; those aged over 65 and under 18, free).

Chiesa di San Siro This church on Via San Siro served as Genoa's cathedral from the 4th to 9th century when, because of its vulnerable location outside the city walls, the ecclesiastical privilege was handed over to San Lorenzo. The church was extensively rebuilt in the 16th century and, as with many Genoese churches, was badly damaged during WWII.

PORTO ANTICO

The 1992 Expo transformed the area known as Porto Antico (Old Port) into Genoa's strongest drawcard. And as Genoa gears up for its role as European City of Culture in 2004, rejuvenation of the ancient Greek port will continue. Unfortunately, nothing can detract from the **Sopraelevata**, a horrendously ugly flyover that slashes straight through the old port area, making one wonder how such a monstrosity could ever have been built.

Just back from the waterfront, frescoed **Palazzo San Giorgio** (1260), Piazza Caricamento, houses the port authority. It previously served as a prison (1298) where inmate Marco Polo worked on *Il Milione*.

Acquario di Genova

Genoa's aquarium (☎ 010 248 12 05, ✉ info@acquario.ge.it), overlooking the water on Ponte Spinola, is the city's star attraction and the largest aquarium in Europe, or so it claims (as does its counterpart in Barcelona). Its stars – oggled at each year by 1.4 million visitors – include sharks, penguins and dolphins (the largest of which is 2.5m long). In all, there are some 500 species and 5000 marine animals swimming around in 61 tanks to be viewed. Detailed captions in English explain what is what.

Feeding time sees 175kg of crustaceans and frozen fish dished out weekly: the common seals are fed at 10 am, noon, 2 and 4 pm; the bottlenose dolphins at 10 am and 12.30, 2.30 and 4.30 pm; and the Humboldt penguins from the Peruvian coast at 3.15 pm.

GENOA

About 1kg of fish and squid per 90kg specimen is fed to the shark tank three times per week, although the speed with which it's snapped up makes viewing tricky.

Since 1998, the floating barge which hosted the Italy pavilion during the 1992 Expo, has housed **Grande Nave Blu**, a 2700 sq m exhibition space. Visitors are taken on a whirlwind voyage through the age of discovery (Darwin, Columbus et al), then whisked off to Madagascar where 90% of species are not known to exist elsewhere. A 150-species reconstruction of Tsingy Forest creeps up one wall, the African island's lagoon environment is recreated in a section of coral reef and there's a 'touch tank' where Madagascan fauna such as the ray, cousin to the shark, can be encountered close-up (yes, you can touch the beasts).

The aquarium opens 9.30 am to 7 or 7.30 pm Tuesday to Friday, and 9.30 am to 8 or 8.30 pm weekends and holidays, October to February; and 9.30 am to 7.30 pm weekdays (11 pm Thursday in July and August), and 9.30 am to 8.30 pm weekends and holidays, the rest of the year. The last admission is 1½ hours before closing. Tickets, which can be reserved in advance, cost L22,000 (those aged three to 12, L13,000). A combination ticket covering admission to the aquarium and Padiglione del Mare e della Navigazione (see later) is L28,000 (children three to 12, L16,000).

Allow at least two to three hours to visit (more in summer when you risk spending up to 45 minutes alone simply queuing to buy an entrance ticket). The aquarium is online at www.acquario.ge.it.

Il Bigo

A hundred metres south of the aquarium on Calata Cattaneo is Il Bigo, '*bigo*' being the Italian naval term for derrick. The waterfront crane was built for the sole purpose of hoisting a cylindrical container 200m into the air and allowing its occupants a bird's-eye view of the city and port. The *ascensore panoramico* (panoramic lift) was designed by Piano (see the boxed text 'Renzo Piano' in the Facts about the Cities chapter) as the symbol of the 1992 Expo.

A ride costs L5000/4000 without/with an aquarium ticket (children aged seven to 12, L4000/3000). It operates 11.30 am to 1 pm and 2.30 to 4 pm Tuesday to Friday, and 11.30 am to 1 pm and 2.30 to 5 pm weekends. Behind is an **ice-skating rink** (see Activities later in this chapter).

Museo Nazionale dell'Antardide

A chilly addition to the waterfront is Museo Nazionale dell'Antardide (☎ 010 254 36 90, e mna@unige.it), behind Il Bigo on Calata Cattaneo. The Antarctic museum occupies the 2nd floor of **Millo**, an old warehouse which was chopped down in size (two storeys were lopped off) and transformed by Piano from 1988 to 1992 into a museum, restaurant and shopping complex. Videos, CD-ROMs and other multi-media devices encourage visitors to explore the 98% ice-covered white continent and learn about Italy's research programme in Antarctica conducted from its base at Terra Nova Bay since 1986.

Free audioguides in English are available at reception. The museum opens 9.45 am to 6.15 pm Tuesday to Saturday, and 10 am to 7 pm Sunday and holidays, October to May; and 10 am to 7 pm Sunday to Thursday, and 10 am to 10.30 pm Friday and Saturday, June to September. Admission costs L10,000 (those aged over 60 and six to 18, L8000) and family tickets are available (L20,000). A combination ticket covering the Museo del Tesoro (see Chiesa del Gesù & Cattedrale di San Lorenzo earlier) too costs L15,000. See also the Web site at Web site at www.mna.it.

La Città dei Bambini & Padiglione del Mare e della Navigazione

Walking west along Calata Mandraccio, you pass **Porta Siberia** (1550), a city gate named not after any gruesome event or geographic location but rather after *cibaria*, a derivation of the Italian word for food (alluding to the port's grain warehouses). Further west along the same waterfront promenade is **Magazzini del Cotone**, one-time cotton warehouses built by English architects in the 19th century. The long hangar-like building has been concerted into a waterside entertainment

GENOA

area and congress centre. A nine-screen **Cineplex Porto Antico** is here, as is a radio station, library and small **shopping centre**. In front, on Piazzale Luigi Durand de la Pierre, is an open-air **swimming pool** (see Activities later in this chapter).

La Città dei Bambini (☎ 010 246 55 35, 010 247 57 02, e cdibimbi@split.it), an interactive space on the 1st floor of Magazzini del Cotone, is aimed at helping kids discover the wonders of 'play, science and technology'. Three zones feature interactive gismos designed to challenge and stimulate differing age groups: three- to five-year-olds (how to construct a house, a building site, etc) and six- to 14-year-olds (ant farm, TV studio, exploring life, etc). The centre opens 10 am to 6 pm Tuesday to Sunday and sessions last 1¼ hours (one hour for children aged three to five). Admission costs L8000; anklebiters must be accompanied by an adult (two accompanying adults per child get in for free).

Equally engaging is 2nd-floor **Padiglione del Mare e della Navigazione** (Sea & Seafaring Pavilion; ☎ 010 246 36 78), dedicated to Genoa's proud maritime history. Life-sized dioramas transport you back to Genoa's busy port days and there's a reconstruction of a 16th-century dockyard and the interior of a transatlantic liner. The museum opens 10.30 am to 6 pm weekdays and 10.30 am to 7 pm weekends, March to September; and 10.30 am to 5.30 pm Tuesday to Friday, and 10.30 am to 6 pm weekends, the rest of the year. Admission costs L10,000 (those aged over 60 and three to 12, L5000) or L30,000 for a family ticket. Aquarium ticket holders get L2000 discount.

A sweeping view of Porto Antico and its **lighthouse** (see the boxed text 'Portly Sights by Boat') can be enjoyed from **Molo Vecchio**, the westernmost tip of the peninsula behind Magazzini del Cotone. A free **electric tourist train** shuttles weary-footed visitors between

---

Portly Sights by Boat

Porto Antico

The Old Port – with its abandoned warehouses, silos, boat yards and military installations – is a grand (albeit industrial) sight in itself, best seen by boat. Boat operators Cooperativo Battellieri del Porto di Genova and Alimar both run trips year-round. See Organised Tours under Getting Around earlier.

Palazzo del Principe

(☎ 010 25 55 09, e doriapamge@mclink.it), Via Adua 6. Built outside the city walls in 1529–33, the Prince's Palace played court to Andrea Doria and his merry band of noble followers who ruled Genoa with fists of gold. Its sumptuous interior and waterfront gardens clad with marble can both be visited. Regular boats yo-yo between Ponte Spinola, next to the aquarium, and the palace. Alternatively, in summer, sail in style aboard **La Fregata dei Doria** (☎ 010 25 55 09, e doria pamge@mclink.it), a reconstruction of a 16th-century frigate which carried messages between vessels during sea battles. It departs from Calata Mandraccio, mid-way between Il Bigo and Magazzini del Cotone, at regular intervals 10.30 am to 4.30 pm Tuesday to Sunday.

The palace opens 10 am to 5 pm Tuesday to Sunday. Admission costs L12,000 (those aged over 60 and students, L9000); a combination ticket covering the museum and boat costs L22,000 (those aged over 60 and students, L18,000).

Faro della Lanterna

Genoa's lighthouse (1543), built on the western side of the port to replace a fire- and later oil-lit structure, is in a military zone off-limits to civilians. Boat trips to its shores and guided tours up the 357 steps to the top of the 117m-tall beacon are organised by the Associazione Culturale Genovese Porta Soprana (☎ 010 246 53 46, e portasoprana@libero.it). Tours (two hours) depart at 2.30 pm on Sunday from in front of Il Bigo on Calata Cattaneo. Tickets cost L15,000. On other days tours (minimum 20 people) can be arranged by telephone.

GENOA

Calata Cattaneo and Piazzale Luigi Durand de la Pierre. Trains stop in front of Il Bigo and Magazzini del Cotone.

PRÈ TO PIAZZA CORVETTO

Commoners lived in seedy **Prè**, wedged between Stazione Principe and Porta dei Vacca at Porto Antico's northern end. Until the 14th century the ramshackle quarter, which continues to exert a lowlife charm, fell outside the city walls (Porta dei Vacca being the westernmost counterpart to Porta Soprana). Its northern edge was gilded in the early 1600s with mansion-studded **Via Balbi**, a thoroughfare built on Balbi family land to link the port with the city. Genoa university occupies many of its sumptuous palaces today. **Santissima Annunziata del Vestato**, on Piazza della Nunziata at the eastern end of Via Balbi, is a rich example of 17th-century Genoese architecture, virtually destroyed by WWII bombing raids. Crane your neck to see the trompe l'oeil in the dome.

Palazzo Reale

The seat of the Savoys from 1824, **Palazzo Reale** (☎ 010 271 02 72), Via Balbi 10, features Renaissance artworks and a fabulous – albeit crumbling – set of 18th-century stuccoed ceilings. Red velvet dating to 1842 plasters the walls of the Sala del Trono (Throne Room) and a panoramic terrace can be accessed from the Salotto dell'Aurora, named after the ceiling fresco by Bolognese painter Jacopo Antonio Boni (1688–1766) which, until 1766, was mistakenly believed to depict the marriage of Aurora and Cephalus – rather than Flora and Zephir!

It opens 8.15 am to 1.45 pm Monday and Tuesday, and 8.15 am to 7.15 pm the rest of the week. Admission costs L8000 (those aged 18 to 25, L4000; those aged over 65 and under 18, free) and a combined ticket to the Reale and Spinola palaces is L12,000 (those aged 18 to 25, L6000; those aged over 65 and under 18, free).

Via Garibaldi

Skirting the northern edge of the former city limits, Via Garibaldi marks a break between the Middle Ages and the Renaissance, and between the poor and rich. Lined with magnificent, if somewhat blackened and unkempt, *palazzi* (palaces), it is the place to admire the pick of Genoa's museums.

Palazzo Rosso (☎ 010 271 02 36), Via Garibaldi 18, boasts works from the Venetian and Genoese schools and several paintings by van Dyck. Across the street, **Palazzo Bianco** (☎ 010 247 63 77), Via Garibaldi 11, features works by Flemish, Spanish and Dutch masters and home-grown material by Caravaggio and Antonio Pisanello. Look also for Dürer's *Portrait of a Young Boy*. Both galleries open 9 am until 1 pm Tuesday, Thursday and Friday; 9 am to 7 pm Wednesday and Saturday; and 10 am to 6 pm Sunday. Admission to each costs L6000 (those aged over 65 and under 18, free) and a combined ticket covering both costs L10,000. Admission is free on Sunday.

Many buildings on Alessi's grand boulevard – off-limits to motorised vehicles – house banks and other public facilities. Wander in if the iron gates are open: **Palazzo Doria Tursi**, Genoa's town hall since 1848 at No 9, was built in 1564 for aristocrat and banker Niccolò Grimaldi. Inside are the relics of two famous Genoese – fragments of Columbus' skeleton (!) and one of Niccolò Paganini's violins (1742), occasionally played at concerts. The palace's elevated courtyard surrounded by open galleries and gardens are worth seeing. **Palazzo del Podestà** at No 7 has magnificent frescoes in its courtyard, as does **Palazzo Spinola** at No 5, home to Deutsche Bank. The Genoa Chamber of Commerce lives at No 4 in **Palazzo Cattega Cataldi** with its splendid Rococo gallery; Banca di Chiavari sits in splendidly frescoed **Palazzo Gambaro** at No 2; and Banca Populare di Brescia is opposite at **Palazzo Cambiaso**, Via Garibaldi 1.

Piazza Corvetto

After strolling the length of Via Garibaldi, continue east along pedestrian Salita Santa Caterina, past the prefecture inside 16th-century **Palazzo Doria Spinola**, to Piazza Corvetto, a busy intersection pierced by a **statue of Vittorio Emanuele II** and flanked on either side by gardens and theatres.

GENOA

From its north-western side, a narrow path staggers up the hillside, through steeply tiered gardens embedded with rock pools and exotic plants, to **Museo d'Arte Orientale** (☎ 010 54 22 85) at Piazzale Mazzini 1. Built in 1971 on the site of the neoclassical Villetta di Negro, the museum displays one of Europe's largest deposits of Oriental art, collected by Genoese painter Eduardo Chiossone when he lived and worked in Japan (1875–98) as director of its finance ministry's banknote department. The pagodas in the terrace gardens behind the museum afford fine views of Genoa's slate rooftops and port. The museum opens 9 am to 1 pm Tuesday and Thursday to Sunday. Admission costs L6000 (free on Sunday).

Steps from the eastern side of Piazza Corvetto lead to **Spianata dell'Acquasola**, tree-pricked public gardens with a children's playground and small lake. When the plague swept through the port city in the 17th century, it was here that its victims were buried. A macabre thought (don't tell the kids).

Heading west, elegant **Via Roma** (1870), with its Art Nouveau boutiques and adjacent glass-covered **Galleria Mazzini**, is Genoa's finest shopping street. It links Piazza Corvetto with Piazza de Ferrari.

EAST OF PIAZZA DE FERRARI

Shop-lined **Via XX Settembre** strides forth in the same elegant fashion as Via Roma, waltzing past ornately carved portals, stone-weary atlantes and other Art-Nouveau ornamentations on an eastbound stroll from Piazza de Ferrari to Piazza della Vittoria. Porticoes embrace its western half. Romanesque **Chiesa San Stefano**, **Ponte Monumentale** (1895), 17th-century **Chiesa della Consolazione** and the covered market of **Mercato Orientale** provide ready landmarks along the way.

The stark face of 1930s Genoa peers out from the rationalist architecture of **Piazza della Vittoria**, an enormous square pierced with **Arco dei Caduti**, an arch honouring those who died during WWI and WWII. South of the square, **Scalinata Millite**

Ignoto (Stairs to the Unknown Soldier) lead through gardens to part of the **Mura Nuove**, built to protect the city in the 17th century (see City Walls & Forts later). About 500m south-west sprawls the waterfront **Fiera Internazionale di Genova**, the city's primary trade fair and exhibition centre built in the 1960s on reclaimed land from the sea.

Museo Civico di Storia Naturale

Duck through the opening between porticoed buildings on the south-western corner of Piazza della Vittoria to reach the Natural History Museum (☎ 010 56 45 67), Via Brigata Liguria 9, founded in 1867 and housed in its own, purpose-built palace since 1912. Its collection is impressive if stuffed monkeys, wild cats, reptiles, turtles, birds and other animals are your kind of thing; there's some 6000 in all. An elephant skeleton, said to be 250,000 years old, fills the central hall on the ground floor.

The museum opens 9 am to 12.30 pm and 3 to 5.30 pm Tuesday to Thursday, Saturday and Sunday; and 9 am to 12.30 pm Friday. Admission costs L6000 (those aged over 60 and under 18, free). On Sunday, it's free.

Museo d'Arte Contemporanea

Steps climb from the seafront to Corso Aurelio Saffi, from where tree-lined Via Jacopo Ruffini leads to the Museum of Contemporary Art (☎ 010 58 00 69, 010 58 57 72) in a 19th-century villa at No 3. Built for Genoese industrialist Giacomo Croce, Villa Croce is surrounded by a ragged park with picnic tables and climbing frames for kids to hurt themselves. Temporary contemporary art exhibitions fill the museum, open 9 am to 6.30 pm Tuesday to Saturday, and 9 am to 12.30 pm Sunday. Admission costs L8000 (those aged under 14, free).

CITY WALLS & FORTS

With the increasing threat posed by both the House of Savoy and France, the Republic built new city walls in 1626–32. These **Mura Nuove** (New Walls), which covered a much larger area than their 12th-century predecessors, stretched west to the lighthouse, east to Piazza della Vittoria and

GENOA

north to **Forte Sperone** (490m), the largest of the remaining defensive forts where open-air plays and concerts are held in summer. The fortress can only be visited by pre-arranged guided tour; ask at the APT office for details.

In all, a 13km-long scar of walls can be traced in the high inland country leaning protectively over the city. The easiest way to get to the wall and inspect its forts is by riding the **funicular** from Largo della Zecca to **Righi** (300m). From Largo Giorgio Caproni, the square in front of Righi funicular station, marked walking trails (red markers) lead to Forte Begato, Forte Sperone, Forte Puin and Forte Diamante.

Another picturesque route offering heady views of Genoa's fort-studded hills is along **Mura di San Bartolomeo**, a section of wall that can be reached from Piazza Manin. Climb the steps leading from the Esso petrol station to Via alla Stazione per Caselle and continue uphill to the wall. Almost immediately on your left you pass the ornate, red-brick facade of **Castello Mackenzie Wolfson** (1896–1906) at Mura di San Bartolomeo 16. The turreted castle, designed by architect Gino Copedé for a Scot called Mackenzie, cannot be visited. Continuing sharply uphill, three forts emerge on the hilly horizon: the abandoned 18th-century **Forte Quezzi** (295m) and **Forte Richelieu** (415m), and the WWII military prison of **Forte Ratti**, rebuilt in 1837.

From Stazione Genova-Piazza Manin (☎ 010 83 73 21, ⓔ fgc@ferroviagenova caselle.it) at Via alla Stazione per Caselle 15, a **narrow-gauge railway** snakes 25km north to **Caselle** (405m), a tiny village in Scrivia Valley. The railway has been in operation since 1929 and offers passengers great views of Cimitero di Staglieno (see the boxed text 'Bury the Dead'), the forts of Sperone, Puin and Dimante on the hilltops and the low-lying Portfino promontory. The journey takes one hour (L3100, nine to 11 daily).

ACTIVITIES
Swimming
In summer the Genoese dip their toes into the Mediterranean from the pebble beaches

Bury the Dead

The best of Genoa's dead – including revolutionary Giuseppe Mazzini (1805–72) and Constance Lloyd (1858–98) who Oscar Wilde wed in 1884 and later abandoned – are buried in **Cimitero di Staglieno**, the city's monumental cemetery tucked in the hills north of town. The sea of graves dates to 1840 and is an extravaganza of ornate marble statues and neoclassical carvings. To get here, take bus No 34 from Stazione Principe to the end of line.

along **Corso Italia**, a promenade that kicks off 500m east of the Fiera Internazionale di Genova and continues for a good 2.5km to the waterfront village of **Boccadasse**. This smooth pedestrian stretch, constructed during the inter-war period, is popular with rollerbladers. From Stazione Brignole, bus No 31 runs the length of Corso Italia. There are plenty more pebble beaches farther east.

The open-air swimming pool (☎ 010 248 57 10), next to Magazzini del Cotone at Porto Antico, opens June to September. The pool inside the Stadio Comunale del Nuolo, Via Mario Galli, with its lovely Rationalist interior dating to 1935, opens all year.

Water Sports
Porto Antico is the hub of Genoa's watersport action, and there's no better place to start than at the harbour office at Marina Molo Vecchio (☎ 010 2 70 11, fax 010 27 01 200, ⓔ pesto@pesto.it), open 8.30 am to 12.30 pm and 2.30 to 6.30 pm inside Magazzini del Cotone on Calata Molo Vecchio. Staff stock lists of local diving and sailing clubs, and always have the latest weather forecast. Yachties can reserve a berth in advance – either in Genoa or along the coast – through the marina's informative Web site at www.mmv.it.

Polo Sub Diving Center (☎/fax 010 247 52 52, ⓔ mail@polosub.it), with an office in Magazzini del Cotone and a Web site at www.polosub.it, runs snorkelling and diving courses as well as guided expeditions.

Ice Skating

The canopy-covered ice-skating rink (☎ 010 246 13 19) at Piazza delle Feste, Porto Antico, opens October to April. Hours are 1 to 11.45 pm Monday, 8 am to 11.45 pm Tuesday to Friday, 8 am to 11 pm Saturday, and 10.30 am to 11.30 pm Sunday. A two-hour twirl on ice costs L8000 (L12,000 during peak hours).

COURSES

The International Language College (☎ 010 553 00 41, fax 010 533 00 40, e i.l .college@ iol.it), Via XX Settembre 20/85; and Benedict School (☎ 010 56 29 41, fax 54 36 48), Via XX Settembre 40, are among the handful of language schools in Genoa that run Italian courses for foreigners. The IAT office has a list of others.

Echo ☎/fax 010 846 18 48, e info@ echolingue.it), Piazza Marsala 2/2, runs Italian language, literature and cultural courses for foreigners.

Places to Stay

The IAT office won't make hotel recommendations or reservations but can provide you with a comprehensive list of accommodation options in the city.

PLACES TO STAY – BUDGET

Although the old city, Porto Antico and Prè have a smattering of budget hotels, you'll get better value and a substantially greater feeling of security east of Piazza de Ferrari, in the newer part of the city.

Camping

Villa Doria *(☎ 010 696 96 00, Via al Campeggio Villa Doria 15)*, en route to Pegli, opens year round and can be reached by bus Nos 1, 2 or 3 from Piazza Caricamento. Several other camp sites and caravan parks are scattered along the coast; ask at the IAT office.

Hostels

The HI ***Hostel Genova*** *(☎/fax 010 242 24 57, Via Costanzi 120)* is in the Righi area,

north of Genoa's old centre. B&B costs L22,000 and a meal costs L14,000. Catch bus No 40 from Stazione Brignole to the end of the line or No 35 from Stazione Principe, after which you have to connect with No 40. The hostel opens February to mid-December and charges L25,000 for B&B and L5000 to L65000 for a plate of pasta (only meal available). Check-in is between 3.30 pm and midnight.

Guesthouses

Arranging B&B around Genoa is ***Columbus Village Bed & Breakfast*** *(☎ 010 530 50 12, fax 010 595 90 76, e columbus_village@ libero.it, Via Galata 33–5)*, with a Web site at www.columbusvillage.com. A single/double/triple room in a family home with shared bathroom costs L35,000/60,000/ 80,000 (65,000/110,000/150,000 with private bathroom). More luxurious and/or charming equivalents cost around L90,000/ 150,000/210,000 and a handful of charming homes are available (from L800,000 for a weekend stay).

Flowers *(☎/fax 010 246 19 18, Via Lomellini 1)*, just off Via del Campo in the northern half of the old city, is a B&B with singles/doubles costing L85,000/140,000 per night.

Hotels – Old City

Hotel Major *(☎ 010 247 41 74, fax 010 246 98 98, e fmorrie@tin.it, Vico Spada 4)* is a friendly place in the old-city heart. Basic but clean singles/doubles cost L45,000/70,000 and singles/doubles/triples with private bathroom and TV will set you back L65,000/ 90,000/110,000. Breakfast is an extra L7000.

Tucked down a dimly lit alley is one-star ***Hotel Doina*** *(☎ 010 247 42 78, Vico dei Garibaldi 2)* which has rooms costing no more than L70,000/90,000. A flight of steps from Via XXV Aprile leads down to the 16-room hotel. Another tucked-away spot, not recommended for solo travellers due to its eerie location, is two-star ***Mini Hotel*** *(☎/fax 010 246 58 03, Via Lomellini 6/1)*.

On the fringe of the old city, ***Hotel Cairoli*** *(☎ 010 246 14 54, fax 010 246 75 12, Via Cairoli 14/4)*, is perched on the 3rd

Size up the fish at Mercato Orientale.

Genoa's alleys are made for scooting around.

A market stall's mountain of molluscs, Genoa

Inside Santissima Annunziata del Vestato

The city of Genoa: what will be your viewpoint?

Trompe l'oeil, Santissima Annunziata del Vestato

A lion crouches outside its Genoese den (Cattedrale di San Lorenzo).

The Ligurian village of Comogli

Ferrying to Cinque Terre

Discovering Columbus in Genoa

The exclusive town of Portofino reels in the glitterati.

floor of a building entrenched on either side by typical Genoese alleys. Two-star singles/doubles kick off at L70,000/110,000.

Hotel Cristoforo Colombo (☎/fax 010 251 36 43, ℮ colombo@libera.it, Via di Porta Soprana 59r) is an extremely charming and welcoming place in what is probably the nicest part of the old city. Quaint singles/doubles/triples with TV, telephone and private bathroom cost L70,000/120,000/150,000. Advance reservations are essential.

Hotels – Porto Antico & Prè

If it's dirt cheap (and occasionally dodgy) you want, prey on Prè, the quarter around Stazione Principe. At 15-room *Pensione Balbi* (☎ 010 247 21 12, Via Balbi 21–3) singles/doubles cost up to L70,000/90,000. Several hotels in a similar category line the same street, including 12-room *Hotel Bernheof* (☎ 010 247 21 66) at No 15 on the 2nd floor; 10-room *Pensione Ginevra* (☎ 010 247 21 09) on the 3rd floor of the same building; and *Hotel Elena* (☎ 010 247 55 09) which has seven rooms and two bathrooms on the 4th. Bang next door to the budget block is a busy university bar-cum-cafe, always packed with students.

One-star *Hotel Bologna* (☎ 010 246 57 72, fax 010 246 54 47, Piazza Superiore del Roso 3), tucked down a narrow alley off Via Balbi, has rooms for one/two for about L50,000/70,000.

Closer to the railway line, solo-starred *Hotel Acquaverde* (☎ 010 26 54 27, fax 010 246 48 39, Via Balbi 29/8) touts 10 single/double rooms costing L70,000/90,000. Neighbouring *Hotel Lausanne* (☎ 010 26 16 34, Via Balbi 33b) is up a flight of stairs from the street and charges similar rates.

Hotels – East of Piazza de Ferrari

Near Stazione Brignole is a hotel in a lovely old building at Via Groppallo 4. Turn right as you leave the train station and go up Via de Amicis to Piazza Brignole. Via Groppallo is on the right. *Pensione Carola* (☎ 010 839 13 40), on the 3rd floor, is clean with well-kept singles/doubles for up to L55,000/85,000. Up the road at No 8,

Albergo Rita (☎/fax 010 87 02 07) offers various one-star rooms from L50,000/75,000 for a single/double without private bathroom to L75,000/95,000 with.

In front of Stazione Brignole, *Albergo Fiume* (☎ 010 59 16 91, 010 570 54 60, fax 010 570 28 33, Via Fiume 9r) is squeaky clean as the reek of disinfectant testifies. Basic singles/doubles with washbasin and bidet cost L45,000/65,000 (L70,000/80,000 with bathroom).

Heading south along Via Fiume, swing right along Via XX Settembre to uncover a handful of good-value places to stay. One-star *Albergo Barone* (☎/fax 010 58 75 78, Via XX Settembre 2/23) is a faintly chaotic 3rd-floor hotel, with large rooms and decorative moulded ceilings, in a building dating to 1910. Only two of its 12 rooms have their own bathroom (L85,000/120,000 for one/two or three people); the rest share at least a toilet and cost L55,000/70,000/100,000/125,000 for one/two/three/four people (L70,000/85,000/110,000/135,000 with shower).

Eclectic, seven-room *Hotel Meublè Suisse* (☎ 010 54 11 76, Via XX Settembre 21/6) is on the 3rd floor of a fabulous building dating to 1850. Crammed with books, vases, photographs and other homely items, singles/doubles with shower and TV clock in at L60,000/80,000.

Albergo Olympia (☎ 010 59 25 38, fax 010 58 13 41, Via XX Settembre 21/8), on the 4th floor of the same building, is more conventional (and orderly), with nine simple but stylishly furnished rooms for L50,000/80,000 per single/double (L60,000/90,000 with private bathroom). If it's space you're seeking, ask for room No 12.

PLACES TO STAY – MID-RANGE
Hotels – Porto Antico & Prè

Three-star *Hotel Veronese* (☎ 010 251 07 71, fax 010 251 06 39, ℮ hlverone@tin.it, Vico Cicala 3), within spitting distance of raucous Piazza Caricamento, has decent singles/doubles with TV and telephone for L90,000/160,000 (more expensive on Friday and Saturday, and nightly April to October). Rates include breakfast.

GENOA

Away from the water, *Hotel Galles* (☎ *010 246 28 20, fax 010 246 28 22, Via Bersaglieri d'Italia 13)* and neighbouring *Hotel Alexander* (☎ *010 26 13 71, fax 010 26 52 57, Via Bersaglieri d'Italia 19)* tout three stars and peer at the ghastly road that rushes past the old port.

Three-star *Hotel Rio* (☎ *010 246 15 94, fax 010 247 68 71, Via Ponte Calvi 5)* charges L90,000/120,000 for singles/ doubles with bathroom, TV and telephone.

Across from Stazione Principe on the corner of Via Balbi, *Hotel Europa* (☎ *010 25 69 55/6, fax 010 26 10 47,* e *europa hotel@mclink.it, Via delle Monachette 8)* carries a trio of stars, a handy car park and decent singles/doubles costing L140,000/ 190,000. Don't miss its roof terrace bar. Next door at No 8 on the same no-through street is *Hotel Agnello d'Oro* (☎ *010 246 20 84, fax 010 246 23 27)*. Equivalent rooms here rock in at L90,000/140,000 (L130,000/ 170,000 in high season). Rates include breakfast at both places.

Hotels – East of Piazza de Ferrari

For a little more money, a reliable option is two-star *Hotel Bel Soggiorno* (☎ *010 54 28 80,* ☎/*fax 010 58 14 18, Via XX Settembre 19)*, in a turn-of-the-century townhouse smack-bang in the middle of Genoa's busy shopping street. Singles/doubles with bathroom, TV and mini-bar start at L90,000/140,000, including breakfast.

A stone-faced pair of weary Atlantes hold up the entrance to *Albergo Soana* (☎ *010 56 28 14,* ☎/*fax 010 56 14 86,* e *soana@ hotelsoana.it, Via XX Settembre 23/8)*, a two-star place favoured by business travellers. Comfortable rooms with mini-bar, TV, etc, cost L90,000/110,000/140,000 (L120,000/ 150,000/190,000 during festivals and holidays. Soana is on the 4th floor.

Hotel Brignole (☎ *010 56 16 51, 010 58 99 15, fax 56 59 90, Via del Corallo 13)*, down a side street off atmospheric Via San Vincenzo, touts acceptable rooms with mod-cons such as air-conditioning and hair dryer for L110,000/130,000, including breakfast.

A short walk north-west from Stazione Brignole along Via De Amicis brings you to Piazza Brignole, a quiet square dominated by the warm ochre facade of *Hotel Astoria* (☎ *010 87 33 16, fax 010 831 73 26, Piazza Brignole 4)*. Grandiose three-star rooms cost L150,000/200,000, including breakfast.

Another popular choice, particularly with guests carrying briefcases, is *Hotel Viale Sauli* (☎ *010 56 13 97, fax 010 59 00 92,* e *htl.sauli@mclink.it, Viale Sauli 5)*, off Via San Vincenzo. A lift whisks guests up to this efficient 1st-floor hotel, clad with marble floors and touting 56 modern single/ double/triple rooms costing L110,000/ 150,000/180,000 from Friday to Sunday (L140,000/180,000/220,000 the rest of the week).

PLACES TO STAY – TOP END

Rates at these pamper pads reflect the almost exclusively business clientele to which they cater: prices are highest in October, November, March to June and during trade fairs and congresses. July and August, coupled with Friday to Sunday nights year-round, usually command the lowest rates.

Those wanting somewhere to sleep at the ferry port could try four-star *Columbus Sea* (☎ *010 26 50 51, fax 010 25 52 26, Via Milano 63)*, a great choice if (a) you're as rich as an ocean liner cruise passenger and/or (b) intend hopping straight off a boat into bed (or out of bed into a boat). Singles/doubles sail in at L160,000/220,000 and max out at a stormy L245,000/390,000.

Hotels – Old City

The hot address is Best Western's 48-room *Hotel Metropoli* (☎ *010 246 88 88, fax 010 246 86 86,* e *metropolis.ge@bestwestern.it, Piazza Fontane Marose)*, strategically set at the entrance to the historic centre. Singles/ doubles cost L190,000/270,000 and include a rash of 'what-you-would-expect' perks.

Hotels – Porto Antico & Prè

Jolly Hotel Marina (☎ *010 2 53 91, fax 010 251 13 20, Molo Ponte Calvi)* sprawls in all its concrete pinkness across Ponte Calvi, the wharf across the water from the aquarium. Inside, characterless but comfortable singles/doubles kick off at L105,000/210,000 (weekends) and peak at L280,000/400,000 (weekdays during trade fairs and festivals).

The top-notch place to stay near Stazione Principe is four-star *Hotel Savoia Majestic* (☎ *010 26 16 41, fax 010 26 18 83, Piazza Stazione Principe)*, a somewhat-dated gilded, marble and wood affair. Rooms for one/two people cost L190,000/220,000 weekdays (L150,000/170,000 weekends). Its equal-starred rival *Hotel Britannia* (☎ *010 2 69 91, fax 010 246 29 42, Via Balbi 38)* commands similar rates.

Hotels – Prè to Piazza Corvetto

A jolly nice choice for anyone into hotel chains is *Jolly Hotel Plaza* (☎ *010 8 31 61, fax 839 18 50, e genova@jollyhotels.it, Via Martin Piaggio 11)*, overlooking the pretty gardens of Piazza Corvetto in an upmarket part of the city. Four-star rooms for one/two cost L265,000/320,000 (L320,000/400,000 in high season).

Hotels – East of Piazza de Ferrari

Across from Stazione Brignole is *Hotel Moderno Verdi* (☎ *010 553 21 04, fax 010 58 15 62, e info@modernoverdi.it, Piazza Guiseppe Verdi 5)*, the plush interior of which provides a stunning contrast to the street bustle outside. Sound-proofed rooms cost L140,000/180,000 (L280,000/360,000 at peak times).

On the other side of the park and next to Genoa's largest theatre looms the concrete, four-star hulk of *Star Hotel President* (☎ *010 57 27, fax 010 553 18 20, e president@ starhotels.it, Corte Lambruschini 4)*. Singles/doubles warranting zero complaint kick in at L280,000/365,000 (L400,000/520,000 at peak times).

One of the grand old establishments of Genoese hospitality is *Bristol Palace* (☎ *010 59 25 41, fax 010 56 17 56, e info@ hotelbristolpalace.com, Via XX Settembre 35)*, a former 19th-century mansion with a breathtakingly beautiful staircase topped by a fabulous stained-glass ceiling. Both are

dramatically visible from reception making for an easy peek for us plebiscites. Singles/doubles start at L330,000/400,000.

Places to Eat

Please see under Food in the Facts for the Visitor chapter for details of Genoa's food.

PLACES TO EAT – BUDGET
Restaurants

Near Stazione Brignole, *Ayers Rock* (☎ *010 58 84 70, Viale Sauli 33)* has a bright self-service buffet, open noon to 3 pm and 7 pm to 2 am. Down by Porto Antico, the waterfront area around Piazza Caricamento is lined with cheap – if unspectacular – restaurants.

Drake, Cook, Silver and other seafaring greats provide the inspiration for *Ugo Il Pirata* (☎ *010 59 37 06, Via Finocchiaro Aprile Camillo 34)*, a pirate den designed like a ship near Piazza della Vittorio. Its L17,000 lunchtime menu (first and second course, dessert, coffee and a 25cl jug of wine) is excellent value, and its home-made pasta dishes are not to be missed. Start off with a hearty bowl of *zuppa di ceci* (chickpea soup), a Genoese speciality, followed by *tagliatelle d'Oriente* (ginger- and saffron-spiced pasta in curry sauce).

Neighbouring *Trattoria Lombarda da Peppino* (☎ *010 59 46 29, Via Finocchiaro Aprile Camillo 26)* is a more traditional dining spot where you can lunch on the cheap for L18,000. *Stoccafisso alla genovese* (stockfish) is one of the fishy delights dished up at this cosy bistro.

Cafes – Old City

Spacious and brightly lit cafes are few and far between in the old city. A welcome exception is *Caffè Loi (Via San Luca 70)*, next to a crumbling palace propped up by two naked men. Another airy place is *Caffè Meridiana (Piazza Meridiana)*, named after the palace it peers at. Well-filled panini cost L3500 to L4000 and a hot dish of the day is L6500. The unpretentious *Doge Bar (Piazza Giacomo Matteotti 5)* commands magnificent views of Palazzo Ducale.

Historic *A Ved Romanengo* (☎ *010 247 29 15, Via degli Orefici 31–3*) has been serving pastries, confectionary and sweet *marroni* (chestnuts) since 1805. Its cafe – clad with three lace-dressed tables – serves lunch. There's no printed menu; just ask what's cooking. *Mangini & C* on Piazza Corvetto is another renowned *pasticceria* (cake shop).

A hop, skip and a jump away from the shaded, old-city alleys is *Le Dolcezze* (*Via XXV Aprile 22*), a sandwich shop which sells an unbeatable range of filled panini, quiches, salads and cakes to take away. Across the square in front of Teatro Carlo Felice is *Caffè Hausbrandt* (☎ *010 54 36 68, Largo Sandro Pertini*), a fine spot to bask in the sun, sip coffee and watch Garibaldi on horseback. The downside? A can of Coke costs L4500.

Piazza Dante throws up a couple of choices for early risers hunting for breakfast: *Bar Grattacielo* at Nos 26–8 serves a L30,000 brunch and has a sprawling terrace which serves pink-and-white-ladies, golden dreams and other cocktails in the evening. Nearby *Rio* (☎ *010 58 00 25, Via Ceccardi 25r*) serves an imaginative range of breakfasts and sandwiches from 5 am to 8 pm. Through Porto Soprana, you hit *Café di Barbarossa* (☎ *010 246 50 97, Piano di Sant'Andrea 21–3r*), a simple but stylish cafe which basks in the shade of the towering 12th-century gate (open until 2 am Wednesday to Sunday).

Cafes – East of Piazza de Ferrari

East of Piazza de Ferrari, the streets around Stazione Brignole and Via San Vincenzo house some of the city's most lip-licking pasticceria, a handful of which serve espresso to a standing-up clientele. Several are listed under What to Buy in the Shopping section.

Actually on Via San Vincenzo, *Le Cantine di San Vincenzo* is an excellent little spot to sit down for a hot or cold panini (L6000), of which there are no less than 27 fillings to choose from. It also serves numerous pizzas and salads, each listed with its ideal wine accompaniment on the user-friendly menu. *Caffè Tubrio* (*Via Settembre 268*) is a pleasant place for coffee and ice cream.

A lovely spot to lunch or down an espresso while waiting for a bus on Piazza della Vittoria is *Al Parador* (☎ *010 58 17 71, Pizza della Vittoria 49*), a modern restaurant-bar which sells well-stuffed panini and full meals (about L8,000/10,000 for a first/second course) on its quiet, sunny terrace beneath the porticoes.

Pizzerias

In summer, munch on wholemeal pizza (from L8000 to L15,000) beneath creeping vines at *Taverna da Michele* (☎ *010 59 36 71, Via della Libertà 41r*), a little-known spot with one of the city's most peaceful and atmospheric terraces. *Pescespada affumicato* (smoked swordfish) and *maialino al forno* (translated as 'baked little pig' on the bilingual menu) are other highlights.

Fast Food

Fast-food places doling out pizza, focaccia and sweet brioches to eat on the move are rampant in the old city. One worthy stop is *Sapore di Pane* (*Via Lucccoli 28*), notable for its brightly lit and modern interior

At the old port, the *no-name outlet* on the corner of Vico Cicala and Piazza Caricamento doles out shrimps, prawns and other fast-food fishy delights deep-fried in batter.

Via San Vincenzo is a short but busy food street lined with several joints selling snacks to munch on the move. Down-to-earth *farinata* specialist *Trattoria da Guglie* at No 64 sells piping-hot slices of Liguria's thin, chickpea-flour bread; *Panificio Mario* at No 61 cooks up focaccia topped with numerous different toppings (L2000 a slice); as does the *focacceria* at No 61a. For moussey *semifreddi* (literally 'semi-frozen') in a rainbow of flavours, *gelato* (ice cream) and *yogurt gelato* (ice-cream yoghurt) try *Bananarama*, a historic ice-cream parlour (with a wholly modern interior) dating to the 1930s.

McDonald's has outlets a short walk from Stazione Brignole at Via XX Settembre 1r (open 10.30 am to 11 pm); farther west along the same street at No 207r (open 10 to 1 to 2 am); at Via Sestri 229r; and at the passenger ferry terminal.

GENOA

Self-Catering

In the old city, several small food shops line Via Maddalena. Near Porto Antico *90 Vegio* *(Via Canneto il Luno 26r)*, with an entrance on Via San Lorenzo too, is a delicatessen with cheese, fresh pasta and cold meat counters.

Just off Via XX Settembre, *Superfresco Standa (Via Cesarea 12)*, with its fresh bread and fish counters, opens 8.30 am to 7.25 pm Monday to Saturday, and 9.30 am to 1 pm and 3.30 to 5.30 pm Sunday. *Supermercato Standa (Via Antonio Cecchi 83)*, a five-minute walk from Piazza della Vittoria, is another large, well-placed supermarket open 8.30 am to 7.30 pm daily.

If you like animal inners, head for *La Tripperia di Colombo (☎ 010 58 90 98, Corso Torino 48)*. The great slabs of stomach that hang from giant hooks in the window of this tripe shop are not for the faint-hearted.

PLACES TO EAT – MID-RANGE
Restaurants – Old City

Hidden in the labyrinthine old city is *La Taverna di Colombo (☎ 010 24 62 447, Vico della Scienza 6)*, a charming, bistro-style place which dishes up simple but delicious cuisine to a hungry clientele. First/second courses average L5500/7000, leaving the cosy red cellar packed out.

Equally tucked away is *Le Chioccole (☎ 010 251 12 89, Piazza Negri 5r)*, an up-market place overshadowed by its monumental neighbours, a candy-striped church and 18th-century Teatro della Tosse. Expect to pay L40,000 per head to dine here.

I Tre Merli (☎ 010 247 40 95, Vico della Maddalena 26), just off Via Garibaldi, touts an interior of uncovered brick and vaults, and is great for a candlelit meal that won't cost over L40,000 per person.

In a really ramshackle area is shabby but tasty *Ostaj dò Castello (☎ 010 29 89 80, Via Santa Maria di Castello 32r)*, an authentic place which prides itself – rightly so – on its *vera cucina genovese* (true Genoese kitchen).

Not far from Piazza Dante, *Da Genio (☎ 010 58 84 63, Salita San Leonardo 61r)* is at the top of a thigh-aching staircase off Via Fieschi. This small and traditional trattoria is always packed and reservations are

essential. Beware the unsmiling staff who speak gun-fire Italian very very fast.

Alternatively, duck through Porto Soprana to *Trattoria Alle 2 Torri (☎ 010 251 36 37, Salita del Prione 53r)*. Enticing pasta dishes such as tagliatelle laced with fresh prawns, and asparagus- or fish-filled ravioli average L15,000. A hearty bowl of *minestrone alla genovese* is L8000.

Continuing west along Salita del Prione and Via San Donato you reach Piazza delle Erbe, the pretty square where Roman Genoa's forum probably was. It has a couple of appealing restaurants and there are several more places along Via San Bernardo, including *Pintori (☎ 010 275 75 07)* at No 68.

If it's *pesce* (fish) you're after, try fishy *Trattoria Rina (☎ 010 246 64 75, Mura delle Grazie 3r)*, a sea-inspired bistro overlooking the highway from its elevated portside perch.

Empty tummies needing replenishment near the cathedral could try *Le Cantine di Squarciafico (☎ 010 247 08 23, Piazza Ivrea 3)*, a vaulted cellar with an excellent-value L12,000 self-service menu (including water or wine) and first/second courses for L14,000/18,000. Classical music adds an elegant touch.

Those on the old city's eastern fringe should make a bee line for *Trattoria da Maria (Vico Testa d'Oro 14)*, a surprisingly simple place with its checked tablecloths fluttering on a washing line outside and a handwritten menu. A filling meal here costs L13,000, including wine.

La Berlocca (☎ 010 247 41 62, Via dei Macelli di Soziglia 45r) is a memorable *enoteca* (wine bar), devoid of pretension and renowned for its traditional dishes with an added twist – sea bass with apples, castelmigno cheese souffle in pear sauce, sweet pear tart without flour, and tiramasu without liqueur! The place has only seven tables, so book ahead.

Restaurants – Porto Antico & Prè

Porto Antico offers some appealing but pricey eating and drinking options, kicking off with *Il Tre Merli (☎ 010 246 44 16)*, a chic restaurant and wine bar, decked out in

GENOA

black and white, and offering winers and diners a blackbird's eye view of the waterfront going-ons. The Three Blackbirds is one of a cluster of mid-range options to languish inside Millo, the former warehouse on Calata Cattaneo.

If tapas is your cup of tea, head west along the waterfront to *Nadamas* (☎ *010 254 33 85, Magazzini del Cotone),* a spacious Spanish restaurant overlooking the fancy yachts bobbing in the marina at the port's westernmost tip.

Al Veliero on Via al Ponte Calvi is a small refined trattoria, set just back from the sea and offering traditional fare for about L12,000 per course. Port views can also be enjoyed from the wharfside places to eat on Ponte Morosini: *La Banchina* at No 1 on the wharf has a great summer terrace, tucked in the shade of a moored galleon. *Old Port* (☎ *010 246 96 25)* at Nos 47–8 is a modern minimalist type of place, again with a waterside terrace.

Restaurants – East of Piazza de Ferrari

Sola, Cucina & Vino (☎ *010 59 45 13, Via Carlo Barabino 120)* is a fabulous wine shop where you can also dine in style – if you're lucky enough to get a table that is. Arrive by 12.30 pm or reserve in advance to guarantee a place to sit. *Torte genovese* (Genoese sponge) is this house's irresistible speciality.

PLACES TO EAT – TOP END

At refined *Le Rhune* (☎ *010 59 49 51, Vico Domoculta 14r)* you can sample tempting creations such as scampi and venus clam gnocchi in tomato sauce or wild mushrooms pan-fried in garlic, olive oil and parsley. The *stoccafisso* (stockfish) dressed in *salsa di noci* (a creamy walnut sauce) is a Genoese speciality. Le Rhune serves a L46,000 menu (including drinks). First/second courses average L17,000/19,000.

At Porto Antico, the upmarket choice is elegant *Restaurant da Coto al Porto Antico* (☎ *010 254 38 79)* on Ponte Morosini where you can enjoy elegant, white-tablecloth dining.

Unstartling from the outside, *Gran Gotto*

(☎ *010 56 43 44, Viale Brigate Bisagno 69)* is a haven of luxury and finesse inside with a price list hovering around the L35,000 mark for pasta and meat dishes. Suited business travellers (predominantly male) or those out to impress (ditto) tend to hang out here.

A short walk north-west of Stazione Brignole is *Le Bon Bec* (Via Gropallo 5), topped with an unusual wooden ceiling and serving French-inspired dishes such as kidneys in wine sauce, oysters, Genoese seafood salad and numerous fish dishes (L30,000). Reservations are recommended.

Entertainment

The weekly *News Spettacolo Liguria* is a free entertainments magazine. It carries cinema schedules and is handy for finding out what concerts and gigs are happening, both in Genoa and along the coast – its regular Top 10 column listing the best disco, DJ, barman, etc, of that week is a great measure of Genoa's 'in' venues of the moment.

Away from the waterfront, central Genoa all but shuts down in the evening – 'better to go home and sleep' was the advice of one local.

BARS & CLUBS

In the old city, a hot choice – day and night – is *Quattro Canti* (☎ *010 25 29 97, Via Ai Quattro Canti di San Francesco 28).* Tucked down a dark and dingy alleyway and hard to find, the cosy red-brick bar dishes up panini, bruschette and *buona musica* (good music) to a mellow crowd. Bring a beer mat if you want to woo the bar staff.

Cocktail fiends can suck through straws to their hearts' content at *Le Corbusier* (☎ *010 246 86 52,* @ *mixersnc@libero.it, Piazza San Donato 36–8),* a cocktail bar and cafe which, despite its name, appears to have nothing to do with the architect. *Café Madeleine* (☎ *010 246 53 12, Via della Maddalena 107)* is a hushed and intimate hideaway for stolen moments over wine, while *Britannia Pub* (☎ *010 247 45 32, Vico della Casana 76)* is the place to go for a pint of Guinness or Kilkenny (L8000 or L7500).

GENOA

Strictly somewhere for after dark is *Hot Vibes (Salita Pollaiuoli 26)*, an alternative club in the eeriest depths of the caruggi. Its walls are plastered with posters advertising what's on where in the clubbing scene.

Live music rocks *Fitzcarraldo (☎ 010 246 11 22, Piazza Cavour 35r)*, wedged between Vico Paggi and Vico dei Mattoni Rossi, well into the wee hours; as it does at *Disco Pub 261*, a food and music bar five minutes' walk away at Mura delle Grazie 21.

Away from the old city, *Liquid Art Café (☎ 0347 488 68 25, Piazza Savonarola 28)* is a hip cafe-cum-music bar with semi-industrial decor and charming bar staff which often star in *News Spettacolo*'s 'top barman' listings. It serves breakfast from 6.30 am and has a DJ spinning tunes from 10 pm; house is played most Saturdays.

American-style *Maddox Rock Café (☎ 010 56 58 96, Via Malta 15)* throws concerts and hosts live bands. Its industrial design is matched by an endless supply of complimentary pizza slices, fries, tortilla chips, olives and other meal-sized 'nibbles' to accompany your aperitif. Cocktails cost L8000 a shake.

Clubs are not Genoa's forte; most places to dance the night away are farther southeast along the coast. *Mako (☎ 010 36 76 52, Corso Italia 28r)*, *New Paips (☎ 010 32 19 25, Via Oberdan 211a)* and *ONIX (☎ 010 254 19 80, Via Targa 12)*, ex Mr Do, are popular discos.

GAY & LESBIAN VENUES

Gay and lesbian venues are thin on the ground. ArciGay or InformaGay (see Gay & Lesbian Travellers in the Facts about the Cities chapter) should be able to be point you in the right direction.

JAZZ

The Italian Jazz Institute (☎ 010 58 52 41, e info@italianjazzinstitute.com), Via Tommaso Reggio 34r, hosts regular jazz soirees at the Jazz museum inside Palazzo Ducale. Details are posted on its Web site at www.italianjazzinstitute.com.

CLASSICAL MUSIC

Classical concerts are held at 5 pm most Sundays in *Palazzo Ducale*. Tickets (from L12,000 to L20,000) and information (☎ 010 58 88 66) are available from the palace box office.

Other venues heaped in history include *Chiesa di San Donato (Piazza San Donato)* which hosts occasional organ concerts; and *Teatro Carlo Felice* (see Opera & Ballet later), Genoa's opera house where concerts are also held. Tickets cost about L50,000; Sunday performances are usually cheaper.

CINEMAS

A handful of cinemas screen films in their original language on selected nights, with the exception of *Multi-Sala Ariston (☎ 010 247 35 49, Vico San Matteo 14–16)*, just off Piazza Matteo, which sports a daily English-language film repertoire – viewable online at www.cinema-online.net. Tickets cost from L5000 to L7000.

Others include *Cineclub Chaplin (☎ 010 88 00 69, Piazza Cappuccini 11)*; *Fritz Lang (☎ 010 21 97 68, Via Acquarone 64)*; and *Cineclub Lumière (☎ 010 50 59 36, Via Vitale 1)*.

Genoa's largest cinema complex is the nine-screen *Cineplex Porto Antico (☎ 010 254 18 20)*, Via al Molo Vecchio, in a converted hangar at Porto Antico.

THEATRE

The Genoa Theatre Company performs at *Politeama Genovese (☎ 010 831 16 56, e info@politeamagenovese.it, Via Piaggio)*, with a Web site at www.politeamagenovese .it, and at the giant modern block of *Teatro di Genova (☎ 010 534 23 00, e info@ teatro-di-genova.it, Piazza Borgo Pila 42)*, of which *Teatro della Corte (☎ 010 534 22 00, Via Duca d'Aosta)* and *Teatro Duse (same tel, Via Bacigalupo)* are part. Tickets (from about L35,000 to L45,000) for Teatro di Genova can be bought in advance by telephone (☎ 010 534 24 00), Internet (www .ticketone.it) or from the theatre box offices. Up-to-date programmes are posted online at www.teatro-di-genova.it. The season runs from January to May.

GENOA

Casanova walked the boards at **Teatro della Tosse** (☎ 010 247 07 93, e info@ teatrodellatosse.it, Piazza Negri 4), dating to 1702. Musicals are often held here; check the Web site at www.teatrodellatosse.it.

In summer, plays and concerts are sometimes held at Forte Sperone (see Things to See & Do earlier). The IAT office has details.

OPERA & BALLET

The curtain first rose at Genoa's opera house, **Teatro Carlo Felice** (☎ 010 538 12 24/7, e info@carlofelice.it, Piazza de Ferrari) in 1828. Heavily bombed during air raids in 1942 and 1943, the current building dates to 1991. An equestrian monument to Giuseppe Garibaldi (1807–82) flanks its reconstructed neoclassical colonnaded facade which is topped by a statue of Harmony.

The four-stage theatre has a year-round programme. Its box office (☎ 010 58 93 29, 59 16 97), in the complex at Galleria Cardinal Giuseppe Siri 6, opens 11 am to 6 pm Tuesday to Friday, 11 am to 3.30 pm Saturday, and one hour before performances start. Tickets can also be booked by credit card over the phone (☎ 010 570 16 50) and online at www.carlofelice.it. Expect to pay about L170,000/40,000 for the best/worst seat in the house for an opera (L90,000/30,000 for equivalent seats at the ballet).

SPECTATOR SPORTS

When it plays at home, Genoa's football team UC Sampdoria kicks off at Stadio Luigi Ferraris, a stadium with a capacity of 40,000. Tickets for home matches cost from L30,000 to L120,000 and are sold at the UC Sampdoria boutique (☎ 010 251 80 42, 010 248 52 52, e segreteria@sampdoria.it) inside Galleria dei Caravana, the shopping mall beneath the aquarium on Ponte Spinola. The club has a Web site at www .sampdoria.it. To join the fan club, send your L50,000 annual membership fee to UC Sampdoria SpA, Fan Club Ufficiale, Campetto 2, 16123 Genova.

UC Sampdoria share their stadium with local rivals Genoa. The club have fallen on hard times of late and are in the lower reaches of Serie B. For tickets contact the club (☎ 010 2 69 21 fax 010 269 24 82) at Via Garibaldi 3. Souvenirs and merchandise are available from Genoa Point Nervi in Via Nervi, or around the stadium on match days.

Shopping

WHAT TO BUY
Sweets & Chocolate

Pietro Romanengo & Stefano has sugared almonds, jellied fruits and moulded chocolate since 1780, as its old-town shop at Via Soziglia 74 (☎ 010 247 45 74), with marble floors and fresco ceiling, clearly attests. It has another outlet at Via Roma 51 (☎ 010 58 02 57).

Casa del Cioccolato Paganini (☎ 010 251 36 62), Via di Porta Soprana 45r, is a chocolate house dating to 1893. Take one step inside this aromatic shop and there's no way you'll leave without buying at least a square.

Pandolce

East of Piazza de Ferrari, Tagliafico at Via Galata 31 has been in business since 1923. It sells exquisitely decorated *torta* (cakes), *kranz* (honey-glazed raison bread baked in a twist and topped with sugar crystals) and traditional *pandolce genovese* (Genoese fruit bread) – the city's answer to *panettone*.

Panarello at Via XX Settembre 156 and Via Galata 67; Marino e Rita at Piazza Paolo da Novi 40–42; and Villa di Profumo at Via del Portello 2, are other typical *panificio* (bread shops) and good places to buy a squat loaf of the sweet bread riddled with candied fruit. It costs L20,000 per kg.

Wine

Most supermarkets (see Self-Catering under Places to Eat earlier) stock a healthy selection of Italian wine.

Rarer, more remarkable bottles of ruby red Rossese di Dolceacqua, aromatic Cinque Terre whites and other Ligurian-produced DOC wines can be chosen with care at Vinoteca Sola (☎ 010 56 13 29, e info@vinotecasola.it), Piazza Colombo 13, a wine shop run by a winemaking family from Piedmont. In the old city, Il

GENOA

Pampino (see Places to Eat earlier) is another place where buying a bottle of wine can be an educational experience.

Old-fashioned Bonanni on Via San Vincenzo and Carmello Petrelli at Via Granello 51 sell fiery grappa and other potent spirits and liqueurs.

WHERE TO SHOP
Books
Libreria Buenos Aires at Corso Buenos Aires 5, Libreria Monadori at Via XX Septembre 210r, the Touring Club Italiano bookshop (see Travel Agencies in the Facts for the Visitor chapter) inside Palazzo Ducale at Piazza Matteoti 62r, Libreria Bozzi (☎ 010 246 17 18, ✉ bozzi@panet.it) at Via Cairoli 2r, and Rizzoli on Piazza delle Feste at Porto Antico, all stock a healthy selection of maps and English-language guides.

English- and French-language novels and other works of fiction, dictionaries and textbooks to learn Italian can be found at Feltrinelli (Web site: www.feltrinelli.it), with branches at Via Bensa 32r (☎ 010 247 76 74) and Via XX Septembre 233 (☎ 010 54 08 30).

The best bet for walking maps and guides is the basement of Assolibro, Via San Luca 5. Art, design and pictorial books about Genoa are sold at Libreria Ducale (☎ 010 59 41 12, ✉ info@tormena.it), inside Palazzo Ducale. Punto di Vista (☎ 010 277 06 61, ✉ puntodivista.libri@libero.it), Stradone Sant'Agostino 58, specialises in architectural titles.

Rare second-hand and antique books are shelved at Libreria di Piazza delle Erbe (☎ 010 247 53 47) at Piazza delle Erbe 25.

CDs
Try Modern Groove (☎ 010 247 40 06, ✉ modgroove@tin.it), off Piazza Fontane Marose at Via Lucculi 77, and Black Widow (☎ 010 246 17 08), Via del Campo 6, for a hip range of CDs and second-hand vinyl LPs, including 1960s sounds, freakbeat, punk, modern jazz and traditional Genoese *trallalleri* (see Arts in the Facts about the Cities chapter).

Music Store, on the ground floor of Magazzini del Cotone at Porto Antico, is a large

---

Market Day

There's no better place to sniff up the scents and pongs of Genoa than at its central market, a sprawling maze of stalls and sellers inside **Mercato Orientale**, with entrances on Via XX Settembre and Via Galata. Flower stalls in front of the covered market on Via XX Settembre sell blooms for your sweetheart. In the old town, fruit and veg stalls are set up on Piazza Banchi and Via degli Orefici, immediately east.

Works by local artists and second-hand books can be picked up from the open-air stalls beneath the arcades on Piazza Colombo, a pretty square at the southern end of Via Galata. On the first Saturday and Sunday of the month from October to July, an antiques market fills the interior courtyards of Palazzo Ducale.

---

music shop where you can listen to the latest releases before purchase. It opens 10 am to 12 midnight.

Fashion
Via Roma is the street for designer fashion: Louis Vuitton (at No 4), Salvatore Ferragoma (at No 23) and Mario Forni (at No 29) are all here. Nearby Nonsense at Via XXV Aprile 24 models fun, off-beat and expensive fashion by young Italian designers, well worth a little drool.

More mainstream fashion stores for both sexes and all ages line Via XX Settembre, the western half of which is bordered by porticoed promenades just made for browsing. Department store Coin.it at No 16a has cosmetics, ladies fashion, accessories and shoes on the ground floor; and home furnishings and a coffee shop-cum-wine bar on the 1st. It opens 9.30 am to 8 pm (from 11 am Sunday).

Other stand-outs include Colours, with its flamboyant knits, bold fur-trimmed skirts and PVC trousers at Via XX Settembre 1; leather king Bruno Magli at Via XX Settembre 138 (shoes, boots and bags); and L'Ultima Volta che Vidi Parigi at Via XX Settembre 137 where you can buy lovely labelled lingerie

GENOA

(Dolce & Gabbana, Anti-Flirt, Armani, Klein) to suit all moods. Lush-legged Calzedonia, with its daring set of stockings and tights, has boutiques at Via XX Settembre 106 and Via San Vincenzo 173.

That all-essential pair of shades to pout behind can be purchased at Salmoiraghi & Vigano at Via XX Settembre 94. Swatch is next door.

Sports Gear

L'Angelo dello Sport (☎ 010 54 51 35), Via Brigata Liguria 64, is a large mainstream sports shop with all the gear. Board Corner, Via Galata 33, sells roller blades, surf- and skate-boards.

Maidre Sport, inside Magazzini del Cotone at Porto Antico, sells micro-scooters, blades and labelled sports clothing. In the same complex, Yacht Chandler is a specialist sailing shop selling everything from compasses and nautical supplies to clothing and basic food provisions.

Design

Italian-designed lamps (and shelves to stand them on) are showcased at Ligur System, a design shop at Via Brigata Liguria 62. Gadgets and accessories designed by Mercedes Benz are dramatically showcased at Mercedes Benz Sport (☎ 010 254 14 34, e mercedes_sport@interbusiness .it), Via XXV Aprile 44.

Classic chair creations by Le Corbusier, Mackintosh et al can be oggled at and bought at Cernaia (☎ 010 240 30 87, e info@ cernaia.it), a 1950s classical and contemporary furniture house with showrooms at Vico Indoratori 13a and on Via degli Orefici.

The latest in hi-tech (TVs, music systems, etc) is screened at Bang & Olufsen, Corso Buenos Aires 96.

Excursions

Any trip out of central Genoa reveals the sheer enormity of this city's unfortunate portside sprawl.

Westwards, the noisy two-lane autostrada speeds past abandoned grain stores and through a blinding succession of tunnels to **Pegli**, distinguishable in this industrial wasteland by the gas storage tanks which scar its rolling green hills. Lavish **Villa Pallavicini**, with its magnificent park modelled on Genoese gardens of the Renaissance, testifies to the 19th-century aristocracy the once-fashionable seaside resort lured. It houses a **Museo Archeologico** (☎ 010 698 40 45, e archligure@mail.it) at Via Pallavicini 11, dedicated to Ligurian prehistory. By bus, take Nos 1, 2 and 3 from Stazione Brignole or No 30 from Piazza Caricamento to Pegli.

Farther west, the congestion eases somewhat, although the **Riviera di Ponente** – the stretch of Ligurian coast between Genoa and France – is substantially more developed than its eastern counterpart. Ponente's most famous resort is **San Remo**, just 17km short of the Italian-French border but a three-hour ride by express train from Genoa, 150km east. An oasis of wealth and prestige, it gained prominence as a resort for Europe's social elite, especially British and Russian, in the mid-to-late-19th century, when Empress Maria Alexandrovna (mother of Nicholas II, the last tsar) held court here. The APT office in San Remo (☎ 0184 57 15 71), Largo Nuvoloni 1, is near the corner of its famous strip, Corso Imperatrice. The other famed stretch, Corso Garibaldi, plays host to Italy's principal **flower market**, held from 6 to 8 am, June to October.

Heading east out of Genoa along the crowded coast you reach **Nervi**, a lesser victim of the port city's growth. Its pretty-in-pink **Villa Grimaldi Fassio** (☎ 010 32 23 96), Via Capolungo 9, is a 17th-century mansion surrounded by a rose garden where an international ballet festival is held in July and an outdoor cinema in August. Inside, is a large art collection. Take bus No 17 from Genoa's Stazione Brignole to Nervi, then bus No 517 to Via Capolungo.

Continuing east, the **Riviera di Levante** unfolds in a sprinkling of seaside villages which, despite their evident popularity (especially Cinque Terre), promise pretty walking, picturesque scenery and a truly unique charm.

GENOA

CAMOGLI
pop 5790 • postcode 16032

Wandering through the alleyways and cobbled streets of Camogli, 25km east of Genoa, it is hard not to be taken aback by the painstaking trompe l'oeil decoration – house after house sports meticulously painted columns, balustrades and windows. This is a feature of many Ligurian towns but Camogli seems to take special pride in this genre of civic art. The esplanade, Via Garibaldi, is a colourful place for a stroll and really comes to life on the second Sunday in May, when local fishermen celebrate the Sagra del Pesce (Fish Festival), frying hundreds of fish for all and sundry in 3m-wide pans along the waterfront.

Camogli, meaning 'house of wives', takes its name from the days when the women ran the town while their husbands were at sea. The town was also a strong naval base and once boasted a fleet larger than Genoa's.

The APT office (☎/fax 0185 77 10 66) at Via XX Settembre 33, to the right when leaving the train station, stocks accommodation lists. There are plenty of touristy places to eat around the waterfront.

Getting There & Away

Camogli is on the Genoa–La Spezia train line (30 minutes from Stazione Principe). Trains run at least hourly between 6.30 am and 9 pm.

Summertime ferries (☎ 0185 77 20 91) connect Camogli with Genoa, Portofino and Cinque Terre (see those sections for details).

Motorists can reach Camogli by the A12 or Via Aurelia (S1) from Genoa.

SAN FRUTTUOSO
pop 850 • postcode 34070

San Fruttuoso is a fascinating village dominated by **Abbazia di San Fruttuoso di Capodimonte**, a Benedictine abbey with medieval origins. Built as a resting place for bishop St Fructuosus, martyred in Spain in 259, it was rebuilt in the mid-13th century with the assistance of the Doria family, who used it as a family crypt. It fell into decay with the decline of the religious community and in the 19th century was divided into small living quarters by local fishermen. It opens 10 am to 6 pm Tuesday to Sunday (to 4 pm in winter, closing altogether in November). Admission costs L5000.

Equally fascinating is the bronze statue of Christ, *Il Cristo degli Abissi*, lowered 15m to the sea bed by locals in 1954 as a tribute to divers lost at sea and to bless the waters. You must dive to see it but locals say it can be viewed from a boat if the waters are calm. A replica, in a fish tank, is on display in the church adjoining the abbey. A religious ceremony is held over the statue each August.

Getting There & Away

San Fruttuoso is accessible by foot from Camogli and Portofino – an exhilarating cliffside walk up to 2½ hours one way from either town. There are year-round ferries to/from Camogli and boat excursions in summer from Genoa (see Organised Tours earlier in this chapter), Santa Margherita and Portofino (see Getting There & Away in those sections).

PORTOFINO
pop 574 • postcode 16034

Dubbed the 'richest promontory in Italy', exclusive Portofino, 40km east of Genoa, is home to the rich, powerful and famous. Petrarca, Maupassant, Truman Capote and English photographer Cecil Beeton all sojourned here.

A haughty disdain on the part of many residents lends the village a healthy air of restraint, and the huddle of pastel-coloured houses around the portside piazza is a delight. In summer the square, fronted by expensive cafes and Cartier-et-al designer boutiques, is full of the glitterati, attracted to Liguria's most chichi spot where Europe's movers and shakers come to wheel, deal, play and pose.

OK, it *is* all very nice but you have to question the motives of the individual responsible for the overblown official sign as you enter town: *Portofino – Gioiello del Turismo Europeo* (Portofino – Jewel of European Tourism). Equally questionable is the queue of summer motorists who sit in the searing heat, waiting to enter the village:

GENOA

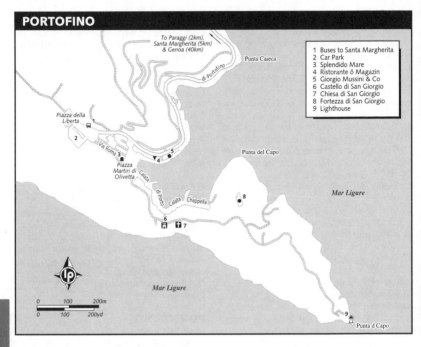

PORTOFINO

To Paraggi (2km),
Santa Margherita (5km)
& Genoa (40km)

Punta Caieca

di Portofino

Piazza della
Libertà

Via Roma

Piazza
Martiri di
Olivetta

Calata

di Porto

Calata

Chappella

Punta del Capo

Mar Ligure

Mar Ligure

Punta d Capo

0   100   200m
0   100   200yd

1 Buses to Santa Margherita
2 Car Park
3 Splendido Mare
4 Ristorante ö Magazin
5 Giorgio Mussini & Co
6 Castello di San Giorgio
7 Chiesa di San Giorgio
8 Fortezza di San Giorgio
9 Lighthouse

a digital clock, 2km north of Portofino in **Paraggi**, flashes how long you can expect to sweat it out. Unlike beachless Portofino, Paraggi sports a small stretch of sand.

Things to See & Do

At the port near **Chiesa di San Giorgio** a flight of stairs marked 'Salita San Giorgio' leads up to the 16th-century **castle** of the same name. Built over an existing fort by the Genoese, under some pressure from their Spanish allies, the castle occasionally saw action, particularly when occupied by Napoleon and taken by the English in 1814. It offers a great view but for an even better outlook continue along the same track through olive groves to the **lighthouse**; it's an hour's walk there and back.

Sailing and motorboats can be hired from Giorgio Mussini & Co (☎ 0185 26 93 27, 0185 26 15 16, e info@giorgiomussini .com), Calata Marconi 38, with a Web site at www.giorgiomussini.com.

Places to Stay & Eat

Accommodation is scarce and expensive. The 'cheapest' is **Eden** (☎ 0185 26 90 91, Vico Dritto 18), with singles/doubles from L170,000/210,000 (double in high season). The priciest – strictly for lira millionaires – is **Splendido Mare** (☎ 0185 26 78 00, e reservations@splendido.net, Via Roma 2).

The handful of waterfront restaurants are horribly overpriced. Decked out like a boat cabin, **Ristorante ö Magazin** (☎ 0185 26 91 78, Calata Marconi 34) is as expensive as the rest but seems the most authentic.

Getting There & Away

Between June and September Alimar, the Cooperativa Battellieri del Golfo Paradiso and Cooperativo Battellieri del Porto di Genova (see Boats and Organised Tours under Getting Around earlier in this chapter) run boat excursions from Genoa to Portofino.

Between April and October, Servizio Marittimo del Tigullio (☎ 0185 28 46 70)

GENOA

runs ferries from Portofino to San Fruttuoso (L9000/14,000 single/return, 30 minutes, twice daily Monday to Saturday and five on Sunday) and Santa Margherita (L6000/10,000 single/return, 15 minutes, twice daily Monday to Saturday and five on Sunday).

Portofino is an easy bus ride from Santa Margherita (see that section later). Motorists must park at the village entrance and pay L7000/25,000 per one/four hours (hard cash only) for the privilege (L1000/3500 per hour for bicycles/motorcycles); vehicles are banned further in.

SANTA MARGHERITA
pop 10,690 • postcode 16038

Once home to a coral-fishing fleet that roamed as far afield as Africa, Santa Margherita, 32km south-east of Genoa, is best known for its orange blossoms and lace today. In a sheltered bay on the eastern side of the Portofino promontory, its waterfront is an eclectic jumble of one-time fishing cottages, elegant four-star hotels with Liberty facades and moored million-dollar yachts.

For details on **sailing**, **water-skiing**, **scuba diving** and other activities, see the IAT office (☎ 0185 28 74 85, e turismo@comune.santa-margherita-ligure.ge.it), Via XXV Aprile 4.Regional information is online at www.portofinobayarea.com. For a green source of information including a list of **walking trails** from Santa Margherita, go to the headquarters of the Parco Naturale Regionale di Portofino (☎ 0185 28 94 79, e enteparco.portofino@libero.it) at Viale Rainusso 1.

For the more leisurely-inclined, there's no better way to while away a few hours than to do what Burton, Taylor and other Hollywood greats did: wine and dine at *Bar Colombo* (☎ 0185 28 70 58), a historic, Art Nouveau place on the waterfront at Via Pescino 13. The more budget-conscious can shop for a gastronomic picnic at delicatessen *Pestarino (Via Palestro 5)* and for pineapple, pear and other sweet tarts at *Dama (Via Palestro 34)*.

Getting There & Away
Santa Margherita (listed as 'Santa Margherita Ligure-Portofino' on timetables) is on the Genoa–La Spezia railway line. From the train station (☎ 0185 28 65 08) on Via Roma head downhill to the palm-clad port, then along the waterfront to Piazza Veneto, from where bus No 82 to/from Portofino (L1700) arrives/departs. Operated by Tigullio Transporti (☎ 0185 28 88 34), it leaves every 20 minutes between 7.10 am and 7.40 pm. There are also buses every 20 minutes to/from Camogli (L1400).

In summer, the Servizio Marittimo del Tigullio (☎ 0185 28 46 70) runs ferries from Santa Margherita to Portofino, San Fruttuoso and Cinque Terre (see those sections for details). To call a boat taxi dial ☎ 0185 28 06 82 or ☎ 0335 33 50 66.

CINQUE TERRE
If you miss the five villages which make up Cinque Terre (literally 'five lands') you will have bypassed some of Italy's most extraordinary countryside. But blink as the train zips between tunnels and miss them you will.

The mountains, covered by terraced vineyards, drop precipitously into the Mediterranean, with local wine growers using ingenious monorail mechanisms to ferry themselves up and the grapes down. Olive groves, tinted orange with nets in November when the black fruits fall, embrace the lower slopes, leaving little room for the Cinque Terre villages cluttering coves, tucked into ravines or perched atop sharp ridges. Fishing and viniculture (along with tourism these days) remain the traditional industries.

Prices in Cinque Terre are neither low nor extortionate. Hotels are scarce but numerous villagers have rooms to rent; look for signs reading *camere* (rooms) or *affittacamere* (rooms for rent). Equally – if not more – seductive than the rooms are Cinque Terre's renowned white and dessert wines *Morasca, Chiaretto del Faro*, its heavenly, sweet *sciacchetrà* and *limoncino*, a lemon liqueur guaranteed to make your heart race.

Getting There & Away
Cinque Terre's greatest asset (particularly for anyone coming from Genoa) is its distinct lack of motorised traffic. Cars are not

GENOA

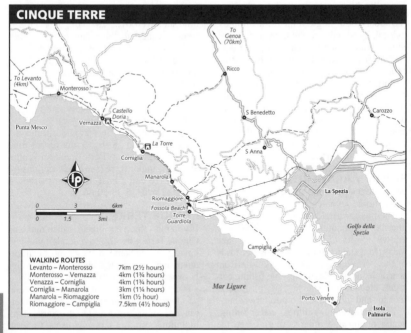

CINQUE TERRE

To Genoa (70km)

Ricco

To Levanto (4km)

Monterosso

Castello Doria

Vernazza

Punta Mesco

S Benedetto

Carozzo

La Torre

Corniglia

S Anna

Manarola

La Spezia

Riomaggiore

Fossola Beach

Torre Guardiola

Golfo della Spezia

Campiglia

Mar Ligure

Porto Venere

Isola Palmaria

0   3   6km
0   1.5   3mi

WALKING ROUTES

Levanto – Monterosso	7km (2½ hours)
Monterosso – Vernazza	4km (1¾ hours)
Venazza – Corniglia	4km (1¾ hours)
Corniglia – Manarola	3km (1¼ hours)
Manarola – Riomaggiore	1km (½ hour)
Riomaggiore – Campiglia	7.5km (4½ hours)

GENOA

permitted beyond village entrances, meaning a hike of up to 1km.

The most convenient way to get to/from and around is the Genoa–La Spezia train service which trundles along the coast every 15 to 30 minutes between 6.30 am and 10 pm. The Biglietto Giornaliero Cinque Terre one-day rail pass costs L5500 and allows unlimited travel on trains between Monterosso and La Spezia.

In summer, Cooperativa Battellieri del Golfo Paradiso and Alimar run ferry and catamaran services from Genoa to Cinque Terre. See Boats and Organised Tours under Getting Around earlier in this chapter.

Between April and 1 November, La Spezia-based Navigazione Golfo dei Poeti (☎ 0187 96 76 76, 0187 73 29 87, ✉ navinfo@navigazionegolfodeipoeti.it), at Viale Mazzini 21, operates shuttle boats (seven to nine daily) between all the villages (*except* Corniglia). A one-day 'village-hopping' ticket costs L20,000 (children

L12,000) and a single/return ticket to one village costs L5000/8000. It also operates boat excursions to Cinque Terre from Porto Venere and La Spezia (see Getting There & Away under those sections).

You can hire bicycles to pedal around in Riomaggiore and Manarola.

Monterosso
pop 1640 • postcode 19016

Huge statues carved into the rocks overlook one of the few decent sized beaches in Cinque Terre, a grey, pebbly affair. The least attractive of the villages, Monterosso gets its name from the unusual red colouring of the nearby cliff faces. In the historic centre, Enoteca Internazionale (☎ 0187 81 72 87) at Via Roma 62, is one of the best places in Cinque Terre to munch on anchovy-topped bruschette and sip sweet sciacchetrà. Other local specialities such as limoncino (made from Monterosso lemons) can be tasted and bought here.

Vernazza

pop 1100 • postcode 19018

This is possibly the most fetching village with its arcaded piazza opening out to sea. Waterfront steps lead to **Castello Doria**, an 11th-century castle with sweeping views from its tower. It opens 10 am to 5.30 pm and admission costs L2000. Heading inland, the road becomes choked with tiny vineyards and patches of lemon grove.

Vernazza's main cobbled lane, Via Roma, links seaside Piazza Guglielmo Marconi with the train station. There's a tasty *focacceria* at No 3, a grocery store at Nos 23–5, a laundrette at No 49 (open 8 am to 10 pm), and Internet access (L300 per minute) at Blue Marlin (☎ 0187 82 11 49, 🄴 bmarlin@ tin.it, Via Roma 43), Vernazza's busiest cafe and bar. The coastal path (see the boxed text 'Lovers' Lane') can be picked up from steps next to (or opposite for westbound walkers) the pharmacy at Via Roma 4.

Vernazza has a couple of hotels and numerous rooms to let. On Piazza Guglielmo *Albergo Barbara (☎ 0187 81 23 98), Francamaria (☎ 0187 81 20 02)* at No 30, and *Da Martina (☎ 0187 81 23 65)* at No 36, are among the handful of idyllically placed on the waterfront piazza. If you dine at *Trattoria da Sandro (☎ 0187 81 22 23, Via Roma 69)* don't miss the huge mixed fried fish platters (L24,000) or the *insalata di polpo* (octopus salad).

The ticket counter at the train station opens 8 am to 6 pm and doubles as a left-luggage desk (L1000 per hour). Regular services link Vernazza with Genoa and Milano.

Corniglia

postcode 16152

Balanced precariously along a ridge high above the sea, charming Corniglia is a picture postcard of four-storey houses, narrow lanes and stairways woven on the hill and topped by **La Torre**, a medieval lookout. Good views of the vines and dry stone walls, distinctive to these terraced parts, can be enjoyed from the central square. From here, Via Fieschi cuts through the village heart to **Belvedere Santa Maria**, another look-out with a coastal panorama.

Near the train station, *La Posada (☎ 0187 82 11 74, Via della Stazione 11)* has a handful of rooms to let and a flower-filled garden restaurant with ocean view. Via Fieschi is sprinkled with homestay options and food shops. *A Cantina de Mananan (☎ 0187 82 11 66)* at No 117 is an especially charming *osteria* with pasta dishes starting at L12,000. Sample Cinque Terre wines next door at *Enoteca Il Pirun (☎ 0187 81 23 15)*; it also has rooms with *vista mare* (sea view) to let.

The four-minute train journey from Vernazza to Corniglia is through one long tunnel. The Corniglia village is a steep 15-minute hike from its train station; bear left (west) and follow the lower red-paved track along the coast to the foot of the 363 steps that zig-zag up the hillside to the village. At the top, bear

GENOA

Lovers' Lane

For those with time or a romance on their hands, there's the Via dell'Amore (Lovers' Lane), a scenic coastal path linking Monterosso with Riomaggiore and the villages in between. The going can get strenuous at times, but reasonably fit walkers can cover the 12km (one way) fairly comfortably in five or so hours. The first stretch between Monterosso and Vernazza (4km, 1¾ hours) is the least scenic and most difficult. Farther east, dramatic coastal views and pretty little coves with crystal-clear water (bring your swimming gear) compensate for any sweat and tears.

Fierce storms, torrential rain and high seas in October 2000 wreaked havoc along this stretch of coastline, causing cultivated terraces to collapse and part of Cinque Terre's lovely lovers' lane – the section between Manarola and Riomaggiore – to close. It should reopen in April 2001; see www.cinqueterre.it for an update in English. In case of emergency, call Emergenza Soccorso in Montagna (Emergency Mountain Rescue; ☎ 0336 68 93 16).

---

left again along Via della Stazione to the central square. In summer, a minibus shuttles tourists between the station and village (L3000 one-way, plus L1000 baggage fee).

Manarola
postcode 19010
More grapes are grown around Manarola than any other Cinque Terre village. A 13th-century church, a bell tower used as a defensive lookout in the 14th century and an oratory that once served as a leper hospital, line its central square, at the northern end of steep Via Discovolo. Those game for a climb can follow a path off nearby Via Rollandi that leads through vineyards to the top of the mountain.

At the foot of the village, Via Birolli (parked up with fishing boats in winter) leads to the water, from where the coastal path twists up to the village cemetery and beyond. Taste and buy Cinque Terre vintages from L'Autëdu at Via Birolli 83 and eat giant slices of pizza and focaccia at *Pizzeria La Cambusa* at No 110.

At the far end of Via Discovolo, *Ostello 5 Terre* (☎ 0187 92 02 15, e ostello@cdh.it, Via Riccobaldi 21) is a private hostel charging L30,000 (L25,000 from October to April) for a bed in a four- or six-bedded room. Breakfast/dinner is L5000/20,000 and the hostel rents out mountain bikes, kayaks and snorkelling gear. Reception opens 7 am to 1 pm and 5 pm to 1 am (4 pm to midnight, October to April). Reservations can be made online at www.cinqueterre.net/ostello.

A tunnel separates the station from the village. At the end of the tunnel turn left to reach the marina; or right onto Via Discovolo, the main shopping drag. Edicola Souvenir at No 235 sells train and boat tickets.

Riomaggiore
pop 1880 • postcode 19017
Riomaggiore is a mess of colourfully painted (and peeling) houses slithering down a ravine that forms the main street, with tiny fishing boats lining the shore and stacked in the small square.

Cinque Terre marine life can be viewed through a mask with divers from the Cooperative Sub 5 Terre (☎ 0187 92 05 96), a diving centre on Via San Giacomo. It also rents out snorkels and canoes/kayaks (L10,000/15,000 for one/two hours or L50,000 per day).

Cycling enthusiasts can hire two wheels from Mar Mar (☎ 0187 92 09 32) at Via Colombo 234, for L10,000/15,000 per hour or L50,000/70,000 per day for one/two people. Walkers with a keen eye for nature should make a beeline for **Torre Guardiola**, a nature observation centre on **Fossola Beach**, immediately south-east of the marina, from where a botanical trail can be followed along the coast. The less energetic can taste and buy local wine at D'Uutu Scintu, a wine shop at Via Colombo 84.

Riomaggiore offers the greatest choice of accommodation. On Via Colombo, the main street which runs from the waterfront through the centre of the village, *La Dolcevita* (☎ 0187 76 00 44) at No 122, *Edi* (☎ 0187 92 03 25, e edi-vesigna@iol.it) at No 111, and *Fazioli* (☎/fax 0187 92 09 04, e robertofazioli@libero.it) at No 94 are agencies which rent rooms and apartments (from L30,000 to L90,000 per person).

Down at the marina, *Enoteca Dau Cila (Via San Giacomo 65)* serves great bruschetta (L12,000) to the sound of crashing waves. *La Lanterna (Via San Giacomo 46)* opens 11 am to 11 pm year-round and fries up the catch of the day for L7000 per 100g.

Riomaggiore village is a few minutes' walk south of its train station through a long tunnel.

PORTO VENERE
pop 4350 • postcode 19025
It is worth a trip to Porto Venere – a boat excursion from Genoa or a wiggly drive 30km south of Riomaggiore via the S530 – simply for the razor-clam soup it has contributed to Ligurian fare. The Romans built Portus Veneris on the western shore of the Golfo della Spezia as a base on the route from Gaul to Spain. From the brightly coloured houses along the waterfront, narrow steps and cobbled paths lead up the hillside to 12th-century **Chiesa di San Lorenzo**. In the church's shadow lies **Cas-**

GENOA

tello Doria, built in the 16th century as part of the Genoese Republic's defence system and offering magnificent views from its terraced gardens. A Pasaà at Piazza Bastreri 2, is the place to **shop for wine**.

At the end of the waterfront quay, a Cinque Terre panorama unfolds from the rocky terraces of **Grotta Arpaia**, a former haunt of Byron who once swam across the gulf from Porto Venere to Lerici. Traces of a pagan temple believed to date to before 6 BC have been uncovered inside **Chiesa di San Pietro** (1277), built in the typical Genoese Gothic fashion with its black and white bands of marble.

Just off the promontory lie the tiny islands of **Palmaria**, **Tino** and **Tinetto** which can be visited by boat. Navigazione Golfo dei Poeti (see Getting There & Away later) runs three-island boat trips (40 minutes) in summer.

Places to Stay & Eat

The IAT office (☎ 0187 79 06 91, ⓔ box@ portovenere.it) at Piazza Bastreri 5, has a list of Porto Venere hotels – all horribly expensive. It's also online at www .portovenere.it.

On Via Cappellini, the main Genoese-style caruggio, *La Piazzetta* at No 56 serves warming pots of tea and plates of *cantuccini* (hard dry almond biscuits to dunk in the tea) and *La Pizzaccia (☎ 0187 79 27 22)* at No 94 has a sterling reputation for its pizza, focaccia and farinata. *Antica Osteria del Caruggio* at No 66 is an old-world place with antique furnishings and a menu featuring traditional cuisine.

Getting There & Away

In summer Alimar runs a catamaran service from Genoa to Porto Venere and the Cooperativo Battellieri del Porto di Genova runs boat excursions. See Getting Around earlier in this chapter.

Between April and October, Navigazione Golfo dei Poeti (see Getting There & Away under Cinque Terre earlier in this chapter) operates boats to/from Cinque Terre (L30,000 return, two to five boats daily) and Lerici (L13,000 return, 30 minutes, seven daily). Day excursions to

Portofino (one boat daily) sail mid-June to mid-September and cost L13,000. In Porto Venere boats use the jetty at the northern end of Calata Doria.

By car, Porto Venere is 13km south-west of La Spezia and 16km south-east of Riomaggiore.

LA SPEZIA
pop 93,300 • postcode 19100

La Spezia, 100km east of Genoa, sits at the head of the gulf of the same name, also known as the Gulf of Poets in deference to Byron, Dante, George Sand and others drawn here by its beauty. **San Torenzo**, on its eastern shores, was a haunt of the Shelleys (Percy Bysshe's boat sank off the coast in 1822) while DH Lawrence hung out in the exclusive summer refuge of **Lerici** and the magnificent bays around **Tellaro** before WWI.

The construction of Italy's largest naval base in 1860–5 propelled La Spezia from minor port to provincial capital. Its city streets, sandwiched between the naval base and **Museo Navale** (☎ 0187 77 07 50) on Piazza Domenico Chiodo to the west and commercial port to the east, buzz with blue naval uniforms. The base opens its doors to the public each year on 19 March, the festival of the town's patron saint, Saint Joseph.

A hand-in-hand *passeggiata* (evening stroll) along **Via Prione**, the main shop-lined promenade linking the train station with palm-lined Viale Italia on the waterfront, remains a ritual for many a sailor-smitten gal in town. Many a bygone romance is captured on canvas in **Pinacoteca Civica Amedeo Lia** (☎ 0187 73 11 00) at Via Prione 234, La Spezia's star attraction with some 2000 art works by masters such as Tintoretto, Tiepolo, Titian, Veronese, Bellini and Sansovino. The museum opens 10 am to 6 pm Tuesday to Sunday. Admission costs L12,000 (reduced L8000).

The IAT office (☎ 0187 77 09 00, ⓔ info .iat@cinqueterre.sp.it), near the waterfront at Viale G Mazzini 47, has a list of scuba-diving schools. *Trattoria da Dino (Via da Poassano 17)* and *Ristorante di Bayon (☎ 0187 73 22 09, Via Felice Cavallotti 23)* are two pleasant places to lunch.

GENOA

LA SPEZIA

PLACES TO EAT
12 Trattoria da Dino
13 Ristorante di Bayon

OTHER
1 Train Station
2 Buses for Lerici
3 Market
4 Museo Civico
5 Pinacoteca Civica Amedeo Lia
6 Castello di San Giorgio
7 Post Office
8 Bank & ATM
9 Cathedral
10 IAT Office
11 Telecom Office
14 Buses for Porto Venere
15 Museo Navale
16 Navigazione Golfo
    dei Poeti

Getting There & Away

La Spezia is on the Genoa–Rome railway line and is also connected to Milan, Turin and Cinque Terre. Porto Venere (from Via Domenico Chiodo) and Lerici (both from the train station) can both be reached by ATC bus (☎ 0187 52 25 22).

Between April and October, Navigazione Golfo dei Poeti (see Getting There & Away under Cinque Terre earlier) runs weekly boat excursions from La Spezia to Genoa (L60,000 including admission to Genoa aquarium), stopping en route at Cinque Terre and Portofino; in Cinque Terre and Portofino (L50,000); and Porto Venere (L30,000).

The A12 links La Spezia with Genoa.

Language

Italian is a Romance language related to French, Spanish, Portuguese and Romanian. The Romance languages belong to the Indo-European group of languages, which include English. Indeed, as English and Italian share common roots in Latin, you will recognise many Italian words.

Modern literary Italian began to develop in the 13th and 14th centuries, predominantly through the works of Dante, Petrarca (Petrach) and Boccaccio, who wrote chiefly in the Florentine dialect. The standard Italian of today is closely founded on this Florentine dialect, and although regional dialects are still commonly used by locals in everyday conversation, standard Italian is the national language of schools, media and literature, and is spoken throughout the country.

Visitors to Italy with more than the most fundamental grasp of the language need to be aware that many older Italians still expect to be addressed in the third person polite, *(lei* instead of *tu)*. Also, it's not considered appropriate to use the greeting *ciao* when addressing strangers unless they use it first; it's better to say *buon giorno* (or *buona sera*, as the case may be) and *arrivederci* (or the more polite form, *arrivederla*). We have used the polite address for most of the phrases in this guide. Use of the informal address is indicated by 'inf' in brackets. Italian also has both masculine and feminine forms (they usually end in 'o' and 'a' respectively). Where both forms are given in this guide, they are separated by a slash, the masculine form first.

If you'd like a more comprehensive guide to the language, get a copy of Lonely Planet's *Italian phrasebook*.

Pronunciation

Italian pronunciation isn't difficult to master once you learn a few simple rules. Although some of the more clipped vowels and the stress on double letters require careful practice for English speakers, it's easy enough to make yourself understood.

Vowels

Vowels are generally more clipped than in English:

a	as in 'art', *caro* (dear); sometimes short, *amico* (friend)
e	as in 'tell', *mettere* (to put)
i	as in 'inn', *inizio* (start)
o	as in 'dot', *donna* (woman); as in 'port', *dormire* (to sleep)
u	as the 'oo' in 'book', *puro* (pure)

Consonants

The pronunciation of many Italian consonants is similar to that of their English counterparts. Pronunciation of some consonants depends on certain rules:

c	as 'k' before **a**, **o** and **u**; as the 'ch' in 'choose' before **e** and **i**
ch	as the 'k' in 'kit'
g	as the 'g' in 'get' before **a**, **o**, **u** and **h**; as the 'j' in 'jet' before **e** and **i**
gli	as the 'lli' in 'million'
gn	as the 'ny' in 'canyon'
h	always silent
r	a rolled 'rr' sound
sc	as the 'sh' in 'sheep' before **e** and **i**; as 'sk' before **a**, **o**, **u** and **h**
z	as the 'ts' in 'lights', except at the beginning of a word, when it's as the 'ds' in 'suds'

Note that when **ci**, **gi** and **sci** are followed by **a**, **o** or **u**, the 'i' is not pronounced unless the accent falls on the 'i'. Thus the name 'Giovanni' is pronounced 'joh-**vahn**-nee'.

Word Stress

A double consonants is pronounced as a longer, more forceful sound than a single consonant.

Stress generally falls on the second-last syllable, as in *spa-**ghet**-ti*. When a word has an accent, the stress falls on that syllable, as in *cit-**tà*** (city).

LANGUAGE

Greetings & Civilities

Hello.	*Buongiorno.*
	Ciao. (inf)
Goodbye.	*Arrivederci.*
	Ciao. (inf)
Yes.	*Sì.*
No.	*No.*
Please.	*Per favore/Per piacere.*
Thank you.	*Grazie.*
That's fine/	*Prego.*
You're welcome.	
Excuse me.	*Mi scusi.*
Sorry (forgive me).	*Mi scusi/Mi perdoni.*
What's your name?	*Come si chiama?*
	Come ti chiami? (inf)
My name is ...	*Mi chiamo ...*
Where are you	*Di dov'è?*
from?	*Di dove sei?* (inf)
I'm from ...	*Sono di ...*
I (don't) like ...	*(Non) Mi piace ...*

Language Difficulties

Please write it down.	*Può scriverlo, per favore?*
I understand.	*Capisco.*
I don't understand.	*Non capisco.*
Do you speak English?	*Parla inglese?*
	Parli inglese? (inf)
Does anyone here speak English?	*C'è qualcuno che parla inglese?*
How do you say ... in Italian?	*Come si dice ... in italiano?*
What does ... mean?	*Che vuole dire ...?*

Paperwork

name	*nome*
nationality	*nazionalità*
date of birth	*data di nascita*
place of birth	*luogo di nascita*
sex (gender)	*sesso*
passport	*passaporto*
visa	*visto consolare*

Getting Around

What time does ... leave/arrive?	*A che ora parte/ arriva ...?*
the boat	*la barca*
the (city) bus	*l'autobus*
the (intercity) bus	*il pullman/corriere*
the plane	*l'aereo*
the train	*il treno*

I'd like a ... ticket.	*Vorrei un biglietto di ...*
one-way	*solo andata*
return	*andata e ritorno*
1st class	*prima classe*
2nd-class	*seconda classe*

I want to go to ...	*Voglio andare a ...*
The train has been cancelled/delayed.	*Il treno è soppresso/ in ritardo.*
the first	*il primo*
the last	*l'ultimo*
platform (three)	*binario (tre)*
ticket office	*biglietteria*
timetable	*orario*
train station	*stazione*

I'd like to rent ...	*Vorrei noleggiare ...*
a bicycle	*una bicicletta*
a car	*una macchina*
a motorcycle	*una motocicletta*

Directions

Where is ...?	*Dov'è ...?*
Can you show me (on the map)?	*Può mostrarmelo (sulla carta/pianta)?*
Go straight ahead.	*Si va sempre diritto.*
	Vai sempre diritto. (inf)
Turn left.	*Giri a sinistra.*
Turn right.	*Giri a destra.*
at the next corner	*al prossimo angolo*
at the traffic lights	*al semaforo*
behind	*dietro*
in front of	*davanti*
opposite	*di fronte a*
near	*vicino*
far	*lontano*

Around Town

I'm looking for ...	*Cerco ...*
a bank	*un banco*
the church	*la chiesa*
the city centre	*il centro (città)*
the ... embassy	*l'ambasciata di ...*
my hotel	*il mio albergo*
the market	*il mercato*
the museum	*il museo*
the post office	*la posta*
a public toilet	*un gabinetto/ bagno pubblico*
the telephone centre	*il centro telefonico*

Signs

Ingresso/Entrata	Entrance
Uscita	Exit
Aperto	Open
Chiuso	Closed
Informazione	Information
Camere Libere	Rooms Available
Completo	Full/No Vacancies
Proibito/Vietato	Prohibited
Polizia/ Carabinieri	Police
Questura	Police Station
Gabinetti/Bagni	Toilets
Uomini	Men
Donne	Women

the tourist office   *l'ufficio di turismo/ d'informazione*

I want to change ...   *Voglio cambiare ...*
   money   *del denaro*
   travellers cheques   *degli assegni per viaggiatori*

Accommodation

I'm looking for ...   *Cerco ...*
   a guesthouse   *una pensione*
   a hotel   *un albergo*
   a youth hostel   *un ostello per la gioventù*

Where is a cheap hotel?   *Dov'è un albergo che costa poco?*
What is the address?   *Cos'è l'indirizzo?*
Could you write the address, please?   *Può scrivere l'indirizzo, per favore?*
Do you have any rooms available?   *Ha camere libere/C'è una camera libera?*

I'd like ...   *Vorrei ...*
   a bed   *un letto*
   a single room   *una camera singola*
   a room with a double bed   *una camera matrimoniale*
   a room with two beds   *una camera doppia*

a room with a bathroom   *una camera con bagno*
to share a dorm   *un letto in dormitorio*

How much is it ...?   *Quanto costa ...?*
   per night   *per la notte*
   per person   *per ciascuno*

May I see it?   *Posso vederla?*
Where is the bathroom?   *Dov'è il bagno?*
I'm/We're leaving today.   *Parto/Partiamo oggi.*

Shopping

I'd like to buy ...   *Vorrei comprare ...*
How much is it?   *Quanto costa?*
I don't like it.   *Non mi piace.*
May I look at it?   *Posso dare un'occhiata?*
I'm just looking.   *Sto solo guardando.*
It's cheap.   *Non è caro/a.*
It's too expensive.   *È troppo caro/a.*
I'll take it.   *Lo/La compro.*
Do you accept credit cards?   *Accettate carte di credito?*

more   *più*
less   *meno*
bigger   *più grande*
smaller   *più piccolo/a*

Time, Date & Numbers

What time is it?   *Che (ora è/ore sono)?*
It's (8 o'clock).   *Sono (le otto).*
When?   *Quando?*
in the morning   *di mattina*
in the afternoon   *di pomeriggio*
in the evening   *di sera*
today   *oggi*
tomorrow   *domani*
yesterday   *ieri*

Monday   *lunedì*
Tuesday   *martedì*
Wednesday   *mercoledì*
Thursday   *giovedì*
Friday   *venerdì*
Saturday   *sabato*
Sunday   *domenica*

January	*gennaio*
February	*febbraio*
March	*marzo*
April	*aprile*
May	*maggio*
June	*giugno*
July	*luglio*
August	*agosto*
September	*settembre*
October	*ottobre*
November	*novembre*
December	*dicembre*

0	*zero*
1	*uno*
2	*due*
3	*tre*
4	*quattro*
5	*cinque*
6	*sei*
7	*sette*
8	*otto*
9	*nove*
10	*dieci*
11	*undici*
12	*dodici*
13	*tredici*
14	*quattordici*
15	*quindici*
16	*sedici*
17	*diciassette*
18	*diciotto*
19	*diciannove*
20	*venti*
21	*ventuno*
22	*ventidue*
30	*trenta*
40	*quaranta*
50	*cinquanta*
60	*sessanta*
70	*settanta*
80	*ottanta*
90	*novanta*
100	*cento*
1000	*mille*
2000	*due mila*

one million	*un milione*

Emergencies

Help!	*Aiuto!*
Call ...!	*Chiami ...!*
	Chiama ...! (inf)
a doctor	*un dottore/*
	un medico
the police	*la polizia*
There's been an accident!	*C'è stato un incidente!*
I'm lost.	*Mi sono perso/a.*
Go away!	*Lasciami in pace!*
	Vai via! (inf)

Health

I'm ill.	*Mi sento male.*
It hurts here.	*Mi fa male qui.*
I'm ...	*Sono ...*
asthmatic	*asmatico/a*
diabetic	*diabetico/a*
epileptic	*epilettico/a*
I'm allergic ...	*Sono allergico/a ...*
to antibiotics	*agli antibiotici*
to penicillin	*alla penicillina*
to nuts	*alle noci*
antiseptic	*antisettico*
aspirin	*aspirina*
condoms	*preservativi*
contraceptive	*anticoncezionale*
diarrhoea	*diarrea*
medicine	*medicina*
sunblock cream	*crema/latte solare (per protezione)*
tampons	*tamponi*

FOOD

breakfast	*prima colazione*
lunch	*pranzo*
dinner	*cena*
a restaurant	*un ristorante*
a grocery store	*un alimentari*
I'd like the set lunch.	*Vorrei il menu turistico.*
Is service included in the bill?	*È compreso il servizio?*

What is this?	*(Che) cos'è?*
I'm a vegetarian.	*Sono vegetariano/a.*
I don't eat ...	*Non mangio ...*
meat	*carne*
chicken	*pollo*
fish	*pesce*

Menu Decoder

This glossary is intended as a brief guide to some basics. Most travellers will already be well acquainted with the various Italian pastas, which include spaghetti, fettucine, penne, rigatoni, gnocchi, lasagne, tortellini and ravioli. The names are the same in Italy and no further definitions are given here.

Useful Words

antipasto	starter
affumicato	smoked
al dente	firm (as all good pasta should be)
alla brace	cooked over hot coals
alla griglia	grilled
arrosto	roasted
ben cotto	well done (cooked)
bollito	boiled
cameriere/a	waiter/waitress
coltello	knife
conto	bill/check
caffè	coffee
cotto	cooked
crudo	raw
cucchiaino	teaspoon
cucchiaio	spoon
dolce	dessert
forchetta	fork
fritto	fried
menù	menu
piatto	plate
primo piatto	first course (often pasta or risotto)
secondo piatto	second course (meat or fish)

Common Food Items

aceto	vinegar
burro	butter
contorno	vegetable side dish
farinata	thin flat bread made from chickpea flour

focaccia	flat bread (usually served with a variety of toppings)
formaggio	cheese
insalata	salad
limone	lemon
marmellata	jam
miele	honey
olio	oil
olive	olives
pane	bread
pane integrale	wholemeal bread
panna	cream
pepe	pepper
peperoncino	chilli
polenta	cooked cornmeal
riso	rice
risotto	rice cooked with wine and stock
sale	salt
uovo/uova	egg/eggs
zucchero	sugar

Soups & Antipasti

brodo – broth
carbonada con polenta – thick Piedmontese soup
carpaccio – very fine slices of raw meat
insalata caprese – sliced tomatoes with mozzarella and basil
insalata di mare – seafood, generally crustaceans
minestrina in brodo – pasta in broth
minestrone – vegetable soup
minestrone alla milanese – a vegetable soup with rice, potatoes and red kidney beans
minestrone alla genovese – same as the Milanese version but with a dollop of pesto
olive ascolane – stuffed, deep-fried olives
prosciutto e melone – cured ham with melon
ripieni – stuffed, oven-baked vegetables
stracciatella – egg in broth
valpellineuntze – a thick soup of cabbage, bread, beef broth and fontina cheese from Valle d'Aosta

First Courses

bianchetti – fried anchovies, sardines or whitebait; typical to Liguria *fondua* – melted fontina cheese, butter and egg yolks on toast, topped with truffle slices and fried

fonduta – a truffle-free version of *fondua*

gnocchi alla bava – potato dumplings with tomato, fontina, cream and truffles

mocetta – dried beef

pizzoccheri – buckwheat pasta with cabbage, potatoes and melted bitto cheese, typical to Milan

risotto alla milanese – traditionally scented with saffron and bone marrow

risotto alla piemontese – risotto with butter, white wine and truffles

risotto con le rane – risotto with small frogs

tartufi bianchi – white truffles

torta di zucca – pumpkin pie stuffed with sweet almond biscuits, eggs, apple and parmesan cheese

torta baciocca – Ligurian pie with potatoes, parmesan cheese, eggs and parsley

torta pasqualina – Ligurian spinach and ricotta cheese pie

trifulin – truffle-filled ravioli in a mushroom sauce

Pasta Sauces

alla matriciana – tomato and bacon

al ragù – meat sauce (bolognese)

arrabbiata – tomato and chilli

carbonara – egg, bacon and black pepper

crema di pomodori secchi – sun-dried tomato sauce

crema di rucola – creamed rocket, best served with gnocchi

gremolata – chopped parsley, garlic and lemon

napoletana – tomato and basil

panna – cream, prosciutto and sometimes peas

pesto genovese – basil, garlic, oil and pine nuts

preboggion – a mix of Ligurian herbs, often used to stuff ravioli

salsa di noci – groundnut sauce

vongole – clams, garlic, oil and sometimes with tomato

Pizzas

All pizzas listed have a tomato (and sometimes mozzarella) base.

capricciosa – olives, prosciutto, mushrooms and artichokes

frutti di mare – seafood

funghi – mushrooms

margherita – oregano

napoletana – anchovies

pugliese – tomato, mozzarella and onions

quattro formaggi – with four types of cheese

quattro stagioni – like a capricciosa, but sometimes with egg

verdura – mixed vegetables; usually courgette (zucchini) and aubergine (eggplant), sometimes carrot and spinach

Meat & Fish

acciughe – anchovies

agnello – lamb

aragosta – lobster

bistecca – steak

boghe in scabescio – floured fish marinated in vinegar with onions, sage, parsley and fried

brasato al Barolo – beef braised in red Barolo wine

burrida – fish stew

busecca – tripe slices boiled with beans

calamari – squid

cassoeula – pork and vegetable stew

cima alla genovese – veal breast stuffed with nuts and vegetables

coniglio alla ligure – Ligurian dish of rabbit cooked with pine nuts and olives

cotoletta alla milanese – cutlet or thin cut of veal, usually crumbed and fried

cozze – mussels

dentice – dentex (type of fish)

fegato – liver

fritto misto alla milanese – slices of bone marrow, liver and lung

gamberi – prawns

granchio – crab

lumache – snails

manzo – beef

merluzzo – cod

ossobuco – Milanese sliced veal shanks

ostriche – oysters

pesce spada – swordfish

pollo – chicken

polpo – octopus

salsiccia – sausage

sarde – sardines
sgombro – mackerel
sogliola – sole
stoccafisso – stockfish
stoccafisso a brandacujun – creamy stockfish stew
stoccafisso accomodato – stockfish cooked
   in a pot with anchovies
tacchino – turkey
tonno – tuna
triglie – red mullet
trippa – tripe
vitello – veal
vongole – clams

Vegetables

asparagi – asparagus
carciofi – artichokes
carote – carrots
cipolle – onions
fagiolini – string beans
melanzane – aubergines (eggplant)
patate – potatoes

peperoni – peppers
piselli – peas
spinaci – spinach

Fruit

arance – oranges
banane – bananas
ciliegie – cherries
fragole – strawberries
mele – apples
pere – pears
pesche – peaches
uve – grapes

Desserts

polenta e ösei – iced sponge cakes with jam
panettone – literally 'little loaf'; light fruit
   loaf known as Italian Christmas cake
torta di tagliatelle – a sweet cake made with
   egg pasta and almonds
torta meneghina – traditional Milanese
   sponge cake
torta paradiso – a soft cake from Pavia

Glossary

See the Food section in the Language chapter for a list of culinary terms

(s) indicates singular, (pl) indicates plural

ACI – Automobile Club Italiano (Italian Automobile Association)
acquario – aquarium
aeroporto – airport
affittacamere – rooms for rent, most common in Cinque Terre
AIG – Associazione Italiana Alberghi per la Gioventù (Italian Youth Hostel Association)
albergo (s), **alberghi** (pl) – hotel (up to five stars)
alimentari – grocery shop
Alleanza Nazionale – National Alliance (neo-Fascist political party)
Alpi – the Alps
ambasciata – embassy
ambulanza – ambulance
annullato – cancelled
APT – Azienda di Promozione Turistica (provincial tourist office)
archivio di stato – state archives
ascensore – lift, elevator
autostrada (s), **autostrade** (pl) – motorway, highway

bancomat – ATM (automated teller machine)
benzina – petrol
benzina senza piombo – unleaded petrol
biglietteria – box or ticket office
biglietto – ticket
birreria – beer bar
borgo (s), **borghi** (pl) – village or district (usually cluttered and little changed over hundreds of years)
BR – Brigate Rosse (Red Brigades; terrorist group)

caffè – cafe
camera – room
camera doppia – double room with twin beds
camera matrimoniale – double room with double bed

camera singola – single room
campanile – bell tower
campeggi – camp sites
cappella – chapel
cappelleria – hat shop
carabinieri – police with military and civil duties
carnevale – carnival period between Epiphany and Lent
carta d'identità – identity card
carta telefonica – phonecard
caruggio (s), **carugi** (pl) – dimly lit alleyways in Genoa's old city
casa – house, home
castello – castle
cattedrale – cathedral
cenacolo – refectory, the place where Christ and the 12 Apostles celebrated the Last Supper, or a mural depicting the latter
centro – city centre
centro storico – historic centre, old city
chiesa (s), **chiese** (pl) – church
chiostro – cloister; covered walkway, usually enclosed by columns, around a quadrangle
cima – summit
cimitero – cemetery
CIT – Compagnia Italiana di Turismo (Italy's national travel agency)
CNMI – Camera Nazionale della Moda Italiana (National Chamber of Italian Fashion)
comune – equivalent to a municipality or county; town or city council; historically, a commune (self-governing town or city)
coperto – cover charge in restaurants
corso – main street
creuse – cobbled lanes
CTS – Centro Turistico Studentesco e Giovanile (Centre for Student and Youth Tourists)
cuccetta – couchette
cupola – dome

DC – Democrazia Cristiana (Christian Democrats; political party)
degustazione – tasting
deposito bagagli – left luggage
diretto – through, slow train

dogate – medieval form of city government, headed by a *doge* and assisted by advisory bodies
doge – city ruler
douja – terracotta wine jug unique to Asti, south of Turin
DS – Democratici della Sinistra (Democrats of the Left; political party)
duomo – cathedral, such as in Milan or Pavia

elicoltura – snail breeding
enoteca – wine bar
ES – Eurostar (very fast train)
esaurito – 'sold out'
espresso – express mail; express train; short black coffee
est – east
estiva – summer

farmacia – pharmacy
fermo posta – poste restante
ferrovia – train station
festa – feast day; holiday
FIAT – Fabbrica Italiana di Automobili Torino
fidanzato – boyfriend
fiera – trade fair and exhibition hall, such Fiera di Milano, Lingotto Fiere or Fiera di Genova
fiume – river
formaggeria – cheese shop
forte – fort
Forza Italia – Go Italy (political party)
frazione – small area
FS – Ferrovie dello Stato (State Railways)
funicolare – funicular railway
funivia – cable car

gabinetto – toilets, WC
gasolio – diesel
gelaterie – ice-cream parlours
Genova – Genoa
golfo – gulf
Golfo di Genova – Gulf of Genoa

ianu – door
IAT – Informazioni e Assistenza ai Turisti (local tourist office)
IC – Intercity (fast train)
interregionale – long-distance train that stops frequently

isola – island

La Scala – opera house in Milan
lago – lake
largo – (small) square
lavanderia – laundrette
Lega Nord – Northern League (federalist political party)
lido – beach
lingua originale – original language
loggia – covered area on the side of a building, porch
Lombardia – Lombardy
lo sci – downhill skiing
lungomare – seafront road, promenade

macelleria – butcher's shop
mar/mare – sea
marito – husband
Mar Ligure – Ligurian Sea
mercato – market
Milano – Milan
Milano Collezioni Donna – Women's fashion week, Milan
Milano Collezioni Uomo – Men's fashion week, Milan
MM – Metropolitana Milanese (Milan underground system)
monte – mountain
Monte Bianco – Mont Blanc
Monte Cervino – Matterhorn
Monte Rosa – Mont Rosa
MSI – Movimento Sociale Italiano (Italian Social Movement; neo-Fascist political party)
municipio – town hall
mura – city wall
musica dal vivo – live music

nave (s), **navi** (pl) – large ferry, ship
navette turistiche – shuttle buses
negozio di alimentari – grocery shop
nudo – nude
numeri verdi – toll-free numbers

oggetti smarriti – lost property
ospedale – hospital
ostello per la gioventù – youth hostel
osteria – cheap restaurant or wine bar offering a small selection of dishes
ovest – west

Pagine Gialle – the *Yellow Pages* (phone directory)

palazzo (s), **palazzi** (pl) – mansion, palace, large building of any type (including an apartment block)

palio – contest

panetteria – bakery

paninerie – sandwich bar

paninoteca – cafe

parcheggi – parking

parco – park

passeggiata – traditional evening stroll

passerelle – raised walkway

pasticceria – cake shop

pastificio – pasta shop

PCI – Partito Comunista Italiano (Italian Communist Party)

PDS – Partito Democratico della Sinistra (Democratic Party of the Left)

pellicola – roll of film

pensione – small hotel, often offering board

permesso di lavoro – work permit

permesso di soggiorno – permit to stay in Italy for a nominated period

pescheria – fish shop

Pianura Padana – Po Plain

piazza (s), **piazze** (pl) – square

piazzale – (large) open square

Piemonte – Piedmont

pietà – literally pity or compassion; sculpture, drawing or painting of the dead Christ supported by the Madonna

pinacoteca – art gallery

piscina – pool

pizzeria (s), **pizzerie** (pl) – pizza restaurant

polizia – police

Polo per le Libertà – Freedom Alliance (right-wing political coalition)

poltrona – airline-type chair on a ferry

ponte – bridge

pontile – jetty

Porta – city gate

portico – portico; covered walkway, usually attached to the outside of buildings

porto – port

Porto Antico – Genoa's historic old port

posta – post office

PRC – Partito Rifondazione Comunista (Refounded Communist Party)

prêt à porter – ready to wear

pronto soccorso – casualty ward

province – provinces into which administrative regions are further divided, such as Provincia di Milano

PSI – Partito Socialista Italiano (Italian Socialist Party)

Quadrilatero d'Oro – Milan's designer shopping district; literally 'Golden Quad'

quartieri – districts

questura – police station

reale – royal

regionale – slow local train

regioni – administrative regions in Italy, such as Lombardy, Liguria and Piedmont

residenze turistico alberghiere – (self-catering residences to rent on a weekly or monthly basis)

rifugi – mountain hut

risotto – (grain) rice

ristorante – restaurant

riva – river bank

rocca – fortress

ronda – roundabout

rosso – red

Sacro Catino – chalice said to have been used by Jesus at the Last Supper, displayed in Genoa

Salone del Mobile – furniture fair

salumeria – delicatessen

santuario – sanctuary

scala – staircase

scala mobile – escalator, moving staircase

scalinata – staircase

sci alpinismo – ski mountaineering

sci di fondo – cross-country skiing

senza piombo – unleaded petrol

servizio – service charge in restaurants

sindone – the Holy Shroud, believed to be the cloth in which Jesus was buried

soccorso stradale – highway rescue

SostaMilano – 'scratch-and-park' card-payment system for parking in Milan

spiaggia – beach

stazione – station

stazione di servizio – petrol or service station

stazione maritime – ferry terminal

strada – street, road

strada provinciale – main road, sometimes just a country lane

strada statale – main road, often multi-lane and toll free
supermercato – supermarket
superstrada – expressway, highway with divided lanes
supplemento – supplement, payable on a fast train

tabaccheria – tobacconist's shop
tavola calda – literally 'hot table'; pre-prepared meat, pasta and vegetable selection, often self-service
TCI – Touring Club Italiano
teatro – theatre
tempio – temple
terminal crociere – cruise terminal
terminal traghetti – passenger terminal
tesoro – treasury
Torino – Turin
torre – tower
traforo – tunnel
Traforo del Frejus – Fréjus Tunnel

Traforo del Monte Bianco – Mont Blanc Tunnel
traghetto (s), **traghetti** (pl) – small ferry
trattoria (s), **trattorie** (pl) – cheap restaurant; less sophisticated version of a *ristorante*
treno – train

UDR – Unione Democratica per la Repubblica (Democratic Union for the Republic; centre political party)
ufficio postale – post office
ufficio stranieri – foreigners office (police)

via – street, road
vico – alley, alleyway
vigili del fuoco – fire brigade
vigili urbani – traffic police, local police
villa – town house or country house; also the park surrounding the house
vineria – wine bar

Zona Rimozione – vehicle removal zone

Lonely Planet Guides by Region

onely Planet is known worldwide for publishing practical, reliable and no-nonsense travel information in our guides and on our Web site. The Lonely Planet list covers just about every accessible part of the world. Currently there are 16 series: Travel guides, Shoestring guides, Condensed guides, Phrasebooks, Read This First, Healthy Travel, Walking guides, Cycling guides, Watching Wildlife guides, Pisces Diving & Snorkeling guides, City Maps, Road Atlases, Out to Eat, World Food, Journeys travel literature and Pictorials.

AFRICA Africa on a shoestring • Botswana • Cairo • Cairo City Map • Cape Town • Cape Town City Map • East Africa • Egypt • Egyptian Arabic phrasebook • Ethiopia, Eritrea & Djibouti • Ethiopian Amharic phrasebook • The Gambia & Senegal • Healthy Travel Africa • Kenya • Malawi • Morocco • Moroccan Arabic phrasebook • Mozambique • Namibia • Read This First: Africa • South Africa, Lesotho & Swaziland • Southern Africa • Southern Africa Road Atlas • Swahili phrasebook • Tanzania, Zanzibar & Pemba • Trekking in East Africa • Tunisia • Watching Wildlife East Africa • Watching Wildlife Southern Africa • West Africa • World Food Morocco • Zambia • Zimbabwe, Botswana & Namibia
Travel Literature: Mali Blues: Traveling to an African Beat • The Rainbird: A Central African Journey • Songs to an African Sunset: A Zimbabwean Story

AUSTRALIA & THE PACIFIC Aboriginal Australia & the Torres Strait Islands •Auckland • Australia • Australian phrasebook • Australia Road Atlas • Cycling Australia • Cycling New Zealand • Fiji • Fijian phrasebook • Healthy Travel Australia, NZ & the Pacific • Islands of Australia's Great Barrier Reef • Melbourne • Melbourne City Map • Micronesia • New Caledonia • New South Wales • New Zealand • Northern Territory • Outback Australia • Out to Eat – Melbourne • Out to Eat – Sydney • Papua New Guinea • Pidgin phrasebook • Queensland • Rarotonga & the Cook Islands • Samoa • Solomon Islands • South Australia • South Pacific • South Pacific phrasebook • Sydney • Sydney City Map • Sydney Condensed • Tahiti & French Polynesia • Tasmania • Tonga • Tramping in New Zealand • Vanuatu • Victoria • Walking in Australia • Watching Wildlife Australia • Western Australia
Travel Literature: Islands in the Clouds: Travels in the Highlands of New Guinea • Kiwi Tracks: A New Zealand Journey • Sean & David's Long Drive

CENTRAL AMERICA & THE CARIBBEAN Bahamas, Turks & Caicos • Baja California • Belize, Guatemala & Yucatán • Bermuda • Central America on a shoestring • Costa Rica • Costa Rica Spanish phrasebook • Cuba • Cycling Cuba • Dominican Republic & Haiti • Eastern Caribbean • Guatemala • Havana • Healthy Travel Central & South America • Jamaica • Mexico • Mexico City • Panama • Puerto Rico • Read This First: Central & South America • Virgin Islands • World Food Caribbean • World Food Mexico • Yucatán
Travel Literature: Green Dreams: Travels in Central America

EUROPE Amsterdam • Amsterdam City Map • Amsterdam Condensed • Andalucía • Athens • Austria • Baltic States phrasebook • Barcelona • Barcelona City Map • Belgium & Luxembourg • Berlin • Berlin City Map • Britain • British phrasebook • Brussels, Bruges & Antwerp • Brussels City Map • Budapest • Budapest City Map • Canary Islands • Catalunya & the Costa Brava • Central Europe • Central Europe phrasebook • Copenhagen • Corfu & the Ionians • Corsica • Crete • Crete Condensed • Croatia • Cycling Britain • Cycling France • Cyprus • Czech & Slovak Republics • Czech phrasebook • Denmark • Dublin • Dublin City Map • Dublin Condensed • Eastern Europe • Eastern Europe phrasebook • Edinburgh • Edinburgh City Map • England • Estonia, Latvia & Lithuania • Europe on a shoestring • Europe phrasebook • Finland • Florence • Florence City Map • France • Frankfurt City Map • Frankfurt Condensed • French phrasebook • Georgia, Armenia & Azerbaijan • Germany • German phrasebook • Greece • Greek Islands • Greek phrasebook • Hungary • Iceland, Greenland & the Faroe Islands • Ireland • Italian phrasebook • Italy • Kraków • Lisbon • The Loire • London • London City Map • London Condensed • Madrid • Madrid City Map • Malta • Mediterranean Europe • Milan, Turin & Genoa • Moscow • Munich • Netherlands • Normandy • Norway • Out to Eat – London • Out to Eat – Paris • Paris • Paris City Map • Paris Condensed • Poland • Polish phrasebook • Portugal • Portuguese phrasebook • Prague • Prague City Map • Provence & the Côte d'Azur • Read This First: Europe • Rhodes & the Dodecanese • Romania & Moldova • Rome • Rome City Map • Rome Condensed • Russia, Ukraine & Belarus • Russian phrasebook • Scandinavian & Baltic Europe • Scandinavian phrasebook • Scotland • Sicily • Slovenia • South-West France • Spain • Spanish phrasebook • Stockholm • St Petersburg • St Petersburg City Map • Sweden • Switzerland • Tuscany • Ukrainian phrasebook • Venice • Vienna • Wales • Walking in Britain • Walking in France • Walking in Ireland • Walking in Italy • Walking in Scotland • Walking in Spain • Walking in Switzerland • Western Europe • World Food France • World Food Greece • World Food Ireland • World Food Italy • World Food Spain **Travel Literature:** After Yugoslavia • Love and War in the Apennines • The Olive Grove: Travels in Greece • On the Shores of the Mediterranean • Round Ireland in Low Gear • A Small Place in Italy

Lonely Planet Mail Order

Lonely Planet products are distributed worldwide. They are also available by mail order from Lonely Planet, so if you have difficulty finding a title please write to us. North and South American residents should write to 150 Linden St, Oakland, CA 94607, USA; European and African residents should write to 10a Spring Place, London NW5 3BH, UK; and residents of other countries to Locked Bag 1, Footscray, Victoria 3011, Australia.

INDIAN SUBCONTINENT & THE INDIAN OCEAN Bangladesh • Bengali phrasebook • Bhutan • Delhi • Goa • Healthy Travel Asia & India • Hindi & Urdu phrasebook • India • India & Bangladesh City Map • Indian Himalaya • Karakoram Highway • Kathmandu City Map • Kerala • Madagascar • Maldives • Mauritius, Réunion & Seychelles • Mumbai (Bombay) • Nepal • Nepali phrasebook • North India • Pakistan • Rajasthan • Read This First: Asia & India • South India • Sri Lanka • Sri Lanka phrasebook • Tibet • Tibetan phrasebook • Trekking in the Indian Himalaya • Trekking in the Karakoram & Hindukush • Trekking in the Nepal Himalaya • World Food India **Travel Literature:** The Age of Kali: Indian Travels and Encounters • Hello Goodnight: A Life of Goa • In Rajasthan • Maverick in Madagascar • A Season in Heaven: True Tales from the Road to Kathmandu • Shopping for Buddhas • A Short Walk in the Hindu Kush • Slowly Down the Ganges

MIDDLE EAST & CENTRAL ASIA Bahrain, Kuwait & Qatar • Central Asia • Central Asia phrasebook • Dubai • Farsi (Persian) phrasebook • Hebrew phrasebook • Iran • Israel & the Palestinian Territories • Istanbul • Istanbul City Map • Istanbul to Cairo • Istanbul to Kathmandu • Jerusalem • Jerusalem City Map • Jordan • Lebanon • Middle East • Oman & the United Arab Emirates • Syria • Turkey • Turkish phrasebook • World Food Turkey • Yemen **Travel Literature:** Black on Black: Iran Revisited • Breaking Ranks: Turbulent Travels in the Promised Land • The Gates of Damascus • Kingdom of the Film Stars: Journey into Jordan

NORTH AMERICA Alaska • Boston • Boston City Map • Boston Condensed • British Columbia • California & Nevada • California Condensed • Canada • Chicago • Chicago City Map • Chicago Condensed • Florida • Georgia & the Carolinas • Great Lakes • Hawaii • Hiking in Alaska • Hiking in the USA • Honolulu & Oahu City Map • Las Vegas • Los Angeles • Los Angeles City Map • Louisiana & the Deep South • Miami • Miami City Map • Montreal • New England • New Orleans • New Orleans City Map • New York City • New York City City Map • New York City Condensed • New York, New Jersey & Pennsylvania • Oahu • Out to Eat – San Francisco • Pacific Northwest • Rocky Mountains • San Diego & Tijuana • San Francisco • San Francisco City Map • Seattle • Seattle City Map • Southwest • Texas • Toronto • USA • USA phrasebook • Vancouver • Vancouver City Map • Virginia & the Capital Region • Washington, DC • Washington, DC City Map • World Food New Orleans **Travel Literature:** Caught Inside: A Surfer's Year on the California Coast • Drive Thru America

NORTH-EAST ASIA Beijing • Beijing City Map • Cantonese phrasebook • China • Hiking in Japan • Hong Kong & Macau • Hong Kong City Map • Hong Kong Condensed • Japan • Japanese phrasebook • Korea • Korean phrasebook • Kyoto • Mandarin phrasebook • Mongolia • Mongolian phrasebook • Seoul • Shanghai • South-West China • Taiwan • Tokyo • Tokyo Condensed • World Food Hong Kong • World Food Japan **Travel Literature:** In Xanadu: A Quest • Lost Japan

SOUTH AMERICA Argentina, Uruguay & Paraguay • Bolivia • Brazil • Brazilian phrasebook • Buenos Aires • Buenos Aires City Map • Chile & Easter Island • Colombia • Ecuador & the Galapagos Islands • Healthy Travel Central & South America • Latin American Spanish phrasebook • Peru • Quechua phrasebook • Read This First: Central & South America • Rio de Janeiro • Rio de Janeiro City Map • Santiago de Chile • South America on a shoestring • Trekking in the Patagonian Andes • Venezuela **Travel Literature:** Full Circle: A South American Journey

SOUTH-EAST ASIA Bali & Lombok • Bangkok • Bangkok City Map • Burmese phrasebook • Cambodia • Cycling Vietnam, Laos & Cambodia • East Timor phrasebook • Hanoi • Healthy Travel Asia & India • Hill Tribes phrasebook • Ho Chi Minh City (Saigon) • Indonesia • Indonesian phrasebook • Indonesia's Eastern Islands • Java • Lao phrasebook • Laos • Malay phrasebook • Malaysia, Singapore & Brunei • Myanmar (Burma) • Philippines • Pilipino (Tagalog) phrasebook • Read This First: Asia & India • Singapore • Singapore City Map • South-East Asia on a shoestring • South-East Asia phrasebook • Thailand • Thailand's Islands & Beaches • Thailand, Vietnam, Laos & Cambodia Road Atlas • Thai phrasebook • Vietnam • Vietnamese phrasebook • World Food Indonesia • World Food Thailand • World Food Vietnam

ALSO AVAILABLE: Antarctica • The Arctic • The Blue Man: Tales of Travel, Love and Coffee • Brief Encounters: Stories of Love, Sex & Travel • Buddhist Stupas in Asia: The Shape of Perfection • Chasing Rickshaws • The Last Grain Race • Lonely Planet ... On the Edge: Adventurous Escapades from Around the World • Lonely Planet Unpacked • Lonely Planet Unpacked Again • Not the Only Planet: Science Fiction Travel Stories • Ports of Call: A Journey by Sea • Sacred India • Travel Photography: A Guide to Taking Better Pictures • Travel with Children • Tuvalu: Portrait of an Island Nation

LONELY PLANET

You already know that Lonely Planet produces more than this one guidebook, but you might not be aware of the other products we have on this region. Here is a selection of titles that you may want to check out as well:

Europe on a shoestring
ISBN 1 86450 150 2
US$24.99 • UK£14.99

Italy
ISBN 0 86442 692 5
US$21.95 • UK£13.99

Italian phrasebook
ISBN 0 86442 456 6
US$5.95 • UK£3.99

Florence
ISBN 0 86442 785 9
US$14.95 • UK£8.99

Mediterrean Europe
ISBN 1 86450 154 5
US$27.99 • UK£15.99

Read This First: Europe
ISBN 1 86450 136 7
US$14.99 • UK£8.99

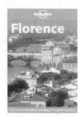

Rome
ISBN 1 86450 311 4
US$15.99 • UK£9.99

Venice
ISBN 0 86442 786 7
US$14.95 • UK£8.99

Walking in Italy
ISBN 0 86442 542 2
US$17.95 • UK£11.99

Western Europe
ISBN 1 86450 163 4
US$27.99 • UK£15.99

World Food Italy
ISBN 1 86450 022 0
US$12.95 • UK£7.99

Rome Condensed
ISBN 1 86450 360 2
US$11.99 • UK£5.99

Available wherever books are sold

Index

Abbreviations

Text

Bold indicates maps.

Places to Stay

Places to Eat

Boxed Text